CONTRACT LAW

PC29

CONTRACT LAW

The Fundamentals

THIRD EDITION

by
RYAN MURRAY
LLB (Hons), PGCHE, Barrister
Principal Lecturer in Law
Course Leader LLB (Hons)
Full Time, Flexible and
Distance Learning,
Nottingham Law School

SWEET & MAXWELL

THOMSON REUTERS

First edition 2008
Second Edition 2011
Third Edition 2014
Published in 2014 by
Thomson Reuters (Professional) UK Limited
trading as Sweet & Maxwell,
Friars House, 160 Blackfriars Road, London, SE1 8EZ
(Registered in England & Wales, Company No 1679046.
Registered Office and address for service:
2nd floor, Aldgate House, 33 Aldgate High Street, London EC3N 1DL)

For further information on our products and services,
visit www.sweetandmaxwell.co.uk

Typeset by Servis Filmsetting Ltd, Stockport, Cheshire
Printed and bound by CPI Group (UK) Ltd, Croydon, CR0 4YY

No natural forests were destroyed to make this product:
only farmed timber was used and replanted

A CIP catalogue record for this book is available from the British Library
ISBN 978-0-41404-817-1

Dedication

For Maya Grace
from Uncle Ryan

Acknowledgements

Grateful acknowledgement is made for permission to reproduce from the undermentioned works:

INCORPORATED COUNCIL OF LAW REPORTING

Law Reports

Weekly Law Reports

REED ELSEVIER (UK) LIMITED, TRADING AS LEXISNEXIS

The All England Law Reports

Preface

The 3rd edition of this text incorporates a number of exciting features that I hope will enhance your understanding of the key legal principles. Most notably, throughout the chapters the "Hear from the Author" feature provides audio / visual commentary to introduce the fundamental legal principles and authorities. This innovative feature can be accessed by scanning the relevant QR code provided in the text or following the link to the supporting website. The end of each chapter also includes a key cases summary grid which should help to consolidate your knowledge and understanding and also provide a useful addition to your revision. Finally, the further reading provided at the end of each chapter now contains additional commentary to help you navigate the relevant resources.

The text has been updated to reflect significant changes in the law relating to exclusion clauses and unfair terms. This area of law is undergoing a process of significant reform in light of the provisions of the Consumer Rights Bill 2013-14, which is expected to become law during the 2014-15 Parliamentary session. At the time of writing, the Bill has completed its Committee Stage in the House of Commons.

For the latest information regarding the Consumer Rights Bill 2013-14, please access the following link:

http://services.parliament.uk/bills/2013-14/con-sumerrights.html

The Bill itself and the accompanying explanatory notes can be accessed at:

http://services.parliament.uk/bills/2013-14/consumerrights/documents.html

Further, there is analysis of the decision in **Progress Bulk Carriers Limited v Tube City** IMS LLC [2012] which provides further consideration of lawful act duress.

Thank you to Sweet & Maxwell for their support during the conception and production of this new edition and a big thank you to my friends and colleagues at Nottingham Law School for their continued support and good humour throughout the writing process.

I hope this books provides and accessible and enjoyable account of the Law of Contract.

I have stated the law, as I believe it to be, as of April 2014.

Ryan Murray
Nottingham Law School.

Contents

◀••

Acknowledgements	vii
Preface	ix
List of Figures	xix
Guided tour	xxi
Table of Cases	xxiii
Table of Statutes	xxxvii

1 Introduction to Contract Law ········· 1

Some introductory points	2
Defining a contract	2
Objectivity in the law of contract	3
A legally binding agreement	4
The sources of contract law	5
The self-regulatory nature of contract law	7
The classical theory of contract	7
● **Summary**	9

2 Offer and Acceptance ········· 11

Introduction	12
Identifying an offer	13
"Ingredients" of an offer	13
Distinguishing an offer from an invitation to treat	15
Acceptance	29
Counter-offers	29
A request for information	31
Cross-offers	31
Statement of minimum price	31
The battle of the forms	31
When will acceptance become effective?	32

Revocation of an offer   50
  Revocation by a third party   51
  Revocation and unilateral contracts   51
A structured approach to offer and acceptance   51

● Summary   53
● Key cases grid   54
● End of chapter question   56
● Further reading   57

3 Certainty and Intention to Create Legal Relations   59

Introduction   60
  The terms of the agreement are too vague   60
  Meaningless phrases   61
  Certainty and negative obligations   61
  Methods of resolving ambiguity   62
  Incomplete agreements   63
Intention to create legal relations   64
  The presumption in domestic and social agreements   65
  The presumption in commercial relationships   66
  Overview of certainty and intention to create legal relations 67

● Summary   68
● Key cases grid   69
● End of chapter question   70
● Further reading   71

4 Consideration and Promissory Estoppel   73

Introduction   74
Defining consideration   74
  Consideration as the "price of the promise"   76
  The "rules" of consideration   76
  "Sufficiency" of consideration   80
  Part-payment of a debt   95
Promissory estoppel: an overview   100
What is an estoppel?   100
  The relationship between consideration and promissory estoppel 101

The development of the modern doctrine of promissory estoppel—
the decision in *High Trees* House   101
The limitations on promissory estoppels   106

● **Summary**   112
● **Key cases grid**   114
● **End of chapter question**   115
● **Further reading**   116

5 Privity of Contract   **119**

Introduction   120
Justifications for the doctrine of privity of contract   120
Exceptions to the doctrine of privity   123
Exceptions at common law   123
Third parties and damages   125
Contracts (Rights of Third Parties) Act 1999   126

● **Summary**   128
● **Key cases grid**   129
● **End of chapter question**   130
● **Further reading**   131

6 Terms   **133**

Introduction   134
Distinguishing between a term and representation   134
The "guiding factors" and "presumptions" in distinguishing a term from
a representation   135
Incorporation of terms   138
Is the term express or implied?   139
Terms implied by law   140
Terms implied by statute   143
Terms implied by custom   143
What type of term?   144
Conditions   144
Warranties   144
Innominate terms   146

● **Summary**   148
● **Key cases grid**   149

● Key cases grid   149
● End of chapter question   150
● Further reading   151

7 : Exclusion Clauses   **153**

Introduction   154
Common law and statutory responses to exclusion clauses   154
A three-stage approach to exclusion clauses   155
Common law   155
   Stage 1: incorporation   156
   Incorporation via a previous course of dealings   162
   Stage 2: the clause must pass the test of "construction"   164
   Stage 3: the clause must satisfy the relevant statutory provisions 170
Unfair Contract Terms Act 1977   171
Unfair Terms in Consumer Contracts Regulations 1999   180
Consumer Rights Bill 2013-14   182
Overview of the Consumer Rights Bill   184

● Summary   190
● Key cases grid   192
● End of chapter question   193
● Further reading   195

8 : Misrepresentation   **197**

Introduction   198
Stage 1: distinguishing a term from a representation   198
   Intention of the maker of the statement   199
   Has the statement been reduced to writing?   199
   Does one party have specialist skill or knowledge?   199
   Lapse of time   200
Stage 2: identifying an actionable misrepresentation   200
   A false statement   201
   Representation by silence   201
   A false statement of fact   204
   A false statement of fact that induced the contract   208
Stage 3: what type of misrepresentation?   211
   Fraudulent misrepresentation   212
   Negligent misrepresentation   212
   Negligent misstatement   212

Innocent misrepresentation 218
Stage 4: the remedies for misrepresentation 219
Rescission 219
Bars to rescission 219
Damages for misrepresentation 223
Damages for fraudulent misrepresentation 223
Damages for negligent misstatement 226
Damages under the Misrepresentation Act 1967 s.2(1) 226
Damages under the Misrepresentation Act 1967 s.2(2) 228
Exclusion of liability for misrepresentation 230
A structured approach to misrepresentation 231

● **Summary** 232
● **Key cases grid** 233
● **End of chapter question** 234
● **Further reading** 236

9 : Mistake 237

Introduction 238
The boundaries of mistake 238
Identifying the type of mistake 239
Common mistake 239
Agreement mistakes 244
Unilateral mistake 246
The House of Lords decision in Shogun Finance v Hudson 253
Documents signed by mistake (non est factum) 258

● **Summary** 259
● **Key cases grid** 260
● **End of chapter question** 261
● **Further reading** 262

10 : Duress and Undue Influence 263

Introduction 264
Threats of physical force or violence 265
Was the nature of the threat sufficient to amount to duress? 265
Effect of the threats on the claimant 266
Economic duress 267

The development of economic duress   267
Economic duress and a lawful act   270
Undue influence   271
Categories of undue influence   271
A singular concept of undue influence?   272
"Presumed" undue influence and Royal Bank of Scotland v Etridge (No.2)   272
Actual undue influence   274
"Presumed" undue influence   275
Undue influence and third parties   281

● **Summary**   284
● **Key cases grid**   286
● **End of chapter question**   287
● **Further reading**   287

11 ┊ **Illegality**   **289**

┊ **Introduction**   290
Illegality and performance   290
The illegal act renders the obligations under the contract unenforceable 291
The illegal act does not affect the obligations under the contract, but the
wrongdoer will be punished for his illegal act.   291
Contracts illegal under statute   291
Competition Act 1998   291
Wagering contracts   292
Breach of statutory requirements   292
Contracts illegal at common law   292
Public policy and immorality   292
Illegality and restraint of trade   294

● **Summary**   301
● **Key cases grid**   302
● **End of chapter question**   303
● **Further reading**   304

12 ┊ **Discharge of Obligations: Agreement, Performance and**
   ┊ **Breach**   **305**

┊ **Introduction**   306
Discharge by agreement   306

Bilateral discharge   306
Unilateral discharge   307
Discharge by performance   307
Performance must be precise and exact   307
Construction of the contract   308
Severable obligations   308
Partial performance   309
Substantial performance   309
Prevention of performance   310
Discharge by breach   311
Anticipatory breach   311

● **Summary**   312
● **Key cases grid**   313
● **Further reading**   313

13 : Frustration   315

Introduction   316
Outline and development of the doctrine of frustration   316
What events can frustrate a contract?   319
Destruction of the subject matter   319
Non-occurrence of an event   319
Illegality   323
Non-availability of the parties owing to death or illness   324
Frustration and leases   324
Limitations on the doctrine of frustration   325
Self-induced frustration   325
Allocation of risk and frustration   326
A radical change of obligations is required; mere delay will not suffice   326
The effect of frustration on the contract   327
The position at common law   327
Law Reform (Frustrated Contracts) Act 1943   330

● **Summary**   336
● **Key cases grid**   337
● **End of chapter question**   338
● **Further reading**   339

14 Damages   **341**

Introduction   342
Limitations on an award of damages   342
   Remoteness of damage   342
The compensatory aim of an award of damages in contract   350
   Assessing the expectation interest   351
   Speculative loss and the expectation interest   352
   The restitutionary interest   354
   The ability to recover for non-pecuniary loss   359
Damages agreed between the parties: "Liquidated damages"   361
   Distinguishing a liquidated damages clause from a penalty clause   362
   The guidelines in Dunlop Pneumatic Tyre   363
Contributory negligence   364
Mitigation of loss   366

  ● Summary   366
  ● Key cases grid   368
  ● End of chapter question   369
  ● Further reading   369

15 Other Remedies   **371**

Introduction   372
Common law   372
   Action for an agreed sum   372
Equitable remedies   373
   Specific performance   373
   Injunctions   377
Restitution   379
   A total failure of consideration   379
Quantum meruit claims   379

  ● Summary   380
  ● Key cases grid   381
  ● Further reading   381

Index   383

List of Figures

2.1	The occurrence of the agreement	12
2.2	Collateral contract in a "without reserve" auction	26
2.3	The decision in **Hyde v Wrench**	30
2.4	Checklist for postal acceptances	40
2.5	Offer and acceptance	52
3.1	Certainty and intention to create legal relations	68
4.1	Consideration: benefit and detriment analysis	75
4.2	Past consideration	81
4.3	Summary of **New Zealand Shipping Co**	93
4.4	Overview of **High Trees House**	102
5.1	**Tweddle v Atkinson**	121
5.2	**Beswick v Beswick**	122
5.3	Agency	123
5.4	Assignment	124
7.1	Incorporation of an exclusion clause	156
7.2	Overview of incorporation and construction	165
7.3	The three-stage approach to negligence following **Canada Steamship**	170
7.4	Summary of UCTA s.2 and liability for negligence	174
7.5	Summary of strict liability under UCTA s.6 and s.7	176
7.6	Overview of UCTA	179
7.7	Application of Legislative Provisions in light of the Consumer Rights Bill 2013	183
7.8	Summary of the Consumer Rights Bill 2013-14	190
8.1	The three main types of misrepresentation	211
8.2	The operation of s.2(1) of the 1967 Act	217
8.3	Summary of types of misrepresentation and damages available	228

8.4	Overview of misrepresentation	231
9.1	A voidable contract	248
9.2	A void contract	248
9.3	**Shogun Finance v Hudson**	254
10.1	Summary of presumed undue influence	280
10.2	Third-party cases and undue influence	282
10.3	Notice and constructive notice of undue influence	284
13.1	**Chandler v Webster**	328
13.2	**The Fibrosa**	329
13.3	The operation of s.1(2) of the 1943 Act	332
13.4	The operation of s.1(3) of the 1943 Act	335
14.1	Summary of the reasoning in **Parsons v Uttley**	349

Guided Tour

Chapter Overview
Each chapter opens with a bulleted outline of the main concepts and ideas to be covered.

Key Extracts
Key extracts are boxed throughout to make them easily identifiable.

Key Cases
All cases are highlighted making your research of the subject easier.

Over to you boxes
A tool to help you develop your critical thinking abilities, Over to you boxes challenge you to engage with and question the subject.

Diagrams, charts, etc.
Included throughout, diagrams, charts and grids enable you to grasp complex legal principles with ease.

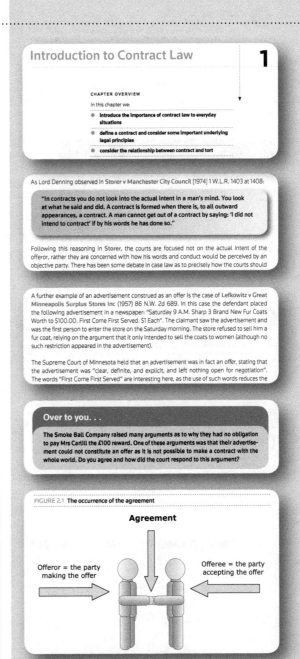

Introduction to Contract Law — 1

CHAPTER OVERVIEW

In this chapter we:

● Introduce the importance of contract law to everyday situations

● define a contract and consider some important underlying legal principles

● consider the relationship between contract and tort

As Lord Denning observed in Storer v Manchester City Council [1974] 1 W.L.R. 1403 at 1408:

"In contracts you do not look into the actual intent in a man's mind. You look at what he said and did. A contract is formed when there is, to all outward appearances, a contract. A man cannot get out of a contract by saying: 'I did not intend to contract' if by his words he has done so."

Following this reasoning in Storer, the courts are focused not on the actual intent of the offeror, rather they are concerned with how his words and conduct would be perceived by an objective party. There has been some debate in case law as to precisely how the courts should

A further example of an advertisement construed as an offer is the case of Lefkowitz v Great Minneapolis Surplus Stores Inc (1957) 86 N.W. 2d 689. In this case the defendant placed the following advertisement in a newspaper: "Saturday 9 A.M. Sharp 3 Brand New Fur Coats Worth to $100.00. First Come First Served. $1 Each". The claimant saw the advertisement and was the first person to enter the store on the Saturday morning. The store refused to sell him a fur coat, relying on the argument that it only intended to sell the coats to women (although no such restriction appeared in the advertisement).

The Supreme Court of Minnesota held that an advertisement was in fact an *offer*, stating that the advertisement was "clear, definite, and explicit, and left nothing open for negotiation". The words "First Come First Served" are interesting here, as the use of such words reduces the

Over to you. . .

The Smoke Ball Company raised many arguments as to why they had no obligation to pay Mrs Carlill the £100 reward. One of these arguments was that their advertisement could not constitute an offer as it is not possible to make a contract with the whole world. Do you agree and how did the court respond to this argument?

FIGURE 2.1 **The occurrence of the agreement**

Agreement

Offeror = the party making the offer

Offeree = the party accepting the offer

Hear from the Author

Scan the QR Tag or follow the link below for an introduction to the topic consideration.

uklawstudent.thomsonreuters.com/category/contract-fundamentals

Hear from the author

On key points the author has provided audio commentary with visual media, use the QR code to hear and see what the author has to say.

 ### Summary

1. The privity of contract rule means that only parties to the contract can enforce the contract, receive a benefit under the contract or be liable on the contract. A third party will have very limited rights indeed under the contract.

2. A third party cannot enforce a contract as he has not provided consideration to support the agreement, nor will he generally have suffered any loss under the contract.

Summary

Each chapter closes with a summary to recap the main points and ensure you haven't missed anything crucial.

Key Cases Grid

Case	Court	Key Issue
Cutter v Powell (1795)	Court of King's Bench	Illustrates the, sometimes harsh requirement, that performance of obligations under a contract must be precise and exact.
Planche v Colbourn (1831)	Court of King's Bench	Generally, there must be full and complete performance in order to discharge the contractual obligation. However, if one party is prevented from performing due to the actions of the other party, then the court may award money on a quantum meruit basis (money had for work done).
Hochster v De La Tour (1853)	Court of Queen's Bench	An example of anticipatory, when one party indicates that he will not be able to meet his obligations under the contract *before* the contract is completed.

Key cases grids

To help with revision of key cases, here's a handy grid with salient points to remember.

End of Chapter Question

Jo books a holiday to Italy for her and her family. She specifies that the accommodation must provide facilities for young children. When Jo and her family arrive they are told that their specified accommodation is no longer available. The tour company offer Jo alternative accommodation located in the city centre. Due to its location the alternative accommodation does not provide any facilities for children; in fact, guests must be at least 18 years old in order to stay at this alternative accommodation.

Q&A

Hone your essay answering skills with the end of chapter questions. Each question comes with guidance on what you should have included in your answer.

Further Reading

Clark, P. "Frustration, Restitution and the Law Reform (Frustrated Contracts) Act 1943" L.M.C.L.Q. [1996] 170
    An analysis of Gamerco SA v ICM / Fair Warning (Agency) Ltd and how expenditure incurred up to time of frustration should be apportioned.
Stone, R. and Cunnington, R. *Text, Cases and Materials on Contract Law* (London: Routledge-Cavendish, 2014), Chapter 12.
Treitel, G. *The Law of Contract*, 13th edn (London Sweet & Maxwell, 2011), Chapter 19.

Further Reading

To help you broaden your perspective we provide selected further reading at the end of each chapter.

Table of Cases

◄ ···

A Schroeder Music Publishing Co Ltd v Macaulay (formerly Instone); sub nom. Macaulay (formerly Instone) v A Schroeder Music Publishing Co Ltd [1974] 1 W.L.R. 1308; [1974] 3 All E.R. 616 HL   11–021, 11–027

Adams v Lindsell, 106 E.R. 250; (1818) 1 B. & Ald. 681 KB   2–028, 2–029, 2–032, 2–033, 2–049, 2–053, 2–060

Ailsa Craig Fishing Co Ltd v Malvern Fishing Co Ltd (The Strathallan); Malvern Fishing Co Ltd v Ailsa Craig Fishing Co Ltd (The Strathallan) [1983] 1 W.L.R. 964; [1983] 1 All E.R. 101 HL   7–021

Ajayi (t/a Colony Carrier Co) v RT Briscoe (Nigeria) Ltd [1964] 1 W.L.R. 1326; [1964] 3 All E.R. 556 P C (Nigeria)   4–045

Alan & Co Ltd v El Nasr Export & Import Co. See WJ Alan & Co Ltd v El Nasr Export & Import Co

Alderslade v Hendon Laundry Ltd [1945] K.B. 189; [1945] 1 All E.R. 244 CA   7–023

Allcard v Skinner (1887) L.R. 36 Ch. D. 145 CA   10–016, 10–019, 10–020, 10–025

Allen v Rescous (1677) 2 Lev. 174   11–010

Alliance & Leicester Building Society v Edgestop Ltd [1994] 2 All E.R. 38   8–040

Anderson Ltd v Daniel [1924] 1 K.B. 138 CA   11–003, 11–004

Anglia Television Ltd v Reed [1972] 1 Q.B. 60; [1971] 3 W.L.R. 528 CA (Civ Div)   14–023

Appleby v Myers; sub nom. Appleby v Meyers (1866–67) L.R. 2 C.P. 651 Ex Chamber   13–020, 13–021, 13–022, 13–024, 13–026, 13–032

Armhouse Lee Ltd v Chappell, Times, August 7, 1996; Independent, July 26, 1996 CA (Civ Div)   11–011

Associated Japanese Bank (International) Ltd v Credit du Nord SA [1989] 1 W.L.R. 255; [1988] 3 All E.R. 902 QBD   9–009, 9–010

Atlantic Baron, The. See North Ocean Shipping Co v Hyundai Construction Co (The Atlantic Baron)

Atlas Express Ltd v Kafco (Importers and Distributors) Ltd [1989] Q.B. 833; [1989]3 W.L.R. 389 QBD (Comm)   10–007, 10–025

Attorney General v Blake [2001] 1 A.C. 268; [2000] 3 W.L.R. 625 HL   14–030, 14–031

Attwood v Lamont [1920] 3 K.B. 571 CA   11–027

Attwood v Small (1863) 6 Cl. & Fin. 232   8–019

Avery v Bowden (1855) 5 El. & Bl. 714   12–013, 13–012

BP Exploration Co (Libya) Ltd v Hunt (No.2) [1983] 2 A.C. 352; [1982] 2 W.L.R.253 HL   13–028, 13–030, 13–032

Balfour v Balfour [1919] 2 K.B. 571 CA   3–011, 3–014

Banco Exterior Internacional v Mann [1995] 1 All E.R. 936; [1995] 1 F.L.R. 602; (1995) 27 H.L.R. 329 CA (Civ Div)   10–025

Bank of Credit and Commerce International SA v Aboody [1990] 1 Q.B. 923; [1989] 2 W.L.R. 759 CA (Civ Div)   10–010, 10–012, 10–013, 10–015, 10–019, 10–020

Bannerman v White (1861) 10 C.B. N.S. 844   6–007

Barclays Bank Plc v Fairclough Building Ltd (No.1) [1995] Q.B. 214; [1994] 3 W.L.R. 1057 CA (Civ Div)   14–037

Barclays Bank Plc v Kennedy (1989) 21 H.L.R. 132; (1989) 58 P. & C.R. 221, CA (Civ Div)   10–017

Barclays Bank Plc v O'Brien [1994] 1 A.C. 180; [1993] 3 W.L.R. 786 HL   10–010, 10–011, 10–019, 10–022, 10–024, 10–025

Barry v Davies (t/a Heathcote Ball & Co); sub nom. Barry v Heathcote Ball & Co (Commercial Auctions) Ltd; Heathcote Ball & Co (Commercial Auctions) Ltd v Barry [2000] 1 W.L.R. 1962; [2001] 1 All E.R. 944 CA (Civ Div)   2–015

Barton (Alexander) v Armstrong (Alexander Ewan) [1976] A.C. 104; [1975] 2 W.L.R. 1050 PC (Aus)   10–003

Bell v Lever Brothers Ltd; sub nom. Lever Bros Ltd v Bell [1932] A.C. 161 HL   9–007, 9–008, 9–009, 9–010, 9–031

Beresford v Royal Insurance Co Ltd [1938] A.C. 586 HL   11–010

Beswick v Beswick [1968] A.C. 58; [1967] 3 W.L.R. 932, HL   5–002, 5–007, 5–009, 5–012, 15–004, 15–015

Bettini v Gye (1875–76) L.R. 1 Q.B.D. 183 QBD   6–027

Bidder v Bridges (No.3) (1888) L.R. 37 Ch. D. 406 CA   4–045

Bigos v Bousted [1951] 1 All E.R. 92 KBD   11–001

Bisset v Wilkinson [1927] A.C. 177 PC (NZ)   8–014, 8–043

Blackpool and Fylde Aero Club v Blackpool BC [1990] 1 W.L.R. 1195; [1990] 3 All E.R. 25 CA (Civ Div)   2–018

Bliss v South East Thames RHA [1987] I.C.R. 700; [1985] I.R.L.R. 308 CA (Civ Div)   14–033

Bolton v Mahadeva [1972] 1 W.L.R. 1009; [1972] 2 All E.R. 1322 CA (Civ Div)   12–010

Brace v Calder [1895] 2 Q.B. 253 CA   14–038

Brimnes, The. See Tenax Steamship Co v Owners of the Motor Vessel Brimnes (The Brimnes); sub nom. Tenax Steamship Co v Reinante Transoceanica Navegacion SA (The Brimnes)

Brinkibon v Stahag Stahl und Stahlwarenhandels GmbH; sub nom. Brinkibon Ltd v Stahag Stahl und Stahlwarenhandelsgesellschaft mbH [1983] 2 A.C. 34; [1982] 2 W.L.R. 264 HL   2–046, 2–047, 2–048, 2–049, 2–060

British & American Telegraph Co Ltd v Colson (1870–71) L.R. 6 Ex. 108   2–035

British Crane Hire Corp Ltd v Ipswich Plant Hire Ltd [1975] Q.B. 303; [1974] 2 W.L.R. 856 CA (Civ Div)   6–011, 6–020, 6–031, 7–014

British Road Services Ltd v Arthur V Crutchley & Co Ltd (No.1) [1968] 1 All E.R. 811; [1968] 1 Lloyd's Rep. 271 CA (Civ Div)   2–026

Butler Machine Tool Co v Ex-cell-o Corp (England) [1979] 1 W.L.R. 401; [1979] 1 All E.R. 965 CA (Civ Div)   2–026

Byrne & Co v Leon Van Tien Hoven & Co (1879–80) L.R. 5 C.P.D. 344 CPD   2–058, 2–060

CIBC Mortgages Plc v Pitt [1994] 1 A.C. 200; [1993] 3 W.L.R. 802 HL   10–010, 10–013

CTN Cash and Carry Ltd v Gallaher Ltd [1994] 4 All E.R. 714 CA (Civ Div)   10–008, 10–025

Canada Steamship Lines Ltd v King, The [1952] A.C. 192; [1952] 1 All E.R. 305 PC (Can)   7–019, 7–059

Caparo Industries Plc v Dickman [1990] 2 A.C. 605; [1990] 2 W.L.R. 358 HL   8–023

Carlill v Carbolic Smoke Ball Co [1893] 1 Q.B. 256 CA   2–013, 2–054, 2–060

Casey's Patents, Re; sub nom. Stewart v Casey [1892] 1 Ch. 104 CA   4–011, 4–012, 4–045

Cehave NV v Bremer Handels GmbH (The Hansa Nord); sub nom. Cehave NV v Bremer Handelgesellschaft mbH (The Hansa Nord) [1976] Q.B. 44; [1975] 3 W.L.R. 447 CA (Civ Div)   6–030

Cellulose Acetate Silk Co Ltd v Widnes Foundry (1925) Ltd; sub nom. Widnes Foundry (1925) Ltd v Cellulose Acetate Silk Co Ltd [1933] A.C. 20 HL   14–035

Central London Property Trust v High Trees House Ltd [1947] K.B. 130; [1956] 1 All E.R. 256 (Note) KBD   4–032, 4–033, 4–035, 4–036, 4–038, 4–039, 4–040, 4–042, 4–043, 4–045

Chandler v Webster [1904] 1 K.B. 493 CA   13–020, 13–021, 13–022, 13–024, 13–025, 13–032

Chapelton v Barry Urban DC [1940] 1 K.B. 532 CA   7–011, 7–059

Chaplin v Hicks [1911] 2 K.B. 786 CA   14–021, 14–032

Chappell & Co Ltd v Nestle Co Ltd [1960] A.C. 87; [1959] 3 W.L.R. 168 HL   4–006

Clarke v Dickson, 120 E.R. 463; (1858) El. Bl. & El. 148 QB   8–035

Collier v P & MJ Wright (Holdings) Ltd [2007] EWCA Civ 1329; [2008] 1 W.L.R. 643   4–045

Collins v Godefroy (1831) 1 B. & Ad. 950   4–014

Combe v Combe; sub nom. Coombe v Coombe [1951] 2 K.B. 215; [1951] 1 All E.R. 767 CA   4–041, 4–044

Condor v The Barron Knights Ltd [1966] 1 W.L.R. 87; (1966) 110 S.J. 71 Assizes (Bedford)   13–013

Cooper v Phibbs (1867) L.R. 2 H.L. 149 HL (UK-Irl)   9–007

Cooperative Insurance Society Ltd v Argyll Stores (Holdings) Ltd [1998] A.C. 1; [1997] 2 W.L.R. 898 HL   15–006

Couturier v Hastie, 10 E.R. 1065; (1856) 5 H.L. Cas. 673 QB   9–006

Crabb v Arun DC [1976] Ch. 179; [1975] 3 W.L.R. 847 CA (Civ Div)   4–030

Craven Ellis v Canons Ltd [1936] 2 K.B. 403 CA   15–015

Cundy v Lindsay; sub nom. Lindsay v Cundy (1877–78) L.R. 3 App. Cas. 459; [1874–80] All E.R. Rep. 1149 HL   9–019, 9–020, 9–026, 9–027, 9–028, 9–029, 9–030, 9–031

Currie v Misa (1874–75) L.R. 10 Ex. 153   4–002, 4–003, 4–045

Curtis v Chemical Cleaning & Dyeing Co [1951] 1 K.B. 805; [1951] 1 All E.R. 631 CA   7–006

Cutter v Powell, 101 E.R. 573; (1795) 6 Term Rep. 320 KB   12–006, 12–008, 12–013

D&C Builders Ltd v Rees [1966] 2 Q.B. 617; [1966] 2 W.L.R. 288 CA   4–025, 4–026, 4–027, 4–043

Dakin & Co v Lee. See H Dakin & Co v Lee; sub nom. Dakin & Co v Lee

Daulia Ltd v Four Millbank Nominees Ltd [1978] Ch. 231; [1978] 2 W.L.R. 621 CA (Civ Div)   2–056

Davies v London and Provincial Marine Insurance Co (1878) L.R. 8 Ch. D. 469; (1878) 26 W.R. 794 Ch D   8–011

Davis Contractors v Fareham Urban DC [1956] A.C. 696; [1956] 3 W.L.R. 37 HL   13–006

Derry v Peek; sub nom. Peek v Derry (1889) L.R. 14 App. Cas. 337; (1889) 5 T.L.R. 625 HL   8–021, 8–024, 8–027, 8–038, 8–041

Dick Bentley Productions Ltd v Harold Smith (Motors) Ltd [1965] 1 W.L.R. 623; [1965] 2 All E.R. 65 CA   6–006, 8–005

Dickinson v Dodds (1875–76) L.R. 2 Ch. D. 463 CA   2–059, 2–060

Dimmock v Hallett (1866–67) L.R. 2 Ch. App. 21; (1866) 12 Jur. N.S. 953 CA in Chancery   8–010

Director General of Fair Trading v First National Bank Plc [2000] Q.B. 672; [2000] 2 W.L.R. 1353 CA (Civ Div) 7–045

DPP for Northern Ireland v Lynch [1975] A.C. 653; [1975] 2 W.L.R. 641 HL   10–004

Doyle v Olby (Ironmongers) Ltd [1969] 2 Q.B. 158; [1969] 2 W.L.R. 673 CA (Civ Div)   8–038, 8–043

Dunlop Pneumatic Tyre Co Ltd v New Garage & Motor Co Ltd [1915] A.C. 79 HL   14–035, 14–036, 14–038

Dunlop Pneumatic Tyre Co Ltd v Selfridge & Co Ltd [1915] A.C. 847 HL   5–002

Dunmore v Alexander (1830) 9 Shaw 190   2–033, 2–038

East v Maurer [1991] 1 W.L.R. 461; [1991] 2 All E.R. 733 CA (Civ Div)   8–038

Ecay v Godfrey (1947) 80 Ll. L. Rep. 286   6–009

Edgington v Fitzmaurice (1885) L.R. 29 Ch. D. 459 CA   8–015, 8–016, 8–019, 8–028, 8–043

Edwards v Skyways [1964] 1 W.L.R. 349; [1964] 1 All E.R. 494 QBD   3–013, 3–014

Entores Ltd v Miles Far East Corp; sub nom. Newcomb v De Roos [1955] 2 Q.B. 327; [1955] 3 W.L.R. 48 CA   2–027, 2–041, 2–045, 2–046, 2–047, 2–048, 2–049, 2–060

Erlanger v New Sombrero Phosphate Co; sub nom. New Sombrero Phosphate Co v Erlanger (1877–78) L.R. 3 App. Cas. 1218 HL   8–035

Errington v Errington and Woods [1952] 1 K.B. 290; [1952] 1 All E.R. 149, CA   2–056

Esso Petroleum Co v Customs and Excise Commissioners [1976] 1 W.L.R. 1; [1976] 1 All E.R. 117 HL   3–013, 3–014

Esso Petroleum Co Ltd v Mardon [1976] Q.B. 801; [1976] 2 W.L.R. 583 CA (Civ Div)   8–014

Esso Petroleum Co Ltd v Niad Ltd [2001] All E.R. 324 Ch D   14–031

Eurymedon, The. See New Zealand Shipping Co Ltd v AM Satterthwaite & Co Ltd (The Eurymedon); sub nom. AM Satterthwaite & Co Ltd v New Zealand Shipping Co Ltd

Experience Hendrix LLC v PPX Enterprises Inc [2003] EWCA Civ 323; [2003] 1 All E.R. (Comm) 830 CA (Civ Div)   14–031

FA Tamplin Steamship Co Ltd v Anglo Mexican Petroleum Products Co Ltd [1916] 2 A.C. 397 HL   13–012

FW Moore & Co Ltd v Landauer & Co; sub nom. Arbitration Between Moore & Co Ltd and Landauer & Co Re [1921] 2 K.B. 519; (1921) 6 Ll. L. Rep. 384 CA   12–006

Farley v Skinner (No.2); sub nom. Skinner v Farley [2001] UKHL 49; [2002] 2 A.C. 732; [2001] 3 W.L.R. 899 HL   14–033

Felthouse v Bindley, 142 E.R. 1037; (1862) 11 C.B. N.S. 869 CCP   2–051, 2–054

Fibrosa Spolka Akcyjna v Fairbairn Lawson Combe Barbour Ltd; sub nom. Fibrosa Societe Anonyme v Fairbairn Lawson Combe Barbour Ltd [1943] A.C. 32; [1942] 2 All E.R. 122 HL   13–022, 13–023, 13–025, 13–031, 13–032, 15–014, 15–015

First Energy (UK) Ltd v Hungarian International Bank Ltd [1993] 2 Lloyd's Rep. 194; [1993] B.C.C. 533 CA (Civ Div)   2–005

Fisher v Bell [1961] 1 Q.B. 394; [1960] 3 W.L.R. 919 DC   2–009, 2–019

Fitch v Dewes; sub nom. Dewes v Fitch [1921] 2 A.C. 158 HL   11–020

Foakes v Beer; sub nom. Beer v Foakes (1883–84) L.R. 9 App. Cas. 605 HL   4–020, 4–024, 4–025, 4–026, 4–027, 4–028, 4–031, 4–035, 4–036, 4–037, 4–038, 4–045

Foley v Classique Coaches Ltd [1934] 2 K.B. 1 CA   3–005, 3–006, 3–008, 3–014

Forsikringsaktieselskapet Vesta v Butcher [1989] A.C. 852; [1989] 2 W.L.R. 290 HL   14–037

Forster v Suggett (1918) 35 T.L.R. 87   11–020, 11–027

G Scammell and Nephew Ltd v HC&JG Ouston [1941] A.C. 251 HL   3–002

Gamerco SA v ICM/Fair Warning (Agency) Ltd [1995] 1 W.L.R. 1226; [1995] C.L.C. 536 QBD   13–025, 13–032

George Mitchell (Chesterhall) Ltd v Finney Lock Seeds Ltd [1983] 2 A.C. 803; [1983] 3 W.L.R. 163 HL   7–015, 7–024, 7–041

Getreide Importgesellschaft mbH v Contimar SA Compania Industrial Commercial y Maritima SA [1953] 1 W.L.R. 793; [1953] 2 All E.R. 223 CA   2–032, 2–033, 2–053, 2–060

Gibbons v Proctor (1891) 64 L.T. 594   2–057

Gibson v Manchester City Council [1979] 1 W.L.R. 294; [1979] 1 All E.R. 972 HL   2–006

Goldsoll v Goldman [1915] 1 Ch. 292 CA   11–026, 11–027

Grainger & Son v Gough (Surveyor of Taxes) [1896] A.C. 325 HL   2–011

Gran Gelato Ltd v Richcliff (Group) Ltd [1992] Ch. 560; [1992] 2 W.L.R. 867 Ch D   8–039, 8–040

Great Peace Shipping Ltd v Tsavliris Salvage (International) Ltd [2002] EWCA Civ 1407; [2003] Q.B. 679; [2002] 3 W.L.R. 1617 CA (Civ Div)   9–002

H Dakin & Co v Lee; sub nom. Dakin & Co v Lee [1916] 1 K.B. 566 CA   12–010

Hadley v Baxendale 156 E.R. 145; (1854) 9 Ex. 341 Ex Ct   14–004, 14–005, 14–006, 14–008, 14–012, 14–014, 14–038

Hall v Wright (1859) 120 E.R. 695   13–013

Hamer v Sidway, 124 N.Y. 538 (1881)   4–006

Hamilton v Al-Fayed (Costs); sub nom. Hamilton v Fayed (Costs); Al-Fayed v Hamilton (Costs) [2002] EWCA Civ 665; [2003] Q.B. 1175; [2003] 2 W.L.R. 128 CA (Civ Div)   11–001

Hanover Insurance Brokers Ltd v Schapiro [1994] I.R.L.R. 82 CA (Civ Div)   11–024

Hansa Nord, The. See Cehave NV v Bremer Handels GmbH (The Hansa Nord); sub nom. Cehave NV v Bremer Handelsgesellschaft mbH (The Hansa Nord)

Hardman v Booth, 158 E.R. 1107; (1863) 1 Hurl. & C. 803 QB   9–022

Harris v Nickerson (1872–73) L.R. 8 Q.B. 286 QBD   2–017

Harris v Sheffield United Football Club Ltd; sub nom. Sheffield United Football Club v South Yorkshire Police Authority [1988] Q.B. 77; [1987] 3 W.L.R. 305 CA (Civ Div)   4–014

Hartley v Ponsonby [1857] 7 El. & Bl. 872   4–016, 4–045

Hartog v Colin & Shields [1939] 3 All E.R. 566   9–015

Harvela Investments Ltd v Royal Trust Co of Canada (CI) Ltd [1986] A.C. 207; [1985] 3 W.L.R. 276 HL   2–018

Harvey v Facey; sub nom. Harvey v Facey [1893] A.C. 552 PC (Jam)   2–025

Hector v Lyons (1989) 58 P. & C.R. 156; [1988] E.G. 170 (C.S.) CA (Civ Div)   9–026

Hedley Byrne & Co Ltd v Heller & Partners Ltd [1964] A.C. 465; [1963] 3 W.L.R. 101 HL   8–023, 8–024, 8–028, 8–029, 8–039, 8–041, 8–043

Heilbut Symons & Co v Buckleton [1913] A.C. 30 HL   6–003, 6–031, 8–003

Henthorn v Fraser [1892] 2 Ch. 27 CA   2–031, 2–037

Herbert Morris Ltd v Saxelby [1916] 1 A.C. 688 HL   11–018, 11–027

Hermann v Charlesworth [1905] 2 K.B. 123 CA   11–012

Herne Bay Steam Boat Co v Hutton [1903] 2 K.B. 683 CA   13–010, 13–011, 13–032

Heron II, The. See Koufos v C Czarnikow Ltd (The Heron II); sub nom. C Czarnikow Ltd v Koufos (The Heron II)

Heyman v Darwins Ltd [1942] A.C. 356; [1942] 1 All E.R. 337 HL   12–012

Hillas & Co Ltd v Arcos Ltd. See WN Hillas & Co Ltd v Arcos Ltd; WN Hillas & Co Ltd v Arcos Ltd (Quantum)

Hochster v De La Tour, 118 E.R. 922; (1853) 2 El. & Bl. 678 QB   12–013
Hoenig v Isaacs [1952] 2 All E.R. 176; [1952] 1 T.L.R. 1360 CA   12–010
Hollier v Rambler Motors (AMC) Ltd [1972] 2 Q.B. 71; [1972] 2 W.L.R. 401 CA (Civ Div)   7–013, 7–023
Holwell Securities Ltd v Hughes [1974] 1 W.L.R. 155; [1974] 1 All E.R. 161 CA (Civ Div)   2–034, 2–035, 2–060
Hongkong Fir Shipping Co Ltd v Kawasaki Kisen Kaisha Ltd (The Hongkong Fir) [1962] 2 Q.B. 26; [1962] 2 W.L.R. 474 CA   6–029, 6–031
Houghton v Trafalgar Insurance Co Ltd [1954] 1 Q.B. 247; [1953] 3 W.L.R. 985 CA   7–016
Household Fire & Carriage Accident Insurance Co Ltd v Grant (1878–79) L.R. 4 Ex. D. 216 CA   2–029
Howard Marine & Dredging Co Ltd v A Ogden & Sons (Excavations) Ltd [1978] Q.B. 574; [1978] 2 W.L.R. 515 CA (Civ Div)   8–026
Hughes v Metropolitan Railway Co (1876–77) L.R. 2 App. Cas. 439 HL   4–037, 4–038, 4–045
Hyde v Wrench, 49 E.R. 132; (1840) 3 Beav. 334 Ct of Chancery   2–022, 2–058, 2–060
Ingram v Little [1961] 1 Q.B. 31; [1960] 3 W.L.R. 504 CA   9–024, 9–025
Interfoto Picture Library Ltd v Stiletto Visual Programmes Ltd [1989] Q.B. 433; [1988] 2 W.L.R. 615   7–043 CA(Civ Div) 7–045
J Evans & Son (Portsmouth) Ltd v Andrea Merzario Ltd [1976] 1 W.L.R. 1078; [1976] 2 All E.R. 930, CA (Civ Div)   6–010
J Lauritzen AS v Wijsmuller BV (The Super Servant Two) [1990] 1 Lloyd's Rep. 1, CA (Civ Div)   13–016
J Spurling Ltd v Bradshaw [1956] 1 W.L.R. 461; [1956] 2 All E.R. 121 CA   7–010, 7–013, 7–051
JA Mont (UK) Ltd v Mills [1993] I.R.L.R. 172; [1993] F.S.R. 577 CA (Civ Div)   11–023
JEB Fasteners Ltd v Marks Bloom & Co [1983] 1 All E.R. 583 CA (Civ Div)   8–018, 8–043
Jackson v Horizon Holidays Ltd [1975] 1 W.L.R. 1468; [1975] 3 All E.R. 92 CA (Civ Div)   5–007, 5–012, 14–033
Jackson v Royal Bank of Scotland [2005] UKHL 3; [2005] 1 W.L.R. 377; [2005] 2 All E.R. 71 HL   14–012
Jackson v Union Marine Insurance Co Ltd (1874–75) L.R. 10 C.P. 125 Ex Chamber   13–017
Jacob & Youngs v Kent (1921) N.Y. 239   14–018, 14–019
Jarvis v Swans Tours Ltd [1973] Q.B. 233; [1972] 3 W.L.R. 954 CA (Civ Div)   14–033
Jordan v Money (1854) 5 H.L. Cas. 185   4–030, 4–039
Karsales (Harrow) Ltd v Wallis [1956] 1 W.L.R. 936; [1956] 2 All E.R. 866; (1956) 100 S.J. 548 CA 7–025
Keir v Leeman (1846) 6 Q.B. 308   11–013

Kings North Trust Ltd v Bell [1986] 1 W.L.R. 119; [1986] 1 All E.R. 423 CA (Civ Div)   10–017

King's Norton Metal Co v Edridge Merrett & Co (1897) 14 T.L.R. 98   9–020

Kleinwort Benson Ltd v Lincoln City Council; Kleinwort Benson Ltd v Birmingham City Council; Kleinwort Benson Ltd v Southwark LBC; Kleinwort Benson Ltd v Kensington and Chelsea RLBC [1999] 2 A.C. 349; [1998] 3 W.L.R. 1095 HL   8–015

Korbetis v Transgrain Shipping BV [2005] EWHC 1345 (QB) QBD   2–032, 2–033, 2–060

Koufos v C Czarnikow Ltd (The Heron II); sub nom. C Czarnikow Ltd v Koufos (The Heron II) [1969] 1 A.C. 350; [1967] 3 W.L.R. 1491 HL   14–008, 14–009, 14–011, 14–012, 14–038

Krell v Henry [1903] 2 K.B. 740 CA   13–010, 13–011, 13–020, 13–021, 13–032

L Schuler AG v Wickman Machine Tool Sales Ltd; sub nom. Wickman Machine Tool Sales Ltd v L Schuler AG [1974] A.C. 235; [1973] 2 W.L.R. 683 HL   6–026

Lampleigh v Braithwaite, 80 E.R. 255; (1615) Hob. 105 KB   4–011, 4–012, 4–045

Lasky v Economy Grocery Stores, 319 Mass. 224, 227, 65 N.E.2d 305 (1946)   2–008

Leaf v International Galleries [1950] 2 K.B. 86; [1950] 1 All E.R. 693 CA   8–034, 9–008, 9–009, 9–010

Lefkowitz v Great Minneapolis Surplus Stores Inc (1957) 86 N.W. 2d 689   2–013, 2–060

L'Estrange v F Graucob Ltd [1934] 2 K.B. 394 KBD   6–004, 6–011, 7–006, 7–011, 7–059, 8–004

Lewis v Averay (No.1) [1972] 1 Q.B. 198; [1971] 3 W.L.R. 603 CA (Civ Div)   9–021, 9–022, 9–023, 9–024, 9–025, 9–027

Lipkin Gorman v Karpnale Ltd [1991] 2 A.C. 548; [1991] 3 W.L.R. 10 HL   4–006

Littlewoods Organisation Ltd v Harris [1977] 1 W.L.R. 1472; [1978] 1 All E.R. 1026 CA (Civ Div)   11–024, 11–027

Liverpool City Council v Irwin [1977] A.C. 239; [1976] 2 W.L.R. 562 HL   6–017, 6–018

Lloyds Bank Ltd v Bundy [1975] Q.B. 326; [1974] 3 W.L.R. 501 CA (Civ Div)   10–019

Lloyds Bank Plc v Waterhouse [1993] 2 F.L.R. 97; (1991) 10 Tr. L.R. 161; [1991] Fam. Law 23 CA (Civ Div)   9–031

London and Northern Bank Ex p. Jones, Re [1900] 1 Ch. 220   2–028

Long v Lloyd [1958] 1 W.L.R. 753; [1958] 2 All E.R. 402 CA   8–033, 8–034

Lowe v Peers (1768) 4 Burr. 2225   11–012

Lumley v Wagner, 42 E.R. 687; (1852) 1 De G.M. & G. 604 QB   15–012

Luxor (Eastbourne) Ltd v Cooper [1941] A.C. 108 HL   2–056

McArdle, Re [1951] Ch. 669; [1951] 1 All E.R. 905 CA   4–009, 4–010

McCutcheon v David MacBrayne Ltd [1964] 1 W.L.R. 125; [1964] 1 All E.R. 430 HL   7–014, 7–059

McRae v Commonwealth Disposals Commission, 84 C.L.R. 377   9–006, 9–009

Mahmoud and Ispahani, Re; sub nom. Mahmoud v Ispahani; Arbitration between Mahmoud and Ispahani, Re [1921] 2 K.B. 716; (1921) 6 Ll. L. Rep. 344 CA   11–008

Manchester Diocesan Council of Education v Commercial & General Investments, Ltd [1970] 1 W.L.R. 241; [1969] 3 All E.R. 1593 Ch D   2–036

Maritime National Fish Ltd v Ocean Trawlers Ltd; sub nom. Ocean Trawlers Ltd v Maritime National Fish Ltd [1935] A.C. 524; (1935) 51 Ll. L. Rep. 299 PC (Can)   13–016, 13–032

May & Butcher Ltd v King, The [1934] 2 K.B. 17; [1929] All E.R. Rep. 679 HL   3–006, 3–007, 3–008

Merritt v Merritt [1970] 1 W.L.R. 1211; [1970] 2 All E.R. 760 CA (Civ Div)   3–011, 3–014

Metropolitan Water Board v Dick Kerr & Co Ltd [1918] A.C. 119 HL   13–012

Midland Bank Plc v Shephard; sub nom. Shephard v Midland Bank Plc [1988] 3 All E.R. 17; [1987] 2 F.L.R. 175 CA (Civ Div)   10–017

Mondial shipping and Chartering BV v Astarte Shipping Ltd [1995] C.L.C. 1011   2–048

Moorcock, The (1889) L.R. 14 P.D. 64; [1886–90] All E.R. Rep. 530, CA   6–014, 6–015, 6–031

Museprime Properties, Ltd v Adhill Properties Ltd (1991) 61 P. & C.R. 111; [1990] 36 E.G. 114 Ch D   8–018

National Carriers Ltd v Panalpina (Northern) Ltd [1981] A.C. 675; [1981] 2 W.L.R. 45 HL   13–014

National Westminster Bank Plc v Morgan [1985] A.C. 686; [1985] 2 W.L.R. 588 HL   10–013, 10–019, 10–020

New Zealand Shipping Co Ltd v AM Satterthwaite & Co Ltd (The Eurymedon); sub nom. AM Satterthwaite & Co Ltd v New Zealand Shipping Co Ltd [1975] A.C. 154; [1974] 2 W.L.R. 865; [1974] 1 All E.R. 1015; [1974] 1 Lloyd's Rep. 534; (1974) 118 S.J. 387 PC (New Zealand)   4–016, 4–021, 4–022, 4–045

Nicholson and Venn v Smith-Marriott (1947) 177 L.T. 189   9–010

Nicolene Ltd v Simmonds [1953] 1 Q.B. 543; [1953] 2 W.L.R. 717 CA   3–003

Nordenfelt v Maxim Nordenfelt Guns & Ammunition Co Ltd; sub nom. Maxim Nordenfelt Guns & Ammunition Co v Nordenfelt [1894] A.C. 535 HL   11–016, 11–027

North Ocean Shipping Co v Hyundai Construction Co (The Atlantic Baron) Atlantic Baron, The [1979] Q.B. 705; [1979] 3 W.L.R. 419   10–006

Nottingham Patent Brick & Tile Co v Butler (1885–86) L.R. 16 Q.B.D. 778 CA   8–010

Occidental Worldwide Investment Corp v Skibs A/S Avanti (The Siboen and The Sibotre) [1976] 1 Lloyd's Rep. 293 QBD (Comm)   10–006

Office of Fair Trading v Abbey National Plc [2009] UKSC 6; [2010] 1 A.C. 696   7–054

Olley v Marlborough Court Ltd [1949] 1 K.B. 532; [1949] 1 All E.R. 127 CA   7–009, 7–059

Oscar Chess v Williams [1957] 1 W.L.R. 370; [1957] 1 All E.R. 325, CA   6–006, 8–005

Overseas Medical Supplies Ltd v Orient Transport Services Ltd [1999] 1 All E.R. (Comm) 981; [1999] 2 Lloyd's Rep. 273 CA (Civ Div)   7–038

Overseas Tankship (UK) Ltd v Morts Dock & Engineering Co (The Wagon Mound); sub nom. Morts Dock & Engineering Co v Overseas Tankship (UK) Ltd [1961] A.C. 388; [1961] 2 W.L.R. 126 PC (Aus)   8–039

Page One Records Ltd v Britton [1968] 1 W.L.R. 157; [1967] 3 All E.R. 822 Ch D   15–012

Pan Atlantic Insurance Co Ltd v Pine Top Insurance Co Ltd [1995] 1 A.C. 501; [1994] 3 W.L.R. 677 HL   8–012

Panayiotou v Sony Music Entertainment (UK) Ltd [1994] Ch. 142; [1994] 2 W.L.R. 241 Ch D   11–021

Pankhania v Hackney LBC [2004] All E.R. (D) 205 (Jan)   8–015

Pao On v Lau Yiu Long [1980] A.C. 614; [1979] 3 W.L.R. 435 PC (HK)   4–012, 4–022, 4–023, 4–045, 10–006, 10–008, 10–025

Paradine v Jane (1674) Aleyn 26   13–003

Parker v South Eastern Railway Co; Gabell v South Eastern Railway Co (1876–77) L.R. 2 C.P.D. 416 CA   7–007, 7–008, 7–059

Parsons (Livestock) Ltd v Uttley Ingham & Co Ltd [1978] Q.B. 791; [1977] 3 W.L.R. 990 CA (Civ Div)   14–010, 14–012, 14–013, 14–014, 14–038

Partridge v Crittenden [1968] 1 W.L.R. 1204; [1968] 2 All E.R. 421 DC   2–010, 2–011, 2–013, 2–020, 2–060

Patel v Ali [1984] Ch. 283; [1984] 2 W.L.R. 960 Ch D   15–007, 15–015

Payne v Cave (1789) 3 T.R. 148   2–015

Payzu Ltd v Saunders [1919] 2 K.B. 581 CA   14–038

Pearce v Brooks (1865–66) L.R. 1 Ex. 213 Ex Ct   11–011

Pharmaceutical Society of Great Britain v Boots Cash Chemists (Southern) Ltd [1953] 1 Q.B. 401; [1953] 2 W.L.R. 427 CA   2–008, 2–009, 2–019, 2–020, 2–060

Phillips v Brooks Ltd [1919] 2 K.B. 243 KBD   9–021, 9–022, 9–023, 9–024, 9–025, 9–027, 9–029, 9–031

Philips Hong Kong Ltd v Attorney General of Hong Kong, 61 B.L.R. 41; (1993) 9 Const. L.J. 202 PC (HK)   14–035

Photo Production Ltd v Securicor Transport Ltd [1980] A.C. 827; [1980] 2 W.L.R. 283 HL   7–025, 12–012

Pinnel's Case, 77 E.R. 237; (1602) 5 Co. Rep. 117a QB   4–024, 4–025, 4–026, 4–028, 4–036

Pitt v PHH Asset Management Ltd [1994] 1 W.L.R. 327; [1993] 4 All E.R. 961 CA (Civ Div)   3–004

Planche v Colbourn, 131 E.R. 305; (1831) 8 Bing. 14 KB   12–011, 12–013, 15–015

Post Chaser, The. See Societe Italo-Belge Pour le Commerce et L'Industrie SA (Antwerp) v Palm and Vegetable Oils (Malaysia) Sdn Bhd (The Post Chaser)

Poussard v Speirs & Pond (1875–76) L.R. 1 Q.B.D. 410 QBD   6–027, 6–031

Price v Strange [1978] Ch. 337; [1977] 3 W.L.R. 943 CA (Civ Div)   15–005

Progress Bulk Carriers Ltd v Tube City IMS LLC [2012] EWHC 273 (Comm); [2012] 2 All E.R. (Comm) 855; [2012] 1 Lloyd's Rep. 501; [2012] 1 C.L.C. 365   10–008

R. v Clarke (1927) 40 C.L.R. 227   2–057

R&B Customs Brokers Co Ltd v United Dominions Trust Ltd [1988] 1 W.L.R. 321; [1988] 1 All E.R. 847 CA (Civ Div)   7–029, 7–036, 7–043, 7–051

Raffles v Wichelhaus, 159 E.R. 375; (1864) 2 Hurl. & C. 906 QB   3–002, 9–012

Ramsgate Victoria Hotel Co Ltd v Montefiore; Ramsgate Victoria Hotel Co Ltd v Goldsmid (1865–66) L.R. 1 Ex. 109 Ex Ct   2–058

Redgrave v Hurd (1881–82) L.R. 20 Ch. D. 1 CA   8–019

Roscorla v Thomas (1842) 3 Q.B. 234   4–009

Routledge v Grant (1828) 4 Bing. 653   2–058, 2–060

Routledge v McKay, Nugent (Third Party), Ashgrove (Fourth Party), Mawson (Fifth Party) [1954] 1 W.L.R. 615; [1954] 1 All E.R. 855 CA   6–008

Rowland v Divall [1923] 2 K.B. 500 CA   15–014

Royal Bank of Scotland Plc v Etridge (No.2); Kenyon-Brown v Desmond Banks & Co (Undue Influence) (No.2); Bank of Scotland v Bennett; UCB Home Loans Corp Ltd v Moore; National Westminster Bank Plc v Gill; Midland Bank Plc v Wallace; Barclays Bank Plc v Harris; Barclays Bank Plc v Coleman [2001] UKHL 44; [2002] 2 A.C. 773; [2001] 3 W.L.R. 1021 HL   10–012, 10–013, 10–014, 10–020, 10–021, 10–024, 10–025

Royscot Trust Ltd v Rogerson; sub nom. Royscott Trust v Maidenhead Honda Centre [1991] 2 Q.B. 297; [1991] 3 W.L.R. 57 CA (Civ Div)   8–040

Ruxley Electronics & Construction Ltd v Forsyth; Laddingford Enclosures Ltd v Forsyth [1996] A.C. 344; [1995] 3 W.L.R. 118 HL   14–019

Ryan v Mutual Tontine Westminster Chambers Association [1893] 1 Ch. 116 CA   15–006

St John Shipping Corp v Joseph Rank Ltd [1957] 1 Q.B. 267; [1956] 3 W.L.R. 870 QBD   11–004

Salomon v Salomon & Co Ltd; Salomon & Co Ltd v Salomon; sub nom. Broderip v Salomon [1897] A.C. 22 HL   7–043, 7–051, 11–015

Saunders (Executrix of the Estate of Rose Maud Gallie) v Anglia Building Society (formerly Northampton Town and County Building Society); sub nom. Gallie v Lee [1971] A.C. 1004; [1970] 3 W.L.R. 1078 HL   9–031

Scally v Southern Health and Social Services Board [1992] 1 A.C. 294; [1991] 3 W.L.R. 778 HL   6–018

Scammell and Nephew Ltd v HC&JG Ouston. See G Scammell and Nephew Ltd v HC&JG Ouston

Schroeder Music Publishing Co Ltd v Macaulay. See A Schroeder Music Publishing Co Ltd v Macaulay (formerly Instone); sub nom. Macaulay (formerly Instone) v A Schroeder Music Publishing Co Ltd

Scotson v Pegg (1861) 6 Hurl. & N. 295   4–016, 4–021, 4–022

Scott v Avery, 10 E.R. 1121; (1856) 5 H.L. Cas. 811 HL   11–013

Scriven Bros & Co v Hindley & Co [1913] 3 K.B. 564 KBD   9–013

Selectmove Ltd, Re [1995] 1 W.L.R. 474; [1995] 2 All E.R. 531 CA (Civ Div)   4–020, 4–027

Shadwell v Shadwell (1860) 9 C.B. N.S. 159   4–021, 4–022

Shanklin Pier Ltd v Detel Products Ltd [1951] 2 K.B. 854; [1951] 2 All E.R. 471 KBD   6–010

Sharneyford Supplies Ltd (formerly Flinthall Farms) v Edge [1987] Ch. 305; [1987] 2 W.L.R. 363 CA (Civ Div)   8–040

Shirlaw v Southern Foundries Ltd. *See* Southern Foundries (1926) Ltd v Shirlaw

Shogun Finance Ltd v Hudson; sub nom. Hudson v Shogun Finance Ltd [2003] UKHL 62; [2004] 1 A.C. 919; [2003] 3 W.L.R. 1371 HL   8–036, 9–026, 9–027, 9–030, 9–031

Shuey v USA (1875) 92 U.S. 73   2–060

Simpkins v Pays [1955] 1 W.L.R. 975; [1955] 3 All E.R. 10 Assizes (Chester)   3–012

Skeate v Beale (1840) 11 Ad. & El. 983   10–005

Sky Petroleum v VIP Petroleum [1974] 1 W.L.R. 576; [1974] 1 All E.R. 954 Ch D   15–004

Smith v Eric S Bush (A Firm); Harris v Wyre Forest DC [1990] 1 A.C. 831; [1989] 2 W.L.R. 790 HL   7–041

Smith v Hughes (1870–71) L.R. 6 Q.B. 597; [1861–73] All E.R. Rep. 632 QB   9–012

Smith v Land & House Property Corp (1885) L.R. 28 Ch. D. 7 CA   8–014, 8–043

Smith New Court Securities Ltd v Citibank NA; sub nom. Smith New Court Securities Ltd v Scrimgeour Vickers (Asset Management) Ltd [1997] A.C. 254; [1996] 3 W.L.R. 1051 HL   8–038, 8–041

Societe Italo-Belge Pour le Commerce et L'Industrie SA (Antwerp) v Palm and Vegetable Oils (Malaysia) Sdn Bhd (The Post Chaser) [1982] 1 All E.R. 19; [1981] 2 Lloyd's Rep. 695 QBD (Comm)   4–042, 4–043

Solle v Butcher [1950] 1 K.B. 671; [1949] 2 All E.R. 1107 CA   8–015

South Caribbean Trading Ltd v Trafigura Beheer BV [2004] EWHC 2676; [2005] 1 Lloyd's Rep. 128 QBD (Comm)   4–020

Southern Foundries (1926) Ltd v Shirlaw [1940] A.C. 701; [1940] 2 All E.R. 445, HL   6–015, 6–031

Spice Girls Ltd v Aprilia World Service BV; sub nom. Spice Girls Ltd v Aprilla World Service BV [2002] EWCA Civ 15; [2002] E.M.L.R. 27; (2002) 25(4) I.P.D. 25024 CA (Civ Div)   8–008, 8–016

Spurling Ltd v Bradshaw. *See* J Spurling Ltd v Bradshaw

Stevenson Jaques & Co v McLean (1879–80) L.R. 5 Q.B.D. 346 QBD   2–023

Stilk v Myrick, 170 E.R. 1168; (1809) 2 Camp. 317 KB   4–015, 4–016, 4–017, 4–018, 4–019, 4–020, 4–025, 4–026, 4–045, 10–005, 12–003

Storer v Manchester City Council [1974] 1 W.L.R. 1403; [1974] 3 All E.R. 824 CA (Civ Div)   2–005, 2–006, 2–060

Sudbrook Trading Estate Ltd v Eggleton [1983] 1 A.C. 444; [1982] 3 W.L.R. 315 HL   6–008

Suisse Atlantique Societe d'Armement SA v NV Rotterdamsche Kolen Centrale [1967] 1 A.C. 361; [1966] 2 W.L.R. 944; [1966] 2 All E.R. 61; [1966] 1 Lloyd's Rep. 529; (1966) 110 S.J. 367 HL 7–025

Sumpter v Hedges [1898] 1 Q.B. 673 CA   12–009

Super Servant Two, The. See J Lauritzen AS v Wijsmuller BV (The Super Servant Two)

Surrey CC and Mole DC v Bredero Homes Ltd [1993] 1 W.L.R. 1361; [1993] 3 All E.R. 705 CA (Civ Div)   14–027, 14–028, 14–029

Sutton v Mishcon de Reya [2003] EWHC 3166 (Ch); [2004] 1 F.L.R. 837; [2004] 3 F.C.R. 142 Ch D   11–011

Sylvia Shipping Co Ltd v Progress Bulk Carriers Ltd [2010] EWHC 542 (Comm); [2010] 2 Lloyd's Rep. 81; [2010] 1 C.L.C. 470   14–014

Taylor v Allon [1966] 1 Q.B. 304; [1965] 2 W.L.R. 598 DC   2–057

Taylor v Caldwell (1863) 32 L.J. Q.B. 164; 3 B. & S. 826   9–006, 13–004, 13–005, 13–006, 13–008, 13–011, 13–030, 13–032

Tenax Steamship Co v Owners of the Motor Vessel Brimnes (The Brimnes); sub nom. Tenax Steamship Co v Reinante Transoceanica Navegacion SA (The Brimnes) [1975] Q.B. 929; [1974] 3 W.L.R. 613 CA (Civ Div)   2–045, 2–046

Thomas v Thomas (1842) 2 Q.B. 851   4–005, 4–045

Thomas Witter Ltd v TBP Industries Ltd [1996] 2 All E.R. 573 Ch D   8–041, 8–042

Thompson v London Midland & Scottish Railway Co [1930] 1 K.B. 41 CA   6–011, 7–008, 7–009

Thornton v Shoe Lane Parking [1971] 2 Q.B. 163; [1971] 2 W.L.R. 585 CA (Civ Div)   2–019, 7–009, 7–010

Tinn v Hoffman (1873) 29 L.T. 271   2–024

Tito v Waddell (No.2); Tito v Attorney General [1977] Ch. 106; [1977] 2 W.L.R. 496 Ch D   14–026

Transfield Shipping Inc v Mercator Shipping Inc (The Achilleas) Achilleas, The [2008] UKHL 48; [2009] 1 A.C. 61   14–014

Tsakiroglou & Co Ltd v Noblee Thorl GmbH; Albert D Gaon & Co v Societe Interprofessionelle des Oleagineux Fluides Alimentaires [1962] A.C. 93; [1961] 2 W.L.R. 633 HL   13–018

Tungsten Electric Co Ltd v Tool Metal Manufacturing Co Ltd (No.3); sub nom. Tool Metal Manufacture Co Ltd v Tungsten Electric Co Ltd [1955] 1 W.L.R. 761; [1955] 2 All E.R. 657 HL
4–042, 4–045

Tweddle v Atkinson, 121 E.R. 762; (1861) 1 B. & S. 393 QB   5–002, 5–009, 5–012

Victoria Laundry (Windsor) v Newman Industries [1949] 2 K.B. 528; [1949] 1 All E.R. 997 CA   14–006, 14–007, 14–008, 14–012, 14–038

Vitol SA v Norelf Ltd (The Santa Clara) [1996] A.C. 800; [1996] 3 W.L.R. 105 HL   12–012

WJ Alan & Co Ltd v El Nasr Export & Import Co [1972] 2 Q.B. 189; [1972] 2 W.L.R. 800 CA (Civ Div)   4–042

WN Hillas & Co Ltd v Arcos Ltd; WN Hillas & Co Ltd v Arcos Ltd (Quantum) (1932) 43 Ll. L. Rep. 359; (1932) 147 L.T. 503 HL   3–005, 3–014

Wakeham v Wood (1982) 43 P. & C.R. 40; [1982] J.P.L. 242 CA (Civ Div)   15–011

Walford v Miles [1992] 2 A.C. 128; [1992] 2 W.L.R. 174 HL   3–004

Walters v Morgan (1861) 45 E.R. 1056   15–007

Ward v Byham [1956] 1 W.L.R. 496; [1956] 2 All E.R. 318 CA   4–014, 4–020

Warlow v Harrison, 120 E.R. 920; (1858) 1 El. & El. 295 QB   2–015

Warner Bros Pictures Inc v Nelson [1937] 1 K.B. 209 KBD   15–012

Watford Electronics Ltd v Sanderson CFL Ltd [2001] EWCA Civ 317; [2001] 1 All E.R. (Comm) 696; [2001] B.L.R. 143 CA (Civ Div)   7–041

Watts v Morrow [1991] 1 W.L.R. 1421; [1991] 4 All E.R. 937 CA (Civ Div)   14–033

Watts v Spence [1976] Ch. 165; [1975] 2 W.L.R. 1039 Ch D   8–040

Webster v Cecil (1861) 30 Beav. 62   15–007

Wenckheim v Arndt (1873) (N.Z.) 1 J.R. 73   2–038

White v Bluett (853) 23 L.J. Ex 36   4–006

White v John Warwick & Co [1953] 1 W.L.R. 1285; [1953] 2 All E.R. 1021 CA   7–024

Williams v Carwardine (1833) 5 C. & P. 566   2–057

Williams v Roffey Bros & Nicholls (Contractors) Ltd [1991] 1 Q.B. 1; [1990] 2 W.L.R. 1153 CA (Civ Div)   4–018, 4–019, 4–020, 4–025, 4–027, 4–045, 12–003

With v O'Flanagan [1936] Ch. 575 CA   8–011, 8–043

Woodar Investment Development Ltd v Wimpey Construction UK Ltd [1980] 1 W.L.R. 277; [1980] 1 All E.R. 571 HL   5–007

Wrotham Park Estate Co Ltd v Parkside Homes Ltd [1974] 1 W.L.R. 798; [1974] 2 All E.R. 321 Ch D   14–028, 14–029, 14–030, 14–031

Wyatt v Kreglinger [1933] 1 K.B. 793 CA   11–019

X v X (Y and Z intervening) [2002] 1 F.L.R. 508; [2002] Fam. Law 98 Fam Div   11–012

Zanzibar v British Aerospace (Lancaster House) Ltd [2000] 1 W.L.R. 2333; [2000] C.L.C. 735 QBD (Comm)   8–041

Table of Statutes

1845   Gaming Act (8 & 9 Vict. c.109)
  s.18   11–007
1873   Supreme Court of Judicature Act (36
       & 37 Vict. c.66)   4–037
1875   Supreme Court of Judicature
       (Amendment) Act (38 & 39 Vict.
       c.77)   4–037
1932   Merchant Shipping (Safety and
       Load Line Conventions) Act (22 & 23
       Geo. 5 c.9)   11–004
1933   Pharmacy and Poisons Act (23 & 24
       Geo. 5 c.25)
  s.18   2–008
1938   Increase of Rent and Mortgage
       Interest (Restrictions) Act (1 & 2 Geo.6
       c.26)   8–015
1943   Law Reform (Frustrated Contracts)
       Act (6 & 7 Geo.5 c.40)   13–024,
       13–032
  s.1(2)   13–024, 13–025, 13–030,
       13–032
    (3)   13–024, 13–026, 13–027, 13–028,
       13–030, 13–031, 13–032
  s.2   13–032
1945   Law Reform (Contributory
       Negligence) Act (8 & 9 Geo. 6
       c.28)   8–039
  s.1(1)   14–037
1954   Protection of Birds Act (2 & 3 Eliz. 2
       c.30) s.6   2–010
1957   Occupiers Liability Act (5 & 6 Eliz. 2
       c.31)   7–010
1959   Restriction of Offensive Weapons
       Act (7 & 8 Eliz. 2 c.37)   2–009

1964   Hire Purchase Act (c.53)
  s.27   9–026, 9–029
1967   Misrepresentation Act
       (c.7)   8–020, 8–022, 8–023, 8–024,
       8–025, 8–026, 8–028 s.2   8–023,
       8–041
    (1)   8–024, 8–025, 8–026, 8–027,
       8–029, 8–030, 8–040, 8–043
    (2)   8–041, 8–043
  s.3   8–042
1968   Trade Descriptions Act
       (c.29)   2–008
1970   Law Reform (Miscellaneous
       Provisions) Act (c.33)   2–035, 11–012
1971   Unsolicited Goods and Services Act
       (c.30)   2–052
1973   Supply of Goods (Implied Terms)
       Act (c.13)   7–042
  ss 9–11   7–042, 7–043
1977   Unfair Contract Terms Act
       (c.50)   7–002, 7–003, 7–025, 7–026,
       7–027, 7–028, 7–042, 7–043, 7–047,
       7–048, 7–051, 7–059
  s.2   7–028, 7–030, 7–031, 7–033, 7–059
    (1)   7–031, 7–055, 7–059
    (2)   7–031, 7–059
  s.3   7–028, 7–029
  s.6   7–028, 7–029, 7–033, 7–034,
       7–037, 7–056, 7–059
    (2)   7–034, 7–036
    (3)   7–034, 7–036
    (4)   7–056
  s.7   7–028, 7–037, 7–056, 7–059
    (2)   7–037

(3)   7–037
s.8   7–028, 8–042
s.11   7–028, 7–038, 7–040, 7–041,
   7–059, 8–042
   (1)   7–038, 7–059, 8–042
   (2)   7–038
   (4)   7–039, 7–059
   (5)   7–038
s.12   7–029, 7–035, 7–051, 7–059
s.14   7–029, 7–033
Sch.2   7–038, 7–040, 7–045,059
1979   Sale of Goods Act (c.54)   1–006,
   6–012, 6–031, 7–029, 7–032, 7–033,
   7–059
s.6   9–005
s.7   13–.32
s.8   3–008, 3–014
   (2)   3–008
s.9   3–008, 3–014
s.12   6–019, 6–025, 9–017, 15–014
   (5A)   6–025
s.13   6–019, 6–025, 7–033
s.14   6–019, 6–025, 7–018, 7–033
s.15   6–025, 7–033
s.51(3)   14–017
s.52   15–004
s.55(3)   7–041
s.57(2)   2–015
1981   Senior Courts Act (c.54)
s.50   14–029
1982   Supply of Goods and Services Act
   (c.29)   6–019, 7–032, 7–059
   ss 8–10   7–044
1989   Law of Property (Miscellaneous
   Provisions) Act (c.34)   1–002
1992   Trade Union and Labour
   Relations (Consolidation) Act
   (c.52)   15–008
1998   Competition Act (c.41)   11–006
1999   Contracts (Rights of Third Parties)
   Act (c.31)   4–007, 5–004, 5–008,
   5–012, 15–004
   s.1   5–008, 5–010, 5–012
   (1)(a)   5–008, 5–009, 5–012

(b)   5–008, 5–009, 5–012
(2)   5–008, 5–009
(3)   5–008, 5–009
s.2   5–010
s.3   5–010, 5–011
(2)–(5)   5–011
(6)   5–011
s.6   5–012
(1)   5–012
(2)   5–012
(3)   5–012
2005   Gambling Act (c.19)   11–007
2006   Companies Act (c.46)
s.33   5–012
2011   Postal Services Act (c.5)   2–028
2014   Consumer Rights Act (c.x)   7–048,
   8–042
Pt 2   7–049
s.2   7–051
   (2)   7–051
   (3)   7–051
ss 9–14   7–056
s.15   7–057
s.31   7–056, 7–057
   (1)   7–059
ss 49–52   7–058
s.57(1)–(3)   7–058, 7–059
s.61   7–049, 7–052
   (1), (2)   7–052
   (6)   7–049
   (8)   7–049
s.62   7–052, 7–053, 7–054, 7–055,
   7–058, 7–059, 8–042
   (3)–(7)   7–052
   (4)   7–059
s.63   7–053
   (6)   7–053
s.64   7–054
   (2)–(5)   7–054
s.65   7–053, 7–055
   (1)   7–055, 7–059
s.68(2)   7–054
s.69   7–059   Sch.2, Pt 1, paras 1, 5, 12,
   14   7–053

Introduction to Contract Law

CHAPTER OVERVIEW

In this chapter we:

- **introduce the importance of contract law to everyday situations**

- **define a contract and consider some important underlying legal principles**

- **consider the relationship between contract and tort**

- **explore the sources and the development of contract law**

- **introduce the principle of freedom of contract**

- **discuss the limitations of freedom of contract**

Summary

1-001 The law of contract is truly remarkable. In fact, it is difficult to think of an area of law that has more impact on everyday life. Each day millions of contracts are formed with few individuals making it through a 24-hour period without entering into a contract of some description. A bus ride to work, the purchase of a sandwich at lunchtime or a ticket to see a film at the cinema are all simple examples of contracts that pass by without us giving further thought as to the legal principles that govern these activities. Most contracts are performed easily with both parties meeting their contractual obligations. Therefore, in the majority of cases, there is no need to challenge the contract, which is why so many of the resulting contractual obligations pass by unnoticed.

Despite the considerable number of contracts that are formed every day, only a tiny proportion will be challenged by the parties and, in turn, even a smaller number will ever reach the courts. To this extent it could be argued that an understanding of the fundamental principles of contract law only becomes necessary when contractual relationships break down or are challenged. However, an understanding of the key contractual principles is important. Not only do they provide a framework for resolving disputes when things go wrong under a contract, but they also provide a framework allowing individuals to regulate their own contractual obligations. The intention of this book is therefore to provide a clear and structured introduction to the fundamental principles of contract law.

Some introductory points

1-002 There are a number of misapprehensions regarding contract law. Perhaps the most common is that a contract must be in the form of a signed written document. From the examples given above it should be clear that this is not the case. A contract can be in the form of an oral agreement that can be as legally enforceable as a formal written document. In fact, there are very limited situations in which a contract *must* be reduced to a formal written document. A contract made by deed provides one example, as in order for such a contract to be enforceable it must be formally reduced to writing and must also pass the formal requirements of the Law of Property (Miscellaneous Provisions) Act 1989.

Contracts that are not required to be made by deed are referred to as "simple contracts". As the majority of contracts made by deed are for the transfer of land or property (which is beyond the scope of this book) our focus will be on simple contracts for which there is no strict requirement of writing.

Defining a contract

1-003 A contract can be simply defined as a legally binding agreement. The parties to the agreement are generally free to agree whatever terms they wish and the court will seek to give legal effect to their agreement should it become necessary to resolve a dispute between them. While a contract is in essence simply an agreement that the court will enforce between the parties, there are some specific legal principles that distinguish a *contract* from an *agreement* in the ordinary sense of the word. Perhaps the most important of these legal principles is the approach the courts take when determining the occurrence of agreement. In deciding whether the parties have formed an agreement the courts apply an *objective* test to determine this issue. In other words, the courts will look at an agreement from the perspective of a reasonable person. If a reasonable person would conclude that, from their words and conduct, the parties have formed an agreement then the courts will seek to give effect to this agreement. This will be the case even if the parties did not believe that they had reached an agreement. The difference between what the parties actually believed (a subjective test) and what the reasonable man would conclude (an objective test) is one of the most unique aspects of contract law. As will become clear, this theme of *objectivity* is a recurrent theme in the study of contract law and permeates most aspects of contract formation and performance.

Objectivity in the law of contract

The courts apply objective principles in many areas of contract law. However, the most impor-   1-004
tant use of these principles relates to the formation of an agreement. An agreement is the first stage towards a legally binding contract and the application of objective principles is fundamental in assisting the courts to identify whether the parties have indeed reached an agreement between themselves. Contractual intent and a clear willingness to be bound in a contractual relationship are key ingredients in the formation of an agreement and the courts deploy an objective test to assess the contractual intent of the parties. Again, the application of an objective test could allow the courts to conclude that *objectively* the parties formed an agreement despite claims from the parties to the contrary that *subjectively* they lacked the necessary contractual intent.

At first glance it may sound rather unfair to hold a party to an agreement that he or she may not have intended to form. However, there are many important justifications for this objective approach. For example, the application of an objective test to the issue of intention promotes certainty in agreements. It prevents parties from arguing that they never intended to enter into a contract when they discover that they have entered into a bad bargain. A *subjective* test would be more open to abuse in that a party could quite easily argue that they did not actually intend to enter into an agreement once it starts to operate to their disadvantage. In such cases the consideration of the evidence would be reduced to the word of one party against the other. This would not provide for certainty in agreements.

A further justification for adopting an objective approach to contractual intent is that it allows factors to be taken into account that, subjectively, may not have been foreseen or considered by the parties. As no party is completely reasonable, they may fail to properly contemplate all the probable consequences that could flow from their actions. For example, by placing an advertisement in the local newspaper offering goods for sale, an individual may, subjectively, argue that he intended to make an offer to sell those goods. However, the application of an objective test would suggest differently. As the individual may only have a limited stock of goods to sell then he would not, objectively, have intended to sell goods to whoever purported to accept his offer. This would create a problem of "multi-acceptance". He would not have intended to expose himself to numerous potential contracts that he would be unable to fulfill. The application of an objective test therefore takes account of these factors which may not have been considered by the individual and as such provides a standard platform to assess contractual intent.

A legally binding agreement

1-005   A contract is defined above as a legally binding agreement. An agreement is the first stage towards a contract, but there are further legal requirements that must be satisfied before an agreement will result in an enforceable contract. The courts require that an agreement is supported by consideration. Consideration will be discussed in more detail in Ch.4, but essentially consideration is the *test of enforceability* in contract law. In order for the parties to be bound by their promises, the parties must have provided consideration in exchange for those promises. If there is no consideration to support the agreement then the courts will not enforce the agreement.

Further, even if the agreement is supported by consideration the courts also require that the parties had an intention to create legal relations. There are a number of circumstances in which the parties will be presumed *not* to have a contractual intent (in domestic agreements for example). This presumption would need to be challenged (or rebutted) before the courts will enforce such agreements.

Finally, the law recognises certain "vitiating factors" that can bring an agreement to an end. For example, the parties may have formed an agreement and provided consideration, but the agreement may have been formed following a misrepresentation by one party or as a result of a mistake and the effect will be to challenge the validity of the agreement. The precise effect on the agreement will depend on the vitiating factor in question. A misrepresentation, for example, will render the contract *voidable*. A voidable contract still binds the parties until the innocent party takes steps to avoid it. A mistake, on the other hand, may render the contract *void*. A void contract is a contract that never in fact existed between the parties, so neither party will have any obligations under the contract.

So, a more detailed analysis of a contract reveals a number of legal rules that determine whether an agreement is legally enforceable:

1. The agreement must be supported by consideration.
2. The parties must have an intention to create legal relations.
3. The agreement must not be affected by any vitiating factors.

We shall adopt a similar structure when assessing the fundamentals of contract law. We shall first look at forming the agreement and the requirements of offer and acceptance. We shall then look at enforcing the agreement and the role of consideration. Next we will examine the ways in which the courts regulate the agreement. Finally, we will consider how the contract can be brought to an end and the available remedies for a breach of contract.

. . . .

The sources of contract law

Contract law is a branch of private law and as such is concerned with the legal relationships between individuals. A breach of contract will be classed as a civil wrong and will give the innocent party the right to claim remedies (usually damages) for the loss suffered as a result of the breach. Contract law is primarily founded in common law. In this context when we refer to "common law" we are essentially referring to *judge-made* law.

1-006

While the common law is the primary source of contract law, there are a few important statutory provisions. The majority of these statutory provisions are quite modern in terms of the development of contract law and many represent an attempt by Parliament to interfere with and regulate certain types of agreement. For example, the Sale of Goods Act 1979 now implies (inserts) terms into contracts for the sale of goods. These terms are implied by statute to prevent a seller from abusing his stronger bargaining position in relation to a consumer and also to recognise the modern realities of contract formation; it is no longer necessary to sit down and agree *all* the terms of an agreement and provide for all eventualities before the agreement will be enforceable.

It is also important to recognise that contract law inevitably overlaps with other areas of law. It is possible that a breach of contract could also result in tortious liability. Understanding the relationship between contract and tort is vital. We will, therefore, briefly discuss the relationship between contract and tort.

THE RELATIONSHIP BETWEEN CONTRACT AND TORT

A tort is also a civil wrong. However, a tort is committed when an individual fails to conduct his actions in accordance with the standards prescribed by the law. The most common example is the tort of negligence. The tort of negligence imposes a duty to act reasonably. The law of tort requires that there exists a "duty of care" between the parties. If one individual owes a duty of care to another and he fails to exercise this duty with reasonable care and skill, and this failure causes loss to the other party, then the injured party can claim compensation for this loss in the tort of negligence.

1-007

A tort and a breach of contract are both civil wrongs, but the obligations in each arise in very different ways. In tort, the duty to act "reasonably" is imposed by the courts and the courts will compensate an injured party for the loss he suffered by the failure of another to act in accordance with this standard. However, obligations under a contract are fundamentally different. It is the *parties* (not the courts) that generally create and define their obligations under a contract. The courts will intervene and compensate an innocent party when the other party fails to meet those obligations to which he agreed to be bound, but generally the courts will not seek to actively regulate the agreement.

- Contractual obligations will bind the parties as they *freely entered* into the contract. The parties have a *choice* as to their legal obligations under the contract. The courts will compensate the parties for a failure to meet these contractual obligations.
- The law of tort *imposes obligations* on individuals to conduct their activities to a certain legal standard. An individual has *no choice* but to meet the standards imposed by law. The courts will compensate the parties for a failure to act in accordance with the standards required by law.

CONCURRENT LIABILITY IN CONTRACT AND TORT

1-008 It is possible that a contract can be breached by a negligent act. In such cases there will be concurrent liability in contract and in tort resulting from a negligent breach of contract. The innocent party could pursue an action in the tort of negligence or he could pursue an action for breach of contract. The cause of action the claimant ultimately chooses to pursue will therefore affect the remedies available. The primary remedy in tort and contract law is damages; the court will award compensation to reflect the loss suffered. However, an award of damages is calculated differently in contract and tort (see Ch.13). Despite these rather artificial distinctions, in practice the claimant will generally not be concerned whether his cause of action rests in contract or tort—he will simply be concerned with the issue of compensation and the chances of success. So, being aware of the potential overlap between contract and tort is vital in order to give the best advice when deciding upon the appropriate cause of action on the particular facts.

THE RELATIONSHIP BETWEEN CONTRACT AND RESTITUTION

1-009 The law of restitution is a further area of law that has the potential to overlap with contract law. However, the key principles of restitution are quite different from those in contract law. First, the law of restitution is not concerned with a mutual exchange of obligations between the parties. The law of restitution operates so as to reverse an unjust enrichment. There is no strict requirement that a contract exists in order for restitution to operate. For example, if money is paid by mistake then the law of restitution will operate to reverse the unjust enrichment of the other party. Secondly, the law of restitution may operate as a way of "filling the gaps" left by contract law. The courts may award restitution in relation to an unjust enrichment under a contract that failed to materialise.

The self-regulatory nature of contract law

A contract agreement is based on the principle of consent. The parties are free to agree to whatever terms they wish and the court will generally seek to give effect to their intentions. The courts are very reluctant indeed to interfere with a private bargain that has been freely agreed between the parties. The parties create the obligations under the contract and the parties are generally free to regulate their agreement. Given the millions of contracts that are created every day it is true to say that contract law can be seen as one of the success stories of self-regulation.

1-010

Whether the reluctance of the courts to interfere with private agreements is driven more by necessity than principle is debatable; it would be impractical (impossible) if the court had to regulate every contractual agreement, but the foundations of this reluctance can actually be traced back many years to the "classical theory" of contract law.

One of the foundations of the classical theory of contract was the recognition that a contract is based on free exchange between the parties. The parties are therefore free to agree to whatever terms they wish and the courts will seek to enforce these obligations. As a result, the courts would not interfere and regulate the agreement for the parties, nor would they enquire as to whether an individual had formed a good bargain. These principles of freedom still survive to some extent within the modern law of contract and this again will form a recurrent theme throughout many of the subsequent chapters. There remains, however, tension between the principle of freedom of contract on the one hand and the desire of the courts to intervene and protect individuals from a potential abuse of this freedom, particularly where one party is of a weaker bargaining position. This uneasy tension between party freedom and judicial intervention will again be highlighted throughout the subsequent chapters.

The classical theory of contract

Until the late eighteenth century there was no distinct body of law that could be labelled as "contract law". Rather, the courts and the State regulated certain activities by imposing legal restrictions on certain transactions. For example, restrictions were imposed as to the price for which certain goods could be sold. Restrictions were also imposed as to the quantity of certain goods that could be produced. It was not until the early nineteenth century that general principles of "contract law" started to emerge. These principles formed a collective body referred to as the "classical theory" of contract.

1-011

There are a number of important elements that make up the classical theory of contract. First, the classical theory of contract is based on a mutual exchange of promises and obligations. This is one reason why the courts will enforce an agreement between the parties, as both parties have contributed something to the agreement. Secondly, the classical theory of contract is based on freedom of contract. The move towards a more industrialised nation in the early nineteenth century brought a new freedom to trade and also new freedom to contract. The courts recognised the freedom of the parties to enter into an agreement with whomever they wished. Further, it was recognised that these parties could agree any terms they wished. If the terms were unfavourable then the presumption was that the parties would not agree to them. If the parties freely accepted the terms of the contract then the court would be very reluctant indeed to interfere with this agreement.

The principle of freedom of contract is firmly rooted in the development of the classical theory of contract law. However, as the law has developed many have questioned its continued significance to modern contract formation. Despite these arguments it is clear that the principle of freedom as the corner stone of the classical theory of contract continues to be reflected in the modern law of contract. The formation of the agreement itself provides a relevant example of this. When trying to identify and enforce an agreement the courts are seeking to give effect to the intention of the parties and by doing so are seeking to ensure that freely negotiated obligations are honoured.

PROBLEMS WITH THE CLASSICAL THEORY OF CONTRACT

1-012   The classical theory of contract certainly influences many areas of modern contract law. However, it is not without flaw and there are a number of problems when trying to reconcile the classical theory with modern contract formation. Particular problems, for example, arise when applying the classical theory to unilateral contracts.

A unilateral contract is not founded on a mutual exchange of promises. Only *one party* makes a promise. The other party will be entitled to the benefit of this promise if he meets the conditions of acceptance. For example, an advertisement offering £500 to the person who finds and returns my lost mobile phone is an example of a unilateral contract. The advertisement does not place an obligation on anyone to go out and find my mobile phone, it is completely one sided. The obligation is for the owner to pay the reward should someone find and return the mobile phone.

In contrast, a bilateral contract imposes obligations on *both parties* and is more in line with the classical theory of contract: the contract is based on a mutual exchange of promises. A simple example can be found in a contract for the sale of goods. Both parties have exchanged promises under the contract. The seller has promised to deliver the goods and the purchaser has in exchange promised to pay for the goods. If either party fails to meet their obligations that party can be sued for breach of contract.

Of course, the classical theory of contract was always based on an assumption that a party would never agree to terms that were unfavourable. In the early nineteenth century when the industrial age was in its infancy this may have been true. However, it is this assumption that has severely limited the role of freedom of contract in modern contract law.

LIMITATIONS ON FREEDOM OF CONTRACT

The agreement was at the heart of the classical theory of contract. The courts would seek to give effect to the intention of the parties on the grounds that they freely entered into an agreement. However, modern contract law adopts a slightly more restrictive approach. The themes of modern contract law are not so much concerned with the freedom of the parties to contract, but rather the focus has shifted towards tighter regulation of the agreement. At common law and under statute several restrictions to freedom of contract have been developed. A number of these have been in response to the concern that a party may exploit their stronger bargaining position. This is particularly so in relation to the common law and statutory responses to the use of exclusion clauses (see Ch.7).

1-013

Further, the courts have been motivated by concerns of unconscionability and have developed specific principles to govern contracts entered into as a result of duress, undue influence or misrepresentation. Again, these developments at common law have generally been supported by Parliament. The past 40 years or so have seen a number of wide-ranging legislative provisions that act so as to limit the principles of freedom of contract.

Despite this attack on freedom of contract by the courts and by Parliament, some of the principles of freedom of contract have survived and are alive within modern contract law. Perhaps the best example of the resilience of freedom of contract can be found in the requirement for offer and acceptance. An offer and acceptance form the first stage of a legally binding agreement and the courts still require that these ingredients are present. It has been questioned whether a strict offer and acceptance are necessary to form an agreement. However, despite these arguments the elements of offer and acceptance are fundamental to modern contract law and it is to these elements of offer and acceptance that we now turn.

◀ ....

Summary

1. A contract can be defined as a legally binding agreement. There are very few formalities as to the form a contract should take; a contract can be a signed written document, but equally an agreement can form the basis of an enforceable contract.

2. In order for an agreement to be enforceable the parties must display a clear contractual intent; an intention to be bound in a legal relationship with the other party. The courts apply an objective test to determine the contractual intent of the parties.

3. Contract law is a branch of private law and as such it regulates agreements between individuals. The law of contract is founded on common law principles but

has later been by supplemented by developments in the law of equity and under statute.

4. The law of contract is largely self-regulatory; the courts are reluctant to interfere and regulate a privately formed agreement. Generally, the role of the courts is to resolve disputes when contractual obligations are not performed in accordance with the agreement.

Offer and Acceptance

2

CHAPTER OVERVIEW

In this chapter we:

- introduce the formation of the agreement
- define and identify the key ingredients of an offer
- distinguish an offer from an invitation to treat
- apply the relevant legal principles of the offer to everyday examples
- discuss the relevant legal principles of acceptance
- consider the revocation of the offer

Summary

Key Cases Grid

End of Chapter Question

Further Reading

Introduction

2-001   A contract is a legally binding agreement. The agreement is the first step towards the forma-tion of a contract. There are few formalities required as to how this agreement is reached. There is no formal requirement that an agreement be reduced to writing, meaning that verbal agreements can equally give rise to contractual obligations. Despite the lack of formal require-ments in reaching an agreement, the courts do require an exchange of offer and acceptance between the parties in order to recognise the agreement. This chapter is therefore concerned with the formation of the *agreement* and the relevant legal principles the court will apply to the exchange of offer and acceptance between the parties.

Offer + Acceptance = Agreement

The person who makes a legally identifiable offer is called the *offeror*. The party to whom the offer is made is called the *offeree*. If the offeree unequivocally accepts the offer then the parties will have formed an *agreement*. Whether this agreement is legally binding (i.e. will be enforce-able by law) will depend on further formalities being met and relevant tests of enforceability being satisfied. In order for a contract to be legally enforceable there is the requirement that the agreement be supported by consideration. However, at this stage we will only concern our-selves with a discussion of offer and acceptance, as without an exchange of offer and accept-ance there will be no *agreement* for the courts to enforce or scrutinise. The occurrence of the agreement is identified in Figure 2.1.

FIGURE 2.1 **The occurrence of the agreement**

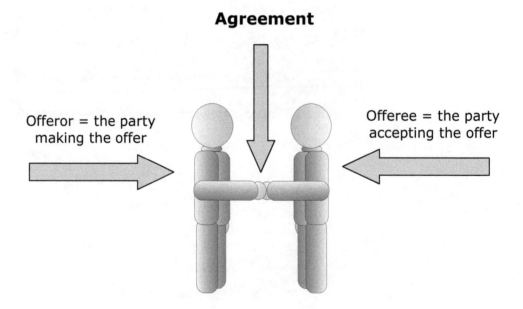

Agreement

Offeror = the party
making the offer

Offeree = the party
accepting the offer

Identifying an offer

Being able to identify an offer may sound a simple task. However, such a simple word   2-002
has received extensive analysis from the courts. Below you will find examples of how the
courts have applied the requirements of offer and acceptance to everyday situations, often
with surprising results. Despite the various situations in which the courts have to consider
the application of offer and acceptance, the contractual principles being applied in all
these situations are very similar and have (to some extent) remained unchanged for many
years.

Ingredients of an offer

A useful way to summarise and structure these principles is to look at the different "ingredi-   2-003
ents" that the court will look for before it will find an offer that is then capable of acceptance.
The ingredients of an offer are as follows:

1. a clear display of contractual intent;
2. on terms that are fixed;
3. on terms that are certain;
4. on terms that once accepted automatically bind both parties to their agreement.

If all these ingredients are present it is likely that the court will find an offer.
(Note: Points (2) and (3) will be considered in more detail in Ch.3 during our discussion of
certainty.)

CONTRACTUAL INTENT

The most important and fundamental ingredient in the formation of an agreement is the   2-004
requirement for a *clear display of contractual intent*. The offeror must display a clear intention to be bound in a legal relationship. If the offeror lacks this necessary contractual intent
then the court will not construe the relevant statement as an offer and instead will interpret
the relevant statement as an *invitation to treat*. An invitation to treat is merely a declaration
that the party is open to the negotiation process but such a statement lacks the necessary
contractual intent to constitute an offer. This negotiation process may ultimately lead to the

formation of a contract, but only once the courts are able to identify a clear exchange of offer and acceptance.

An invitation to treat is usually lacking in all of the necessary ingredients noted above. An invitation to treat lacks contractual intent; such statements are usually quite vague so that no reasonable person would assume they displayed an intention to be bound. It is not possible to accept an invitation to treat and so no contractual obligations can flow from it. The first stage, therefore, in determining whether an agreement has been formed is being able to distinguish an offer from an invitation to treat. The distinction will ultimately turn on an assessment of contractual intent.

ASSESSING CONTRACTUAL INTENT

2-005   In assessing whether an offer has been made the courts adopt an *objective* approach to the issue of intention. Rather than being concerned with *actual* intent of the offeror (a subjective approach) the courts adopt a more impartial stance and apply an objective standard to determine the issue of contractual intent.

As Lord Denning observed in **Storer v Manchester City Council** [1974] 1 W.L.R. 1403 at 1408:

> **"In contracts you do not look into the actual intent in a man's mind. You look at what he said and did. A contract is formed when there is, to all outward appearances, a contract. A man cannot get out of a contract by saying: 'I did not intend to contract' if by his words he has done so."**

Following this reasoning in **Storer**, the courts are focused not on the actual intent of the offeror, rather they are concerned with how his words and conduct would be perceived by an objective party. There has been some debate in case law as to precisely how the courts should apply this objective standard. The modern approach to assessing contractual intent has been to apply the standard of a reasonable person. If, by their words or conduct, the offeror acts in such a way so that the reasonable person would conclude that the offeror has an intention to be bound, then the courts will find such contractual intent even if in fact the offeror (subjectively) had no such intent at all.

Applying an objective standard to determine the issue of contractual intent does present some difficulties. No person can claim to be completely reasonable or impartial in every sense. However, to ensure consistency in decisions and to prevent unscrupulous abuse by parties who find themselves in a bad bargain, the courts continue to view the formation of the agreement from the perspective of a reasonable person. This is illustrated by the comments of Steyn L.J. in **First Energy (UK) Ltd v Hungarian International Bank Ltd** [1993] B.C.C. 533:

"A theme that runs through our law of contract is that the reasonable expectations of honest men must be protected. It is not a rule or a principle of law. It is the objective which has been and still is the principal moulding force of our law of contract. . . The court must take into account surrounding circumstances which reasonable persons in the position of the parties would have had in mind."

While the application of this objective standard is initially difficult to conceptualise, viewing contractual formation through the eyes of a completely reasonable man does allow the courts to avoid many impractical and often absurd results—such as the parties being bound by an agreement that is in itself impossible to satisfy.

Distinguishing an offer from an invitation to treat

2-006

It is important to distinguish an *offer* from an *invitation to treat*. As noted above, an *offer* displays a clear intention to be bound. As such only an offer is capable of being accepted, giving rise to contractual obligations between the parties. In contrast, an *invitation to treat* is merely an indication that the party is open to negotiation. The party is not making a statement of contractual intent, but is demonstrating his willingness to open the negotiation process or he may even be inviting offers from another party. Therefore, the fundamental distinguishing factor between an *offer* and an *invitation to treat* is that an *offer* displays a contractual intent (our first "ingredient" from the list above and an ingredient that is lacking in an *invitation to treat*).

Case law provides many examples of how the courts assess this requirement of contractual intent, but a useful starting point is to compare the two cases of **Gibson v Manchester City Council** [1979] 1 W.L.R. 294 and **Storer v Manchester City Council** [1974] 1 W.L.R. 1403.

In **Gibson**, the claimant enquired as to whether he could purchase the council house in which he lived. The council responded to this enquiry by sending a letter that stated that the council "may be prepared to sell the house to you" at a fixed price. Shortly after, the Conservative-controlled council was taken over by Labour and the decision was taken to withdraw the house from the market. Mr Gibson claimed that the letter from the council constituted an offer and that he had accepted that offer before control of the council changed. However, the House of Lords held that the letter was merely an *invitation to treat*. The words "may be prepared to sell" displayed no contractual intent and were intended only to invite Mr Gibson to make an offer for the property.

In contrast, in the **Storer** case, which arose out of the same decision to withdraw council houses from sale as did **Gibson**, the claimant received a letter from the council labelled "Agreement for sale". The claimant signed and returned the document before political control of the council changed. The council then revised its policy on selling council houses and refused to sell the property to the claimant. In this case the Court of Appeal held that the letter was in fact an *offer* that the claimant had accepted before the property was withdrawn from sale.

Looking at both of these cases and all of the surrounding circumstances, it is interesting to see how the courts approach the issue of contractual intent. Even the indication of a price contained in the letter to Mr Gibson was not sufficient to constitute an offer, owing to the words "may be prepared to sell", which negated any argument that there was an intention to sell the property.

THE USE OF "PRESUMPTIONS"

2-007 As noted above, the courts apply an objective standard to the issue of contract formation. This approach seeks to provide consistency and to give effect to the perceived intention of the parties. In order to maintain a consistent approach to the analysis of contractual intent, the courts have developed a number of presumptions to assist when distinguishing between an offer and an invitation to treat. In certain cases the court will start with a strong presumption that the offeror displayed the necessary contractual intent to make an offer and will require substantial evidence to rebut this presumption. In other cases the court will presume that the offeror lacked the necessary contractual intent unless there is strong evidence to the contrary.

The nature of the presumption will vary depending on the different categories of contracts recognised by the courts. We shall consider some of the more everyday examples in further detail:

- display of goods;
- advertisements;
- auctions; and
- tenders.

DISPLAY OF GOODS

2-008 In **Pharmaceutical Society of Great Britain v Boots Cash Chemists** [1953] 1 Q.B. 401, Boots were charged with infringing s.18(1)(a)(iii) of the Pharmacy and Poisons Act 1933, which required that the sale of proscribed poisons be "effected by or under the supervision of a registered pharmacist". In deciding whether there had been such an infringement of the Act, the Court of Appeal had to decide how the requirements of offer and acceptance applied to the system of a self-service shop. The Pharmaceutical Society argued that the display of goods in the self-service shop constituted an offer for sale which the customer accepted by picking an item they wished to purchase off the shelf and placing it into their basket. As the contract was formed at the time when the item was placed in the basket the pharmacist did not have the ability to veto the transaction and had therefore neither supervised nor effected the transaction and thus had failed to satisfy the duty imposed by s.18 of the Act.

The Court of Appeal rejected these arguments and found that the display of goods was an *invitation to treat*. In fact, it was the customer who made the *offer* which was then accepted by the cashier when the items were presented at the cash desk. At this point the transaction was supervised by the pharmacist and therefore there was no infringement of the Act. This decision may sound strange and even contrary to the way in which we would assume offer and acceptance works in relation to shops. To understand the decision of the Court of Appeal it is helpful to consider the consequences that would have flowed if the court had accepted the argument that the display of goods was an *offer*.

■ Why is the display of goods generally an invitation to treat?

Over to you. . .

It was held in *Pharmaceutical Society of Great Britain v Boots Cash Chemists* that the display of goods in a self-service shop should be construed as an invitation to treat. Can you explain the legal reasoning of the court? When analysing the distinction between an offer and an invitation to treat it is always important to consider both sides of the legal argument. What consequences would have followed if the display of goods had been held to be an offer?

If the display of goods were an *offer* then this could have quite impractical and absurd consequences for both the customer and the shopkeeper. For example, if by displaying items, the shop is making an offer, then the customer would accept that offer by removing the item from the shelf. At this point the customer has accepted an offer so there will be an agreement to purchase between the customer and the shop. If the customer changes their mind they will not be able to return the item to the shelf and exchange it for another item. The obligation to purchase that item has arisen so they will be in breach of contract if they do not meet that obligation. Further, as the customer is obliged to purchase that particular item they will also be obliged to pay the price marked on that item. There will be no room for negotiation.

If we look at this situation from the perspective of the shopkeeper then we can see that he will also be obliged to sell to anybody who enters his shop and removes an item from the shelf. Once acceptance has taken place he will not be able to refuse the sale of that item, as by doing so he in turn will be in breach of contract. If the display of goods were held to be an offer then this would limit the freedom of both the contracting parties. The customer would lose their freedom to browse goods and to change their mind once an item had been removed from the shelf. The freedom of the shopkeeper to pick and choose his customers would also be reduced. For these reasons the Court of Appeal, applying an objective assessment of contractual intent, held that the display of goods should be construed as an invitation to treat.

■ **Problems with the decision in** *Boots*

Over to you. . .

Can you identify any problems with the decision of the Court of Appeal in *Pharmaceutical Society of Great Britain v Boots Cash Chemists?* **Can you think of any alternative ways in which the court could have applied the principles of offer and acceptance to the display of goods in a self-service shop to avoid the problems noted above?**

There are certainly criticisms that can be levelled at the decision in the **Boots** case. The argument that items displayed in a self-service shop were to be construed as *offers* and that acceptance took place when the items were placed in the basket was largely driven by the desire of the Pharmaceutical Society to establish that the contract was formed at a time and a place that was not under the supervision of a registered pharmacist (and hence establish an infringement of the legislation). A more convincing argument would have been that the display of items in a shop is actually an *offer* for sale and that *acceptance* only takes place when the customer presents an item for purchase at the cash desk. This was the approach of the court in the American case of **Lasky v Economy Grocery Stores**, 319 Mass. 224, 227, 65 N.E.2d 305 (1946).

However, had this approach to contract formation been adopted then the transaction would either have been effected by, or was under the supervision of, the pharmacist. The Pharmaceutical Society could not, therefore, have pursued this argument as it would have completely undermined their allegation that there had been an infringement of the legislation. As a result we are left with a rather artificial application of the legal principles of offer and acceptance to the display of goods. Further, the decision of the Court of Appeal in the **Boots** case also appears to conflict with relevant consumer protection legislation (for example, the Trade Descriptions Act 1968). Despite these criticisms, the courts have continued to construe the display of goods as an *invitation to treat* to maintain the relevant freedoms of both the customer and the shopkeeper.

THE DISPLAY OF GOODS IN A SHOP WINDOW

2-009   In **Fisher v Bell** [1961] 1 Q.B. 394 the defendant displayed a flick knife in his shop window with a price tag attached. He was charged with "offering for sale" the flick knife in contravention of the Restriction of Offensive Weapons Act 1959. The court held that the display of a flick knife in a shop window (even with a price tag attached) was an *invitation to treat*. As he had not made an *offer* he was not guilty of the offence of "offering for sale" the knife.

Again, this decision is founded on principles similar to those of the **Boots** case. If the display of an item in a shop window were an *offer* then the shopkeeper would again lose his right to refuse sale to anybody who accepted. Further, there is also a "quantity argument" in that the shopkeeper may have only a limited (or totally depleted) stock of that item. If a customer saw an item displayed in a shop window and then demanded to purchase that item the shopkeeper would be obliged to sell even if his stock of that item was exhausted and he would again be in breach of contract if he refused.

Over to you. . .

Read the case of *Fisher v Bell*. Notice that the Restriction of Offensive Weapons Act 1959 created numerous offences in relation to manufacture, sale and hire of flick knives, but following the court's interpretation of the words "offer for sale" it was not an offence to display the item for sale in a shop window. Why do you think the court refused to apply a wider interpretation to the words "offer for sale" so as to address the mischief of the Act?

ADVERTISEMENTS

The general rule relating to advertisements is that they are merely *invitations to treat*. However, this is only a general rule and is again based on a presumption (which of course is capable of being challenged).

2-010

Hear from the Author

Scan the QR Tag or follow the link below for an overview of the legal principles relating to advertisements.

uklawstudent.thomsonreuters.com/category/contract-fundamentals

In **Partridge v Crittenden** [1968] 2 All E.R. 421 the defendant placed an advertisement in the periodical **Cage and Aviary Birds**, under the general heading "Classified Advertisements". The advertisement stated: "Bramblefinch cocks, Bramblefinch hens, 25s each". Mr Thompson saw the advertisement and wrote to Mr Partridge requesting a bird. A bird was subsequently delivered to Mr Thompson. Mr Partridge was then charged with offering for sale a wild bird contrary to s.6 of the Protection of Birds Act 1954.

The central issue in this case was whether Mr Partridge had "offered" the bird for sale and was therefore guilty under the legislation. In order to answer this question the court had to apply the ordinary rules of contract law. At first instance, the magistrates found that the advertisement constituted an offer for sale and fined Mr Partridge £5 for breach of the legislation. On appeal, the High Court came to a different conclusion and held that the advertisement was an *invitation to treat*. Therefore, the offence with which Mr Partridge had been charged, "offering for sale" a wild bird, had not been made out as the advertisement did not constitute an *offer* for sale.

As Lord Parker C.J. concluded:

> "I think when one is dealing with advertisements and circulars, unless they indeed come from manufacturers, there is business sense in them being construed as invitations to treat and not offers for sale."

■ Advertisements and the issue of "multi-acceptance"

2-011   The decision from **Partridge** is clear, that advertisements are generally to be construed as *invitations to treat*. However, to understand *why* this is the case it is necessary to consider the consequences that would flow if the court had decided that the advertisement constituted an *offer* for sale. By doing so the court would have opened up the possibility of "multi-acceptance". In other words, Mr Partridge would have been obliged to sell to anybody who saw the advertisement and purported to accept by placing their money in the post. As Mr Partridge did not have an unlimited supply of birds he would have been in breach of contract with every person to whom he was unable to supply a bird.

Lord Parker identifies this problem in **Partridge** by referring to the case of **Grainger & Son v Gough (Surveyor of Taxes)** [1896] A.C. 325, a case that concerned the distribution of a catalogue by a wine merchant accompanied by a price list:

> "The transmission of such a price-list does not amount to an offer to supply an unlimited quantity of wine described at the price named, so that as soon as an order is given there is a binding contract to supply that quantity. If it were so, the merchant might find himself involved in any number of contractual obligations to supply wine of a particular description which he would be quite unable to carry out, his stock of wine of that description being necessarily limited." (per Lord Herschell at 334).

The decisions in **Partridge** and **Grainger** provide clear illustrations of the *objective* test of contractual intent. There can be little doubt that Mr Partridge, by placing the advertisement, subjectively intended to offer the birds for sale. This can be evidenced by him selling the bird to Mr Thompson in the first place. However, *objectively*, the court held that he lacked the necessary contractual intent. Applying the standards of a reasonable person, he would not have intended to contract with everybody that responded and accepted the advertisement. His limited stock would mean that he would be unable to meet all such acceptances and would be in breach of contract for every bird that he was unable to supply.

Over to you. . .

It is interesting to note that the wording of the advertisement in *Partridge v Crittenden* did not contain the words "offer for sale". Do you think it would have made any difference to the decision had the advertisement used the words "offer for sale"?

Remember, the courts apply an objective test to determine the issue of contractual intent. While the words "offer for sale" may be some evidence of the offeror's intention to be bound, it will not be conclusive on the matter. The problem of multi-acceptance would still remain and objectively the court will presume that the reasonable person would not intend to enter into a contract with every person who purported to accept his offer. When there is limited stock the offeror will be unable to meet all the possible acceptances that may follow. Unless the problem of multi-acceptance can be avoided, it is unlikely that the words "offer for sale" would have altered the decision on the facts of **Partridge**.

As Ashworth J. commented:

> "In no place, so far as I can see, is there any direct use of the words 'Offer for sale'. I ought to say I am not for my part deciding that that would have the result of making this judgment any different, but at least it strengthens the case for the appellant that there is no such expression on the page."

Advertisements from manufacturers

2-012

Interestingly, Lord Parker appears to suggest that if an advertisement or circular came from a manufacturer then the position might be different. The presumption is that a manufacturer will be able to respond to the number of people who accept their offer by producing more of the item in question, hence eliminating (or at least substantially reducing) the limited stock problem. However, this should be treated with some caution as these considerations will only be a *factor* used by the court in deciding whether or not the advertisement constitutes an offer or an invitation to treat; it by no means creates a general rule that an advertisement originating from a manufacturer should be automatically construed as an offer.

Advertisements construed as offers

2-013

The general rule established in **Partridge v Crittenden** is that advertisements are generally held to be *invitations to treat*. However, this is only a general rule and there are some instances of when the courts have construed an advertisement as in fact being an offer. Providing the court can identify a clear objective display of contractual intent then there is nothing to prevent an advertisement being held to be an offer.

That said, unfortunately, very few English authorities that have actually construed an advertisement to be an offer. The case of **Carlill v Carbolic Smoke Ball Co Ltd** [1893] 1 Q.B. 256, however, provides one such example. In this case the defendants placed an advertisement in the newspaper advertising their Carbolic Smoke Ball, a device that they claimed could cure many common ailments. Specifically, the advertisement promised that:

> "£100 reward will be paid to any person who contracts the increasing epidemic influenza . . . after having used the ball three times daily for two weeks according to the printed directions supplied with each ball. £1000 is deposited with the Alliance Bank, Regent Street, showing our sincerity in the matter."

On the strength of this advertisement Mrs Carlill bought a smoke ball and used it as prescribed for several months but then caught influenza. When Mrs Carlill tried to claim her "reward" the Smoke Ball Company refused to honour its promise. In resisting Mrs Carlill's claim the Smoke Ball Company advanced many defences, among them the argument that the advertisement amounted to no more than a "mere puff". In other words, this was a mere marketing device which no reasonable person would take as displaying any contractual intent. However, the Court of Appeal thought differently:

> "We must first consider whether this was intended to be a promise at all, or whether it was a mere puff that meant nothing. Was it a mere puff? My answer to that question is 'No', and I base my answer upon this passage: '£1000 is deposited with the Alliance Bank, showing our sincerity in the matter'. Now, for what was that money deposited or that statement made except to negative the suggestion that this was a mere puff and meant nothing at all? The deposit . . . is proof of his sincerity in the matter—that is, the sincerity of his promise to pay this £100 in the event which he specified" (per Lindley L.J. at 261–262).

Therefore, if the court can find a clear display of contractual intent then it may find an *offer* despite the arguments to the contrary from the defendants that they lacked the necessary intent. This also reaffirms the objective approach that the courts take when assessing the issue of intention: *subjectively*, the Smoke Ball Company may never have intended to honour its promise, but *objectively* there was clear evidence to the contrary.

Over to you. . .

The Smoke Ball Company raised many arguments as to why they had no obligation to pay Mrs Carlill the £100 reward. One of these arguments was that their advertisement could not constitute an offer as it is not possible to make a contract with the whole world. Do you agree and how did the court respond to this argument?

Initially, there would seem to be some merit to the Smokeball's argument. We have already considered potential issues that could result from advertising to the public generally, such as the problem of multi-acceptance. However, the nature of the promise in **Carlill** was interpreted quite differently. As Bowen L.J. commented, at 268:

"It was also said that the contract is made with all the world—that is, with everybody; and that you cannot contract with everybody. It is not a contract made with all the world. There is the fallacy of the argument. It is an offer made to all the world; and why should not an offer be made to all the world which is to ripen into a contract with anybody who comes forward and performs the condition? It is an offer to become liable to anyone who, before it is retracted, performs the condition, and, although the offer is made to the world, the contract is made with that limited portion of the public who come forward and perform the condition on the faith of the advertisement."

The case of **Carlill v Carbolic Smoke Ball Company** provides an example of a particular type of contract, referred to as a *unilateral* contract. The contract is described as being *unilateral* as only one party has obligations under the contract. Mrs Carlill was under no obligation to purchase or use the smoke ball. The Smoke Ball Company would, however, have an obligation to pay £100 if Mrs Carlill used the ball as prescribed and caught influenza. The Smoke Ball Company's obligations would therefore depend on the conduct of Mrs Carlill. As Mrs Carlill came forward and accepted their offer by performing the conditions required then the Smoke Ball Company had an obligation to pay the £100 reward.

In unilateral contracts, acceptance occurs by the *performance* of the acts stipulated by the offeror. For this reason, unilateral contracts are sometimes referred to as "if" contracts. Using the facts of **Carlill**, the Smoke Ball Company promised that "if" you used their smoke ball as prescribed and caught influenza, then they would pay £100 reward. The acceptance in this case would therefore be using the ball as prescribed *and* catching influenza. The breach of contract therefore occurred when the Smoke Ball Company failed to perform their obligations by refusing to pay the £100 promised.

A further example of an advertisement construed as an offer is the case of **Lefkowitz v Great Minneapolis Surplus Stores Inc** (1957) 86 N.W. 2d 689. In this case the defendant placed the following advertisement in a newspaper: "Saturday 9 A.M. Sharp 3 Brand New Fur Coats Worth to $100.00. First Come First Served. $1 Each". The claimant saw the advertisement and was the first person to enter the store on the Saturday morning. The store refused to sell him a fur coat, relying on the argument that it only intended to sell the coats to women (although no such restriction appeared in the advertisement).

The Supreme Court of Minnesota held that an advertisement was in fact an *offer*, stating that the advertisement was "clear, definite, and explicit, and left nothing open for negotiation". The words "First Come First Served" are interesting here, as the use of such words reduces the problem of "multi-acceptance". The store did not have an obligation to sell to every customer who saw the advertisement and accepted the offer. Rather, they were only required to sell to those customers who performed the conditions of acceptance—being any of the first customers to enter the shop. The problem of multi-acceptance is avoided as the store will have sufficient stock to meet demand; they are only required to sell three coats to the first three customers. Once the coats have been sold and the stock depleted then the offer will lapse.

The decision in **Lefkowitz** again highlights the application of an objective test to the issue of contractual intent. By advertising "fur coats" to the "first people" on the "first come, first served basis", the court was able to infer the necessary contractual intent. The wording of the advertisement implied that the store had waived their right to pick and choose their customers; they were not concerned with whom they contracted, rather their intention was simply to sell to the first three customers. Limiting the offer to three fur coats had also avoided the problem of multi-acceptance. Therefore, the reasonable person would construe the advertisement as an offer.

Over to you. . .

Following the legal reasoning illustrated above in *Lefkowitz v Great Minneapolis Surplus Stores*, can you think how the wording of the advertisement in *Partridge v Crittenden* could be altered so as to amount to an offer? Remember, the courts are seeking to identify an objective display of contractual intent, so simply using the words "offer for sale" may not be sufficient in such cases.

AUCTIONS

2-014   The example of an auction often reveals a number of misconceptions as to the application of offer and acceptance. The most common of these misconceptions is that when you bid for an item you have bought it. As we will see, this is not strictly the case. However, when assessing how offer and acceptance apply to auctions it is necessary to distinguish between the different types of auction.

■ A "without reserve" auction

2-015   At a "without reserve" auction the auctioneer undertakes to sell the item to the highest bidder. The auctioneer acts as an agent between the owner of the item and the bidders. The *offer* is made by a person placing a bid (**Payne v Cave** (1789) 3 T.R. 148). This offer is then *accepted* when the auctioneer's hammer falls. As acceptance only takes place upon the fall of the hammer a person may withdraw his bid before this point (a position that can be found in statutory form, Sale of Goods Act 1979 s.57(2)). However, what if the auctioneer refuses to accept your bid? Generally there is no obligation placed on the offeree to accept the offer. However, in this situation there will be a separate contract, referred to as a collateral contract, between the auctioneer and the highest bidder (**Warlow v Harrison** (1859) 1 El. & El. 295). If the auctioneer refuses to accept the highest bid he will be in breach of this implied obligation and will be in breach of contract to that bidder.

The use of a collateral contract in this way was affirmed by the Court of Appeal in **Barry v Davies** [2000] 1 W.L.R. 1962. In this case the owners of two machines instructed the defendants to auction these machines "without reserve". The machines had a market value of £14,000 each.

At the auction the highest bid was £200 for each machine. The auctioneer therefore withdrew the machines from sale. The auctioneer then advertised the machines for sale and sold them for £700 each. The highest bidder brought an action against the auctioneer arguing that there had been a breach of contract when the auctioneer refused to accept his bid.

The court held that there had been a breach of a collateral contract between the auctioneer and the highest bidder. When the machines were auctioned "without reserve", this created an obligation that the auctioneer would accept the highest bid. When the auctioneer withdrew the machines from sale he was in breach of contract to the highest bidder. The highest bidder was therefore awarded damages for this breach.

In calculating damages in these situations, the court will make an award on the expectation interest. In other words, the court will look to the position the highest bidder would have been in had the contract not been breached. Had the auctioneer met his obligations and sold the machines to the highest bidder then the bidder would have received machinery worth £28,000 in total. The bidder would have paid £400 for these machines (a very good bargain indeed). The court will award the difference between the price bid (£400) and the market value of the machines (£28,000). On the facts, this resulted in substantial damages, £27,600.

The decision in **Barry v Davies** and the use of collateral contracts has further consequences for auctioneers. If the *owner* of the item decides to withdraw the item from sale then he will not be in breach of contract to the bidder. As it is the bidder who makes the offer, which is only accepted by the auctioneer (the owner's agent) when the hammer falls, the owner will have no liability to the bidder in this situation. The auctioneer, however, will be in breach of his collateral contract to the highest bidder to accept his bid.

The use of a collateral contract in a "without reserve" auction is illustrated in Figure 2.2.

■ A "with reserve" auction

Sometimes the owner of the goods may state a minimum price to the auctioneer below which they are not prepared to sell. If this price is not met at auction then the auctioneer has no obligation to sell the item to the highest bidder. If the auctioneer were to accept a bid that fell below the reserve price then the auctioneer would actually be in breach of their contract with the owner of the goods.

2-016

■ Advertisement of an auction

An interesting problem arises in connection with the advertisement of an auction. If an advertisement states that an auction will take place on a particular day can potential bidders claim for breach of contract if the auction does not in fact take place or if particular items are withdrawn from sale? This question was addressed in **Harris v Nickerson** (1872–73) L.R. 8 Q.B. 286. In this case the claimant travelled to an auction on the strength of an advertisement intending to bid for certain items of furniture. In fact the items for which he intended to bid were withdrawn from sale and the claimant tried to claim for his loss of time and for his travel

2-017

FIGURE 2.2 **Collateral contracts in a "without reserve" auction**

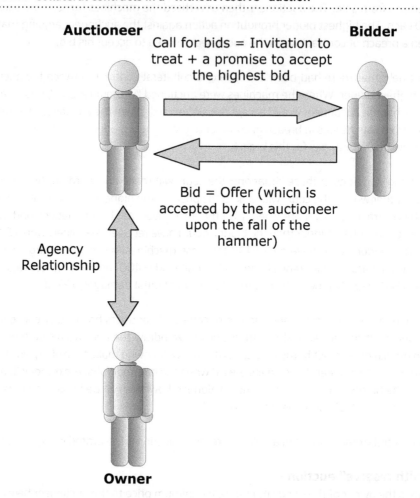

However, the advertisement may in a very limited way also constitute an *offer*. An advertisement that an auction will take place and that it will be "without reserve" will be construed as an

expenses. Unsurprisingly, the court held that the advertisement was an *invitation to treat* and as such no action for breach contract could be brought. To have decided otherwise would have placed an intolerable burden on the auctioneer and other parties advertising the occurrence of events. As Blackburn J. commented:

> "It amounts to saying that anyone who advertises a sale by publishing an advertisement becomes responsible to everybody who attends the sale for his cab hire or travelling expenses."

However, the advertisement may in a very limited way also constitute an *offer*. An advertisement that an auction will take place and that it will be "without reserve" will be construed as an *invitation to treat*. But what if the auction does not take place? While a person may not be able to claim breach of contract if the auction does not take place, the wording of the advertisement may create an *implied offer* that the auction will take a particular form, that it will be without reserve and that goods will be sold to the highest bidder. If the auctioneer then refuses to sell to the highest bidder he will be in breach of contract. In other words, the advertisment takes on an increased significance once the auction takes place.

TENDERS

A tender operates in a very similar way to an auction. A person may seek specific goods **2-018** or services and will put the job or service out to tender. By doing so the individual making the request will be seeking that people submit offers in response. The request for tender is therefore an *invitation to treat*. The response to this request (the tender itself) will be an *offer*. The person making the request will then be able to accept the offer that meets his requirements.

However, there are circumstances in which a request for tender may be construed as an offer. For example, in **Harvela Investments v Royal Trust Co of Canada** [1986] A.C. 207, the first defendants sought to sell their shares in a company by tender with the intention that they would accept the highest offer. The plaintiff made an offer of $2,175,000. The second defendants made an offer of "$2,100,000, or C$101,000 in excess of any other offer . . . whichever is the higher". This type of offer is known as a referential bid. The first defendants accepted the referential bid.

The House of Lords then had to decide which party was entitled to the purchase of the shares. In resolving this issue the House looked to the intention of the party making the invitation. Was their intention to participate in a fixed bidding sale (in which case only fixed bids would satisfy) or was their intention to enter in an auction sale (in which case each party could alter their bids by reference to the other bidders)? The House of Lords held that upon a true construction of the invitation, the intention of the party making the invitation was to participate in a fixed bidding sale. Therefore, the referential bid of the defendants was not the "highest offer" and the plaintiff's bid of $2,175,000 should have been accepted.

Similarly, in **Blackpool and Fylde Aero Club Ltd v Blackpool BC** [1990] 1 W.L.R. 1195, the council made it clear that it would consider all tenders submitted before the specified deadline. The Aero Club posted its tender in the Town Hall post box before this deadline. However, the post box was not emptied that day resulting in the council refusing to consider the club's late bid. It was held that the request for tender was an invitation to treat, so there was no obligation to accept any of the tenders submitted. However, the request also contained a collateral *offer* to *consider* all the bids that were received by the deadline, which the Aero Club had accepted by placing its tender in the Town Hall post box before the deadline. This collateral contract was therefore breached when the council failed to consider the Aero Club's bid.

AUTOMATED MACHINES

2-019   Although not strictly one of the "categories" of contracts referred to above, the use of auto-mated machines poses a novel problem for the principles of offer and acceptance. If we take the example of a vending machine, it would seem logical that a display of items for sale in a vending machine would be considered *invitations to treat* following the general principles as laid down in **Pharmaceutical Society of Great Britain v Boots and Fisher v Bell**. However, this conclusion fails to take account of the objective standard that the courts will apply to contract formation. The application of an objective test is likely to conclude that such a display is to be construed as an *offer*.

If the intention in displaying the items for sale is assessed, then the intention would appear to be to enter into a contract with anyone who is able to provide the correct money in return for the item. In other words, the machine is not open to the negotiation process. As Lord Denning observed in **Thornton v Shoe Lane Parking** [1971] 2 Q.B. 163, a case that concerned an auto-mated ticket machine:

> **"The customer pays his money and gets a ticket. He cannot refuse it. He cannot get his money back. He may protest to the machine, even swear at it. But it will remain unmoved."'**

Over to you. . .

If a machine being ready to accept your money is making an offer, then how and when does the customer accept the offer?

One argument is that the acceptance will take place once your money is inserted into the machine. However, at this point it may still possible for the customer to change their mind and press the coin return button. Therefore, it is more likely that the acceptance takes place once the customer inserts their money and makes a product selection. If the machine then refuses to vend, or vends the incorrect product, then this is when the breach of contract will occur. Of course, the machine itself is not in breach of contract (and the machine will remain unmoved should you wish to take issue with it) so it would be necessary to pursue the owner/operators of the machine.

INTERNET TRANSACTIONS

2-020   Given that there is no strict requirement that the "simple" contracts be reduced to writing, there is no reason why a contract cannot be formed over the internet. Further, the application of the principles of offer and acceptance should not necessarily change simply because the contract is being formed electronically.

Take the example of an online shop on a website. Will items displayed for sale on the site be offers or invitations to treat? Applying the same principles as in the **Boots** case and **Partridge v Crittenden**, the display of goods or advertising those goods for sale should be construed as an invitation to treat. The customer therefore has the ability to freely browse the items on the website. Once they make their selection, the item is placed in their virtual shopping basket. The goods are then taken to the virtual checkout where the goods are presented for purchase. Following the decision in **Boots**, the customer makes the offer and this is either accepted or rejected by the seller. The precise point of acceptance could, however, vary in such cases. Many websites require the customer to accept their standard terms and conditions before allowing them to proceed to the checkout. These terms and conditions will usually determine the point of acceptance. In most cases the point of acceptance will usually be upon the despatch of the goods (and not necessarily at the point at which payment is taken).

Acceptance

So far we have just been concerned with the first stage towards the formation of the agreement; being able to identify an offer and to distinguish it from an invitation to treat. The next stage towards the formation of an agreement is to consider the relevant legal principles of acceptance. If a legally recognisable offer has been made then in order for this to develop into an agreement there needs to be an unequivocal acceptance of that offer.

2-021

Offer + Unequivocal Acceptance = Agreement

We have seen that an objective test is applied in determining the existence of an offer. The same objective approach is also applied in relation to acceptance. The law requires that the offer and acceptance must match; that they should be mirror images of one another. The offeree must unequivocally accept the terms of the offer. We will now look at the importance of this mirror image rule in relation to the issue of acceptance.

Counter-offers

The offer and acceptance must match. If the offeree tries to introduce new terms to the offer or to vary the existing terms then this will not constitute an acceptance. An attempt to vary the terms will be considered a counter-offer. A counter-offer is not an acceptance and has the effect of destroying the original offer.

2-022

In **Hyde v Wrench** (1840) 3 Beav. 334, the defendant offered his land for sale for £1,000. The plaintiff responded by offering £950, which was rejected by the defendant. The plaintiff then sought to accept the defendant's offer of £1,000. It was held that by making an offer of £950 the plaintiff had rejected the original offer of £1,000 and had replaced this with an offer of £950. As this new offer was rejected by the defendant there was no contract. It was not possible for the plaintiff to revive the defendant's original offer of £1,000 as that offer has been destroyed and a new offer of £950 had been substituted by his counter-offer. The original offer of £1,000 was therefore no longer capable of being accepted and the counter-offer was now the *new offer* which was capable of being accepted or rejected.

The effects of the decision in **Hyde v Wrench** are illustrated in Figure 2.3.

A counter-offer will destroy the original offer and any new terms proposed will constitute a new offer which can then be accepted or rejected by the other party. The recipient of the "new" offer can of course make a further counter-offer which then itself becomes the new offer. This process of negotiation between the parties could be quite lengthy and could almost become like a game of tennis, with both parties exchanging offers and counter-offers until they finally reach consensus as to the agreement.

FIGURE 2.3 The decision in *Hyde v Wrench*

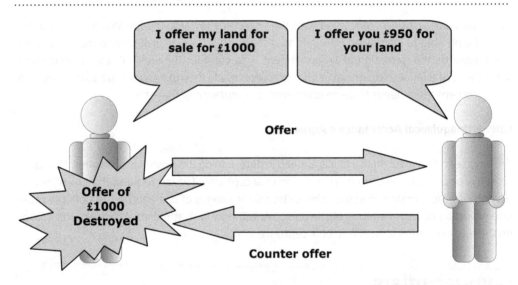

Hear from the Author

Scan the QR Tag or follow the link below for further guidance on the case of *Hyde v Wrench*.

uklawstudent.thomsonreuters.com/category/contract-fundamentals

A request for information

A counter-offer must be distinguished from a request for information. This distinction is impor-   2-023
tant and a request for information will not have the effect of destroying the original offer. In
Stevenson v McLean (1879–80) L.R 5 Q.B. 346, the defendants offered to sell a quantity of
steel to the plaintiffs at 40s per ton. The plaintiffs responded by enquiring as to whether the
defendants would accept 40s for delivery over two months, or if not, what was the longest time
that they would give? It was held that this response by the plaintiffs constituted a request for
information. The plaintiffs in this case were not seeking to introduce new terms into the offer,
but rather were seeking clarification of the existing terms. The offer of 40s per ton was therefore still open to acceptance.

You will have realised that it is sometimes difficult to distinguish a counter-offer from a request
for information. The distinction will ultimately depend on the manner of interpretation adopted
by the court. If the response of the offeree is framed as an enquiry then the court may construe
this as a request for information as the intention of the offeree was not to seek to introduce new
terms into the original offer. Conversely, if the offeree's response is framed in such a way as to
reject the original offer and to substitute new terms into the original offer, then it is likely this
will be construed as a counter-offer.

Cross-offers

An interesting application of the principles of offer and acceptance arises in relation to cross-   2-024
offers. These occur when both parties make the same offer, each party in ignorance of the
other's offer. In terms of an agreement, it is arguable that both parties display a contractual
intent, but a meeting of the minds as to an agreement appears to be lacking. Of course, either
party is free to accept the other's offer, but until this stage there will be no contract. There is
obiter authority for this position in **Tinn v Hoffman** (1873) 29 L.T. 271.

Statement of minimum price

Finally, an offer needs to be distinguished from a statement of a minimum price. In **Harvey**   2-025
v Facey [1893] A.C. 552, the plaintiff sent a telegram to the defendant stating: "Will you
sell Bumper Hall Pen? Telegraph lowest cash price". The defendant replied stating that his
lowest price was £900. The court, unsurprisingly, held that there was no contract here. The
defendant's response was neither an offer nor an acceptance. The response was more akin to
a request for information, with the defendant merely providing clarification in response to the
plaintiff's request.

The battle of the forms

The courts require a clear and unambiguous offer and acceptance before any contractual obli-   2-026
gations will be enforced. If there is ambiguity as to the fact of agreement then the court will

be reluctant to bind the parties to an agreement. A particular problem in relation to offer and acceptance has arisen owing to the increased use of the "standard form" contract by business. As the name suggests, a standard form contract is a model document that contains the standard terms and conditions on which each business is prepared to contract.

The increasing popularity of such contracts has resulted in the need for the courts to clarify the position when two companies attempt to contract on one another's standard terms. Of course, each business would ideally like to contract on its standard terms and conditions and a battle as to which terms prevail may ensue.

This battle between the parties usually arises when one business makes an offer on its standard terms and the other business seeks to impose its own standard terms when accepting. In such cases it could be questioned whether the parties have reached an agreement at all. However, the courts have developed specific rules to deal with such disputes.

One approach is to apply the "last shot" principle. The party that sought to introduce its standard terms the latest would prevail (**British Road Services Ltd v Arthur Crutchley & Co** [1968] 1 All E.R. 811). However, this "last shot" approach is best viewed as a starting point in resolving such disputes.

A more detailed analysis of the law was conducted in **Butler Machine Tool Co v Ex-cell-o Corp** [1979] 1 W.L.R. 401. In this case, the plaintiffs offered to sell some machinery to the defendants for £75,535. The plaintiffs sought to impose their standard terms, which included a price variation clause. The defendants sought to accept the plaintiffs' offer and impose their own standard terms (which did not include such a clause). The plaintiffs completed and signed a tear-off slip stating that they accepted the defendants' terms. The court therefore had to decide which terms governed the agreement.

The Court of Appeal held that it was the defendants' terms that prevailed. The plaintiffs' initial offer was rejected by the defendants and was substituted by a counter-offer from the defendants. The plaintiffs accepted this counter-offer when they signed and returned the tear-off slip.

. . . .

When will acceptance become effective?

2-027   If there is an unequivocal acceptance of the offer then the next issue is to determine *when* that acceptance will become effective. The general rule is that acceptance must be *communicated* to the offeror (**Entores Ltd v Miles Far East Corp** [1955] 2 Q.B. 327). Therefore an acceptance will only become effective (and therefore form a binding agreement) when it comes to the attention of the offeror. However, there are a number of exceptions to this basic rule.

THE POSTAL RULE

For nearly two hundred years the courts have applied a special rule in relation to postal accept- **2-028** ances. The precise rationale for such a rule, however, remains one of the greatest mysteries in contract law and it has to be questioned whether such a rule has a continued role to play in modern contract law in light of developments in technology and the more recent changes to the postal system itself.

The case of **Adams v Lindsell** (1818) 1 B. & Ald. 681 established the rule that a postal accept- ance will be effective as soon as it enters the postal system. This rule sought to address a number of problems that may arise when accepting an offer using the postal system. Firstly, there is the obvious delay between the acceptance being sent and that acceptance arriving with the offeror. Secondly, the acceptance may get lost in the postal system and never arrive at all. Finally, once the letter of acceptance has been posted it is out of the control of the offeree and there is little else they can do to ensure their acceptance gets through. As a result, it could be argued that the postal rule developed as a way of mitigating these potential problems.

It cannot be in doubt that the postal rule is at best a rather archaic principle. Not only is the rule nearly two hundred years old, but it was conceived at a time in which the postal system, specifically the Royal Mail, was a very different creature to its modern equivalent. The modern postal service is a long way from the days of Charles I when the Royal Mail was conceived and operated as a State owned monopoly. Further, the Postal Services Act 2011 and the subse- quent privatisation of the Royal Mail in 2013 means there is now little to distinguish it from any other private courier service.

Interestingly, the postal rule has not been explicitly extended to cover acceptances sent by pri- vate courier. The courts have consistently limited the application of the postal rule to accept- ances using Royal Mail. The case of **Re London & Northern Bank** [1900] 1 Ch 220 suggests that if a postal acceptance is handed to an agent, or a private courier then letter of acceptance has not been properly posted and the postal rule will not apply to such acceptances. It is now very difficult to see why this distinction between Royal Mail and private courier services should be maintained. In a modern marketplace in which competition between private companies is encouraged, the postal rule could operate to penalise those individuals or companies who choose a swifter and more efficient means of delivery, such as a courier. The earlier justifica- tions for the postal rule concerning the delay between the acceptance being sent and it being received by the offeror and the fact that a postal acceptance is out control of the offeree are equally relevant to acceptances sent by private courier. Further, the development of modern, instantaneous methods of communication means that the postal rule has, in any event, a diminishing role to play in relation to modern contract formation. At the time of writing, it is the case that the postal rule has not been expressly overruled or challenged by the courts, but the arguments for its continued existence seem limited. What follows below is therefore an account of the legal principles developed so far in relating to the postal rule until such time as the rule is expressly abolished.

■ Development of the postal rule

2-029 As noted above, the postal rule was first established in the case of **Adams v Lindsell** (1818) 1 B. & Ald. 681, where the defendants wrote to the plaintiffs offering wool for sale. However, the letter sent by the defendants (the offer) was misaddressed and as a result the delivery of the letter to the plaintiffs was delayed. The plaintiffs posted an acceptance on the same day that they received the offer. Before the plaintiffs' acceptance arrived the defendants sold the wool to another party. The court held that the plaintiffs' acceptance was effective once posted. As this acceptance was effective before the wool was offered to another party, the defendants were in breach of contract when they in fact sold the wool to another party.

The rule in **Adams** will therefore have the effect of favouring the offeree. Provided that the letter of acceptance was posted while the offer was still open to acceptance, the contract will be formed once the acceptance has been posted. This will still be the case even if the letter is delayed through the fault of the Post Office, or even if the acceptance never reaches the offeror at all (**Household Fire Insurance Co Ltd v Grant** (1878–79) L.R. 4 Ex. D.216).

■ Rationale for the postal rule

2-030 In reality, it could be argued that with postal acceptances the courts are generally going to be faced with a difficult choice. Is it fair to bind the offeror into a contract of which he may have no knowledge? Is it fair to allow the offeror to manipulate the circumstances to his advantage by saying that he never received the letter of acceptance at all, therefore allowing him to "pick and choose" from various acceptances? If a balance were to be struck it could be argued that favouring the offeree in these circumstances is perhaps the lesser of two evils in that it prevents the offeror from arbitrarily revoking his offer after the acceptance has been sent and prevents him from arguing that the letter of acceptance never reached him.

LIMITATIONS ON THE POSTAL RULE

2-031 Given the difficulties identified above, the application of the postal rule has been limited over the years, with a number of requirements introduced before the postal rule will apply.

■ It must be reasonable to use post as a method of acceptance

One of the limitations on the postal rule is that it must be reasonable to use post as a method of acceptance. If an offer is sent by post then it may be reasonable to accept via post. This will be especially so if the parties live at a distance from one another and it is likely that post will be a reasonable method of acceptance in these cases even if the original offer was not made by post. As Lord Herschell made clear in **Henthorn v Fraser** [1892] 2 Ch. 27:

> "Where the circumstances are such that it must have been within the contemplation of the parties that, according to the ordinary usages of mankind, the post might be used as a means of communicating the acceptance of an offer, the acceptance is complete as soon as it is posted."

Certain situations, however, may make it unreasonable to use post as a method of acceptance. For example, if the offeree knows that there is going to be some delay to his acceptance due to an event such as a postal strike, then it may not be reasonable to use post in these circumstances as a method of acceptance and the postal rule may not apply.

■ The letter of acceptance must be properly posted

Following **Adams** a letter of acceptance will become effective once posted. There also appears to be a further requirement that the letter has to be properly posted. It is interesting to consider how the postal rule would apply to a misaddressed letter. Curiously enough, the postal rule began with a misaddressed letter in **Adams** itself, although note that in **Adams** it was the *offer* that was misaddressed, not the letter of acceptance, so the fact that there was a delay in that case caused by a misaddressed letter is not precisely on point.

2-032

In **Getreide Importgesellschaft mbH v Contimar (Contimar's Case)** [1953] 1 W.L.R. 793, the Court of Appeal addressed a similar issue albeit in the context of an arbitration agreement. The plaintiffs entered into a contract with the defendants to purchase a quantity of wheat. The contract was governed by a clause requiring that all disputes arising out of the contract were to be referred to arbitration. A right of appeal following the arbitration process was available provided that notice of an intention to appeal was given to the other party within 14 days of the date of award.

On July 30, 1952, an award was made in favour of the plaintiffs. On August 12, 1952, the defendants notified the plaintiffs of their intention to appeal (so, within the 14-day notice period). However, while the letter was addressed to the town in which the plaintiffs carried on business, the address gave the wrong company and street name. As a result, the letter was delivered to a different company in that town, which had a similar name to the plaintiffs. The letter was eventually forwarded to the plaintiffs but arrived after the 14-day notice period had expired. The court held that, as the notice had not arrived within the 14-day period, the notice of intention to appeal was ineffective.

The decision in the **Contimar** Case is a long way from forming any general principle in relation to a misaddressed acceptance. Treitel would favour a rule that takes account of the particular facts of each case. In some instances, for example, a misaddressed acceptance could actually benefit the party responsible for the delay. He gives the example of a contract where the prevailing market price is to be set at the time of acceptance. If the market price falls after a misaddressed acceptance has been sent, but before it arrives, then this will obviously be to the benefit of the offeree.

Treitel suggests that the better approach would be to treat a misaddressed acceptance as being effective at the time *least favourable* to that party. Therefore, in the example above, the time *least favourable* would be the time at the acceptance is posted. This analysis received recent approval from the High Court in **Korbetis v Transgrain Shipping BV** [2005] EWHC 1345.

■ A general rule for postal acceptances?

2-033 In the light of the decisions in **Contimar** and **Korbetis** above it is now difficult to argue convincingly that there exists a general rule relating to postal acceptances. Following **Adams**, to say that acceptance is effective upon posting would therefore not allow an offeree to withdraw their acceptance once it has entered the postal system. Indeed, it may seem illogical not to allow an offeree to revoke his acceptance via a swifter method of revocation given that the offeror may not have suffered any discernible loss as a result. Rather than the offeree being favoured, as is usually the case with the postal rule, the offeree may be disadvantaged if he were prevented from revoking his acceptance in this way. There is no clear authority on this point, although the decision in **Dunmore v Alexander** (1830) 9 Shaw 190 appears to suggest that it may be possible to revoke an acceptance via a swifter method of revocation (although it is debatable whether the letter in that case was an acceptance, or whether it was in fact an offer). However, **Adams** seems to remain as authority for the position that once a letter of acceptance has been posted it will not be possible for the offeror to revoke his offer.

■ The offeror can explicitly displace the postal rule

2-034 Given that the operation of the postal rule can favour the offeree, especially in situations where a letter of acceptance is delayed (or even lost completely) in the postal system, an offeror will be well advised to guard against such problems by excluding the operation of the postal rule. Therefore, a further, if rather more obvious limitation on the postal rule is that an offeror through the wording of his offer can explicitly displace the postal rule.

It may simply be that the offeror states that acceptance should not be by post (or should be by a means "other than" post). However, a more subtle method of interpretation has been applied by the courts. In the case of **Holwell Securities Ltd v Hughes** [1974] 1 W.L.R. 155 the defendants made an offer to the plaintiff for the sale of land requiring "notice in writing" of their acceptance. The plaintiff posted a letter of acceptance but it never arrived. The Court of Appeal held that the postal rule did not apply in this case. As the defendants stipulated that "notice" was a condition of acceptance then the acceptance will be effective when it arrives rather than when it was posted. The reasoning behind this decision is quite plain. To have "notice" of acceptance the defendants made it clear through the wording of their offer that they never intended the postal rule to apply to the transaction. As the defendants would only have "notice" of acceptance once they receive the letter, then the general requirement that an acceptance must be communicated applies.

As Lawton L.J. summarised in his judgment:

> **"First, it does not apply when the express terms of the offer specify that the acceptance must reach the offeror. The public nowadays are familiar with this exception to the general rule through their handling of football pool coupons."**

◼ The postal rule will not apply if it would produce an absurd result

In the case of **Holwell** Lawton L.J. referred to a further limitation to the postal rule. He stated   2-035
that the postal rule would probably not apply if its application would produce "manifest inconvenience and absurdity."

Lawton L.J. cites the case of **British & American Telegraph Co v Colson** (1871) LR 6 Exch 108, and considers the examples provided by Bramwell B in that case:

> **"Is a stockbroker who is holding shares to the orders of his client liable in damages because he did not sell in a falling market in accordance with the instructions in a letter which was posted but never received? Before the passing of the Law Reform (Miscellaneous Provisions) Act 1970 (which abolished actions for breach of promise of marriage), would a young soldier ordered overseas have been bound in contract to marry a girl to whom he had proposed by letter, asking her to let him have an answer before he left and she had replied affirmatively in good time but the letter had never reached him? In my judgment, the factors of inconvenience and absurdity are but illustrations of a wider principle, namely, that the rule does not apply if, having regard to all the circumstances, including the nature of the subject-matter under consideration, the negotiating parties cannot have intended that there should be a binding agreement until the party accepting an offer or exercising an option had in fact communicated the acceptance or exercise to the other."**

Lawton L.J.'s observations on this issue are particularly interesting. If the application of the postal rule would result in "manifest inconvenience and absurdity" then the courts may refuse to apply the rule in order to give effect to the intention of the parties. This provides further support for the view espoused above that it may be incorrect to speak of a general rule of postal acceptance to be applied to all cases.

◼ Prescribed method of acceptance

As described above, an offeror can explicitly displace the postal rule by stating that accept-   2-036
ance *must not* be via post. This is exclusionary in nature and may mean that other methods of acceptance are acceptable. However, given the difficulties in identifying a general rule relating to postal acceptance it can be argued that the role of the courts in such cases should be to give effect to the intention of the parties. If an offeror makes it clear that acceptance should *only* be in a particular manner, then it is unlikely that acceptance via a different method will result in a binding agreement.

When explicit words are used in the offer such as "exclusively" or "compulsory" it will be difficult to argue that any other methods of acceptance will be effective. Things become less certain, however, when the wording of the offer is less prescriptive. In such cases unless the offeror has made it explicitly clear that only a particular form of acceptance will be sufficient the courts are willing to recognise an equally swift method of acceptance as valid (see **Manchester Diocesan Council of Education v Commercial and General Investments Ltd** [1970] 1 W.L.R. 241).

■ The postal rule and the withdrawal of an *offer*

2-037   The postal rule will only apply to acceptances. Given the favourable application of the postal rule to the offeree it is unsurprising that the courts have refused to extend the postal rule to the revocation of an offer (**Henthorn v Fraser** [1892] 2 Ch.27). The general rule of revocation will apply and such withdrawals will only be effective once communicated to the offeree (see p.50 below).

■ The postal rule and the withdrawal of an *acceptance*

2-038   It has been argued that the postal rule does not apply to the withdrawal of an offer, but what about the withdrawal of an acceptance? The postal rule operates in a way that provides that the offeror may be bound by an acceptance of which he is completely ignorant. The delay between the postal acceptance being sent and it arriving creates the possibility that an offeree may seek to withdraw their acceptance by using a swifter method of communication. Given that the postal rule already favours the offeree in terms of acceptance then there is an argument that it could also do so in relation to a withdrawal.

Unfortunately, the authorities on this issue are contradictory and are a long way from providing any definite conclusions. In fact, we have to look to other jurisdictions for guidance. For example, in **Wenckheim v Arndt** (1873) (NZ) 1 J.R. 73 the court held that it was not possible to withdraw an acceptance once it had been posted. The purpose of the postal rule is to determine the point of acceptance. The acceptance is complete once posted and it is at this point that the contract is formed. Once the contract is formed then it cannot be unravelled by the actions of one of the parties.

However, there is contrary authority in **Dunmore v Alexander** (1830) 9 Shaw 190. Here the court suggested that it may be possible to withdraw an acceptance by using a swifter method of communication (a horse and cart for example!). This decision should be treated with a fair amount of caution as there was some disagreement between the judges as to whether the communication in question was actually an acceptance or whether it was an offer.

There are certainly arguments to consider either way. On the one hand, it could be argued that allowing the offeree to withdraw his acceptance by a swifter method causes no actual loss to the offeror. As the offeror will generally not be aware of a postal acceptance until it arrives, he will be in no worse position and none the wiser if the offeree seeks to withdraw their acceptance.

The counter-arguments are that this allows the offeree to hedge his bets. The operation of the postal rule means that once the letter of acceptance is posted the offeror will be prevented from withdrawing his offer. The offeree can then use the delay in communication to assess the merits of the agreement. If they become unfavourable then the offeree has the option to withdraw using a swifter method.

On balance it would seem unjust to allow the postal rule to apply to the withdrawal of an offer. The postal rule already favours the offeree in that it prevents the offeror from withdrawing his offer once acceptance is posted. To give the offeree the added benefit of being able to withdraw his acceptance by a swifter method of communication would seem to create a *double* risk for the offeror. He faces the risk of an action for breach of contract if he attempts to withdraw his offer once a letter of acceptance has been posted. Additionally, he faces the risk that the offeree may seek to escape from a contract despite the fact that he has demonstrated his intention to be bound. The offeror does not have this option and granting it to the offeree would thus seem a step too far.

SUMMARY OF POSTAL ACCEPTANCE

As we have seen, there are many issues that need to be considered before the postal rule of acceptance will apply. The grid in Figure 2.4 summarises these issues and presents them as a checklist for each stage. Each issue must be satisfied before progressing to the next stage. Only once all the issues and limitations have been satisfied will acceptance be effective upon posting.

2-039

MODERN METHODS OF COMMUNICATION

One of the key criticisms of the postal rule is that it is outdated and fails to reflect the realities of modern forms of communication. We have already mentioned that the modern postal system is significantly different from the postal system in operation when the rules relating to postal acceptance were first developed. Therefore, attempting to apply the postal rule to modern forms of communication would seem particularly unsatisfactory.

2-040

Further, modern forms of communication present different problems in relation to offer and acceptance. When considering methods such as faxes, emails, voice messages, there will be some inevitable delay between the acceptance being *sent* and the acceptance being *received*. Also, being able to identify the precise timing of such acceptances presents further difficulties.

An email may take a few seconds to travel from the computer of the offeree to the computer of the offeror. However, once on the offeror's computer the email could remain unread for hours/ days/weeks. The basic general rule that acceptance must be communicated to the offeror therefore becomes difficult to apply to these modern forms of communication.

■ The rules relating to instantaneous methods of communication

In response to the difficulties outlined above, the courts have developed further principles relating to "instantaneous" methods of communication.

2-041

FIGURE 2.4 **Checklist for postal acceptances**

Stage	Authority	Yes?	No?
1. Did the letter of acceptance enter the postal system?	*Adams v Lindsell* *Household Fire Insurance v Grant*	Proceed to next stage.	Postal rule will not apply—acceptance effective when received.
2. Was it reasonable to use post as a method of acceptance?	*Henthorn v Fraser*	Proceed to next stage.	Postal rule will not apply—acceptance effective when received.
3. Did the offeror explicitly displace the postal rule?	*Holwell Securities v Hughes*	Postal rule will not apply—acceptance effective when received.	Proceed to next stage.
4. Was letter of acceptance "properly posted"?	*Contimar's Case* *Korbetis* *Adams v Lindsell* *Household Fire Insurance v Grant*	Proceed to next stage.	Postal rule will not apply—acceptance effective "at the time least favourable" to the offeree.
5. Would the application of the postal rule produce "manifest inconvenience and absurdity?"	Lawton L.J: *Holwell Securities v Hughes*	Postal Rule will not apply.	Postal rule applies—acceptance effective when posted.

The starting point is to consider the case of **Entores Ltd v Miles Far East Corp** [1955] 2 Q.B. 327. Here, the plaintiffs were based in London and the defendants in Holland. The plaintiffs communicated to the defendants using a telex machine and the issue for the court was to determine *where* the contract was formed. The Court of Appeal held that the contract was formed where the acceptance was *received*.

However, it is the obiter of **Entores** that is of particular interest in relation to instantaneous methods of communication. Denning L.J. highlighted the many different problems posed by such methods of communication. In doing so Denning L.J. considers how the issue of acceptance would be determined in three broad scenarios:

1. The offeree *realises* that his acceptance has not got through.
2. The offeree *reasonably believes* that his acceptance has got through when it has *not*.
3. The offeree *reasonably believes* that his acceptance has got through and it is the *fault of the offeror* that it has not.

We shall consider each in turn.

■ The offeree *realises* that his acceptance has not got through

If the offeree realises that his acceptance has not got through to the offeror (and neither party is at fault), then in this case there is no contract. It remains the responsibility of the offeree to communicate his acceptance to the offeror.

2-042

Denning L.J. provided a hypothetical scenario to illustrate his reasoning:

> "Let me first consider a case where two people make a contract by word of mouth in the presence of one another. Suppose, for instance, that I shout an offer to a man across a river or a courtyard but I do not hear his reply because it is drowned by an aircraft flying overhead. There is no contract at that moment. If he wishes to make a contract, he must wait till the aircraft is gone and then shout back his acceptance so that I can hear what he says. Not until I have his answer am I bound."

■ The offeree *reasonably believes* that his acceptance has got through when it has not

Again, this scenario is quite straightforward. If the offeree reasonably believes that his acceptance has got through when it has not (and neither party is at fault), then again there is no contract. As Denning L.J. observed:

2-043

> "If there should be a case where the offeror without any fault on his part does not receive the message of acceptance—yet the sender of it reasonably believes it has got home when it has not—then I think there is no contract."

Again, it remains the responsibility of the offeree to resend his acceptance. Until the acceptance is communicated to the offeror there is no contract. Denning L.J. further illustrated this point using the example of a telephone conversation:

> "Now take a case where two people make a contract by telephone. Suppose, for instance, that I make an offer to a man by telephone and, in the middle of his reply, the line goes 'dead' so that I do not hear his words of acceptance. There is no contract at that moment. . . The contract is only complete when I have his answer accepting the offer".

■ The offeree reasonably believes that his acceptance has got through and it is the fault of the offeror that it has not

2-044   This final scenario is the most problematic. If the offeree reasonably believes that his acceptance has got through and it is the fault of the offeror that it has not, then the offeror will be estopped (or prevented) from saying that he did not receive the message of acceptance.

Denning L.J. emphasises that the issue of *fault* has an important part to play in determining the issue of acceptance and it is this aspect that is of fundamental importance in relation to modern forms of communication such as faxes and answer-machine messages. For example, if an acceptance is sent to the offeror but this is never received owing to the fault of the offeror in failing to replace a toner cartridge in his fax machine, or in failing to clear the tape in his answer-machine, then the fault will lie with the offeror and he will be prevented from arguing that he never received the acceptance.

■ *When* is the contract formed?

2-045   It is important to note that the principles discussed above in **Entores** are concerned with *where* the contract was formed. The precise issue of *when* acceptance is effective when considering instantaneous methods of communication was not addressed in detail until much later.

In **Tenax Steamship Co v Owners of the motor Vessel Brimnes (The Brimnes)** [1975] Q.B. 929, although this case concerned a revocation of an offer as opposed to an acceptance, the court offered some guidance as to how to address the delay between a message being sent and it being received. In this case a revocation of an offer was sent via telex to the defendants during office hours. The message was not read by the defendants until the next day. The Court of Appeal held that the revocation was effective at the time it was received on the defendants' machine (and not when it was read).

This decision is interesting as it provides some clarification as to how the normal rules of offer and acceptance apply to instantaneous methods of communication. The general rule for both acceptance and revocation of an offer is that both must be communicated to the other party. In **The Brimnes**, the issue of "communication" was given a more flexible interpretation and on the facts of the case was taken to mean when the message was received as opposed to read by the other party.

■ The importance of "fault"

2-046   The decision in **The Brimnes** can partly be explained by adopting an assessment of fault. It was the fault of the office staff that the message was not read until the next day. The fault therefore rested with the defendants. However, the decision in **The Brimnes** was purely concerned with the *revocation* of an offer. Further analysis is therefore required in relation to *acceptances*.

The leading case here is **Brinkibon v Stahag Stahl und Stahlwarenhandels GmbH** [1983] 2 A.C. 34, in which the House of Lords approved the reasoning in **Entores**. Most notably, the obiter comments of Lords Wilberforce and Fraser provide some useful guidance as to when such acceptances will become effective.

Lord Wilberforce recognises the problems that may arise in relation to instantaneous methods of communication:

> **"The message may not reach, or be intended to reach, the designated recipient immediately: messages may be sent out of office hours, or at night, with the intention; or upon the assumption, that they will be read at a later time. . . And many other variations may occur: No universal rule can cover all such cases: they must be resolved by reference to the intentions of the parties, by sound business practice and in some cases by a judgment where the risks should lie"**

Lord Wilberforce's approach was to adopt a rather flexible, but of course, less precise rule in relation to difficult cases, including the problems created by the use of instantaneous methods of communication. If one party fails to adopt sound business practice in relation to the handling of his messages then the risk may rest with him. As Lord Fraser comments, obiter, in Brinkibon:

> **"Once the message has been received on the offeror's telex machine, it is not unreasonable to treat it as delivered to the principal offeror, because it is his responsibility to arrange for prompt handling of messages within his own office."**

◼ Acceptances sent inside office hours

Say, for example, that a letter of acceptance was faxed to the offeror at his place of business. The fax was sent at 1pm on Monday. However, the fax was not actually read until 11am the next day. There are a number of possible arguments as to when the acceptance will become *effective*.

2-047

Firstly, it could be argued that the acceptance is effective when read (11am Tuesday). This is consistent with the general rule that acceptance is effective when it is *communicated*. However, this argument ignores the particular characteristics of the method of acceptance. Once the fax has been sent and is received on the offeror's machine, then the offeree has no control over when that acceptance will be read. It could stay on the machine for days/weeks, or may never actually be read. It would seem unfair that the position of the offeree should be determined by the actions of the offeror in failing to check his machine.

Secondly, it could be argued that the acceptance is effective when it is sent. The message is out of the control of the offeree, there is nothing more that he can do to ensure that his acceptance gets through, so acceptance should be effective when it is sent. However, using this argument would mean applying the principles of the postal rule to fax acceptances and would be inconsistent with the general rule that acceptance must be *communicated*. It would seem unfair to bind the offeror at the point when the fax is received given the inevitable delay between the message being sent and the message being read.

Finally, applying the rules of instantaneous methods of communication established in **Entores** and **Brinkibon**, the acceptance will be effective when it could *reasonably* have been expected that it be read. Applying "sound business practice" it would be reasonable to expect that the message would have been read by the close of business. It is the offeror's responsibility to arrange for the prompt handling of his messages. If the message is not read until the next working day the fault should lie with the offeror who is responsible for this unreasonable delay.

This final approach seems the preferable one and takes account of the principles relating to instantaneous methods of communication.

◼ Acceptances sent outside office hours

2-048   We have considered the problems of an instantaneous method of communication sent within office hours. However, if such an acceptance was sent outside office hours then when would that acceptance be effective? Again, we have to apply the principles identified in **Entores** and **Brinkibon** (above) to decide this issue.

Let us slightly modify the example above. Say that a letter of acceptance was faxed to the offeror at his place of business. The fax was sent at 6pm on Friday. However, the fax was not actually read until 3pm the next Monday. In this case, if usual office hours are taken to be 9am–5pm Monday to Friday, then it would be unreasonable to expect the offeror to read the message at 6pm Friday. However, it may be reasonable to expect the message of acceptance to be read at the opening of business on Monday. If this is the case then it could be argued that the acceptance will be effective at 9am on Monday and not when it is read at 3pm. Of course, as Lord Wilberforce reminds us, "there is no universal rule" to cover these situations, so the precise time of acceptance will of course differ depending on the particular facts and the nature of the business in question.

Lord Wilberforce's reasoning was subsequently applied in the case of **Mondial Shipping and Chartering BV v Astarte Shipping Ltd** [1995] C.L.C. 1011. This case concerned a notice of withdrawal by telex machine. The telex was sent at 23:41 on Friday December 2. The message was not read until several days later. As the telex had not been sent within ordinary business hours then the recipients could not have been expected to receive the telex instantaneously. The court held that the withdrawal was not "received" by charterers until the opening of business on December 5. As Gatehouse J. observed, at 1014:

> **"What matters is not when the notice is given/sent/despatched/issued by the owners but when its content reaches the mind of the charterer. If the telex is sent in ordinary business hours, the time of receipt is the same as the time of despatch because it is not open to the charterer to contend that it did not in fact then come to his attention."**

■ Email

Is email an instantaneous method of communication? If the answer to this question is yes, then it would seem that the postal rule would not apply to email in view of the decision in **Entores** above. On the other hand, it could be argued that there are striking similarities between postal acceptance and email that would justify the application of the postal rule. For example, while the delivery of an email may be very quick there is inevitably some delay between the email being sent and it being delivered to the recipient's computer. Factors such as available bandwidth, the time of day and place in the world from which it is sent all play a part in the relevant delivery time. Further, as with a postal acceptance, once the email is sent it is then out of the control of the sender. There is nothing more the sender can do to ensure that his acceptance is delivered.

2-049

These "control" arguments, however, seem to ignore the rather narrow application of the postal rule. Following **Adams**, if the postal rule is only to apply to a letter that enters the Royal Mail postal system (and not for example a private courier) then it is not just an issue of *what* control the offeree has over the letter of acceptance, but more importantly, *who* has control over that postal acceptance. Drawing an analogy with email, yes the offeree loses control of delivery of the message once sent, but that control is then relinquished to the internet service provider. To extend the postal rule to email would therefore have the effect of radically expanding the very narrow application of the postal rule, which is currently limited to the use of the Post Office.

Further, once the email arrives there is no guarantee as to when it will be read. It may remain on the recipient's computer for days or even weeks before it is finally brought to the attention of the recipient. These problems could be resolved if the sender requested a delivery and read receipt with their message. In this case the sender would be able to ascertain the precise moment at which the message was received, even if it was not read for some time later. Following **Entores** and **Brinkibon**, if it was the fault of the recipient that the message was not read then the message of acceptance may be effective when it would be reasonable to expect it to have been read. This solution would of course take into account any delay in the message reaching the recipient's machine, but also any delay in the message being read.

SILENCE

The general rule is that acceptance must be communicated to the offeror. It would therefore seem unlikely that silence could ever amount to a valid acceptance. Silence is not an effective communication. There are many justifications for this approach. First, the law requires an unequivocal acceptance. If the courts were to try and determine the issue of acceptance from silence then there is scope for confusion and uncertainty as to the issue of acceptance, the acceptance itself not being made explicitly clear. This is particularly the case in bilateral contracts.

2-050

■ Silence and bilateral contracts

2-051 In **Felthouse v Bindley** (1862) 11 C.B. N.S. 869, a nephew and an uncle negotiated for the sale of the nephew's horse. The uncle sent a letter to his nephew, offering a specific amount for the horse, stating that "If I hear no more, I consider the horse mine". The nephew did not reply and the horse was sold to a third party at auction. The uncle then pursued an action for breach of contract against the auctioneer. In resolving the issue the court had to decide whether the uncle had entered into a contract with the nephew before the sale at auction. Unsurprisingly, the court held that there was no contract between the uncle and the nephew as the nephew had failed to communicate his acceptance to his uncle.

■ Silence and the problem of inertia selling

2-052 The second justification for the postal rule is that it limits the potential for abuse by the offeror. This is particularly so in relation to the practice of inertia selling.

The practice of inertia selling usually involves a company sending goods to individuals and requiring that the goods are paid for unless returned within a certain time. Subsequent products are then sent unless the recipient expressly directs otherwise. Book clubs and record clubs are typical examples (this practice is now regulated by the Unsolicited Goods and Services Act 1971, which provides protection to recipients and may allow certain products to be kept as gifts).

■ Exceptions to the rule on silence

Despite the general rule that an acceptance is effective once communicated, there are limited ways in which the need for communication may be waived.

The key exceptions to the rule on silence are:

1. acceptance by post; and
2. acceptance in unilateral contracts.

■ Acceptance by post

2-053 If the postal rule applies then acceptance will be effective when posted (**Adams v Lindsell** (1818) 1 B. & Ald. 681). As has been discussed, this rule can obviously operate quite harshly on the offeror. If the letter is lost, delayed or never received by the offeror he will still be bound by the acceptance, despite the fact that he may be completely ignorant of the acceptance. Again, the lapse of time between the letter being posted and the letter arriving means that the offeror could also face an action for breach of contract if he attempts to withdraw his offer or to contract with another party in that interim period.

Again, this calls into question the validity of the so-called "postal rule" and its role within modern contract law. Perhaps an alternative approach to postal acceptances would be to adopt similar principles to those of instantaneous methods of communication in which the issue of *fault* will be relevant. The general rule would therefore be that a postal acceptance will be effective when it would be reasonable for the offeror to have received and read the acceptance. This approach would take account of any delay to the acceptance due to the fault of the offeree (**Contimar**'s Case [1953] 1 W.L.R. 793). If the reason for delay rests with the offeror (for example, there is an unreasonable delay in reading the letter) then again, as the acceptance should be effective when it would have been reasonable for the acceptance to have been read, the fault will lie with the offeror.

◼ Acceptance in unilateral contracts

The position in relation to bilateral contracts has been explained above when discussing **Felthouse v Bindley** (p.46) However, the position in relation to unilateral contracts is slightly more complex. Generally, silence cannot constitute an effective acceptance. The general rule is that acceptance must be communicated to the offeror in order to be effective so it would seem unlikely that silence could constitute a valid acceptance. However, in relation to *unilateral* contracts, the offeror will have implicitly *waived* the need for acceptance to be communicated. Acceptance will be by *performing* the act required as a condition of acceptance.

2-054

For example, think back to the case of **Carlill** (see p.21 above) In this case there was no need for Mrs Carlill to *communicate* her acceptance. It was her *conduct* that constituted her acceptance (her use of the ball and catching influenza). If this was decided differently, and the need for communication was applied to unilateral contracts, it could produce a number of undesirable and absurd results which would be contrary to the intention of the parties. As Bowen L.J. observed in **Carlill** itself:

> "If I advertise to the world that my dog is lost, and that anybody who brings the dog to a particular place will be paid some money, are all the police or other persons whose business it is to find lost dogs to be expected to sit down and write me a note saying that they have accepted my proposal? Why, of course, they at once look after the dog, and as soon as they find the dog they have performed the condition. . . It follows from the nature of the thing that the performance of the condition is sufficient acceptance without the notification of it, and a person who makes an offer in an advertisement of that kind makes an offer which must be read by the light of that common sense reflection. He does, therefore, in his offer impliedly indicate that he does not require notification of the acceptance of the offer."

As the condition of acceptance is *performance* of the required act, the offeror has waived the need for the offeree to communicate the fact of acceptance.

While the requirement of performance in a unilateral contract seems a logical exception to the rule on silence it also creates particular problems in relation to the issue of acceptance. Most notably, it can be very difficult to identify at what point the acceptance is *effective*.

◼ The problems of acceptance in unilateral contracts

2-055 Unilateral contracts pose unique problems for the issue of acceptance. Firstly, the offeror may have waived the need for communication by requesting that an act be performed as a condition of acceptance. Secondly, it is difficult to identify the precise point at which an acceptance is effective. The consequences of these problems are that an offeror may be in complete ignorance of the fact that someone has purported to accept his offer by performing the required act of acceptance. Further, the difficulty in identifying the precise point of acceptance has a knock-on effect in the context of revocation. An offer cannot be revoked once acceptance is effective. This therefore creates uncertainty for both parties: the offeror cannot be certain that he is bound to an agreement; the offeree cannot be certain that he is entitled to enforce the contract.

The courts have responded to these problems by recognising that acceptance in a unilateral contract can be a "continuing act".

◼ Acceptance in unilateral contracts—the "continuing act" of acceptance

2-056 Imagine, for example, that I promise you £5,000 if you walk from Manchester to Piccadilly Circus, London. At what point is your acceptance effective and at what point will I be prevented from withdrawing my offer? If you sit at home and contemplate accepting, then there will be little argument that I will be free to revoke my offer; you have not taken steps to accept. However, if you have spent several days walking and are approaching the outskirts of London there can be little doubt that you have *embarked* upon performance. In this case your acceptance can be seen as a "continuing act". Your acceptance starts when you embark upon performance and ends when you complete the required act (arrive at Piccadilly Circus).

The notion of a continuing act of acceptance was recognised in **Errington v Errington** [1952] 1 K.B. 290. In this case the father promised his son and daughter-in-law that he would give them the family home if they continued to pay the mortgage on the property. The father subsequently died and the representatives of his estate sought to revoke the father's offer. The Court of Appeal held that the offer could not be withdrawn as the parties had embarked upon performance. The continuing act of acceptance meant that the son and daughter-in-law could not be *prevented* from completing performance. If they failed to fully complete (full completion meaning that all the mortgage payments must have been met) then their acceptance would not have been effective and there would be no contract. However, *if* they met the conditions of acceptance then the father's promise would be enforceable. As all the instalments were paid, the promise was enforceable.

As Denning L.J. observed:

> **"The father's promise was a unilateral contract—a promise of the house in return for their act of paying the instalments. It could not be revoked by him once the couple entered on performance of the act, but it would cease to bind him if they left it incomplete and unperformed, which they have not done."**

The reasoning in **Errington** was accepted obiter in **Daulia Ltd v Four Millbank Nominees Ltd** [1978] Ch. 231 in which it was argued that the offeror has an *implied obligation* not to revoke once performance has started. Further, the offeror will be unable to act in a way so as to prevent the acceptance from being completed. So, for example, if I were to run up beside you when you were only a few metres away from Piccadilly Circus and tell you that the offer has been withdrawn, this revocation will be ineffective. The effort you have exerted in performance will outweigh my attempt to revoke my offer.

However, the courts will also look to the intentions of the parties and the commercial realities of such agreements when considering the issue of revocation. For example, in **Luxor (Eastbourne) v Cooper** [1941] A.C. 108, the seller of some land was able to revoke his offer to pay the estate agent £10,000 if he could find a buyer for his land. Given the rather minimal effort required by the estate agent, it would be within the contemplation of the parties that such an offer could be revoked before the sale of land was completed.

There remain some difficulties in applying the above principles. Identifying when an offeree *embarks* upon performance can be difficult. Using our example of walking to Piccadilly, when does the offeree embark upon performance? The offeree may go out and buy new sports clothes and trainers for the journey; has he embarked upon performance at this stage? What if the offeree leaves his house and walks to the end of his street with the intention of continuing on to London? The offeree is still miles away (literally!) from meeting the conditions of acceptance, but in the latter example he may have *embarked* upon the act of performance. The offeror will then not be able to revoke his offer at this point.

■ Acceptance in ignorance of an offer

We have established that silence will generally not be recognised as a valid acceptance. One of the key reasons is that the offeror will be unaware that his offer has been accepted and that he is thus bound by contractual obligations. Similar principles also apply to the offeree. The court generally requires that the offeree is aware of the offer before his acceptance will be effective. However, there is some disagreement in the authorities on this point.

2-057

It may sound improbable that a person may accept in ignorance of an offer, but it does happen. This usually arises in contracts for reward. In **Gibbons v Proctor** (1891) 64 L.T. 594, a police officer gave information for which a reward was offered. The police officer was not aware of the reward when he gave the information. It was only later that he discovered that a reward might be payable. The court held that the officer was entitled to the reward. Part of the reasoning seems to be based on the fact that by the time the information reached its intended recipient, the officer had become aware of the offer. Even though he was not aware of the offer for reward when giving the information, he became aware of the offer before the information had been relayed to the appropriate recipient.

This decision should be treated with a fair amount of caution. The courts have never followed it and subsequent decisions call the validity of **Gibbons v Proctor** into question. One of the few

English authorities on this point is **Taylor v Allon** [1966] 1 Q.B. 304. This case suggests that the offeree should at least be aware of the offer in order to accept. Applying this reasoning to **Gibbons**, it is unlikely that the officer would have been entitled to the reward.

There are also a number of cases from other jurisdictions that address this issue, although, unfortunately, there is again disagreement as to the relevant principles that apply. In the American case of **Williams v Carwardine** (1833) 5 C. & P. 566, the plaintiff gave information to the police which led to the conviction of a murderer. She gave this information to satisfy her conscience; she was not motivated by the promise of reward. The court held that her motive was irrelevant. She was aware of the offer of reward when giving the information so she was entitled to the reward.

In contrast, the Australian case of **R v Clarke** (1927) 40 C.L.R. 227 suggests that if an offeree has an awareness of the offer of reward, but happens to forget about it, then he will not be entitled to claim the reward.

If it is possible to draw any conclusions from these cases, it appears that the offeree must be aware of the offer at the time of accepting, in order for the acceptance to be effective.

Revocation of an offer

2-058   An offer is capable of being accepted until it is withdrawn (or revoked). Equally, an offer can be revoked at any point before acceptance (**Routledge v Grant** (1828) 4 Bing. 653). Being able to apply the rules above as to when an acceptance becomes effective is therefore fundamental in deciding whether an offer can be revoked. If acceptance is effective before the offer is revoked, then the offeror may face an action for breach of contract if he refuses to recognise the acceptance.

As with an acceptance, the general rule is that in order to be effective the revocation of an offer must be *communicated*. This is demonstrated in **Byrne & Co v Leon Van Tien Hoven** (1879–80) L.R. 5 C.P.D. 344. In this case the defendants sent an offer by letter to the plaintiffs in New York. The plaintiffs accepted the offer by telegram. After the telegram was sent the defendants sent a letter revoking their offer. The court held that the offer was accepted when the telegram was sent and therefore the defendants could not revoke their offer without being in breach of contract.

Besides communicating a revocation there are further ways in which an offer can lapse. An offer may have only been open for a fixed period of time. Once that time has lapsed then so will the offer. Even if the offer has no fixed time period for acceptance, the court may find that the offer is only open for a *reasonable* time (**Ramsgate Victoria Hotel Co Ltd v Montefiore** (1865–66) L.R. 1 Ex. 109). It is unlikely that the offeror intended his offer to be open for an unlimited period of time so the courts may intervene to give effect to the apparent intent of the offeror.

Further, a counter-offer, for example, will have the effect of destroying the original offer (**Hyde v Wrench**). The original offer is then not capable of being accepted.

· ·

Revocation by a third party

The law requires that the revocation of an offer must be communicated. However, there is no strict requirement that this communication must come from the offeror directly. The courts have accepted that a reliable third party may be able to communicate the revocation of an offer (**Dickinson v Dodds** (1875–76) 2 Ch. D. 463). The third party must be "objectively reliable", which creates some problems for the offeree. If the offeree (*subjectively*) does not believe the third party is reliable, but the court concludes that he is *objectively* reliable, then the offeree may incur time and expense in pursuing an offer that is no longer capable of being accepted.

2-059

· ·

Revocation and unilateral contracts

We have discussed the problems of acceptance in unilateral contracts above (see p.48). However, unilateral contracts also present a number of problems in relation to the revocation of an offer. The advertisement of a unilateral contract will generally be open to the public at large and this creates problems for the offeror. Firstly, he will not be aware if anyone has started to perform the conditions of acceptance. Secondly, the offeror will not be able to communicate the revocation of his offer to everybody who may have seen the advertisement.

2-060

In such cases the courts will waive the *strict* need for actual communication. Instead, the court will insist that the offeror takes *reasonable steps* to communicate the revocation of his offer. The American case of **Shuey v USA** (1875) 92 U.S. 73 would suggest that if the offer was advertised in a particular way then it would be reasonable to revoke it by the same method. So, if the advertisement was placed in a local newspaper then it would be reasonable to publish the revocation of that offer in the same newspaper. Providing that the offeror takes reasonable steps to revoke his offer it will not be necessary that everybody who saw the original advertised offer sees the subsequently published revocation.

A structured approach to offer and acceptance

When considering questions of offer and acceptance it may be useful to follow the basic structure outlined in Figure 2.5.

FIGURE 2.5 **Offer and acceptance**

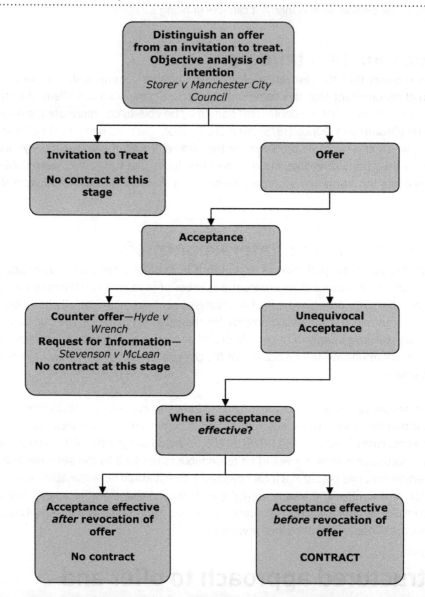

Hear from the Author

Scan the QR Tag or follow the link below for guidance on a structured approach to the topic of offer and acceptance.

uklawstudent.thomsonreuters.com/category/contract-fundamentals

Summary

Offer

1. A contract is a legally binding agreement. The first stage towards a binding agreement is to identify an *offer* and *acceptance*.

2. Whether there is a legally recognisable offer will depend on the intention of the offeror. The courts apply an *objective* test of intention to determine this fact (**Storer v Manchester City Council**).

3. It is necessary to distinguish an offer from an invitation to treat. An invitation to treat is an indication that the party is open to the negotiation process. There is no contractual intent so an invitation to treat does not form part of a legally binding agreement, as it is not capable of being accepted.

4. The courts use a number of "presumptions" when applying the objective test of intention to particular types of contract.

5. The presumption with advertisements is that they are invitations to treat (**Partridge v Crittenden**). This conclusion is usually based on the multi-acceptance problem. *Objectively*, the party who placed the advertisement could not have intended to enter into a contract with everybody who attempts to accept his offer as he will not have an unlimited supply to meet demand.

6. Similar presumptions also apply to the display of goods. The display of goods is presumed to be an invitation to treat as the owner of the goods wishes to reserve his right to pick and choose his customers (**Pharmaceutical Society of Great Britain v Boots**).

7. These presumptions can be rebutted if the court is able to identify a clear display of contractual intent. This is particularly the case in relation to unilateral contracts (**Carlill v Carbolic Smoke Ball Co**).

Acceptance

1. There must be an unequivocal acceptance of the terms of the offer to form an agreement. A counter-offer, for example, is not a valid acceptance and will destroy the original offer (**Hyde v Wrench**).

2. The general rule is that an acceptance will only be *effective* when communicated to the offeror. A notable exception to this is the postal rule, which states that an acceptance will be effective once posted (**Adams v Lindsell**).

3. The rules relating to instantaneous methods of communication require an analysis of fault in deciding where the risk should lie with such acceptances (**Brinkibon**).

Revocation

1. An offer can be revoked at any time before acceptance (**Routledge v Grant**).

2. In order to be effective a revocation must also be *communicated* (**Byrne v Van Tien Hoven**).

3. It is possible for a third party to revoke an offer provided that the party is *objectively reliable* (**Dickinson v Dodds**).

4. Finally, with advertisements of unilateral contracts the need for *actual* communication may be waived. The offeror must take *reasonable steps* to revoke his offer. This may include revoking the offer by the same method by which it was advertised (**Shuey v USA**).

Key Cases Grid

Case	Court	Key Points
Storer v Manchester City Council [1974]	Court of Appeal	This case confirms the objective approach that courts adopt to the issue of contract formation. The courts are not concerned with the actual intent of the parties, but how the words, conduct, actions of the party would appear to a reasonable man.
Partridge v Crittenden [1968]	Divisional Court	In distinguishing between and an offer and an intention to treat, the court will use a number of presumptions to help them determine the contractual intent of the parties. In relation to advertisements, the courts will presume that an advertisement is an invitation to treat. This is based on the problem of "multi-acceptance" that would arise if the advertisement were an offer.
Pharmaceutical Society of Great Britain v Boots Cash Chemists [1953]	Court of Appeal	The courts will presume that the display of goods in a self-service shop is an invitation to treat. Applying an objective approach to contractual intent, the court will seek to preserve the freedom of both parties. The freedom of the shopkeeper to pick and choose their customers and the freedom of the customer to change their mind and/or substitute items before entering into a contract at the cash desk.

Carlill v Carbolic Smoke Ball Co Ltd [1893]	Court of Appeal	An advertisement of reward was held to amount to an offer. The wording of the advertisement displayed sufficient contractual intend to bind the parties to the promises contained within it. As a separate issue, Carlill is also an example of a unilateral contract. In such cases, there is no need to communicate acceptance. The acceptance is through the performance of the required act.
Hyde v Wrench (1840)	Court of Chancery	In order to form a valid agreement, the exchange of offer and acceptance must match. If one party seeks to vary the terms of the offer or to introduce new terms, this will constitute a counter-offer that will have the effect of destroying the original offer.
Enotres Ltd v Miles Far East Copr [1955]	Court of Appeal	As a general rule, an acceptance will be affective when it is communicated to the offeror. It will be communicated when it is brought to the attention of the offeror.
Brinkibon v Stahag Stahl und Stahlwarenhandels GmbH [1983] 2 A.C. 34	House of Lords	The House of Lords approved the approach in Entores, acceptance is generally effective when communicated. However, this is not a universal rule and there will be difficult cases when it is not appropriate to apply this general rule. Refer the dicta of Lord Wilberforce and Fraser as to the factors that could determine when such acceptances become effective. These factors have been applied to the use of instantaneous methods of communication.
Byrne & Co v Leon Van Tien Hoven (1879–80)	Common Pleas Division	This case concerns the revocation of an offer. As a general rule, in order for the revocation to be effective, it must have been communicated to the offeree

End of Chapter Question

Simon places the following advertisement in the local newspaper: "Bargain offer, Black Vauxhall Corsa, 12,000 miles, one careful owner, £5,000. The car will go to the first person to notify me of their intention to purchase by May 15".

Vicki sees the advertisement and posts a letter accepting Simon's offer on May 12. Vicki misaddresses the letter and because of this her letter is delayed in the post. The letter finally arrives on May 15.

Later that evening Vicki talks to Amy, Simon's girlfriend, who tells Vicki that the car has now been sold. Vicki now brings an action against Simon for breach of contract.

Advise Simon.

Points of Answer

The first issue is to decide whether Simon's advertisement is an offer or an invitation to treat.

♦ The courts apply an objective test to decide whether the party has displayed the necessary contractual intent to be bound.

♦ The court will presume that the advertisement is an invitation to treat (**Partridge v Crittenden**). This is due to the problem of "multi-acceptance" that would result if the advertisement was construed as an offer.

♦ However, by using the words "car will go to the first person", Simon may have waived his right to pick and choose who he contracts with and has also addressed the problem of multi-acceptance. He has *one* car and it will go to the *first person*. See the case of **Lefkowitz** for further guidance as to this issue.

♦ If the court is satisfied that the advertisement displays the necessary contractual intent then the court can construe the advertisement as an offer (**Carlill v Carbolic Smoke Ball Co**).

♦ In relation to Vicki's acceptance, discuss whether the postal rule applies here (**Adams v Lindsell**). Simon may have displaced the postal rule by requiring "notice" (see **Holwell Securities v Hughes**). Further, as Vicki has misaddressed the letter then the postal rule may not apply (see the approach of the courts in **Contimar** and **Korbetis**).

♦ Amy may have communicated revocation of Simon's offer to Vicki—she would seem to be objectively reliable (**Dickinson v Dodds**).

♦ As such, Simon's offer may have been revoked before Vicki's acceptance is effective so there is no contract between the parties.

Further Reading

Howarth, W. "The Meaning of Objectivity in Contract" (1984) 100 L.Q.R. 265

    This article provides a comprehensive analysis of what is meant by "objectivity" in contract law, providing critical commentary on supporting authorities to explain the approach of the courts when considering "promisor" and "promisee objectivity.

Vorster, J.P. "A Comment on the Meaning of Objectivity in Contract" L.Q.R. 1987, 103(Apr), 274-287

    This article provide a critical response to Howarth's article above, with particular analysis of the case of **Gibson v. Manchester City Council**

Kadir, R. "Rules of Advertisement in an Electronic Age." Int. J.L.M. 2013, 55(1), 42–54

    This article considers the relevant authorities relating to "paper advertisements" and how they may apply to web advertisements in a virtual environment.

Stone, R. and Cunnington, R. *Text, Cases and Materials on Contract Law* (London: Routledge-Cavendish, 2014), Chapter 2.

Treitel, G. *The Law of Contract*, 13th edn (London Sweet & Maxwell, 2011), Chapter 2.

Certainty and Intention to Create Legal Relations

3

CHAPTER OVERVIEW

In this chapter we:

- explain the importance of certainty of terms to the formation of the agreement

- consider the approach of the courts in relation to an intention to create legal relations

- discuss the relevant presumptions in relation to domestic and social agreements

- discuss the relevant presumptions in relation to commercial relationships

Summary

Key Cases Grid

End of Chapter Question

Further Reading

Introduction

3-001   As with so many aspects of the agreement, the issue of certainty will only become a problem when one party wishes (or both parties wish) to challenge the validity of the agreement and bring the issue before the court. The courts will not enforce an agreement and thus the agreement will not be binding if there is a lack of certainty.

Again, the aim of the courts is to give effect to the intention of the parties. The courts will assess whether there has been a "meeting of the minds" so as to demonstrate consensus ad idem as to the agreement. If the parties have for all intents and purposes reached an agreement then the court will seek to resolve any uncertainty to give effect to that agreement. However, if the agreement is too vague or incomplete then the court cannot enforce such an agreement.

There is an obvious tension between the principle of freedom of contract and the role of the courts when assessing issues of certainty. On the one hand, the role of the courts is to give effect to the intention of the parties. On the other, the courts should not go so far so as to create and write the contract for the parties. A balance between these two competing factors therefore needs to be struck. In response the courts have developed a number of methods by which they approach the need for certainty as to the terms of the agreement.

The terms of the agreement are too vague

3-002   If the terms of the agreement are too vague or too ambiguous then the court cannot enforce the agreement. A classic example can be found in **Raffles v Wichelhaus** (1864) 2 Hurl. & C. 906. In this case the agreement for the delivery of goods stated "the goods to arrive ex Peerless from Bombay". However, there were two ships named *Peerless*. One ship sailed from Bombay in October and the other sailed in December. The defendants thought that the goods were being carried by the ship that sailed in October; they were in fact being carried by the ship that sailed in December. When the goods arrived the defendants refused to accept them and claimed damages for breach of contract.

As there were two ships that carried the same name the court felt that there was sufficient ambiguity to justify refusing to enforce the agreement. The key issue here is that the ambiguity went right to the heart of offer and acceptance. The role of the courts is to assess whether there has been a "meeting of the minds" between the parties. If the parties are at cross-purposes with one another then there will be no contract as the parties never reached a consensus as to their agreement.

In fact, the case of **Raffles v Wichelhaus** can also be explained by reference to the law of mistake (see p.244). Such mistakes are referred to as common mistakes or "agreement mistakes" and will negative any agreement between the parties, because there is a lack of certainty or a fundamental confusion as to the terms of the agreement.

In **Scammell & Nephew Ltd v Ouston** [1941] A.C. 251, Ouston was negotiating the sale of a motor-van from Scammell on "hire-purchase terms over two years". Before the sale was complete Scammell withdrew from the sale. Ouston then pursued an action for damages against Scammell for breach of contract in failing to supply the vehicle. The House of Lords held that the phrase "on hire-purchase terms over two years" was too vague and further agreement was required between the parties as to the precise terms before the parties could be said to have reached an enforceable agreement.

Meaningless phrases

3-003

Some phrases may be so meaningless that it is possible to sever (or remove) them from the contract altogether. If it is possible to give effect to the rest of the agreement after removing the meaningless phrase, but without altering the nature of the contract itself, then the court may sever the meaningless phrase from the agreement. In **Nicolene Ltd v Simmonds** [1953] 1 Q.B. 543, the contract for the purchase of steel was subject to "the usual conditions of acceptance". However, there were no such "usual conditions of acceptance" between the parties. The Court of Appeal held that this meaningless phrase should be severed and ignored leaving an enforceable contract between the parties.

Certainty and negative obligations

3-004

Most contracts contain positive obligations which require the parties to act in a particular way. However, some agreements may contain negative obligations, obligations to refrain from acting in a particular way. Such agreements have the potential to be unclear and ambiguous. The approach of the courts in such cases is illustrated in **Walford v Miles** [1992] 2 A.C. 128. Here, the agreement was between the seller and the buyer of a house. The seller agreed not to negotiate with any other party for the sale of the house. This meant that the buyer was the only party that could purchase the house during the negotiations. The seller breached the agreement by selling the house to a third party.

Before the House of Lords the buyer argued that the agreement contained two limbs, each of which should be enforceable: first an *express* agreement that the seller would not negotiate with any other purchaser; secondly, an *implied* term that the seller would negotiate with the buyer in "good faith". The House of Lords considered that these two obligations overlapped to such an extent and that there was such ambiguity that neither could be enforceable.

First, the agreement not to negotiate with another party was unenforceable as it was too vague as to its duration. There was no specific time period for which the negative obligation, not to negotiate with another party, should last. Usually, in such cases the court would be prepared to imply a term that the obligation should run for a "reasonable time". However, in this case it was not possible to do so since the *second* (implied) obligation to negotiate "in good faith" was also too vague to be enforceable. The difficulty in assessing "good faith" in relation to the agreement meant that neither obligation could therefore be enforced.

Interestingly, had a fixed time limit been agreed between the parties then the agreement not to negotiate might have been enforceable (as was the case in **Pitt v PHH Asset Management Ltd** [1994] 1 W.L.R. 327). It would then also have been possible to interpret the obligation to negotiate in "good faith" in the light of the agreed time limit.

. . . .

Methods of resolving ambiguity

3-005   Even though the terms of the agreement may be particularly ambiguous the court may still be able to resolve such uncertainty and give effect to the intention of the parties. The court may be prepared to imply terms into the agreement to give effect to this intention.

In **WN Hillas & Co Ltd v Arcos Ltd** (1932) 147 L.T. 503, the plaintiffs entered into a contract with the defendants to purchase timber. The agreement also gave the plaintiffs the option "for the purchase of 100,000 standards". When the plaintiffs sought to enforce this option the defendants did not have any timber to meet their request. The plaintiffs therefore sued for breach of contract. The difficulty for the House of Lords was, of course, in interpreting the phrase "100,000 standards".

Over to you. . .

Focusing on the basic facts of *Hillas*, can you think of how the court resolved the ambiguity as to the subject matter of the contract? In relation to the option to purchase "100,000 standards", why could it be relevant that the parties already had an existing and enforceable contract for the purchase of timber?

The parties had not explicitly agreed upon the meaning of the phrase "100,000 standards", but nevertheless the House of Lords was prepared to imply a term into the contract that this phrase be interpreted in the light of the agreement for the purchase of the timber (which was enforceable and which both parties had already performed). The agreement relating to the initial sale of the timber was therefore of fundamental importance in interpreting the phrase "100,000 standards" and resolving the ambiguity in the agreement.

The contract itself may also provide a mechanism by which any ambiguity can be resolved. This was the case in **Foley v Classique Coaches Ltd** [1934] 2 K.B. 1, in which the contract expressly provided that any ambiguity would be referred to and resolved by arbitration.

Incomplete agreements

The primary issue for the court is to assess whether the parties have managed to reach an agreement as to the fundamental terms of the contract. This means that the court may enforce an agreement in which the parties have failed to agree on *all* the elements of the contract. A failure to reach an agreement will be fatal to the contract. However, a mere dispute about the terms of the agreement that have been agreed may not. To examine the way in which the court approaches such incomplete agreements it is useful to contrast the case of **May & Butcher v The King** [1934] 2 K.B. 17, with that of **Foley v Classique Coaches Ltd** [1934] 2 K.B. 1.

3-006

In **May & Butcher v The King** [1934] 2 K.B. 17, the contract for the purchase of some surplus military equipment provided that the price was to be agreed "from time to time" between the parties. Again, in such cases the court may imply a term that a "reasonable price" should be paid. However, the House of Lords refused to imply such a term in this case, as the parties had not reached a complete agreement. All that the parties had agreed was that in the future they would agree the price. This is in fact an "agreement to agree" and as such is not enforceable owing to lack of certainty.

In such cases the contract may provide a mechanism by which such uncertainty can be resolved. If this is so then the courts will refer to the mechanism as a way of giving effect to the intention of the parties. This is demonstrated in **Foley v Classique Coaches Ltd** [1934] 2 K.B. 1. This case concerned the purchase of petrol from the defendant "at a price to be agreed by the parties in writing from time to time". At first glance this sounds a very similar agreement to that in **May & Butcher**. However, the contract also provided that any ambiguity should be referred to and resolved by arbitration. The Court of Appeal held that the contract was enforceable as the parties had reached an agreement as to key elements of the contract. The parties had agreed that any ambiguity over the price could be resolved by arbitration and the court was prepared to give effect to this intention.

RECONCILING *FOLEY* WITH *MAY & BUTCHER*

Given the similarity between these two cases and the way in which the agreement was expressed—"a price to be agreed from time to time"—it is difficult to understand how the courts managed to reach such different conclusions regarding the enforceability of the agreements. This is even more difficult when you take account of the fact that the contract in **May & Butcher** also contained an arbitration clause.

3-007

However, the availability of arbitration in the case of **May & Butcher** would not have resolved the problem that the parties had still failed to agree as to the price. In other words, the agreement was that the price would be agreed between the parties. They had not progressed beyond a mere "agreement to agree". In **Foley**, the parties had agreed that the price could be decided by arbitration. Further, the level of performance of the contract also needs to be taken into account. In **May & Butcher**, there had been no performance under the contract at all, whereas in **Foley** a plot of land had been transferred following the agreement. Both of these facts illustrated that the parties in **Foley** had actually formed an agreement as to fundamental terms of the contract and the ambiguity regarding price could easily be resolved by arbitration.

SALE OF GOODS ACT 1979 SS.8 AND 9

3-008   A final issue flowing from the decisions in **May & Butcher and Foley** is the effect of ss.8 and 9 of the Sale of Goods Act 1979. First, s.8 provides that for the sale of goods, the price in the contract may be fixed in the contract, or in a manner agreed by the contract, or may be determined by the course of dealing between the parties. Where the contract does not provide for the price, then s.8(2) states that the buyer must pay a "reasonable price" for the goods.

A harsh interpretation of this section would mean that a "reasonable price" will only be paid when the contract is *completely* silent as to price. For example, in the case of **May & Butcher**, the contract provided that the price was to be agreed "from time to time". Strictly, the contract is not silent as to price and s.8(2) would not apply, even if the method of resolving the price is not effective (as was the case in **May & Butcher**). However, a more lenient interpretation of this section was adopted by the House of Lords in **Sudbrook Trading Estate Ltd v Eggleton** [1983] 1 A.C. 444, in which one of the parties refused to name an arbiter for the valuation of a plot of land. The agreement was not avoided by this refusal and it was held that a reasonable price should be paid for the land.

Secondly, s.9 of the Sale of Goods Act 1979 states that if the contract provides that the price is to be fixed by a third party, but that party fails to make such a valuation, then the contract will be avoided. If we were to apply this to the case of **Foley**, and the arbiter failed to reach a conclusion as to the contract price, then there would be no enforceable agreement between the parties.

Intention to create legal relations

3-009   An intention to create legal relations is the final key ingredient of a binding agreement. It may be that the parties have demonstrated a contractual intention to be bound, but nevertheless the court will refuse to give effect to such an intention on the basis that they lacked an intention to create legal relations. As with the issue of offer and acceptance, the courts assess whether the parties have an intention to create legal relations by applying an *objective* test of intention and by applying two key presumptions.

The court uses two key presumptions when assessing an intention to create legal relations.

1.   There is a presumption in domestic and social agreements that there is *no intention* to create legal relations (the presumption is rebuttable).

2. There is a strong presumption in commercial agreements that there *is an intention* to create legal relations (again, this can be challenged, but strong evidence will be required in rebuttal)

The presumption in domestic and social agreements

The presumption in domestic and social agreements is that there is no intention to create legal relations. However, this is only a presumption and it can be rebutted (disproved) if other evidence is presented to the contrary.

3-010

DOMESTIC AGREEMENTS

A classic example, in the context of husband and wife, is found in **Balfour v Balfour** [1919] 2 K.B. 571. In this case, the husband promised his wife that he would pay her £30 per month for living expenses while he was working abroad. When the relationship broke down the husband refused to continue making the payments and the wife sued for breach of contract. The promise to pay the £30 per month was not enforceable as the court held that there was no intention to create legal relations.

3-011

Over to you. . .

At first glance the decision in *Balfour* may seem rather harsh. Can you think of any justifications for why the courts are reluctant to enforce such promises?

First, if all such agreements between husband and wife were enforceable then the courts could be faced with a tremendous number of claims that they would have to resolve. This then leads to the second justification, namely that the courts are always reluctant to interfere with private and domestic agreements.

Atkin L.J. recognised these problems in **Balfour v Balfour**:

"All I can say is that the small Courts of this country would have to be multiplied one hundredfold if these arrangements were held to result in legal obligations. They are not sued upon, not because the parties are reluctant to enforce their legal rights when the agreement is broken, but because the parties, in the inception of the arrangement, never intended that they should be sued upon. Agreements such as these are outside the realm of contracts altogether. The common law does not regulate the form of agreements between spouses."

Further support for this approach can be found in the decision of **Merritt v Merritt** [1970] 1 W.L.R. 1211. The facts of this case are very similar to those of **Balfour** in that the husband promised the matrimonial home to his wife, plus a payment of £40 per month. However, this promise was made *after* their relationship had broken down and they were in the process of separating. Therefore Lord Denning M.R. was prepared to accept that this promise was enforceable as it fell outside the realm of a social agreement and took on more of the form of a business agreement between the parties.

SOCIAL AGREEMENTS

3-012   As has been established, domestic agreements are generally not enforceable as the parties are presumed to be lacking contractual intent. The same presumption applies in relation to social agreements. Again, applying an objective test of intention it is unlikely that the parties in a social agreement intend their agreement to be legally binding. To hold the parties to their agreement would mean that the courts would have to intervene and regulate numerous contracts contrary to the intention of the parties.

However, this presumption can also be rebutted. In **Simpkins v Pays** [1955] 1 W.L.R. 975, three parties regularly entered newspaper competitions, rotating the costs of entry and postage between them. The competition in question was entered in the name of the defendant. The parties were successful in the competition but the defendant refused to share the prize with the others. She argued that their agreement to enter the competition was a purely social one and as such there was no intention to create legal relations.

The court disagreed and held that the agreement was binding. There was mutuality in the arrangement between the parties and an intention to create legal relations could be inferred from this fact. The prize had to be shared between all three parties in line with their intentions.

· ·

The presumption in commercial relationships

3-013   In commercial agreements there is a strong presumption that there is an intention to create legal relations (this presumption can be rebutted but very strong evidence is needed).

The strong presumption of a contractual intent in commercial agreements is demonstrated in **Edwards v Skyways** [1964] 1 W.L.R. 349. This presumption will apply even if the wording of the agreement is ambiguous. In **Edwards** the plaintiff (an airline pilot) was made redundant and on being dismissed the plaintiff elected to reclaim his payments that had been made under the employee pension scheme. The plaintiff's trade union had agreed with the employer that should an employee elect to claim back these payments then the employer would make an ex gratia payment to the employee (an ex gratia payment is given out of generosity rather than any legal obligation to do so). The employer failed to make the payment and the plaintiff sued for breach of contract.

The court held that the employer had not rebutted the presumption of contractual intent and as such the plaintiff was entitled to the additional payment. The words "ex gratia" in this context did not indicate a lack of contractual intent, but merely recognised that there was generally no obligation to make such a payment.

Further, in **Esso Petroleum Co v Customs and Excise Commissioners** [1976] 1 W.L.R. 1, the plaintiffs ran a promotion by which customers could collect a number of collectable coins commemorating the 1970 World Cup. A customer who purchased four gallons of petrol would be entitled to a free coin. Customs and Excise Commissioners claimed that the coins were goods liable to be taxed as they were being "produced in quantity for general sale".

The House of Lords had to decide whether the coins were simply intended to be a free gift with every purchase of four gallons of petrol or whether there was a contract between the customer and the plaintiff for the supply of a coin. The plaintiffs argued that they did not have an intention to create legal relations and that the coins were simply intended to be a gift. On this basis, they argued, the coins were not liable to be taxed. By a majority, the House of Lords held that Esso did have a contractual intent, but this would have been rebutted from the perspective of the customers who would have claimed a coin on the basis that they were being given away free.

. . . .

Overview of certainty and intention to create legal relations

The flowchart at Figure 3.1 illustrates the relationship between the different elements we have introduced so far. This chart is not complete as we still have to analyse the further tests of enforceability (particularly that of consideration, which we will look at in the next chapter). However, in the meantime, the chart highlights the necessary ingredients required to form an agreement.

3-014

FIGURE 3.1 **Certainty and intention to create legal relations**

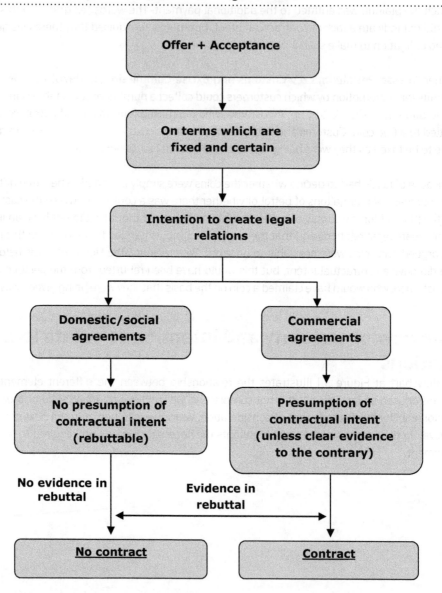

Summary

1. In assessing an agreement the court will seek to give effect to the intention of the parties. If there is uncertainty as to the terms of the agreement then the court may not be able to enforce the agreement.

2. There are, however, a number of ways in which the court can resolve ambiguity in the agreement. The court can make reference to previous dealings between the parties (**Hillas & Co Ltd v Arcos**) and will also look to whether the parties have agreed as to the fundamental terms of the agreement (**Foley v Classique Coaches Ltd**).

3. Statutory provision can also resolve certain ambiguity relating to price (Sale of Goods Act 1979 ss.8 and 9).

4. An agreement will not be enforced if the parties do not display an intention to create legal relations. In assessing this issue the courts use a number of (rebuttable) presumptions.

5. The presumption in domestic and social agreements is that there is *no* intention to create legal relations (**Balfour v Balfour**).

6. There is a strong presumption in commercial agreements that there *is* an intention to create legal relations (**Edwards v Skyways**).

Key Cases Grid

Case	Court	Key Points
Hillas & Co Ltd v Arcos Ltd (1932)	House of Lords	The court may be prepared to imply terms into a contract to resolve any ambiguity in the agreement and to give effect to the intention of the parties. The court may make reference to any previous agreement between the parties to resolve such ambiguity.
Foley v Classique Coaches Ltd [1934]	Court of Appeal	If the contract provides a mechanism by which uncertainty in the agreement can be resolved (such as an arbitration clause) courts will refer to the mechanism as a way of giving effect to the intention of the parties.
Balfour v Balfour [1919]	Court of Appeal	The presumption in domestic and social agreements is that there is no intention to create legal relations. However, this is only a presumption and it can be rebutted (disproved) if other evidence is presented to the contrary.

| Balfour v Balfour [1919] | Court of Appeal | The presumption in domestic and social agreements is that there is no intention to create legal relations. However, this is only a presumption and it can be rebutted (disproved) if other evidence is presented to the contrary. |
| Esso Petroleum Co v Customs and Excise Commissioners [1976] | House of Lords | In commercial agreements there is a strong presumption that there is an intention to create legal relations, even if the wording of the agreement is ambiguous. This is a rebuttable presumption but strong evidence is required. |

End of Chapter Question

Jeremy promises Sophie, his estranged wife, that she can live in the matrimonial home if she pays him a rent of £500 per month. Sophie accepts and moves into the property. Jeremy also agrees to sell Sophie his Constable watercolour for £15,000. The purchase takes place and Sophie takes possession of the painting. As part of the agreement for the purchase of the painting Jeremy also promises Sophie that she can purchase any or all of his remaining water-colours in that series at a price to be agreed in the future. Jeremy and Sophie's relationship breaks down even further and Jeremy is now refusing to honour his promise to allow Sophie to live in the matrimonial home. He is also refusing to sell Sophie any further paintings.

Advise Sophie.

Points of Answer
- As this agreement arose out of a domestic agreement then the court may presume that Jeremy lacked an intention to create legal relations.
- Compare and contrast the cases of **Balfour v Balfour** and **Merritt v Merritt**. As the parties are estranged, this agreement may be construed as being akin to a business transaction rather than a purely domestic agreement following **Merritt**.
- If court is satisfied that Jeremy had an intention to create legal relations then the next step is to consider whether the terms of the agreement are sufficiently certain to be legally binding.
- In relation to the paintings, there are a number of issues to note. First, question whether the option to purchase is sufficiently certain, as Jeremy does not give precise details of which paintings can be purchased. Is the phrase "paintings in the same series" sufficiently certain? However, as the parties have previously con-

tracted with each other then the courts could makes reference to this previous transaction to resolve this ambiguity—**Hillas v Arcos**.

♦ Finally, is the promise sufficiently certain as to price—"a price to be agreed"? Again, as the parties have already started to perform the agreement, the courts may hold that a reasonable price has to be paid for any future purchases—**Foley v Classique Coaches**.

Further Reading

Turner, J. "Developments in the Doctrine of Intention to Create Legal Relations." S.L. Rev. 2012, 66(Sum), 16-17

> This article provides a brief analysis of whether the principles relating to domestic agreements established in **Balfour v Balfour** are in need of review.

Graznak, P. "The good, the bad and the ugly: the **Spandau Ballet** case and oral agreements in the entertainment industry". Ent. L.R. 1999, 10(6), 175–179

> This article provides an interesting an entraining account of the law relating to oral agreements and intention to create legal relations in light of the decision in Hadley v Kemp [1999] E.M.L.R. 589 (Ch D)

Stone, R. and Cunnington, R. *Text, Cases and Materials on Contract Law* (London: Routledge-Cavendish, 2014), Ch.4

Treitel, G. *The Law of Contract*, 13th edn (London Sweet & Maxwell, 2011), Ch. 2 (Certainty) and 4 (Contractual Intention)

Consideration and Promissory Estoppel

4

CHAPTER OVERVIEW

In this chapter we:

- introduce the doctrine of consideration as the test of enforceability of agreements at common law

- define consideration

- consider the key "rules" of consideration

- analyse examples of when consideration will be insufficient to enforce the promise of another party

- discuss the relationship between the common law doctrine of consideration and the equitable doctrine of promissory estoppel

- analyse the development, the availability and the application of the equitable doctrine of promissory estoppel

Summary

Key Cases Grid

End of Chapter Question

Further Reading

Introduction

4-001 An offer and acceptance form an agreement between the parties. For this agreement to be *legally enforceable* the courts require it to be supported by consideration. Consideration, therefore, provides the common law test for the enforceability of agreements.

Offer + Acceptance = Agreement

Offer + Acceptance + Consideration = Legally Enforceable Agreement

It is difficult to identify the precise origins of the requirement for consideration. As the courts moved away from the strict formal requirements of a contract by deed, the recognition of "simple contracts" (those contracts not contained in deed) required the development of alternative principles by which to enforce promises between the parties. While the origins of the requirement of consideration remain somewhat of a mystery, it would appear that consideration has its foundations in the classical theory of contract law. The classical theory of contract was founded on a mutual exchange between the parties. In order for the courts to enforce this exchange, the courts required that there be something of value given or promised as part of the exchange. The *promise* of something of value in *exchange for the promise* of the other party would provide the courts with a justification to enforce and hold the parties to their relevant promises. The requirement for a mutual exchange of something of value between the parties has developed into the modern doctrine of consideration.

If identifying the origins of consideration is difficult, then providing a clear, workable definition of consideration is perhaps even more challenging. We will consider various definitions which seek to explain the requirement of consideration, but as we will see, the ability to recognise the contentious issues relating to consideration will become easier the more you familiarise yourself with the relevant legal principles and case law. To this extent, this what Stewart Smith L.J. referred to as the "elephant test"; consideration is difficult to define, but you know it when you see it.

Hear from the Author

Scan the QR Tag or follow the link below for an introduction to the topic consideration.

uklawstudent.thomsonreuters.com/category/contract-fundamentals

Defining consideration

4-002 Providing a clear and all-encompassing definition of consideration is not an easy task. For this reason it is not surprising that many students struggle when trying to define and identify consideration within the context of an agreement. Many theoretical definitions are somewhat disconnected from modern contract formation. This disconnection makes some traditional definitions difficult to apply to everyday situations. However, the classic starting point in defining consideration is the definition provided by Lush J. in **Currie v Misa** (1874–75) L.R. 10 Ex. 153:

> **"A valuable consideration, in the sense of the law, may consist either in some right, interest, profit, or benefit accruing to the one party, or some forbearance, detriment, loss, or responsibility, given, suffered, or undertaken by the other."**

This definition requires that one party suffers a detriment or the other party receives a benefit as a result of what is promised under the contract. In most cases there will be both a benefit and a detriment, but strictly only one of these is required to enforce the agreement.

Take a simple example for the sale of goods. The purchaser will suffer a detriment: he will have to part with his money in exchange for the goods. The seller will also receive a benefit: payment for the goods. Of course, you could turn this round and say that the seller has suffered a detriment: he will lose ownership of his goods. The purchaser receives a benefit: he receives the goods under the contract. Either analysis will result in the promise being enforceable as the agreement to purchase the goods is supported by consideration. The "benefit and detriment" analysis of consideration is illustrated in Figure 4.1.

FIGURE 4.1 **Consideration: benefit and detriment analysis**

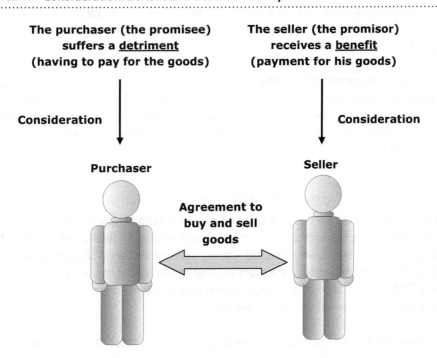

Consideration as the "price of the promise"

4-003   The definition of consideration in **Currie v Misa** is founded on the principle that consideration is a mutual exchange under which one party must suffer a detriment or receive a benefit as a result of what is promised or given under the contract. However, this "benefit/detriment" analysis of consideration is often confusing and difficult to apply to particular cases. For example, what if the seller *promises* to deliver goods in exchange of the purchaser's *promise* to pay for the goods? Applying the definition from **Currie v Misa**, it is difficult to identify any benefit conferred or detriment suffered simply by the exchange of promises. The seller will only suffer a detriment if he honours his promise and delivers the goods. The purchaser will only receive a benefit if the seller performs his obligations and delivers the goods, and vice versa. In practice, an exchange of promises can well amount to valid consideration, so perhaps this would be an appropriate point at which to discuss an alternative approach to defining consideration.

Sir Frederick Pollock famously defined consideration as being "the price of the promise". What must one party promise in order to secure the promise of the other party (and vice versa)? In our simple example for the sale of goods the purchaser promises to pay for the goods in exchange for the seller's promise to sell the goods. There has been a mutual exchange of promises which will be the valid consideration to support the agreement.

Defining consideration as "the price of the promise" has many attractions. First, it recognises the need for a mutual exchange of promises. Both parties contribute something of legal value to the agreement and it is for this reason that the court will enforce the agreement. If only one party gives his promise and the other party provides nothing of value in exchange, that promise will not be enforceable. This would be an example of a *gift* rather than an enforceable agreement.

Secondly, it also recognises that a promise in itself can be valid consideration. Using our example of a contract for the sale of goods, a *promise* of payment in exchange for the *promise* to sell goods will be valid consideration. If the seller delivers the goods and the purchaser breaks his promise and refuses to pay, then the seller will be able to enforce the agreement and sue for breach of contract.

The "rules" of consideration

4-004   Defining consideration is the first step in being able to determine whether an agreement will be legally enforceable. Once familiar with the various definitions of consideration the next step is to analyse the relevant "rules" of consideration. A simple exchange of promises will not be enough to enforce an agreement if the promises themselves are not recognised as being *legally sufficient*. This is one of the key principles of consideration. If what is promised is not legally sufficient then the courts will not enforce the agreement.

This key principle is made up of many elements and we shall discuss three as follows:

- Consideration must be sufficient, but need not be adequate
- Consideration must have some economic value
- Consideration must move from the promisee

CONSIDERATION MUST BE SUFFICIENT, BUT NEED NOT BE ADEQUATE

The first rule of consideration is that "consideration must be sufficient but need not be adequate". Sufficient consideration must be provided in order for the courts to enforce the agreement. In this context when we refer to consideration being *sufficient* we are really asking whether something that is legally recognisable as consideration has been provided. When we refer to the *adequacy* of consideration we are analysing whether that which has been provided relates to the value of that which is being contracted for.

4-005

As the courts are only concerned with *sufficiency* of consideration, then provided they are able to identify *some* consideration in some shape or form this will be the justification for why the courts will hold the parties to their agreement. The promise of £1, 1p or even a peppercorn would be generally be sufficient as consideration. This highlights that consideration is simply a legal requirement for a legally binding agreement and one which often fails to reflect the true nature of the bargain between two contracting parties.

An example of this principle can be found in the case of **Thomas v Thomas** (1842) 2 Q.B. 851. In this case the executors of a will promised the deceased's widow that she could live in the matrimonial home if she paid £1 ground rent and continued to maintain the property. The court held that as the widow had provided something of value (£1) in exchange for the executor's promise, then such a promise was enforceable. Of course, £1 in no way related to the actual value of the lease of the property—in other words, it was by no means adequate in relation to what was being contracted for, but the promise of payment was nevertheless legally sufficient.

The decision in **Thomas v Thomas** also highlights the self-regulatory foundations on which contract law is based. It is not the role of the courts to protect individuals from entering into bad bargains. The role of the courts in this context is simply to determine whether relevant promises are enforceable in law. For example, if I promise to sell you my Aston Martin car for £1,000 (the actual value being £60,000) then, at this point leaving aside any issue as to whether I had an intention to enter into legal relations, the courts will have no reluctance in holding me to my promise. The promise of payment in exchange for my car will be *sufficient* consideration even though it is nowhere near adequate for what is being bargained for. The agreement is supported by consideration and the courts will not enquire into or interfere with the nature of my bargain.

CONSIDERATION MUST HAVE SOME ECONOMIC VALUE

4-006   As we will recall, consideration has to be sufficient but does not have to be adequate. In order for consideration to be legally sufficient the court requires that it must have at least *some* economic value. The promise to perform an act which carries no economic value will generally not be sufficient and therefore not enforceable as consideration. This is illustrated in the case of **White v Bluett** (1853) 23 LJ Ex 36. In this case a dispute arose between a father and son. The son owed his father money and the father promised not to enforce the debt if the son promised to stop complaining about how the father intended to distribute money to the rest of the family in his will. The father died and the executor of his estate sought to enforce the debt against the son.

In his defence, the son argued that by not complaining he had provided consideration to support his father's promise to waive the debt. The court, however, held that the promise was unenforceable. The son's promise not to complain had no economic value and as such the son had not provided valid consideration to enforce the father's promise.

Pollock CB provides further justification for this decision, at p.73:

> "It is said, the son had a right to an equal distribution of his father's property, and did complain to his father because he had not an equal share, and said to him, I will cease to complain if you will not sue upon this note. Whereupon the father said, If you will promise me not to complain, I will give up the note. If such a plea as this could be supported, the following would be a binding promise: A man might complain that another person used the public highway more than he ought to do, and that other might say, do not complain, and I will give you five pounds. It is ridiculous to suppose that such promises could be binding.
>
> The son had no right to complain, for the father might make what distribution of his property he liked; and the son's abstaining from doing what he had no right to do can be no consideration."

While the courts require that consideration some have *some* economic value, the actual value of what is being provided may be very minimal indeed. For example, in **Chappell & Co Ltd v Nestlé Co Ltd** [1960] A.C. 87, it was held that something of such little value as a chocolate wrapper could be *sufficient* consideration. In this case the defendants manufactured chocolate bars and devised a promotional scheme by which customers could claim free songs on records by sending 1s. 6d plus three chocolate wrappers. The wrappers received were completely worthless and were thrown away by the defendants. The plaintiffs owned the copyright in the songs being distributed and brought an action to restrain the defendants from manufacturing and selling the records on the grounds that the transactions involved breaches of their copyright.

The key issue for the House of Lords was whether the chocolate wrappers formed part of the consideration. This fact would determine the amount of royalties that were due to the plaintiffs. By a majority the House of Lords held that the chocolate wrappers did form part of the consideration. The promotional offer was not just for the sale of the records in exchange of payment; the offer was for the sale of the records in exchange for payment and the chocolate wrappers. Even though the wrappers were of hardly any value at all (they were thrown away by the defendants) it was held that they were sufficient to form part of the consideration for the sale of the records.

In contrast, in the case of **Lipkin Gorman v Karpnale Ltd** [1991] 2 A.C. 548, it was held that gambling chips were not a valid form of consideration; they did not have any economic value (but surely the same can be said of chocolate wrappers!).

Finally, the American case of **Hamer v Sidway** 124 N.Y. 538 (1881) provides an interesting (and also rather amusing) analysis of the requirement that consideration must have some economic value. In this case an uncle promised to pay his nephew $5,000 if the nephew refrained from activities such as drinking, smoking and swearing until he reached the age of 21. Surprisingly, the court held that refraining from these activities was valid consideration to support the promise of payment. It is arguable whether the uncle received sufficient benefit in knowing that his nephew was free from such vices. Moreover, it is difficult to reconcile this decision with cases such as **White v Bluett** that require that consideration must have some economic value. The decision in **Hamer** therefore illustrates the sometimes contradictory approach the courts have applied in relation to the requirement of consideration. Some cases turn very much on their particular facts, with the courts being able to adopt a very flexible approach when they so desire.

CONSIDERATION MUST MOVE FROM THE PROMISEE

In order for a person to enforce a promise it is often said that consideration must "move from the promise". In other words, as it is the promisee that wishes to enforce the promise it was logical to require them to provide justification for allowing them to do this. However, modern developments have to some extent eroded this historically strict position. Applying the strict requirement that consideration must move from the promisee means that a party who receives a *benefit* under a contract, but is not a party to the contract, would not be able to avail themselves of that benefit. As they are not privy to the contract, they cannot enforce an obligation under that contract.

4-007

The Contracts (Rights of Third Parties) Act 1999 now makes provisions for contracts that are made for the benefit of a third party and in such situations the third party will be able to enforce this benefit—even though they may not have strictly provided any consideration to enable them to enforce such a promise. In view of these developments it is not strictly true to say that consideration must be provided by the promisee. It is certainly the case that consideration must be provided (or supplied) by an individual in order for an agreement to be enforceable, but not necessarily by the party who is seeking to enforce a promise.

"Sufficiency" of consideration

4-008   We have briefly discussed some of the "rules" of consideration. One of the most fundamental principles is that consideration must be legally sufficient. We now, therefore, turn to address certain examples that the courts have identified as being *insufficient* as consideration.

PAST CONSIDERATION

4-009   The general rule is that past consideration is no consideration. If we remind ourselves of our basic definition of consideration we will recall that the test of enforceability can be defined as the "price of the promise". What does one party have to promise in order to secure the other party's promise? The exchange of promises will be the reason the parties are bound by their obligations. As consideration is concerned with the mutual exchange of promises, it follows that consideration must be provided at the time the contract is formed, or at some time in the future, but not before the contract is formed.

Circumstances in which consideration will be deemed to be "past" arise where one party provides an act or a promise *before* the other party's promise is given in exchange. For example, in the case of **Roscorla v Thomas** (1842) 3 Q.B. 234 the plaintiff negotiated with the defendants for the purchase of a horse. After the transaction had been completed the defendants told the plaintiff that the horse was "sound and free from vice". This statement subsequently turned out to be false and the claimant brought an action against the defendant for breach of warranty. The issue for the court was whether this promise that the horse was indeed sound and free from vice was enforceable. The court held that such a promise was not enforceable because at the time that promise was given the plaintiffs provided no consideration in return. In order to be enforceable, the warranty as to temperament of the horse should have been given at the time of the sale, not after.

Similarly, in **Re McArdle** [1951] Ch. 669 a promise to pay a sum of money for improvements completed on the property was not enforceable as the work had already been carried out before the promise of payment was made. The work was not undertaken in exchange for the promise of payment and was therefore "past consideration".

The problem of past consideration is illustrated in Figure 4.2.

FIGURE 4.2 **Past consideration**

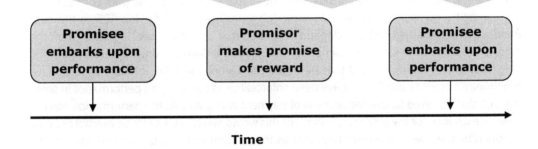

Promise or reward <u>NOT</u> enforceable
Promisee embarks upon performance *before* promise of reward = Past Consideration

Promise or reward <u>enforceable</u>
Promisee embarks upon performance in exchange for the promise of reward

| Promisee embarks upon performance | Promisor makes promise of reward | Promisee embarks upon performance |

Time

■ The Exception to the past consideration rule

Over to you. . .

Analysing the case of *Re McArdle*, can you identify how the strict application of the past consideration rule has the potential to operate harshly in certain situations?

The past consideration rule has the potential to operate quite harshly. The case of **Re McArdle**   4-010
provides an example of this. You will recall that in **Re McArdle** the refurbishment of a property was undertaken before the agreement to compensate the party for their expenses was formed. As such the party who had incurred considerable time and expense in refurbishing the property was unable to enforce the promise of compensation. There was little doubt that the parties had the necessary contractual intent to form the agreement for compensation, but as the promisee had not strictly provided consideration at the time the agreement was formed they were unable to enforce the agreement.

Generally, the aim of the courts is to try and give effect to the intention of the parties. However, the rule on past consideration can prevent the courts from being able to enforce an agreement that was clearly intended to be binding due to the technical requirement that consideration should be provided at the time the agreement was formed. The past consideration can in some circumstances also appear to be disconnected from the commercial realities of contract formation. For example, a purchaser may request that certain goods be delivered, but does not specify a price. The seller delivers the goods and the purchaser then agrees payment. In these cases a strict application of the past consideration rule could result in the seller being unable to enforce the promise of payment. The seller's consideration (delivering the goods) was provided before the promise of payment was given. The courts have therefore recognised an exception to avoid the application of the past consideration rule. This is referred to as the "Requested Performance" exception.

The Requested Performance Exception

4-011 If the act in question was undertaken at the *request* of the promisor then the courts may waive a strict application of the past consideration rule. This exception to the past consideration rule can be traced back to the case of **Lampleigh v Braithwaite** (1615) Hob. 105. In this case Braithwaite was charged with murder and requested that Lampleigh seek a pardon from the King. In response to this request Lampleigh sought and indeed obtained a pardon from the King. Braithwaite then promised that he would pay Lampleigh £100 for his efforts. Strictly, Braithwaite's promise should not have been enforceable as Lampleigh's performance in seeking a pardon occurred before the promise of payment was given. As the performance was not given in exchange for the promise of payment this would seem to be a classic example of past consideration. However, the court held that as the performance in this case had come at the request of the promisor then such performance constituted valid consideration.

In **Lampleigh** not only was the performance at the request of the promisor, but also both parties would have understood payment was to follow from such performance. This further requirement was discussed in **Re Casey's Patents** [1892] 1 Ch. 104. In this case the owner of some patents appointed a manager to manage and collect the royalty payments. The owner then promised the manager that in return for his services he could have a share of a third of the patent rights. The court held that the manager could enforce the promise as the act was done at the promisor's request and due to the commercial relationship between the parties both parties would have understood that payment was to follow this performance.

Bowen L.J. offers further explanation of this decision:

> "Even if it were true, as some scientific students of law believe, that a past service cannot support a future promise, you must look at the document and see if the promise cannot receive a proper effect in some other way. Now, the fact of a past service raises an implication that at the time it was rendered it was to be paid for, and, if it was a service which was to be paid for, when you get in the subsequent document a promise to pay, that promise may be treated either as an admission which evidences or as a positive bargain which fixes the amount of that reasonable remuneration on the faith of which the service was originally rendered. So that here for past services there is ample justification for the promise to give the third share".

Pao On v Lau Yiu Long

The exception to the past consideration rule was consolidated and restated by Lord Scarman in **Pao On v Lau Yiu Long** [1980] A.C. 614. This restatement creates a three-stage test, all stages of which must be satisfied before the courts will recognise an exception to the past consideration rule:

4-012

1. that an act done before the giving of a promise could be valid consideration for that promise if the act had been done at the promisor's request (this is a restatement of the principle established in **Lampleigh v Braitwaite**);
2. the parties had understood that the act was to be remunerated either by payment or by conferment of a benefit (this is a restatement of the principle in **Re Casey's Patents**); and
3. the payment or conferment of a benefit would have been enforceable had it been promised in advance.

Lord Scarman's first two requirements are restatements of the principles established in **Lampleigh** and **Re Casey's Patents**. The final requirement simply states that the ordinary principles of consideration still apply to such promises. In other words, had the promise been given in exchange for the act of another would it have been legally sufficient as consideration? If, for example, the benefit conferred by performance of the requested act had no economic value then the promise would not be enforceable. This example would fail under Lord Scarman's third requirement as consideration that has no economic value will be insufficient as consideration and the fact that the act may have been performed at the promisor's request would not alter this position.

PERFORMANCE OF EXISTING DUTIES

Generally, performance of an existing duty will be insufficient as consideration.

4-013

The reasoning is quite clear. As a matter of *law*, there will be no additional detriment suffered, or no additional benefit conferred, if a party is only performing an act that they are already under an existing duty to perform.

However, as we shall see, the courts have departed from this general rule on a number of occasions. To focus the discussion we shall consider the various ways in which a duty to perform an obligation can arise and then explore the approach of the courts as to whether performance of such a duty can amount to sufficient consideration. We shall consider the following duties:

1. performance of an existing public duty;
2. performance of an existing duty owed to the same promisor;
3. performance of a duty owed to a third party;

■ Performance of an existing public duty

4-014   As the law imposes a number of obligations and requirements upon individuals in the way that they conduct their everyday activities it is not surprising that performance of a duty required by law will not constitute valid consideration.

In the case of **Collins v Godefroy** (1831) 1 B. & Ad.950, a promise was made to pay a witness in return for giving evidence at trial. Such a promise was not enforceable as the witness was already required by law to give such evidence. Therefore, the performance of an existing public duty did not constitute valid consideration, as the witness was only doing what the law required him to do. Of course, in this case there are also underlying policy issues that have to be factored into this decision. The courts will not, as a matter of policy and public interest, allow such a promise to be enforceable.

However, if by your actions you exceed the duty imposed by law then by going beyond what is required your conduct may constitute valid consideration. In **Ward v Byham** [1956] 1 W.L.R. 496 the Court of Appeal held that the father's promise to pay the mother £1 per week to maintain the child and to ensure that the child was "well looked after and happy" was enforceable, despite a statutory duty imposed on the mother to look after the child properly. The mother, in ensuring that the child was *well* looked after and happy, had exceeded the existing duty imposed by law to simply maintain the child.

Similarly, in **Harris v Sheffield United FC** [1987] 2 All E.R. 838, police officers by providing extra and specialist services at a football match to ensure the safety of the spectators had gone beyond their basic existing public duty owed to the general public.

Over to you. . .

Reflect on the decision of the court in *Ward v Byham*. Think about how the court applied the basic principles of consideration in this case. Can you identify any problems with this decision in the application of these principles?

Few would argue that it was unfair to hold the father to his promise of additional payment in **Ward v Byham**. After all, as a matter of policy, the type of promise would be one that the courts would be anxious to enforce to give effect to the clear intention of the parties. However, in terms of a strict application of the principles of consideration there is much criticism that can be levelled at this decision. Primarily, the court seemed to ignore the requirement that in order to be legally sufficient, consideration must have some economic value. The father may well have received an emotional benefit—peace of mind that his child was being well looked after—but such benefits are generally insufficient as consideration.

Interestingly, Denning L.J. suggested that even if the mother had not exceeded her existing public duty he would have still enforced the promise between the parties:

"I approach the case, therefore, on the footing that the mother, in looking after the child, is only doing what she is legally bound to do. Even so, I think that there was sufficient consideration to support the promise. I have always thought that a promise to perform an existing duty, or the performance of it, should be regarded as good consideration, because it is a benefit to the person to whom it is given. Take this very case. It is as much a benefit for the father to have the child looked after by the mother as by a neighbour. If he gets the benefit for which he stipulated, he ought to honour his promise; and he ought not to avoid it by saying that the mother was herself under a duty to maintain the child."

It is important to note that Denning's views outlined above were not endorsed by the other members of the court. However, Denning's comments provide us with a glimpse of a more flexible approach that the courts may be willing to adopt in relation to the performance of existing duty. With these comments in mind we now turn to the next issue of whether performance of an existing duty owed to the same promisor can constitute valid consideration.

■ Performance of existing contractual duty owed to the same promisor

4-015

Take a very basic example of where two parties are already bound by an existing contract. In order for the contract to have been formed there will need to have been an agreement that was supported by consideration. If the parties wish to vary this agreement then fresh consideration will need to be furnished in order for this variation to be enforceable. The problem to which we now turn is whether the performance of an existing contractual duty owed to the same promisor can constitute valid consideration.

The general rule is that performance of an existing contractual duty to the same promisor is not good consideration. This general rule was established in the case of **Stilk v Myrick** (1809) 2 Camp. 317, 170 E.R. 1168. In this case the crewmen of a ship were contracted to sail a vessel, but during the voyage two crew members deserted the ship. The captain was unable to find replacement crewmembers, so the captain promised that he would distribute the wages of the men who had deserted among the remaining crew if they sailed the ship back home. The crew accordingly sailed the ship back home, but on arrival the captain refused to honour his promise of additional payment. The court held that the promise of extra payment was not enforceable as the crew had provided no consideration to support the promise. By sailing the ship back home the crew had done no more than was already required of them as part of their existing contractual duties.

Exceeding an existing contractual duty

4-016

It is interesting to compare **Stilk v Myrick** with the case of **Hartley v Ponsonby** [1857] 7 El. & Bl. 872 as the two cases are both based on very similar facts. In **Hartley** the captain also promised additional payment if the crew sailed the ship back home, but in this case the court held that the crewmen by sailing the ship back *had* provided valid consideration. The reason is that in **Hartley** so many crewmen had deserted the ship and it was so dangerous for such a small crew to sail the ship back, that by doing so the crew had *exceeded* their contractual duties. They had gone beyond what was required of them under their original contract and had therefore provided fresh consideration to support the promise of additional payment.

The principle in **Stilk v Myrick** has the potential to operate in a harsh manner. Further, it appears very difficult to reconcile this principle with cases such as **Scotson v Pegg and The Eurymedon**, which were concerned with a duty owed to a *third party* which we will consider later in the chapter. In order to fully understand the decision in **Stilk v Myrick** it is necessary to look deeper at the legal reasoning in this case.

Performance of an existing duty and the role of economic duress

4-017 The principle from **Stilk** is that performance of an existing contractual duty *to the same promisor* is *not* good consideration. However, as we have seen, performance of an existing contractual duty owed *to a third party* may well constitute valuable consideration. So, the question has to be asked: why can performance of a duty owed to a third party constitute valid consideration, but not in relation to the same promisor?

There are a number of arguments and criticisms that need to be analysed in attempting to answer this question. First, it is necessary to look at the context and the historical background in which **Stilk** was decided. It is also important to note that an accurate and reliable report of the case is difficult to find. For example, Espinasse's report indicates that the ratio of **Stilk** was to ensure that crewmen were prevented from obtaining additional payment by improper methods. In other words, the courts were trying to clamp down on the practice of crewmen essentially holding captains to ransom by refusing to sail the vessel back home unless additional payment was promised.

Of course, as a matter of policy, the courts were not willing to enforce such promises induced as a result of blackmail or economic duress (although at the time **Stilk** was the courts had yet to develop the doctrine of economic duress). Place this in the historical context in the midst of the Napoleonic Wars, which made it a very dangerous time to be sailing across the North Sea, then again it can be seen that the courts were trying to protect captains and owners of vessels from being exploited by crewmen trying to take advantage of their stronger bargaining positions. In such cases the captain may have *no realistic alternative* but to make the promise of additional payment in order to ensure that the crew sail the ship home. The decision in **Stilk** is therefore based on policy and the risk that the captain's promise was induced by duress.

■ The decision in *Williams v Roffey*

4-018 It has already been established that the general rule is that performance of an existing duty to the same promisor is not good consideration (**Stilk v Myrick**). However, the decision of the Court of Appeal in **Williams v Roffey Bros** [1991] 1 Q.B. 1, makes considerable inroads into the decision in **Stilk**.

The defendants entered into a contract with a housing association to refurbish a number of flats. The defendants subcontracted the work to the plaintiffs. Before all the flats were completed the plaintiffs got into financial difficulties and would not be able to complete the work by the agreed date in the contract. This had significant consequences for the defendants as their contract with the housing association contained a penalty clause. The defendants would be penalised financially if the flats were delivered late. The defendants therefore promised the plaintiffs an extra £575 per flat to ensure that the work was completed on time. The plaintiffs completed eight further flats and then brought an action against the defendants claiming the extra payments that were promised.

The defendants argued that their promise of additional payment was not enforceable as the plaintiffs had not provided consideration in support. They argued that **Stilk v Myrick** should apply on the grounds that performance of an existing contractual duty is not good consideration; the plaintiffs were doing no more than the existing contract required of them.

The Court of Appeal disagreed with the defendants and held that the plaintiffs were entitled to the additional payment. The court held that performance of an existing contractual duty can amount to valid consideration if that performance confers a "practical benefit" on the other party. The defendants received a practical benefit by the plaintiffs' performance. The work was completed on time, they avoided the time and expense of having to find alternative contractors to complete the work and, most importantly, they avoided the *disbenefit* of the penalty clause being enforced.

Glidewell L.J. set out the following "criteria" that help to clarify the application of the principles in **Williams v Roffey**:

> **"The present state of the law on this subject can be expressed in the following proposition:**
>
> (i)   if A has entered into a contract with B to do work for, or to supply goods or services to, B in return for payment by B; and
>
> (ii) at some stage before A has completely performed his obligations under the contract B has reason to doubt whether A will, or will be able to, complete his side of the bargain; and
>
> (iii) B thereupon promises A an additional payment in return for A's promise to perform his contractual obligations on time; and
>
> (iv) as a result of giving his promise, B obtains in practice a benefit, or obviates a disbenefit; and
>
> (v)   B's promise is not given as a result of economic duress or fraud on the part of A; then
>
> (vi) the benefit to B is capable of being consideration for B's promise, so that the promise will be legally binding.

Reconciling Williams with Stilk v Myrick

4-019   At first glance it seems difficult to reconcile the decision of the Court of Appeal in **Williams v Roffey** with the decision in **Stilk v Myrick**. As you will recall, the principle in **Stilk v Myrick** is that performance of an existing contractual duty to the same promisor *is not* good consideration to support the promise of additional payment. However, the principle in **Williams** is that performance of an existing contractual duty *can be* good consideration if the performance confers a practical benefit (or avoidance of a disbenefit) on the promisor. It is difficult to see how these two authorities can co-exist given that they seem to arrive at two very different conclusions as to whether performance of an existing contractual obligation can constitute valid consideration.

Further, it could be argued that the captain in **Stilk** also received a "practical benefit" as a result of his promise of additional payment. His ship was sailed back to port and he avoided the time and expense of having to recruit new crew members. However, the promise was binding in **Williams** but not in **Stilk**.

The Court of Appeal in **Williams** was quite clear that its decision in **Williams** did not overrule **Stilk**. Glidewell L.J. stated that the principles in **Williams** "refine and limit the application of that principle, but they leave the principle unscathed". In this context Glidewell L.J. was referring to those situations where the promisor receives no benefit as a result of his promise. However, as we have already identified, surely it could be argued that the captain did in fact receive a "practical benefit" as a result of his promise of additional payment?

In those cases where a "practical benefit" is received by a promise of additional payment then further analysis is required to reconcile the cases of **Stilk** and **Williams**. The starting point perhaps should be to refer back to Glidewell L.J.'s criteria in **Williams**. As you will recall, Glidewell' L.J.'s fifth criterion in **Williams** is that: B's promise must not have been given as a result of economic duress or fraud on the part of A. The decision in **Stilk** could therefore be distinguished on the basis of economic duress; the captain *had no realistic alternative* but to make the promise of additional payment. The facts of **Williams** are slightly different. The defendants realised that the plaintiffs were not going to meet their contractual obligations and it was the defendants that approached the plaintiffs with the promise of additional payment. The differences in the two cases can therefore be explained on the basis of duress; the presence of duress in **Stilk** meant that the promise was not enforceable; the absence of duress and receipt of a practical benefit in Williams meant that the promise was enforceable.

Glidewell L.J.'s fifth criterion can therefore be seen as a way of confining (but not overruling) the decision in **Stilk** to cases where no practical benefit is conferred or where the promise of additional payment was induced by duress or fraud. For example, in **Williams**, had the plaintiffs simply put down tools and refused to work unless they were paid extra, then the principle in **Stilk v Myrick** may have applied and the promise would not have been enforceable as it was induced by duress.

The limitations on Williams v Roffey

There are a number of problems that could flow from the decision of the Court of Appeal in **4-020** Williams v Roffey. Most notably, the "benefits" identified in **Williams** as constituting valid consideration could appear quite trivial in contrast to the usually strict principles of consideration. If something as simple as ensuring that the work is completed on time, or avoiding the time and expense of having to find contractors that are capable of doing the job for which they have been hired could constitute a "practical benefit", then the principle in **Williams** will significantly broaden the scope of promises that the courts will enforce.

However, the counter-argument is that **Williams** now provides the courts with a more flexible approach that reflects the commercial realities of such promises. In forming his statement of law in **Williams**, Glidewell L.J. relied heavily on the reasoning of Denning in **Ward v Byham**. If a party freely promises additional payment to ensure the performance of contractual obligations, and the courts are satisfied that they had the necessary contractual intent to be bound, then the courts should seek to hold that party to their promise. Applying this reasoning to the facts of **Williams**, it was clear in this case that **Roffey** had a choice when they realised that the work would not be completed on time. They had the option of suing for breach of contract when those obligations were not met and would seek recovery of their loss through an action for damages. In the circumstances, however, **Roffey** freely chose to promise additional payment to ensure that the work would be completed on time. In a commercial context, having the work completed, avoiding the time and expense of finding other contractors and avoiding the time and expense of pursuing legal action may have been a more commercially attractive alternative than commencing legal proceedings. Providing this promise of additional payment was freely given then the courts should recognise such promises as being enforceable.

The decision in **Williams** signifies an important change of emphasis by the courts in relation to the requirement of consideration. It signifies a move away from the strict interpretation as consideration being a *legal* benefit and recognises that a *practical, factual* benefit can constitute valid consideration.

However, this recognition of a factual benefit as being valid consideration has not been extended to cover all types of contracts. The scope of **Williams v Roffey** has been limited somewhat by the decision of the Court of Appeal in **Re Selectmove Ltd** [1995] 1 W.L.R. 474. This case concerned a purported agreement to pay debts to the Inland Revenue by instalments. When the Inland Revenue demanded full and immediate payment of the debt, the debtor argued that he had provided consideration for the promise by the Revenue to accept payment by instalments. He argued that payment by instalments was a practical benefit to the Inland Revenue in that it allowed the Revenue to recover more money than if the debtor simply went insolvent (after all, some money is better than no money).

The Court of Appeal rejected this argument and held that the purported promise to accept payment by instalments would not have been enforceable as the debtor had provided no consideration to support this promise. The principles established in **Williams v Roffey** do not apply to the part-payment of a debt. The court was bound by the decision in **Foakes v Beer** (1883–84) L.R. 9 App. Cas. 605, and the debt could be claimed in full.

The decision in **Re Selectmove** limits the application of **Williams v Roffey** to contracts for the provision of goods and/or services. This restriction is consistent with the first of Glidewell L.J.'s "criteria" in **Williams**: "A has entered into a contract with B *to do work for, or to supply goods or services to*, B in return for payment by B'". [emphasis added]

Williams v Roffey will therefore not apply to the part-payment of a debt. The decision of the House of Lords in **Foakes v Beer** is the leading authority on this issue and clearly states that part-payment of a debt is not valid consideration for a promise to discharge the debt.

Further doubt has now been cast over the decision in **Williams** by the recent decision in **South Caribbean Trading Ltd v Trafigura Beheever BV** [2004] EWHC 2676. In this case Coleman J. stated:

> "The authorities on this issue starting with *Stilk v Myrick* . . . indicate a firmly established rule of law that a promise to perform an enforceable obligation under a pre-existing contract between the same parties is incapable of amounting to sufficient consideration. The decision of the Court of Appeal in *Williams v Roffey Bros* appears to have introduced some amelioration to the rigidity of this rule in cases where there has been refusal to perform not amounting to economic duress by the party who might otherwise be in breach of any existing contract and where the other party will derive a practical benefit from such performance. But for the fact that *Williams v Roffey Bros* was a decision of the Court of Appeal, I would not have followed it. That decision is inconsistent with the long-standing rule that consideration, being the price of the promise sued upon, must move from the promisee."

Given that **Williams** has successfully withstood the scrutiny of the Court of Appeal in **Re Selectmove**, it seems unlikely that this criticism from the High Court in **South Caribbean Trading Ltd** will limit the application of **Williams** in recognising factual benefits as constituting valid consideration in contracts for goods and/or services.

■ Performance of a duty owed to a third party

4-021 An interesting problem arises where a party promises payment in return for the other party performing a duty that he is already under an obligation to perform to a third party. Such a situation arose in **Shadwell v Shadwell** (1860) 9 C.B. N.S. 159 where an uncle promised his nephew £150 per year if the nephew married his fiancée (note that at the time this case was decided the agreement to marry created an enforceable legal obligation on the nephew).

Therefore, the existing contractual duty owed by the nephew was to marry the fiancée and as there was no contract between the uncle and the fiancée, the fiancée was a third party to the agreement. In other words, the nature of the uncle's promise was that he would pay the nephew £150 if the nephew performed a duty that was already owed to a third party (the duty to marry the fiancée). Surprisingly, the court held that by marrying his fiancée the nephew had provided good consideration to support the uncle's promise of payment.

However, the decision in **Shadwell** should be treated with a fair amount of caution. First, as we discussed in Ch.3, there is presumed to be no intention to create legal relations in such domestic agreements. It is therefore doubtful that the agreement should have been enforceable at all. Secondly, the court approached the issue of consideration in this case by focusing on the requirement of a detriment to the nephew, which then in turn conferred a benefit onto the uncle. It is also doubtful whether the nephew's marriage to his fiancée could be construed as a detriment that in turn conferred a benefit on the uncle (the great joy he received by seeing his nephew married). Such a conclusion also ignores the basic principle that consideration must have some economic value.

Further, in **Scotson v Pegg** (1861) 6 Hurl. & N. 295, Scotson entered into a contract with X to deliver coal to Pegg. Pegg then promised Scotson that if he delivered the coal to him he would unload the coal at a fixed rate. In an action by Scotson to enforce Pegg's promise, Pegg argued that his promise was not binding as Scotson had provided no consideration—Scotson was already obliged under his contract with X to deliver the coal. Again, it was decided that Scotson's performance of an existing contractual duty owed to X did constitute valuable consideration for Pegg's promise. The precise reasoning as to why this performance could be valid consideration is not entirely clear from the case report, although the court did seem to suggest that Scotson suffered a detriment in delivering the coal to Pegg (as Scotson could always have breached his duty to X and faced the consequences for such a breach) and in turn the delivery of the coal conferred a benefit on Pegg. In the light of the criticisms and lack of clarity from both **Shadwell** and **Scotson**, it is perhaps more useful to look at the modern and more commercial application of these principles.

The leading case regarding third parties is **New Zealand Shipping Co Ltd v AM Satterthwaite & Co Ltd (The Eurymedon)** [1975] A.C. 154. The facts of this case are particularly challenging and as such the facts and the decision are summarised at Figure 4.3 below. In this case, an expensive drilling machine was received on board a ship, the *Eurymedon*, for transportation to Wellington in New Zealand. The contract between the shippers and carriers contained a clause exempting the liability of the carriers for damage to the machine when being unloaded. The carriers then entered into a contract with the stevedores who undertook to unload the drill once it arrived at its destination. The shippers of the drilling machine also promised the stevedores that they could take the benefit of the exemption clause if they unloaded the machine. Owing to the negligence of the stevedores the drill was damaged during unloading. The Court of Appeal of New Zealand held that the stevedores could not take advantage of the exemption clause as they already had an existing duty to the carriers to unload the machine. They had not provided consideration to support the shipper's promise as they were simply performing a duty that they already owed to the carriers (a third party to the agreement between the shippers and the stevedores).

On appeal, the Privy Council had to decide whether the stevedores, by unloading the goods, had provided consideration to enforce the shipper's promise to exclude them of liability. The Privy Council held that the stevedores, in performing their existing contractual duty owed to a third party (the carriers), had provided valid consideration to support the promise of the shippers to exclude their liability.

The reasoning behind this decision was expressed by Lord Wilberforce:

> **"An agreement to do an act which the promisor is under an existing obligation to a third party to do, may quite well amount to valid consideration and does so in the present case: the promisee obtains the benefit of a direct obligation which he can enforce. This proposition is illustrated and supported by *Scotson v. Pegg* (1861) 6 H. & N. 295 which their Lordships consider to be good law."**

So, the shippers received the benefit of being able to enforce a *direct and enforceable obligation* against the stevedores. This benefit was the consideration provided by the stevedores that enabled them to rely upon the exclusion clause.

This decision is also an example of the inventive way in which the courts deploy the idea of a collateral contract as a means of creating legal rights and obligations. As there was no direct contract between the shippers and the stevedores, the court had to "invent" a contract so that the stevedores could enforce the limitation clause against the shippers. Lord Wilberforce describes it as follows:

> **"The bill of lading brought into existence a bargain initially unilateral but capable of becoming mutual, between the shipper and the stevedore, made through the carrier as agent, which became a full contract when the stevedore performed services by unloading the goods; and the performance of those services for the benefit of the shipper was the consideration for the agreement by the shipper that the stevedore should have the benefit of the exemptions in the bill of lading."**

The Eurymedon is also an example of how the court can sometimes disregard the doctrine of privity of contract, which appears to have been ignored completely in the decision at the expense of business efficacy and giving effect to the intention of the parties.

FIGURE 4.3 **Summary of *New Zealand Shipping Co***

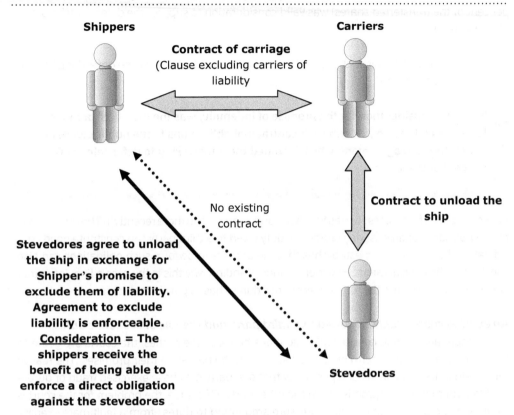

A *promise* to perform a duty to a third party

A further and interesting issue is raised in the case of **Pao On v Lau Yiu Long** [1980] A.C. 614.   **4-022**
Pao On differs slightly from **The Eurymedon** as the latter case was primarily concerned with
whether the *performance* of an existing obligation owed to a third party could constitute valid
consideration. The Privy Council in **Pao On** had to analyse whether the *promise to perform* such
a duty could constitute valid consideration.

The facts of **Pao On** are that the plaintiffs were the owners of the issued share capital of a
private company whose principal asset was a building under construction. The defendants
were the majority shareholders of a public company which wished to acquire the building.
The plaintiffs agreed to sell their shares to the public company. In return the public company
agreed to issue shares to the plaintiffs as part of the same agreement. A separate agreement
was then formed between the plaintiffs and the defendants, where the defendants agreed to
indemnify the plaintiffs against any decrease in the value of the shares if the plaintiffs agreed
to hold on to 60 per cent of the transferred shares from the public company. The issue, therefore, for the Privy Council was whether the promise to perform an existing contractual duty

owed to a third party (the promise made by the plaintiffs to the public company to retain 60 per cent of the transferred shares) was valid consideration to support the defendants' promise of an indemnity.

The Privy Council held that such a promise was valid consideration for the defendants' promise. As the court observed:

> "The real consideration for the promise of indemnity was the plaintiffs' promise to the defendants to perform their contractual obligations to the public company under the main agreement, which included the undertaking to defer sale of 60 per cent of the shares."

So, we have seen from cases such as **Shadwell** and **Scotson** and more recently in **The Eurymedon** that *performance* of an existing contractual duty owed to a third party can constitute good consideration. Further, **Pao On** establishes that the *promise to perform* such obligations can also constitute valid consideration. However, in understanding *why* this is the case a final issue that is worthy of discussion is the role that economic duress has to play in such cases.

An existing contractual duty owed to a third party and the role of economic duress

4-023   Where there are existing contractual obligations between the parties, the courts are going to be extra vigilant when determining whether to hold the parties to their promises. The reason for this vigilance is the increased possibility that one party may have exercised fraud or duress in obtaining that further promise from the other party. Of course, the problem for the court is whether it can distinguish improper pressure amounting to duress from a legitimate exercise of bargaining pressure. However, despite these problems, if the court finds that the promise of the other party has been induced by improper pressure amounting to duress, the court may refuse to enforce the promise.

While a full-blown doctrine of economic duress was still in its infancy when **Pao On** was decided, Lord Scarman makes significant mention of the role that such a doctrine may play in the context of existing legal duties:

> "Their Lordships' conclusion is that where businessmen are negotiating at arm's length it is unnecessary for the achievement of justice, and unhelpful in the development of the law, to invoke such a rule of public policy. It would also create unacceptable anomaly. It is unnecessary because justice requires that men, who have negotiated at arm's length, be held to their bargains unless it can be shown that their consent was vitiated by fraud, mistake or duress. If a promise is induced by coercion of a man's will, the doctrine of duress suffices to do justice. The party coerced, if he chooses and acts in time, can avoid the contract. If there is no coercion, there can be no reason for avoiding the contract where there is shown to be a real consideration which is otherwise legal."

While Lord Scarman's comments arose in the context of an existing duty owed to a third party, these principles espoused by Lord Scarman also appear to have an increased significance in relation to existing duties owed to the same promisor, and this is the issue to which we now turn.

Part-payment of a debt

Finally, there is the common law rule that part-payment is not good consideration to support a promise to discharge a debt. This is an ancient rule and can be traced back to the decision in **Pinnel's Case** (1602) 5 Co. Rep. 117 in which it was stated that:

> **"Payment of a lesser sum on the day in satisfaction of a greater cannot be any satisfaction for the whole, because it appears to the judges that by no possibility a lesser sum can be a satisfaction to the plaintiff for a greater sum."**

4-024

The rule in **Pinnel's Case** was approved by the House of Lords in **Foakes v Beer** (1883–84) L.R. 9 App. Cas. 605. In this case, Mrs Beer obtained judgment against Dr Foakes. The total judgment sum was in the region of £2,000. Mrs Beer agreed to accept payment by instalments if Dr Foakes made a payment of £500. Dr Foakes made the payment and continued to pay the instalments as they fell due over the next five years. When the full £2,000 had been paid, Mrs Beer then sought to claim the interest that had accrued on the debt. The House of Lords held that Dr Foakes was liable to pay the outstanding interest. The full debt was not discharged until the full amount, plus interest, had been paid. Dr Foakes had not provided any consideration for Mrs Beer's promise to accept payment by instalments. Following the rule in Pinnel's Case, the part-payments were not valid consideration so Mrs Beer was free to demand the full amount due on the debt.

THE CONSEQUENCES OF THE RULE IN *PINNEL'S CASE*

The rule in **Pinnel's Case**, as confirmed by the House of Lords in **Foakes v Beer**, can operate harshly against the debtor. For example, say you owed me £1,000 and I promised that if you paid me £500 I would waive the outstanding amount. On the strength of this promise you pay me £500. At common law I would not be bound by my promise to accept £500 in full satisfaction of £1,000. Your part-payment is not good consideration to support my promise, so my promise will not be enforceable. I can therefore change my mind and demand that you pay the outstanding £500 due on the debt.

4-025

To this extent the reasoning in **Pinnel's Case** and **Foakes v Beer** is very closely linked to that in **Stilk v Myrick**. Although these cases addressed different legal issues, the legal reasoning is very similar. Part-payment of a debt is not good consideration as the debtor is doing no more than the contract already demands of him. The credit agreement requires that the full amount be paid (plus interest) so by simply making the payments as they fall due under the agreement, this confers no additional benefit to the creditor and the debtor suffers no additional benefit, in law. The part-payment is therefore insufficient as consideration.

Over to you. . .

As we have seen, the decision of the House of Lords in *Foakes v Beer* has the potential to operate harshly from the debtor's perspective. A debtor who makes a part-payment in the reliance on a promise that the debt has been discharged will be unable to enforce that promise at common law; his part-payment is insufficient as consideration. Given these potentially harsh consequences can you think of a justification for the principle in *Foakes v Beer*?

Despite the harsh consequences that the rule can have on debtors, it could be argued that the rule provides necessary protection from the debtor exploiting the financial position of the creditor. For example, in **D&C Builders Ltd v Rees** [1966] 2 Q.B. 617, the claimants had completed some building work for the defendants. The claimants sent an invoice for payment of £482. Some months later (and realising that the claimants were in financial difficulties), Mrs Rees offered to pay the claimants £300 in full satisfaction of the debt. The claimants reluctantly accepted this payment. The claimants then brought an action to recover the outstanding £182.

The court held that the claimants were entitled to the outstanding amount. Following the decision of the House of Lords in **Foakes v Beer**, applying the rule in **Pinnel's Case**, meant that Mrs Rees had not provided any consideration to support the promise to accept £300 in full satisfaction of the debt. In this case, Mrs Rees was prevented from unjustly exploiting her strong bargaining position.

However, this justification for application of **Foakes v Beer** fails to take account of agreements that are freely agreed between the debtor and the creditor. In some cases, the ability to recover some money under a contract may be more commercially beneficial to the creditor than insisting that the whole amount be paid. In the absence of duress, the courts should seek to give effect to the intention of the parties and hold them to their freely agreed promises. This approach would seem preferable and is also consistent with developments at common law that recognise that a factual benefit (as opposed to a legal benefit) may be sufficient as consideration (as illustrated in the case of **Williams v Roffey**). Despite the obvious merits of such an approach the courts have fallen short of developing such flexible principles in relation to the part-payment of a debt. Instead, the courts have provided some more restrictive exceptions to the rule in **Pinnel's Case** as to when part-payment of a debt may be sufficient as consideration.

THE EXCEPTIONS TO THE RULE IN *PINNEL'S CASE*

It has been established that the rule in **Pinnel's Case** has the potential to operate very harshly on the debtor. However, the court in **Pinnel's Case** recognised that there are limited exceptions to this rule. Part-payment of a debt is not good consideration, however:

4-026

> "... the gift of a horse, hawk, or robe in satisfaction is good, for it shall be intended that a horse, hawk, or robe, might be more beneficial to the plaintiff than the money, in respect of some circumstance, or otherwise the plaintiff would not have accepted it in satisfaction."

This is interesting, as something of little value promised in exchange for the discharge of a debt could be valid consideration, but payment of 99 per cent of the debt itself will be insufficient as consideration. For example, if I promised to accept a payment of £990 to discharge a debt of a £1,000, then I will still be able to claim the outstanding £10. Your part-payment is not valid consideration to support my promise to accept a lesser amount. However, if I promised to accept £10 plus your mobile phone (which is, say, only worth £90) to discharge a debt of £1,000, then my promise will be enforceable. I cannot go back on my promise and claim the outstanding amount due on the debt. The reasoning is based on the presumption that your mobile phone has some value to me that goes beyond the mere repayment of the debt. Of course, £10 plus your mobile phone in no way reflects the nature of promise to discharge you of an obligation to pay £990, but as consideration must only be sufficient (not adequate) then I will be bound by my promise to discharge the debt.

As you will recall, when analysing the case of **Foakes v Beer** we drew an analogy between the reasoning in Foakes and the reasoning in **Stilk v Myrick**. Part-payment of a debt will generally be insufficient as consideration as the debtor is only doing what his original obligations required him to do. We can also draw an analogy between the reasoning in **Pinnel** and the case of **Hartley v Ponsonby**. Part-payment is insufficient as consideration, but if you provide something *in addition* to what was originally contracted for (you exceed the terms of your existing duty) then this could amount to sufficient consideration to support the promise to discharge the debt.

In accordance with this reasoning, the court in **Pinnel's Case** also recognised that payment in a different form or at a different time could amount to valid consideration:

> "... so if I am bound in £20 to pay you £10 at Westminster, and you request me to pay you £5 at the day at York, and you will accept it in full satisfaction for the whole £10, it is a good satisfaction for the whole, for the expenses to pay it at York is sufficient satisfaction."

In the same way that a promise of goods in exchange for the discharge of a debt can be valid consideration, the promise of payment in a different form or at a different time can therefore amount to valid consideration to support a promise to discharge a debt. The reasoning again appears to be based on the fact that the promise is going beyond the obligations of the original agreement, which, presumably, will be more valuable to the promisor than full payment in the form as promised and on the date previously agreed.

Interestingly, however, in the case of **D & C Builders v Rees** [1966] 2 Q.B. 617 the court held that part-payment of a debt by cheque would not be considered as a different form of payment from payment by cash. As Lord Denning M.R. stated at 623:

> **"No sensible distinction can be taken between payment of a lesser sum by cash and payment of it by cheque. The cheque, when given, is conditional payment. When honoured, it is actual payment. It is then just the same as cash. If a creditor is not bound when he receives payment by cash, he should not be bound when he receives payment by cheque."**

PART-PAYMENT OF A DEBT AND THE DECISION IN *WILLIAMS V ROFFEY*

4-027   It has been argued that the principle in **Williams v Roffey** should extend to the part-payment of debts. As you will recall, the principle in **Williams v Roffey** is that performance of an existing contractual duty owed to the same promisor may be valid consideration if the promisor receives a "practical benefit" (or the avoidance of a disbenefit). Given the breadth of what the courts seem prepared to accept as constituting a "practical benefit", it could be argued that the part-payment of a debt confers a "practical benefit" on to the creditor. Surely, receiving some money under the contract is better than receiving nothing at all.

However, this argument was rejected by the Court of Appeal in **Re Selectmove Ltd**. The court considered itself bound by the House of Lords decision of **Foakes v Beer**: that part-payment of a debt is not good consideration. The decision in **Williams v Roffey** is therefore limited to contracts for the provision of goods and/or services and will not apply to the part-payment of debt.

It is unfortunate that the courts have developed more flexible principles in relation to contracts for the provision of goods and/or services, but due to strict principles of precedent they are unable to extend such principles to the part-payment of a debt. The recognition of "practical benefits" as being sufficient consideration reflects the commercial realities of such agreements. If the promisor freely agrees to promise additional payment to ensure that work is completed on time, then he will be held to his promise if the promisee confers to him a "practical benefit" by their performance. It is arguable that the same principle should also extent to the part-payment of a debt.

Further, given that the courts have now developed a more robust doctrine of economic duress (as illustrated in the case of **D & C Builders**, above) then this could provide a way of reconciling the approach in **Williams** with that in **Foakes v Beer**. Irrespective of the subject matter of the contract, whether it be for goods and/or services or whether it be a debt between the parties, the courts should seek to enforce a freely given promise between the parties if they received something of factual benefit as a result of that promise.

Despite the merits of such an approach it is clear that as a matter of precedent the Court of Appeal is unable to extend the principle in **Williams** to cover the part-payment of a debt. The Court of Appeal is bound by the House of Lords authority of **Foakes v Beer**. As Peter Gibson L.J. observed in **Re Selectmove**:

> "If the principle of *Williams v. Roffey Bros. & Nicholls (Contractors) Ltd.* [1991] 1 Q.B. 1 is to be extended to an obligation to make payment, it would in effect leave the principle in *Foakes v. Beer*, 9 App.Cas. 605 without any application. When a creditor and a debtor who are at arm's length reach agreement on the payment of the debt by instalments to accommodate the debtor, the creditor will no doubt always see a practical benefit to himself in so doing. In the absence of authority there would be much to be said for the enforceability of such a contract. But that was a matter expressly considered in *Foakes v. Beer* yet held not to constitute good consideration in law. *Foakes v. Beer* was not even referred to in *Williams v. Roffey Bros. & Nicholls (Contractors) Ltd.* [1991] 1 Q.B. 1, and it is in my judgment impossible, consistently with the doctrine of precedent, for this court to extend the principle of Williams's case to any circumstances governed by the principle of *Foakes v. Beer*, 9 App.Cas. 605. If that extension is to be made, it must be by the House of Lords or, perhaps even more appropriately, by Parliament after consideration by the Law Commission."

REMAINING PROBLEMS WITH THE PART-PAYMENT OF DEBT

The rule in **Pinnel's Case** makes no allowance for the fact that a debtor may have *relied* upon the creditor's promise to discharge a debt. In many cases this reliance will operate harshly and to the detriment of the debtor. The House of Lords itself in **Foakes v Beer** felt somewhat uneasy about approving such an approach. The speech of Lord Blackburn is most notable:

4-028

> "What principally weighs with me in thinking that Lord Coke made a mistake of fact is my conviction that all men of business, whether merchants or tradesmen, do every day recognise and act on the ground that prompt payment of a part of their demand may be more beneficial to them than it would be to insist on their rights and enforce payment of the whole. Even where the debtor is perfectly solvent, and sure to pay at last, this often is so. Where the credit of the debtor is doubtful it must be more so. I had persuaded myself that there was no such

> long-continued action on this dictum as to render it improper in this House to reconsider the question. I had written my reasons for so thinking; but as they were not satisfactory to the other noble and learned Lords who heard the case, I do not now repeat them nor persist in them."

Unfortunately, Lord Blackburn did not go as far to dissent with the majority of the House and as such the position at common law is quite clear. The test of enforceability of promises at common law is that of consideration and part-payment of a debt is insufficient as consideration. At common law the courts do not recognise reliance as a test of enforceability at common law and instead insist on applying the strict and sometimes artificial requirement of consideration.

While the common law adopts a restrictive approach to the part-payment of debts, the courts of *equity* have responded by developing more flexible (more equitable) principles that focus on *reliance* as being the key to enforcing promises between the parties. At this point we will turn to consider these equitable principles and most notably we shall analyse the doctrine of promissory estoppel.

Promissory estoppel: an overview

4-029 The doctrine of promissory estoppel is an area of contract law that students tend to find very difficult. This is in part due to the slightly intimidating (and confusing) terminology used to express quite straightforward principles. The difficulties in understanding the principles of promissory estoppel are also due to the overlap that arises between two different areas of law; the common law and equity. The doctrine of promissory estoppel is founded on equitable principles; therefore, a basic understanding of the background and operation of such equitable principles is required.

Hear from the Author

Scan the QR Tag or follow the link below for an introduction the doctrine of promissory estoppel.

uklawstudent.thomsonreuters.com/category/contract-fundamentals

What is an estoppel?

4-030 An estoppel is simply a device developed by the courts which has the effect of preventing (or estopping) a party from acting in a particular way when the other party has *relied upon* the facts that were represented to him. There are different types of estoppel but the key principle that runs through them all is the issue of reliance. For example, an estoppel by representation will have the effect of preventing (or estopping) a party from denying the truth of their representation of fact (**Jordan v Money** (1854) 5 HL Cas 185).

A *proprietary* estoppel will have the effect of preventing a party from denying that they led another to believe that they had acquired rights in a plot of land (**Crabb v Arun District Council** [1976] Ch 179).

A *promissory* estoppel can be described as an equitable device that will have the effect of preventing (or estopping) a party from going back on their promise where the other party has *relied upon* that promise.

The relationship between consideration and promissory estoppel

We have established that consideration is the test of enforceability of promises at common law for all contracts not contained in a deed (simple contracts). The strict requirement of consideration at common law can operate in a harsh and unjust manner. If the other party has relied upon a promise but that promise is not supported by consideration, then it will not be enforceable at common law. This will be the case even if both parties intended the promise to be binding. This problem is best illustrated by the cases such as **Foakes v Beer** (1883–84) L.R. 9 App. Cas. 605, in the context of part-payment of a debt. At common law a promise to accept a smaller amount in satisfaction of the whole was not enforceable, because part-payment was not good consideration to support such a promise. The promisee is doing no more than was already required under the contract.

4-031

Therefore, the courts of equity identified the need to develop further principles that could lead to promises being enforceable, even in the absence of consideration, when there has been reliance upon the promise. So, while the test of enforceability of a promise at common law is that of consideration, the test of enforceability of a promise at equity is that of *reliance*.

The development of the modern doctrine of promissory estoppel—The decision in *High Trees House*

For many years the strict approach at common law was that a promise will only be enforceable if supported by consideration. However, this ignored the developments that had taken place in the law of equity which had the effect of enforcing promises in the absence of consideration. The application of these equitable principles and the development of the modern doctrine of promissory estoppel can be traced to the obiter of Denning J. in **Central London Property**

4-032

Trust Ltd v High Trees House Ltd [1947] K.B. 130. The facts of this case and the relevant legal issues are illustrated in Figure 4.4.

In this case the defendants leased a block of flats from the plaintiffs. The lease for the flats was signed in September 1937 with a rent of £2,500 per year payable by the defendants to the plaintiffs. In January 1940, owing to the outbreak of the Second World War, it became difficult for the defendants to let out all of the flats. The plaintiffs therefore agreed to accept a reduced amount of rent, £1,250, while the difficulties in letting the flats continued. In September 1945, the war had ended and it was no longer difficult for the defendants to let the flats. The plaintiffs therefore sought to enforce the original agreement that rent of £2,500 per year should be payable. Further, the plaintiffs enquired whether it would be possible to recover the arrears for the reduced rent during the war years (the arrears being £1,250 per year).

FIGURE 4.4 **Overview of *High Trees House***

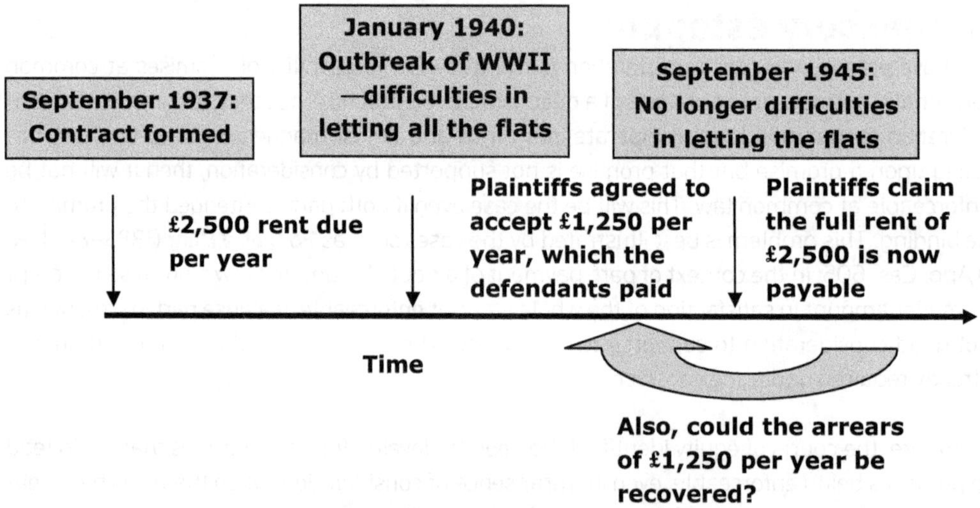

THE JUDGMENT OF DENNING J.

4-033   Denning J., in the High Court, only had to consider the issue of whether the full rent could be reinstated once the war had ended. It is therefore important to distinguish the *decision* in High Trees from Denning's *obiter* comments (which are particularly controversial and interesting).

THE DECISION IN *HIGH TREES*

4-034   The *decision* of the case is that the plaintiffs could reinstate the original agreement of £2,500 per year as the promise to accept a lesser amount was only intended to be binding while the difficulties in letting the flats continued. When the war ended these difficulties no longer existed so they could enforce the original terms of the agreement.

THE OBITER IN *HIGH TREES*

However, in his obiter, Denning J. had to decide whether the arrears on the rent during the war years were recoverable. This strictly forms part of the obiter as the plaintiffs only brought a test case to enquire whether it might be possible to claim the arrears; the claim itself was as to whether the full amount of £2,500 per year could be reinstated after the war. Denning J. was of the opinion that had the plaintiffs sought to claim the arrears in the rent during the war then they would have been *estopped* from doing so. The arrears in rent during the war were therefore not recoverable.

4-035

These obiter comments are startling. As you will recall, the House of Lords in **Foakes v Beer** made it clear that part-payment of a debt is not good consideration. Applying this reasoning to High Trees, the promise to accept a lesser amount (the reduced rent during the war years) would not be enforceable as the defendants had not provided any consideration for this promise. Their part-payment would not be a sufficient reason to bind the plaintiffs to their promise.

However, Denning was prepared to accept that a promise could be enforceable even in the absence of consideration. His obiter comments therefore challenge the strict requirement for consideration as a test of enforceability.

The fundamental principle in **High Trees** was expressed by Denning as follows:

> **"A promise intending to be binding, intended to be acted on and in fact acted on, is binding so far as its terms properly apply".**

Applying this principle to the facts of **High Trees**:

- The full rent of £2,500 could be claimed from the end of the War as this promise was only intended to be binding so far as the difficulties in letting the flats continued;
- The arrears in rent during the war years could not be recovered, as the promise to accept a reduced amount was intended to be binding, intended to be acted on and was in fact acted upon by the defendants when they paid the reduced amount of rent. The plaintiffs would therefore be estopped from going back on their promise.

PROMISSORY ESTOPPEL AND PART-PAYMENT OF A DEBT: THE CONFLICT WITH *FOAKES V BEER*

It has been established that the rule in **Pinnel's Case** has the potential to operate very harshly on the debtor. Part-payment of a debt will not be good consideration to support a promise to discharge a debt. The debtor may rely on this promise and suffer hardship if the creditor goes back on his agreement and seeks to recover the outstanding amount.

4-036

The effect of the Denning J.'s obiter comments in **High Trees** was to hold that a promise to accept a lesser amount (£1,250) in satisfaction of the whole (£2,500) was enforceable and that the plaintiffs would be prevented from going back on this promise. However, such an approach would seem to contradict the House of Lords decision in **Foakes v Beer** (1883–84) L.R. 9 App. Cas. 605 (which confirmed the long-standing principle in **Pinnel's Case** (1602) 5 Co. Rep. 117a) that part-payment of a debt is not good consideration to support such a promise (see p.95 above). In other words, why did Denning J. (in the High Court!) not consider himself bound by the House of Lords authority of **Foakes v Beer**? The answer can be found by analysing the fusion of common law and equity that occurred in the late nineteenth century.

"THE FUSION OF COMMON LAW AND EQUITY"

4-037   Denning J. argued that the decision in **Foakes v Beer** was not binding on him because the House of Lords in **Foakes** did not take account of the developments in the law of equity when reaching its decision. In other words, Denning J. saw the decision in **Foakes** as incomplete and defective with regard to the application of equitable principles.

In order to fully understand Denning J.'s arguments as to the deficiencies with **Foakes v Beer**, it is necessary to provide an overview of some historical developments in this area of law culminating with the fusion of common law and equity. The development of the common law can be traced back to the Norman conquest of England in 1066 which deposited a common law for the entire country. However, there were many problems with the common law; for example, it was rigid and inflexible in terms of the remedies that it could award. The courts of equity developed as a way of providing a remedy when the common law was unable to do so. There existed, therefore, two separate bodies of law, the common law and equity and two separate court structures, the common law courts and the courts of equity.

These two separate bodies of law were finally brought together with the passing of the Judicature Acts 1873–75. As a result, an individual could claim both a common law and an equitable remedy in the same court. Further, the courts were required to take account of both common law and an equitable principles in reaching their decisions.

Denning J. argued that the House of Lords in **Foakes v Beer** failed to take account of the effects of the Judicature Acts and as a result failed to take account of the developments in the law of equity. In particular, the decision of **Hughes v Metropolitan Railway Co** (1876–77) L.R. 2 App. Cas. 439, provided authority in the law of equity which would have the effect of preventing a party from going back on their promise in such situations. The failure of the House of Lords to consider such equitable principles gave Denning J. his justification for not being bound by **Foakes v Beer**. He expressed his argument as follows:

"The decisions are a natural result of the fusion of law and equity: for the cases of *Hughes v. Metropolitan Ry Co* . . . afford a sufficient basis for saying that a party would not be allowed in equity to go back on such a promise. In my opinion, the time has now come for the validity of such a promise to be recognised. The logical consequence, no doubt, is that a promise to accept a smaller sum in discharge of a larger sum, if acted upon, is binding notwithstanding the absence of consideration: and if the fusion of law and equity leads to this result, so much the better. That aspect was not considered in *Foakes v. Beer*."

THE DECISION IN *HUGHES V METROPOLITAN RAILWAY CO*

In refusing to accept the binding authority of **Foakes v Beer**, Denning J. preferred instead to rely upon the authority of **Hughes v Metropolitan Railway Co** (1876–77) L.R. 2 App. Cas. 439. This case concerned a clause in a lease that required the holder of the lease to conduct repairs of the property on being given notice to that effect. Notice was given which required the repairs to be carried out within six months. Discussions regarding the sale of the property then began between the two parties. When the discussions broke down, Hughes sought to take possession of the property on the grounds that the necessary repairs had not been carried out within the six-month period. The House of Lords held that Hughes had "waived" his right to seek possession owing to an implied promise that the repairs need not be carried out while the discussions regarding the sale were taking place.

4-038

The consequence of this decision is that the House of Lords recognised that a promise could be binding even if it is not supported by consideration. This concept was referred to as "equitable waiver" and it was this concept that Denning J. developed into his doctrine of promissory estoppel in **High Trees**.

THE LIMITATIONS ON *JORDAN V MONEY*

As mentioned above (see p.101), the courts recognised in the case of **Jordan v Money** (1854) 5 H.L. Cas. 185 that an estoppel by representation (a common law estoppel) will have the effect of preventing a party from denying the truth of their representation of fact. However, the House of Lords made it clear that such a principle will only apply to a representation of existing fact. The principle could not be used so as to give effect to a statement about the future. As a result, it would again seem that Denning J. should have been bound by this decision and thereby prevented from extending the operation of an estoppel to apply to situations such as that in **High Trees**.

4-039

Denning responded to this problem as follows:

"The law has not been standing still since *Jordan v Money*. There has been a series of decisions over the last fifty years which, although they are said to be cases of estoppel are not really such. They are cases in which a promise was made which was intended to create legal relations and which, to the knowledge of the person making the promise, was going to be acted on by the person to whom it was made and which was in fact so acted on. In such cases the courts have said that the promise must be honoured."

The limitations on promissory estoppel

4-040 At first glance, it may seem that in the obiter of **High Trees** Denning J. effectively abolished the need for consideration as he recognised that a promise could be enforceable even in the absence of consideration, provided that the promise was relied upon by the other party. The obiter in **High Trees** therefore would seem to mark a move away from consideration as a test for the enforceability of promises and a shift towards *reliance* as being the key test of enforceability.

However, despite these initial concerns, there are a number of limitations to the doctrine of promissory estoppel, to the extent that it can be argued that promissory estoppel merely *supplements* the law of consideration, rather than abolishing it.

The key restrictions to the operation of promissory estoppel are:

- There must have been an existing legal relationship between the parties.
- There must have been (detrimental) reliance on the promise.
- The doctrine operates as a "shield not a sword".
- It must not be inequitable to allow the promisor to go back on his promise.
- The doctrine merely suspends rights, it does not extinguish them.

THERE MUST HAVE BEEN AN EXISTING LEGAL RELATIONSHIP BETWEEN THE PARTIES

4-041 This first restriction is not too controversial. It simply clarifies that promissory estoppel does not exist in isolation; it is not an all-encompassing doctrine that can apply to all promises. The doctrine of promissory estoppel will only apply where there is an existing legal relationship between the parties. In most cases the existing legal relationship between the parties will be a contract. For this reason it is said that the doctrine of promissory estoppel does not abolish the need for consideration as a test of enforceability. As promissory estoppel in this context will operate in relation to the variation of an *existing contract* then the operation of promissory estoppel will depend on there being consideration to support the original agreement.

Denning L.J. conceded this very point in **Combe v Combe** [1951] 2 K.B. 215:

> "The principle, as I understand it, is that, where one party has, by his words
> or conduct, made to the other a promise or assurance which was intended to
> affect the legal relations between them and to be acted on accordingly, then,
> once the other party has taken him at his word and acted on it, the one who
> gave the promise or assurance cannot afterwards be allowed to revert to the
> previous legal relations as if no such promise or assurance had been made by
> him, but he must accept their legal relations subject to the qualification which he
> himself has so introduced, even though it is not supported in point of law by any
> consideration but only by his word.
>
> *Seeing that the principle never stands alone as giving a cause of action in itself, it
> can never do away with the necessity of consideration when that is an essential part
> of the cause of action."* [Emphasis added]

THERE MUST HAVE BEEN (DETRIMENTAL) RELIANCE ON THE PROMISE

Reliance is fundamental to the operation of promissory estoppel. The need for reliance is **4-042** what distinguishes promissory estoppel from the harsh common law rules of consideration, especially in relation to part-payment of debts. However, there remains some uncertainty as to whether the party must rely upon the promise to his *detriment*.

Denning was always of the opinion that detriment was not a requirement for promissory estoppel to operate. For example, in **High Trees** the defendants *relied* upon the plaintiff's promise by making reduced payments during the war years. There was no suggestion that these part-payments were *detrimental* to the defendants (quite the opposite in fact, they would seem to have benefitted from the agreement). Further, in **WJ Alan & Co Ltd v El Nasr Export & Import Co** [1972] 2 Q.B. 189, Denning stated that it would be sufficient if a party merely altered his position as a result of the promise.

As Denning argued in **Alan & Co Ltd**:

> "I know that it has been suggested in some quarters that there must be
> detriment. But I can find no support for it in the authorities cited by the judge.
> The nearest approach to it is the statement of Viscount Simonds in the *Tool
> Metal* case [1955] 1 WLR 761, 764, that the other must have been led 'to alter his
> position' . . . But that only means that he must have been led to act differently
> from what he otherwise would have done and if you study the cases in which the
> doctrine has been applied, you will see that all that is required is that the one
> should have 'acted on the belief induced by the other party'."

The test of reliance would appear to be very low indeed: the party must have been "led to act differently from what he otherwise would have done". So, while detrimental reliance is not fundamental to the availability of promissory estoppel, its relevance should be noted as to when a party seeks to go back on their promise. The court may use promissory estoppel to prevent a party from enforcing a strict legal right where the other party has altered their position to the extent that it would be inequitable for the party to go back on their promise.

As Robert Goff J observed in **The Post Chaser** [1982] 1 All E.R. 19:

> "It is not necessary to show detriment; indeed the representee may have
> benefitted from the representation, and yet it may be inequitable, at least
> without reasonable notice, for the representor to enforce his legal rights. . .
> it would be open to the court, in any particular case, to infer from the
> circumstances of the case that the representee must have conducted his affairs in
> such a way that it would be inequitable for the representor to enforce his rights,
> or to do so without reasonable notice."

The need for "reliance" as to the availability of promissory estoppel needs to be considered in light of the next requirement that it must not be inequitable to allow the promisor to go back on their promise.

IT MUST NOT BE INEQUITABLE FOR THE PROMISOR TO GO BACK ON HIS PROMISE

4-043   The underlying principles of equity on which promissory estoppel is based are concerned with equality and fairness. The courts will hold a party to their promise, even in the absence of consideration, if it would be unfair (or inequitable) for them to go back on their promise. In deciding this issue the court will have regard to the surrounding circumstances and the conduct of each party in deciding whether to grant equitable relief.

As discussed above, if a party has relied on a promise and has altered their position accordingly, then this will be a relevant factor in deciding the availability of promissory estoppel. While *detrimental* reliance is not necessary, if the promise has altered their position to their detriment then this will certainly strengthen the case that it would be inequitable to allow the promisor to go back on their promise. It may be that in some cases it will be equitable to go back on such a promise providing reasonable notice is given of this intention.

The facts of **High Trees** provide a useful illustration. In that case it is questionable whether the promisee suffered any *detriment* by relying on the promise of the other party to accept a reduced rent during the war years. However, it would be *inequitable* for the promisor to go back on their promise and claim the arrears that were due during those years. The promisee had altered their position on the basis of the promise and, as such, were not conducting their affairs on the basis that the arrears would need to be paid upon demand by the promisor. In contrast, both parties understood that the promise was only intended to be binding while the difficulties in letting the flats continued. It was therefore not inequitable to allow the promisor to reinstate this right by giving reasonable notice of their intention to do so. The extent of reliance is therefore one relevant factor as to whether it would be inequitable to allow the promisor to go back on their promise.

The court will also look to the conduct of both parties in deciding whether it would be inequitable to enforce a strict legal right. If the promisee has acted inequitably then the court will not allow them to use promissory estoppel in their defence. In **D&C Builders Ltd v Rees**, the claimants had performed building work for the defendants. The claimants issued an invoice for work which totalled £482. Mrs Rees offered the builders £300 in full satisfaction of the work. Owing to their financial position the claimants had no choice but to accept this offer. When the claimants sought payment of the extra £182 Mrs Rees claimed that they should be estopped from going back on their promise to accept £300 in full satisfaction of the debt.

The court held that it would not be inequitable to allow the claimants to go back on their promise. As Mrs Rees had knowingly exploited the claimants' financial position she could not rely on the doctrine of promissory estoppel. Mrs Rees had acted *inequitably* by exploiting the financial position of the builders, so she in turn could not claim the protection of equity when the claimants sought to go back on their promise. This reasoning is based on the famous equitable *maxim*: "He who comes to equity must do so with clean hands".

There are further circumstances in which it will not be inequitable for the promisor to go back on his promise. For example, if there is a only a short amount of time between a promise being made and the promise being withdrawn, then it may not be inequitable to allow the promisor to withdraw his promise. This position was considered in **Société Italo-Belge Pour le Commerce et L'Industrie SA (Antwerp) v Palm and Vegetable Oils (Malaysia) Sdn Bhd (The Post Chaser)** [1982] 1 All E.R. 19, in which the court allowed a promise to be withdrawn given that there had been a lapse of a only few days since the offer was made. This decision can also partly be explained on the basis that the short lapse of time meant that it was unlikely that the promisee had *relied* upon this promise.

THE DOCTRINE OPERATES AS A "SHIELD NOT A SWORD"

It has famously been said that promissory estoppel operates as a shield and not a sword (**Combe v Combe**). This rather dramatic language sometimes complicates for students what is actually quite a straightforward limitation to promissory estoppel. Essentially, promissory estoppel can only be used as a defence (a shield) and not as a cause of action (a sword).

4-044

For example, say that you owe me £1,000. I promise that if you pay me £600 I will not demand payment of the outstanding £400. In reliance on this, you go out and spend the £400 on clothes and shoes. I then attempt to go back on my promise and demand that you pay me the outstanding £400. In this example you cannot use promissory estoppel as a way of *enforcing my promise* ("you must not claim back the £400"). Rather, you may rely on promissory estoppel *as your defence* to my action if I seek to claim back the £400 ("you promised that you would not demand payment of the £400").

Again, the limitation that promissory estoppel operates as a shield not a sword has the effect of preserving the requirement for consideration. In its strict sense, promissory estoppel is not used to enforce promises (although its effect in most cases will be just that); rather, promissory estoppel is a device that is deployed when the promisor seeks to enforce a strict legal right that he promised he would not enforce.

THE DOCTRINE MERELY SUSPENDS RIGHTS, IT DOES NOT EXTINGUISH THEM

4-045   Once the limitations on promissory estoppel above have been met, there is still some confusion as to the precise way in which promissory estoppel operates in relation to the strict legal rights of the parties. In **High Trees**, Denning was of the opinion that promissory estoppel operates merely to suspend these strict legal rights. Applying this reasoning to the facts of **High Trees**, it can be seen that the right to claim the full rent of £2,500 was *suspended* during the war years and while the difficulties continued with letting the flats. As you will recall, a promise intending to be binding, intended to be acted upon and in fact acted upon is binding so far as its terms properly apply.

> ### Over to you. . .
>
> **Denning was insistent that promissory estoppel operates only to suspend rights and not to extinguish them. However, reflecting on Denning's obiter in** *High Trees* **do you agree with this analysis? Can you think how some rights may have actually have be extinguished in** *High Trees***?**

An analysis of the facts of **High Trees** reveals that in that case promissory estoppel had the effect of both suspending some rights and extinguishing others. Denning's obiter in **High Trees** was that the plaintiffs would be estopped from claiming the arrears during the war years. They had lost the right to claim the additional £1,250 per year. Therefore, the right to claim the full rent during this period had not been suspended, this right had been *extinguished*.

The case of **Hughes v Metropolitan Railway Co** (on which Denning placed so much reliance in **High Trees**) merely had the effect of suspending rights. The notice to repair was suspended during the negotiations. There was no evidence to suggest that the landlord had intended to extinguish his right to give notice of repair. It was this case that Denning applied as his authority for departing from the House of Lords decision in **Foakes v Beer**. In doing so Denning argued that **Foakes v Beer** failed to take account of the fusion between law and equity and therefore did not bind him on the issue of part-payment. As Treitel observes, this reasoning is unsatisfactory as equity had previously recognised that part-payment would not be cause to discharge a debt (**Bidder v Bridges** (1888) L.R. 37 Ch. D. 406). So, perhaps the best way to reconcile **High Trees** with **Foakes** is to accept the default position that promissory estoppel operates merely to *suspend* the debtor's rights under the contract. If it is the case that rights are merely suspended by the operation of promissory estoppel, then it would seem that these rights can be reinstated.

This reasoning was adopted by the House of Lords in **Tungsten Electric Co Ltd v Tool Metal Manufacturing Co Ltd** [1955] 1 W.L.R. 761. In this case Tool Metal entered into a licence agreement with Tungsten Electric. The agreement allowed Tungsten to sell a number of alloys that Tool Metal had patented. The agreement also provided that Tungsten would pay Tool Metal an amount of compensation if they sold more alloys than the agreement allowed. Tungsten breached this agreement but Tool Metal agreed to waive the compensation payments because of the outbreak of the war. After the war, Tool Metal sought to reinstate their right to claim compensation.

The House of Lords held that Tool Metal's right to claim compensation had been *suspended*. This right could be reinstated by giving reasonable notice of their intention to enforce this right. However, Tool Metal did not claim for the compensation that was due during the war years (in identical fashion to **High Trees**). The House of Lords therefore did not have to consider whether that amount would have been recoverable. It is unfortunate that the House did not address this issue, albeit obiter. As such, the operation of promissory estoppel remains somewhat uncertain.

The approach of the **Privy Council Ajayi v RT Briscoe (Nigeria) Ltd** [1964] 1 WLR 1326 was that the promisor will be unable to reinstate a strict legal right if the promisee "cannot resume his original position". If this reasoning is followed, then if the promisee is able to resume their original position then the promisor will be able to reinstate a strict legal right by providing reasonable notice of their intention to do so. To this extent, the rights of the promisor have been suspended. However, if the promisee is *unable* to resume their original position then the promisor will not be able to insist on enforcing the strict legal right at all. To this extent it would seem that promissory estoppel would operate so as to *extinguish* the rights of the promisor. Again, this approach highlights the continued significance reliance. The court will seek to avoid unduly disadvantaging the promisee where they have relied upon the clear promise of another.

The case of **Collier v P & MJ Wright (Holdings) Ltd** [2007] EWCA 1329 demonstrates the continued uncertainty as to operation of promissory estoppel. In this case a debtor argued that the creditor's promise to accept a part-payment in full settlement of the debt should extinguish the creditor's right to claim any further outstanding payments. The Court of Appeal did not have to decide whether promissory estoppel could operate in this case (the claim was to enforce a statutory demand), but the Court did decide that the debtor's argument did present a "triable issue" on the facts as to the operation of promissory estoppel.

The culmination of these authorities makes the application of promissory estoppel difficult in particular cases. The House of Lords decision in **Tool Metal Manufacturing** does not, for example, explain how promissory estoppel will operate in relation to a debt that is due to be paid by instalments. For example, imagine that you owe me £1,000 and you agree to pay by 10 monthly instalments of £100. If after the first five payments I promise to discharge the debt and release you of your obligation to pay the remaining five instalments, will I be able to reinstate this obligation in two months' time and claim the remaining three instalments plus the two that are in arrears? It would certainly sound inequitable for me to claim the arrears; you may have relied on my promise and as such were not expecting to be required to pay this amount. If you are unable to resume your original position then it could be argued that my right to claim the arrears has been extinguished.

In relation to the five remaining instalments, if you are able to resume your position upon being given reasonable notice of my intention to do so then my right to claim the instalments has merely been suspended.

The conclusion therefore seems to be that promissory estoppel can operate to suspend rights *and* to extinguish rights. The precise effect of promissory estoppel will therefore depend on the facts of the particular case, the intentions of the parties and whether it would be inequitable for the promisor to go back on their promise.

Summary

1. For an agreement to be legally enforceable it must be supported by consideration. Consideration can be defined as "the price of the promise".

2. Consideration must be legally sufficient, although it need not be adequate (**Thomas v Thomas**). It must have some economic value and consideration must pass from the promisee (the party seeking to enforce the promise).

3. The courts have recognised different situations in which consideration will not be legally sufficient to enforce a promise. Past consideration is said to be "no consideration". The rule on past consideration is subject to an exception; "The requested performance" exception. The requirements of this exception were restated by Lord Scarman in **Pao On**:

(a) the act must have been done at the promisor's request (**Lampleigh v Braithwaite**);

(b) the parties understood that the act was to be remunerated (**Re Casey's Patents**); and

(c) the payment or conferment of a benefit would have been enforceable had it been promised in advance.

4. Performance of an existing contractual duty is generally not good consideration. However, if by performance of a *duty owed to a third party* the promisee obtains the "benefit of a direct obligation which he can enforce" this can be valid consideration (**New Zealand Shipping Co—The Eurymedon**).

5. Performance of an existing duty *to the same promisor* is also generally not good consideration (**Stilk v Myrick**). However, if a party exceeds their contractual obligations (**Hartley v Ponsonby**) or confers a "practical benefit" on the other party (**Williams v Roffey**), then providing the promise was not induced by duress or fraud, the performance of the duty can be valid consideration.

6. Part-payment of a debt is not good consideration to support a promise to accept a lesser amount in satisfaction of the whole (**Foakes v Beer**).

7. If a promise is not binding at common law owing to a lack of consideration, then the equitable doctrine of promissory estoppel may have the effect of preventing a party from going back on their promise (**High Trees House**).

8. The doctrine of promissory estoppel is subject to a number of limitations, so as to preserve the need for consideration in most contracts.

(a) There must have been an existing legal relationship between the parties.

(b) There must have been (detrimental) reliance on the promise.

(c) The doctrine operates as a "shield not a sword".

(d) It must not be inequitable to allow the promisor to go back on his promise.

(e) The doctrine merely suspends rights, it does not extinguish them.

Key Cases Grid

Case	Court	Key Issues
Currie v Misa (1874–75)	Court of Exchequer Chamber	This case provides the classical definition of consideration, with the emphasis on the need for an exchange of something of legal vale between the parties, whether that be "some right, interest, profit, or benefit accruing to the one party, or some forbearance, detriment, loss, or responsibility, given, suffered, or undertaken by the other."
Stilk v Myrick (1809)	Assizes	The performance of an existing contractual duty to the same promisor is generally insufficient as consideration. If one party is simply performing a duty that they are contractually obliged to perform to the promisor, then as a matter of law, there is no additional detriment suffered or no additional benefit conferred.
Williams v Roffey Bros [1991]	Court of Appeal	The performance of an existing contractual obligation may amount to sufficient consideration if the performance of that duty confers a practical benefit to the promisor. In contract to Stilk v Myrick, this case signifies an important shift in emphasis from consideration having to be something of legal value, and recognises that factual / practical benefits may constitute valuable consideration, subject to the application of the "Glidewell Criteria"
Foakes v Beer (1883–84)	House of Lords	The part-payment of a debt is generally insufficient as consideration. This case approved the earlier reasoning in Pinnel's Case that: "Payment of a lesser sum on the day in satisfaction of a greater cannot be any satisfaction for the whole, because it appears to the judges that by no possibility a lesser sum can be a satisfaction to the plaintiff for a greater sum."

Central London Property Trust Ltd v High Trees House Ltd [1947]	High Court	By his obiter comments, Denning J, provided an alternative method of enforcing promises between the parties that does not depend on the existence of consideration at common law. These comments have developed into what is now referred to as the doctrine of promissory estoppel. *"A promise intending to be binding, intended to be acted on and in fact acted on, is binding so far as its terms properly apply".*
New Zealand Shipping Co Ltd v AM Satterthwaite & Co Ltd (The Eurymedon) [1975]	Privy Council (New Zealand)	The performance of an existing construal duty owed to a third party may constitute valuable consideration as "the promisee obtains the benefit of a direct obligation which he can enforce."
Pao On v Lau Yiu Long [1980]	Privy Council (Hong Kong)	This case provides a modern restatement of the exception to the past consideration rule, the "requested performance exception": 1. that an act done before the giving of a promise could be valid consideration for that promise if the act had been done at the promisor's request (this is a restatement of the principle established in Lampleigh v Braitwaite); 2. the parties had understood that the act was to be remunerated either by payment or by conferment of a benefit (this is a restatement of the principle in Re Casey's Patents); and 3. the payment or conferment of a benefit would have been enforceable had it been promised in advance.

◄ ....

End of Chapter Question

The Nottingley Train Company enters into a contract with Fix-it Ltd under which Fix-it Ltd agrees to service the train company's carriages in time for the busy summer period. The contract price is £50,000 and Fix-it Ltd agrees to complete the service by July 10.

On July 1, Fix-it Ltd approach the train company and say that they will be unable to complete the service on time due to a shortage of mechanics. Fearing the financial consequences of running a reduced service during the summer, the train company promises to pay Fix-it Ltd an additional £10,000 to enable them to hire additional mechanics.

The work is completed on time and the train company are refusing to pay the additional £10,000.

Advise Fix-it Ltd.

Points of Answer

♦ This question concerns the common law principles of consideration. The train company will argue that they have no obligation to pay the additional amount as Fix-it Ltd were doing no more than their existing contractual obligations required (**Stilk v Myrick**). There is no evidence that Fix-it Ltd have exceeded their existing duty (**Hartley v Ponsonby**) so in *law* Fix-it Ltd have no provided consideration to support the train company's promise of additional payment.

♦ However, following the principle in **Williams v Roffey**, if performance of the existing duty confers a "practical benefit" to the train company then this can be valid consideration to support the train company's promise.

♦ Clearly state and apply the "Glidewell" criteria to determine whether the promise of additional payment is enforceable.

♦ On the facts it would seem that the train company receive the benefit of having the service completed on time which means they avoid the disbenefit of having to find other contractors to complete the work and also avoid the financial consequences of having to run a reduced service.

♦ These *factual benefits* could constitute valid consideration enabling Fix-it Ltd to enforce the promise of additional payment.

Further Reading

Austen-Baker, A strange sort of survival for Pinnel's case: Collier v P & MJ Wright (Holdings) Ltd, M.L.R. 2008, 71(4), 611–620.

An article that assesses the impact of the decision of **Collier v Wright** on the principle established by Re Pinnel's case regarding part-payment of a debt.

Blair, Minding your own business, Williams v Roffey re-visited: consideration re-considered, [1996] J.B.L. 254.

This article focuses on the relationship between the decision in **Williams v Roffey** and the relevant principles relating to part-payment of a debt in light of the decision in **Re Selectmove**.

Knight, C. A plea for (re)consideration, C.S.L.R. 2006, 2(1), 17–23
    A very accessible examination the law of consideration following the decision of the Court of Appeal in **Williams v.Roffey Bros. & Nicholls (Contractors) Ltd**.

Stone, R. and Cunnington, R. *Text, Cases and Materials on Contract Law* (London: Routledge-Cavendish, 2014), Ch.3

Treitel, G. *The Law of Contract*, 13th edn (London Sweet & Maxwell, 2011), Ch.3

Privity of Contract

5

CHAPTER OVERVIEW

In this chapter we:

- **introduce the doctrine of privity of contract**

- **explain the justifications for the doctrine of privity**

- **consider the exceptions to the doctrine of privity**

- **introduce the key provisions of the Contracts (Rights of Third Parties) Act 1999**

Summary

Key Cases Grid

End of Chapter Question

Further Reading

Introduction

5-001 A contract is a two-way street and is based on a mutual agreement between two parties. Each party will have obligations under the contract and each party will have the right to sue if the other party fails to meet those obligations. An individual who is not a party to a contract is referred to as a third party. A third party will not have any of these rights described above. Only parties that are *privy* to the contract will be able to exercise these rights. This is referred to as the doctrine of *privity of contract*.

Privity of contract has three broad effects:

1. A third party *cannot receive a benefit* of a contract if he is not party to that contract.
2. A third party *cannot be liable* under a contract if he is not a party to that contract.
3. A third party *cannot enforce* a contract if he is not a party to that contract.

Justifications for the doctrine of privity of contract

5-002 As outlined above, a third party to a contract has no rights in that contract. To understand *why* this is the case it is important to consider two closely connected justifications. First, as a contract is based on a mutual agreement, it would be unfair to impose obligations on a party who may not have given his consent to be bound. Secondly, a third party to a contract will not have provided consideration to support the agreement. Even if the intention of the parties is that a third party shall have some rights under the contract the courts will not enforce this agreement. A key requirement of enforceability, that consideration must move from the promisee, has not been satisfied.

These principles were described as "fundamental" by Viscount Haldane L.C. in **Dunlop Pneumatic Tyre Co Ltd v Selfridge and Co Ltd** [1915] A.C. 847.

> **"In the law of England certain principles are fundamental. One is that only a person who is a party to a contract can sue on it . . . A second principle is that if a person with whom a contract not under seal has been made is to be able to enforce it, consideration must have been given by him to the promisor or to some other person at the promisor's request."**

A familiar example of these principles in action can be found in **Tweddle v Atkinson** (1861) 1 B. & S. 393. Essentially, the plaintiff was engaged to be married to his fiancée. The father and future father-in-law agreed between them to pay the plaintiff sums of money. The father agreed to pay his son £100 and the father-in-law agreed to pay his future son-in-law £200.

The father-in-law died before the payment was made. The plaintiff then brought an action against the executors to enforce the promise of payment.

The court held that the plaintiff could not enforce the father-in-law's promise of payment. The agreement was between the father and father-in-law. This is illustrated in Figure 5.1.

FIGURE 5.1 *Tweddle v Atkinson*

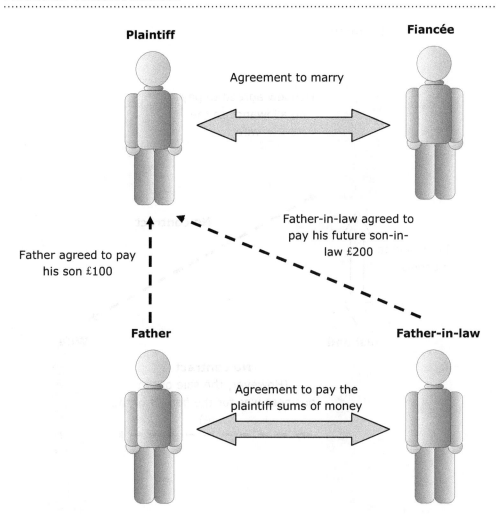

Tweddle v Atkinson provides a classic example of the operation of privity of contract. The contract is between the father and the father-in-law. The plaintiff is not a party to this contract. Further, the plaintiff has not provided consideration in exchange for their promises of payment. The plaintiff therefore cannot enforce the agreement for payment.

The decision in **Tweddle v Atkinson** therefore creates a particular problem for third parties. The third party may often have an *interest* in seeing the contract performed, but will not be able to enforce this. Further, the contracting parties may have intended to confer rights to the third party as part of their agreement. Again, the strict principles of privity of contract would prevent this. This problem was evident in **Beswick v Beswick** [1968] A.C. 58, which is illustrated in Figure 5.2.

FIGURE 5.2 *Beswick v Beswick*

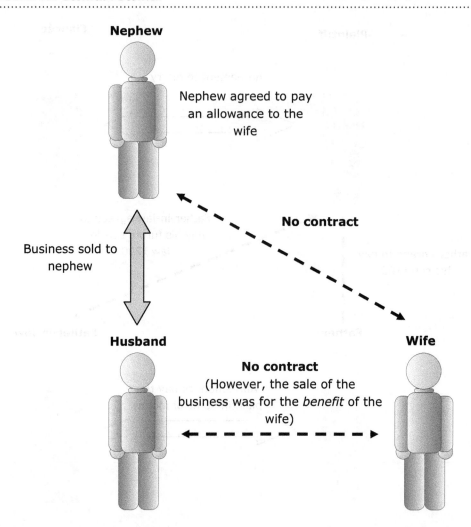

Nephew

Nephew agreed to pay an allowance to the wife

No contract

Business sold to nephew

Husband

Wife

No contract
(However, the sale of the business was for the *benefit* of the wife)

In this case a husband sold his business to his nephew in exchange for the nephew's promise that he would pay his wife an allowance after his death. The nephew refused to make these payments. The court held that the doctrine of privity of contract prevented the wife from enforcing the agreement. The wife was not a party to the contract. The contract was between her husband and the nephew. This was despite the fact that the husband clearly intended that the contract for the sale of the business would be for the *benefit* of the wife.

Exceptions to the doctrine of privity

The doctrine of privity of contract has the potential to operate in a very harsh and unfair manner. This is particularly so in relation to contracts made for the *benefit* of a third party. In these cases the doctrine of privity was given priority over the clear intentions of the parties. Given this potential unfairness and inflexibility a number of exceptions to the privity rule have been developed.

5-003

Exceptions at common law

A number of common law exceptions have been developed which have eased the strict application of the privity rule. These will be addressed briefly below as the primary focus in modern contract law should be on the operation of the Contracts (Rights of Third Parties) Act 1999.

5-004

AGENCY

An agent has the authority to act on behalf another (the principal). The agent has the authority to enter into a contract on behalf of his principal. If the principal is disclosed to the third party (in other words, the third party is aware that the agent is contracting on behalf of the principal) then the agent generally drops out of the agreement leaving an enforceable contract between the principal and the third party and this basic position is illustrated in Figure 5.3.

5-005

However, if the principal is undisclosed (the third party is not aware of the principal), then the third party may well believe that he is contracting directly with the agent, rather than with the principal. In this case there will be a true exception to the privity rule. The third party will be able to enforce a contract against the principal (and vice versa) even though he was not aware that the principal was a party to the contract.

FIGURE 5.3 **Agency**

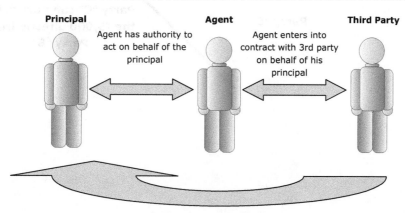

Principal

Agent has authority to act on behalf of the principal

Agent

Agent enters into contract with 3rd party on behalf of his principal

Third Party

The contract is enforceable between the *3rd party* and the *principal*.

ASSIGNMENT

5-006 It is possible for a party to assign (hand over) some of his rights under a contract to a third party. Take the example in Figure 5.4.

In the example in Figure 5.4 Party A has the right to claim £5,000 from Party B. This right can be transferred like most other kinds of property and Party A chooses to assign the right to claim the £5,000 to Party C as part-payment of Party A's debt. The effect is that Party C can then directly enforce this right against Party B, which is effectively an exception to the privity of contract rule.

FIGURE 5.4 Assignment

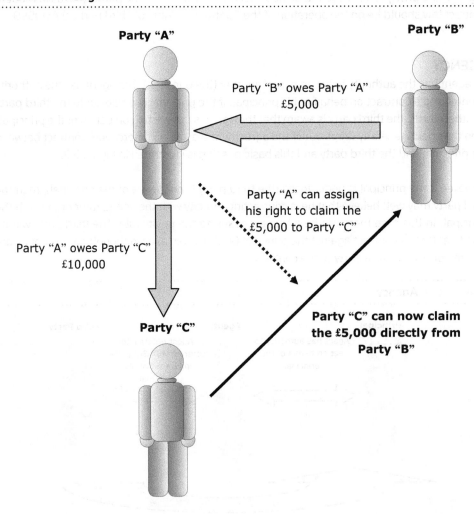

Third parties and damages

As a third party is not a party to the contract the third party cannot enforce the contract and they cannot receive a benefit under the contract. Therefore, if a contract is breached only a party under the contract can claim damages for this breach. This was essentially the position in **Beswick v Beswick** (above): the widow had not actually suffered any loss under the contract so she was not able to claim damages for the breach of contract. This obviously has the potential to operate quite harshly and has led to the courts developing a rather flexible approach to the privity rule.

In **Jackson v Horizon Holidays Ltd** [1975] 1 W.L.R. 1468, a husband booked for himself and his family. The holiday proved to be a disaster. Before leaving, the family were told that their choice of accommodation was not available and they were offered a substitute. The alternative accommodation fell well below the standard promised and the husband sued the holiday company for breach of contract. The court found for the husband and awarded him £1,100 damages. The holiday company appealed on the basis that the amount of damages awarded was excessive. As only the husband was a party to the contract then £1,100 seemed excessive to reflect his loss under the contract.

Lord Denning confirmed the amount of damages award and held that the husband was able to recover not just for his own loss but also for the loss suffered by his family. The contract was made for the benefit of the family as a whole and as such the husband could recover on their behalf. However, Denning went further and held that the family members could also enforce the agreement and require the holiday company to pay the money due to them for their loss. This is quite a remarkable decision as Denning circumvented two of the most fundamental principles of the privity of contract rule.

Over to you. . .

There is no doubt that the decision of Lord Denning in *Jackson* appears to be *fair* in terms of the final decision, but his reasoning is less than clear. Read the case of *Jackson* and try to identify any differences in terms of the reasoning the judges adopted in reaching their decision.

As you will see from reading the case of **Jackson**, there was in fact disagreement between the judges themselves as to precisely why damages were awarded on behalf of the family. James L.J. seemed to explain the decision based on principles of agency, rather than accepting that a contract made for the benefit of the family could be *enforced* by the family.

Some doubt was cast on the reasoning in **Jackson** in the case of **Woodar Investment Development Ltd v Wimpey Construction UK Ltd** [1980] 1 W.L.R. 277. In this case the purchasers of some land agreed to pay part of the purchase price to the vendor, plus an extra payment to a third party. In an action for breach of contract the vendor claimed the purchase price plus the additional payment that was promised to the third party. The court decided that there was no breach of contract in this case, so the reasoning is strictly obiter, but the court was of the opinion that the vendor could not recover the extra payment owed to the third party. The vendor had not actually suffered any loss in relation to this payment so he was not able to claim damages on behalf of a third party.

While the decision certainly challenges the reasoning in **Jackson**, the House of Lords in **Woodar** did not overrule this decision. Interestingly, the Package Travel, Package Holidays and Package Tours Regulations 1992 (SI 1992/3288) now cover these types of contract and have the effect of giving rights to third parties in relation to package holidays. However, the gap left by the Regulations could still be filled by the decision in **Jackson** should the Regulations not apply to a particular contract.

Contracts (Rights of Third Parties) Act 1999

5-008　While common law has recognised some exceptions to the privity rule, the Contracts (Rights of Third Parties) Act 1999 provides some *additional* exceptions. The provisions of the Act supplement the common law. Therefore, if the Act does not apply to a particular contract then the courts can revert to the position at common law. It is for this reason that it is advisable to briefly consider the position at common law before referring to the Act. The common law exceptions represent the default position and any additional exception provided by the Act will be a bonus to the third party.

Following many years of gestation, the Contracts (Rights of Third Parties) Act 1999 came into force on November 11, 1999. The broad effect of the Act is to allow a third party to enforce a contract that was made for their *benefit*. The Act falls short of giving *every* third party a right to claim under a contract as this would lead to a multiplicity of claims. Rather, the Act provides that a third party may be able to enforce a contract in two situations:

- if the contract expressly provides that the party can enforce the contract;
- if the contract purports to confer a benefit on that third party.

These two grounds are provided in s.1, as follows:

> **"1. (1) Subject to the provisions of this Act, a person who is not a party to a contract (a "third party") may in his own right enforce a term of the contract if—**
> **(a)　the contract expressly provides that he may, or**
> **(b)　subject to subsection (2), the term purports to confer a benefit on him.**
> **(2) Subsection (1)(b) does not apply if on a proper construction of the contract it appears that the parties did not intend the term to be enforceable by the third party.**
> **(3) The third party must be expressly identified in the contract by name, as a member of a class or as answering a particular description but need not be in existence when the contract is entered into."**

It is important to note the effect of s.1(2). This subsection acts so as to limit the parties who might otherwise fall within s.1(1)(b)—a term that *purports* to confer a benefit on a third party. We shall now consider the operation of s.1(1)(b) in more detail.

A TERM THAT PURPORTS TO CONFER A BENEFIT ON A THIRD PARTY (S.1(1)(B))

5-009

If a contractual term expressly provides that a third party will be able to enforce the contract then s.1(1)(a) will allow that party to do so. Cases such as **Tweddle v Atkinson** would not fall within this section as the section requires the contract expressly to provide that the third party may sue. This is not too controversial and there is limited scope for confusion. Section 1(1)(b) is slightly more contentious. This provides that a third party can enforce a contract if the contract purports to confer a benefit on that party. Cases such as **Beswick v Beswick** would now fall within this section.

However, the Act imposes a specific restriction on these types of contract. There is a presumption that a party under a contract will be able to enforce the contract if it purported to confer a benefit on that party. This presumption can be rebutted under s.1(2) if a proper construction of the contract reveals that the parties did not intend to confer such a benefit. This also needs to be read in the light of s.1(3), which provides that the party must be expressly identified in the contract. Again, the effect of this subsection is to limit the number of third parties who will be able to enforce the contract and to prevent the floodgates opening to multiple claims.

VARIATION AND RESCISSION OF THE CONTRACT (S.2)

5-010

Once the parties have formed an agreement they are generally free to vary or alter this agreement as they wish. Provided that any variation is supported by consideration the courts will usually bind the parties to their new agreement. The exceptions to the privity of contract rule provided by s.1 create particular problems for the third party. Most importantly, can the original parties to the contract vary the agreement so as to limit or destroy the right of the third party to enforce the contract?

The answer to this question is provided by s.2, as follows:

> **"2. (1) Subject to the provisions of this section, where a third party has a right under s.1 to enforce a term of the contract, the parties to the contract may not, by agreement, rescind the contract, or vary it in such a way as to extinguish or alter his entitlement under that right, without his consent if—**
>
> **(a) the third party has communicated his assent to the term to the promisor,**
>
> **(b) the promisor is aware that the third party has relied on the term, or**
>
> **(c) the promisor can reasonably be expected to have foreseen that the third party would rely on the term and the third party has in fact relied on it."**

It should be noted that the focus of s.2 is still firmly on the original contracting parties. Consent of the third party to vary the agreement is only needed should one of the three exceptions above apply. If none of these conditions is satisfied then the parties will be free to vary their agreement.

DEFENCES (S.3)

5-011   As the third party has the right to enforce the contract, the promisor may find that he faces an action for breach of contract from the third party. The relevant defences available to the promisor are provided by s.3. Essentially, the promisor will be able to claim the same remedies that would be available to him against the promisee.

On the flip side of the coin, s.3(6) provides that the third party will not be able to exercise any remedy or defence that he would not have been entitled to had he been an original party to the contract. So, if the promisor brings an action against the third party then the third party will be limited as to the remedies available to him in the same way that the promisor is limited under s.3(2)–(5).

EXCEPTIONS TO THE ACT (S.6)

5-012   Not all contracts are covered by the Act. Section 6 provides a list of specific contracts to which the Act will not apply. For example, the Act will not apply to a bill of exchange, promissory note or other negotiable instrument (s.6(1)). Nor will it apply to a contract binding on a company and its members under s.14 of the Companies Act 1985 (s.6(2)). (This section should now be read in the light of s.33 of the Companies Act 2006.) Also, the Act will not give a third party the right to enforce a contract of employment against an employee (s.6(3)).

Summary

1.   The privity of contract rule means that only parties to the contract can enforce the contract, receive a benefit under the contract or be liable on the contract. A third party will have very limited rights indeed under the contract.

2.   A third party cannot enforce a contract as he has not provided consideration to support the agreement, nor will he generally have suffered any loss under the contract.

3.   The privity of contract rule was quite inflexible in relation to contracts that were made for the *benefit* of a third party. Following the decision in **Beswick v Beswick** it was clear that a third party cannot enforce a contract to which they are not a party.

4. At common law a number of exceptions to the rule of privity were developed. Principles of agency and assignment had the effect of circumventing the privity rule, although the ability to claim damages on behalf of a third party is less convincing.

5. The Contracts (Rights of Third Parties) Act 1999 provides additional exceptions to the privity of contract rule and allows a third party to enforce a contract that was made for the *benefit* of the third party.

6. In order for the Act to apply the two broad conditions in s.1 must be satisfied:

   (a) either the contract expressly provides that the party can enforce the contract (s.1(1)(a)); or

   (b) the contract purports to confer a benefit on that third party (s.1(1)(b)).

Note that s.1(1(b) is rebuttable and the court must decide as a matter of construction whether the contract purported to confer a benefit on the third party before it can enforce the contract.

Key Cases Grid

Case	Court	Key Issues
Tweddle v Atkinson (1861)	Court of Queen's Bench	This case illustrates that as a general principle of law, only a party that is privy (party to) the contract may enforce a legal obligation arising under that contract: "In the law of England certain principles are fundamental. One is that only a person who is a party to a contract can sue on it . . . A second principle is that if a person with whom a contract not under seal has been made is to be able to enforce it, consideration must have been given by him to the promisor or to some other person at the promisor's request."
Beswick v Beswick [1968] A.C. 58	House of Lords	The House of Lords confirmed that only a party to the contract can enforce rights under that contract. This is the case even if there is evidence that eh contract was made for the *benefit* of the third party.

Jackson v Horizon Holidays Ltd [1975] 1 W.L.R. 1468	Court of Appeal	This case provides a more flexible interpretation of the privity of contract rule when assessing damages in light of breach of contract. Although the contract in this case was between the husband and the holiday company, the husband was able to recover damages to reflect the loss suffered by his family. The contract was made for the benefit of the family as a whole and as such the husband could recover on their behalf.

End of Chapter Question

Jo books a holiday to Italy for her and her family. She specifies that the accommodation must provide facilities for young children. When Jo and her family arrive they are told that their specified accommodation is no longer available. The tour company offer Jo alternative accommodation located in the city centre. Due to its location the alternative accommodation does not provide any facilities for children; in fact, guests must be at least 18 years old in order to stay at this alternative accommodation.

Jo brings an action for breach of contract against the tour company claiming damages for the ruined holiday for herself and on behalf of her family.

Discuss the legal issues.

Points of Answer

♦ From the facts it would seem that accommodation with family facilities was a condition of the contract. As the tour company are unable to provide alternative company for Jo's children then there would seem to be a breach of contract.

♦ As Jo is a party to the contract then she can claim damages for this breach.

♦ However, as her family are not strictly parties to the contract, in order to claim damages on their behalf Jo will need to circumvent the rule of privity of contract.

♦ Compare and contrast the approaches in **Jackson v Horizon Holidays and Woodar Investment Development Ltd**. Also, in light of statutory developments consider the application of s.1 (1) (b); the contract was for the benefit of the whole family (not just Jo) which may give Jo the ability to recover damages on their behalf.

Further Reading

Stevens, R. "The Contracts (Rights of Third Parties Act) 1999." L.Q.R. 2004, 120(Apr), 292—323.
A comprehensive and critical review of the Law The Contracts (Rights of Third Parties Act) 1999 which draws from various jurisdictions to analyse whether the provisos of the Act are appropriate in light of development of other remedies available to the promisee.

Stone, R. and Cunnington, R. *Text, Cases and Materials on Contract Law* (London: Routledge-Cavendish, 2014), Chapter 5.

Treitel, G. *The Law of Contract*, 13th edn (London Sweet & Maxwell, 2011), Chapter 14.

Terms

6

CHAPTER OVERVIEW

In this chapter we:

● **distinguish a term of the contract from a representation**

● **discuss express and implied terms of the contract**

● **distinguish a condition from a warranty**

● **consider the development and use of innominate terms**

Summary

Key Cases Grid

End of Chapter Question

Further Reading

Introduction

6-001 So far we have looked at formulating the agreement with the requirements of offer and acceptance. Further, we have looked at the key test of enforceability of that agreement with the requirement of consideration. However, we now need to look at the terms of the agreement.

Terms of a contract identify the obligations of each party. They determine what each party is expected to perform or provide under the contract as part of their bargain. If one party fails to meet these obligations then he may face an action for breach of contract. It is therefore important to be able to identify the terms of the agreement.

Identifying the terms of the agreement is not always straightforward. The parties may make numerous statements as part of their contractual negotiations; however not all of these statements will form terms of the contract. Further, not all those statements would have been *intended* to form terms of the agreement.

The courts have therefore developed a number of tests and hurdles that a statement must overcome before it will be classed as a term of the contract. Once the courts have identified a statement as a term of the contract then the next task will be to identify the *type* of term in question.

This chapter will therefore adopt the following structure in assessing contractual terms:

1. Distinguish between a term and a representation.
2. Is the statement a term and has it been incorporated into the contract?
3. Is the term express or implied?
4. What is the type of term in question?

Distinguishing between a term and representation

6-002 Not all statements will form part of the contract. Terms form part of the contract and will bind the parties to the obligations they create. However, a representation does not form part of the contract and will generally not give rise to any contractual obligations.

It is therefore important to distinguish between a term and a representation for two reasons. First, it is important for the parties to be able to identify a term that creates a contractual obligation so that they are aware of what action they should take to meet the obligation.

Secondly, if a party fails to meet an obligation provided for by a term in the contract then that party may face an action for breach of contract. As a representation does not form part of the contract there can be no action for breach of contract. The appropriate cause of action in relation to a representation will generally be for misrepresentation. The distinction between a term and a representation will therefore establish the relevant cause of action and will determine the remedies available to the innocent party.

Only statements that are deemed to be terms will form part of the contract. A breach of a term will entitle the innocent party to sue for breach of contract.

A representation does not form part of the contract and therefore the appropriate cause of action for the innocent party will generally be for misrepresentation.

The distinction between a term and representation is also discussed in relation to misrepresentation in (see p.198), but will also be discussed here as the first stage in our assessment of contractual terms.

. . . .

The "guiding factors" and "presumptions" in distinguishing a term from a representation

The courts distinguish between a term and a representation by looking *objectively* at the intention of the parties (**Heilbut Symons & Co v Buckleton** [1913] A.C. 30). This can be a difficult task so the courts have developed a number of "guiding factors" and "presumptions" to assist them with this distinction. If the court decides that the maker of the statement intended that statement to form part of the agreement then the court will treat that statement as a term of the contract.   **6-003**

There are four key guiding factors and presumptions to assist with the term/representation distinction.

1. Has the statement been reduced to writing?
2. Does one party have specialist skill or knowledge?
3. The importance placed upon the statement.
4. Has there been a lapse of time between the statement being made and the contract being formed?
5. Was there an invitation to verify the statement?

We shall consider each in turn.

HAS THE STATEMENT BEEN REDUCED TO WRITING?

6-004   If the relevant statement has been reduced to writing there will be greater presumption that it will form a term of the contract. What better evidence of the intention of the maker of the statement than it being contained in a written document? If this document is signed, the parties will find it very difficult to argue that they didn't intend the contents of that document to form part of their agreement (**L'Estrange v F Graucob Ltd** [1934] 2 K.B. 394).

THE "PAROL EVIDENCE" RULE

6-005   The parties may try to introduce oral evidence that the contents of the document do not reflect their true intentions at the time of entering into the agreement. The courts, however, will not be receptive to such claims. This is known as the "parol evidence" rule, which provides that where clear evidence of the parties' intentions is provided (such as a signed written document) then no further evidence in rebuttal should be accepted. The obligation imposed by, and the effect of, the parol evidence rule is therefore to ensure that the written document containing the parties' agreement is presented in a very clear and precise manner so that no oral evidence of their intentions is required (nor will it generally be accepted).

This does not mean that an oral statement can never form a term of the contract. It is quite possible for parties to enter into a legally binding oral agreement and there is no strict requirement that this agreement be reduced to writing. However, the fact that an agreement has been reduced to writing will be a guiding factor for the courts in ascertaining the intention of the parties in relation to the term/representation distinction.

DOES ONE PARTY HAVE SPECIALIST SKILL OR KNOWLEDGE?

6-006   If the party making a statement has specialist skill or knowledge and the other person relies upon this as a factor when entering into the contract, then the greater the presumption that such a statement will be a term of the contract.

In **Dick Bentley Productions Ltd v Harold Smith (Motors) Ltd** [1965] 1 W.L.R. 623, a car dealer stated that a car had done 20,000 miles. Relying upon this statement the plaintiff purchased the car for his wife. Almost immediately there were problems with the car and it was eventually discovered that the car had done nearer 100,000 miles. The plaintiff brought an action for breach of contract arguing that the statement as to the mileage was a term of the contract. The Court of Appeal held that, as the statement was made by a car dealer—a person with specialist knowledge of the motor industry who, as a result, was in a better position to find out the true mileage of the car—the statement regarding the mileage was indeed a term of the contract.

Compare this decision to that of **Oscar Chess v Williams** [1957] 1 W.L.R. 370 which is based on very similar facts. In **Oscar Chess**, a private seller described a car he had for sale as a "1948 Morris 10 saloon". In fact, it turned out to be a 1939 model and as a result was worth considerably less. The court held that the statement as to the car's age was a representation. The distinguishing factors here between **Oscar Chess** and **Dick Bentley** are that in **Oscar Chess** the private seller did not have any specialist skill or knowledge, nor was that relied upon by the purchaser. If anything, the purchasers in **Oscar Chess** (who were car dealers themselves) were in a better position than the private seller to discover the truth of the statement.

THE IMPORTANCE PLACED UPON THE STATEMENT

Here the court will look to the importance of the statement taking account of the position as far as both parties are concerned. First, the maker of the statement must have realised that the statement was important to the other party. For example, before the statement is made the other party could have expressly communicated such importance to the maker.

6-007

Further, the surrounding circumstances could also indicate the importance placed upon the statement. In **Bannerman v White** (1861) 10 C.B. N.S. 844, the seller of some hops stated to the purchaser that no sulphur had been used in their production (which was untrue). The statement regarding the use of sulphur was held to be a term given. If this statement had not been made then the purchaser would not have entered into the contract.

LAPSE OF TIME

As the key test is that of intention and the relative importance that is given to pre-contractual statements, the courts will also look to the timing of the statement. The greater the lapse of time between a statement being made and the contract being entered into, the greater the presumption that the statement will be a representation (**Routledge v McKay** [1954] 1 W.L.R. 615). The lapse of time between the statement being made and the final contract being formed gives the courts an indication of the true intention of the parties (and also the relative importance of that statement as an influential factor in entering into the contract).

6-008

INVITATION TO VERIFY THE STATEMENT

If the maker of the statement invites the other party to verify the truth of the statement, then this could provide evidence that the party did not intend the statement to form a term of contract. In **Ecay v Godfrey** (1947) 80 Ll. L. Rep. 286, the contract concerned the purchase of a motor boat. During the negotiations, the defendant said that the boat was in sea-going condition, but advised that the plaintiff should conduct their own independent survey to determine its overall condition. The plaintiff did not conduct a survey to verify the condition of the boat. After the sale, the plaintiff discovered that the boat was not in a sea-going condition and this dramatically affected the value of the boat. In a claim for breach of contract, the court held that the statement regarding the condition of the boat was not intended to form a term of the contract. The statement was held to be a representation. The purpose of the defendant's

6-009

request to have the boat surveyed was to avoid responsibility for his statement regarding the condition of the boat.

COLLATERAL CONTRACTS

6-010   The concept of a "collateral contract" has already briefly been explained in relation to auctions (see p.24). In the context of a "with reserve" auction it is established that there are in fact two contracts between the auctioneer and the bidder. The first contract relates to the sale of the lot. The bidder makes an offer that is accepted with the fall of the hammer. There will also be a separate collateral contract, between the auctioneer and the highest bidder. The auctioneer has an implied obligation under the contract to accept the highest bid and will be in breach of this contract if he refuses.

In some cases the courts may decide that a representation (so not a term of the contract) could give rise to a breach of a collateral contract. The use of collateral contracts in this situation was predominantly to avoid unjust conclusions. For example, the "parol evidence" rule meant that a party could not produce evidence to supplement or vary a written document. In the case of a partially written and partially oral agreement, the court can avoid the operation of the parol evidence rule by use of a collateral contract (**J Evans & Son (Portsmouth) Ltd v Andrea Merzario Ltd** [1976] 1 W.L.R. 1078). The written and the oral statements will be assessed separately. If the oral statement induced the other party to enter into the written document the court will allow evidence of the oral statement to be adduced if the terms of the written agreement are challenged.

Further, the use of a collateral contract may allow the courts to overcome the rules of privity of contract (**Shanklin Pier Ltd v Detel Products Ltd** [1951] 2 K.B. 854).

Incorporation of terms

6-011   Once a statement has been identified as a term the next requirement is that the term has been incorporated into the contract. If a term has been incorporated into the contract it will form part of the contract. Only a term that has been incorporated into the contract and forms a part of the contract will bind the parties.

There are three primary methods by which a term can be incorporated:

1.   by signature (**L'Estrange v Graucob** [1934] 2 K.B. 394);
2.   by notice (**Thompson v London, Midland and Scottish Railway Co** [1930] 1 K.B. 41); and
3.   by a previous course of dealings (**British Crane Hire Corp Ltd v Ipswich Plant Hire Ltd** [1975] Q.B. 303.)

These methods of incorporation are explained in more detail at p. 156 during the discussion of exclusion clauses.

. . . .

Is the term express or implied?

Express terms are not too problematic. As the name suggests, an "express" term will have been expressly communicated between the parties by words or in writing. There will be little doubt as to what the parties actually intended as there will usually be some record of what was agreed.   **6-012**

However, it is not always possible, or necessary, to expressly agree on all the terms of the contract. For example, think of purchasing an item from a shop. About the only term that will have been expressly agreed relates to the price. It is not necessary to thrash out all the details of the contract with the sales assistant (and it would be very time consuming if you did). Rather, the courts will automatically *insert* terms into the agreement (which in this scenario would be an example of a term implied by law under the Sale of Goods Act 1979). These are referred to as implied terms and even though such terms have not been expressly agreed between the parties, the courts will nevertheless insert such terms into the contract to reflect the *intentions* of the parties.

Terms can be implied into a contract in a number of ways:

1. terms implied in fact;
2. terms implied in law;
3. terms implied by custom.

TERMS IMPLIED IN FACT

The court will imply a term as a matter of fact in order to fill the gaps left by the parties and in order to make the contract workable. As a matter of fact the parties must have intended such terms to form part of their agreement but in the circumstances neither party thought it important to expressly agree these terms.   **6-013**

The courts have developed several methods and justifications for inserting such terms into the agreement. The most important of these are:

1. to give the contract "business efficacy";
2. the "officious bystander" test.

"BUSINESS EFFICACY"

The courts will imply a term into the contract to give the contract what is referred to as "business efficacy". In other words, they will imply a term into the contract in order to make it workable between the parties so as to reflect their commercial intent.   **6-014**

Such an approach was first adopted by the courts in **The Moorcock** (1889) L.R.14 P.D. 64. In this case the defendants undertook to repair the plaintiffs' ship. The ship was damaged during low tide when the ship hit the bottom of the river in the repair dock. The court implied a term into the contract that the defendants had undertaken to act with reasonable care in ensuring that the river bed was in a suitable condition so as not to damage the plaintiffs' ship. The court thought it necessary as a matter of fact to imply such a term. Of course, the defendants knew about the low tide, the condition and the risk of damage faced by the plaintiffs' ship. The plaintiffs knew of none of these facts. In order to make the contract workable based on what must have been the presumed intention of the parties, the court had to imply a term. Had the plaintiffs known about the risk of damage they would have insisted upon such a term in the contract.

THE "OFFICIOUS BYSTANDER" TEST

6-015   Another approach of the courts is to imply a term by applying the "officious bystander" test. This test is perhaps best understood by referring to the judgment of MacKinnon L.J. in **Shirlaw v Southern Foundries Ltd** [1939] 2 K.B. 206:

> "Prima facie that which in any contract is left to be implied is something so obvious that it goes without saying; so that, if, while the parties were making their bargain, an officious bystander were to suggest some express provision for it in their agreement, they would testily suppress him with a common 'Oh, of course!'"

Imagine that two parties were sitting at a table negotiating a contract. An officious bystander overhears their negotiations and asks whether they intended a certain term to form part of their agreement. If the response of both parties is "Of course", then the court will imply that term as a matter of fact. Such terms will only be implied on this basis if the clause is so obvious that it "goes without saying".

It is important to note the approach of the courts in relation to a term implied in fact. The courts adopt a very strict approach to such terms and will only imply a term in fact if it is *necessary* to the contract, either to give it "business efficacy" (**The Moorcock**) or to give effect to the intentions of the parties (**Shirlaw**).

. . . .

Terms implied by law

6-016   In our discussion of terms implied in fact we have seen that the surrounding circumstances and intentions of the parties are fundamental in determining whether to imply terms into the contract. The courts will also imply terms in law, but they will do so for quite different reasons.

Generally the courts are reluctant to regulate the agreement between the parties. However, when the court implies a term into the contract in law then the intention of the court is to do just that. In such cases the intervention of the court has the effect of displacing the actual intention of the parties and replacing it with a legal interpretation of their obligations. This may sound dramatic (and contrary to the principle of freedom of contract) but the courts are motivated by the need to prevent an abuse of obligations under the contract.

There are two ways in which a term will be implied in law:

1. a term implied in law by the court;
2. a term implied in law by statute.

A TERM IMPLIED IN LAW BY THE COURT

The leading case of **Liverpool City Council v Irwin** [1977] A.C. 239, illustrates why (and how) **6-017** the court will imply a term in law. This case concerned a tenancy agreement between the council and the tenants of a block of flats. The agreement was clear as to the obligations of the tenants but made no reference to the obligations of the council. The communal areas of the flats fell into disrepair and the tenants refused to pay their rent until the council made the necessary repairs. The council then sought to evict the tenants arguing that the tenancy agreement imposed no repairing obligation on the council.

In response, the tenants claimed that the council itself was in breach of the tenancy agreement in failing to maintain the block of flats. In order to establish whether this was the case, the House of Lords had to assess the terms of the tenancy agreement. In this case, the House of Lords implied a term into the contract that that council was "to take *reasonable* care to keep in reasonable repair and usability'" the communal areas of the flats.

It is interesting that such an innocuous word, "reasonable", generated so much debate surrounding the extent of the obligation imposed by the court and the reason *why* such a term was implied in law.

THE TENSION BETWEEN THE COURT OF APPEAL AND THE HOUSE OF LORDS

In the House of Lords in **Irwin**, Lord Wilberforce was of the opinion that a term should be **6-018** implied in law as a matter of necessity given the nature of a tenancy agreement. It was therefore necessary that the council had some obligations under the tenancy agreement and the term was implied in law to reflect this. However, Lord Denning in the Court of Appeal maintained that the appropriate test should be one of "reasonableness".

The distinction between a test of necessity and a test of reasonableness raises an interesting debate as to the appropriate test for implying a term in law and the appropriate test for implying a term in fact. Remember, a term will be implied in *fact* if it is *necessary*, taking into account the intentions of the parties and the surrounding circumstances. The tension between Denning in the Court of Appeal and Wilberforce in the House of Lords therefore raises a further issue. Was the term in **Irwin** implied in fact or in law?

Lord Wilberforce's argument in the House of Lords was that the test of *necessity* brought the implied term clearly within the realm of *law* and not of fact. While this obviously conflicts with the reasoning of Denning in the Court of Appeal, such reasoning is also consistent with the approach of Lord Cross in the House of Lords.

Lord Cross was of the opinion that the term was implied in law (agreeing with Lord Wilberforce); however, he explained this on the basis that it was *reasonable* given the nature of the contract between the parties. As the contract fell into a particular category (a tenancy agreement) it was *reasonable* to imply a term in *law* that was consistent with such contracts.

Over to you. . .

Analyse the approaches of Lord Wilberforce and Lord Fraser in relation to the use of implied terms. Which approach do you favour?

It seems whatever approach or test is adopted in relation to terms implied in fact or terms implied in law, the result is a deliberate intervention by the court to regulate the agreement. Given the reluctance of the court to do this, it is unfortunate that courts have failed to agree upon the precise reasoning for implying a term in law.

On many levels it seems that the reasoning of Lord Cross is more attractive. A solution would therefore be to establish a test that represents the *level of interference* of the court in relation to the contract.

On this basis it would be logical for the court to imply a term in *fact* when it is *necessary* in order for the contract to work or to give effect to the intentions of the parties. This is a high test and reflects that fact that the courts are effectively interfering with the *intentions* of the parties when formulating their agreement (something which the court is very reluctant to do).

In order to imply a term in *law*, it must therefore be *reasonable* given the nature of the contract. This is a lower test than that of *necessity* and represents the fact that the courts are intervening to regulate the type of contract in question (and not the intention of the parties).

Despite these arguments and the attraction of the reasoning of Lord Cross in **Irwin**, the authorities have tended to favour the reasoning of Lord Wilberforce. For example, in **Scally** v **Southern Health and Social Services Board** [1992] 1 A.C. 294, the test of *necessity* was applied when implying a term in law.

In view of this perhaps the time has come to clarify the interpretation of the word "necessity". The following interpretation takes account of the relevant arguments above, but is at best a "half-way house".

> Terms implied in fact: is it *necessary* to imply a term in *fact* in order to give effect to the intention of the parties?
> Terms implied in law: is it *necessary* to imply a term in law in relation to the particular *type* of contract?

Terms implied by statute

A term can also be implied by the operation of statute. Parliament has decided that in certain contracts terms should be automatically implied into the agreement despite the fact that they have not been expressly agreed between the parties. The most common examples are to be found in the area of consumer protection.

6-019

For example, the Sale of Goods Act 1979 will automatically imply terms into a contract for the sale of goods. These implied terms relate to title (s.12), description (s.13) and quality (s.14). Whether or not these terms have been expressly agreed (which will be unlikely in most cases) the court will automatically imply such important terms into the agreement—giving effect to the "statutory rights" of the parties.

It is also useful to note that the Supply of Goods and Services Act 1982 implies similar terms to in contracts for the *supply* of goods and services. This Act would therefore cover contracts where goods are leased (or hired) rather than where the goods pass under a contract of sale.

Implied terms by custom

Finally, it is possible that a term can be implied into a contract by custom. If both contracting parties are within the same trade or industry then the court may imply terms into the contract that are consistent with that trade custom. The justification for this approach is that when the parties are in the same industry and are of equal bargaining position then as a matter of habit, such terms should automatically be implied into the contract on the basis that both parties should be aware of them.

6-020

For example, in **British Crane Hire Corp Ltd v Ipswich Plant Hire Ltd** [1975] Q.B. 303, both parties were in the plant hire business and the court was prepared to imply a term into an oral agreement based on trade custom that the cost of recovering a crane (after it had sunk on marsh land) rested with the defendants.

What type of term?

6-021   The importance of identifying a statement as a term has been discussed above; most notably that a term will give the innocent party the right to pursue damages for breach of contract. However, not all terms are equal; some terms are more important than others.

Terms can be classified as:

1.   conditions;
2.   warranties; or
3.   innominate (or intermediate) terms.

As we will see, an innominate term is not really a separate classification of term at all. An innominate term is rather a name the court uses to describe a term that does not fall within the broad categories of a condition or a warranty at the point that the contract is formed. The court will decide whether the breach of an innominate term is a breach of a condition or a warranty at the time the term is breached.

Conditions

6-022   Conditions are at the top of the hierarchy of terms. A breach of a condition will bring the contract to an end and will give the innocent party the right to claim damages. In order to be classed as a condition the term must be of fundamental importance to the contract. A breach of a condition therefore goes to the root of the contract. For this reason a breach of a condition is usually referred to as a "repudiatory" breach. Such a breach will discharge the parties of their future obligations under the contract.

Warranties

6-023   Warranties are of less importance to the contract. For this reason a breach of warranty will not bring the contract to an end. A breach of warranty will simply allow the innocent party to claim damages for breach of contract; it will not discharge the parties of their obligations under the contract.

IDENTIFYING A TERM AS A CONDITION OR A WARRANTY

6-024   While a breach of a term will give the innocent party the right to claim damages, only a breach of condition will bring the contract to an end. For this reason it is important to understand how and why the courts distinguish between a condition and a warranty.

STATUTE IDENTIFIES A TERM AS A CONDITION OR A WARRANTY

As discussed above, terms can be implied by statute. In some cases the statute may contain **6-025** express guidance as to whether these terms are to be classed as conditions or warranties. If this is the case then there is little problem in identifying whether a term is a condition or a warranty. The courts will simply give effect to the intention of Parliament.

Examples of such guidance can be found in the Sale of Goods Act 1979:

1. s.12: An implied term as to title;
2. s.13: An implied term that goods must match their description;
3. s.14: An implied term that goods must be fit for purpose; and
4. s.15: An implied term that goods must be of satisfactory quality.

All these terms are expressly stated to be *conditions*.

However, s.12(5A) provides that an implied term that the goods shall be free from encumbrances and that the owner will enjoy quiet possession are both *warranties*.

THE PARTIES IDENTIFY THE TERM AS A CONDITION OR A WARRANTY

If statute does not provide guidance as to the classification of the term then the courts will **6-026** again look to the intention of the parties. If the parties describe a term as either a condition or a warranty or indicate the particular consequences of a breach, the courts can use such evidence in determining the intentions of the parties. However, simply because a party labels a term as either a condition or a warranty; the classification will not be conclusive.

In **L Schuler AG v Wickman Machine Tools Sales Ltd** [1974] A.C. 235, a contract giving Wickman the exclusive right to sell equipment on behalf of Schuler stated that "it shall be a condition of this agreement" that Wickman must make a minimum number of visits to particular customers. The House of Lords refused to accept this term as a "condition" and instead interpreted it as being a warranty. If the House of Lords had accepted the labelling of this term as a condition then if Wickman failed to make even one visit the contract would be brought to an end as a result of the breach. The House of Lords therefore looked at the importance of the term and the seriousness of the breach in deciding whether to classify a term as a condition or a warranty. To treat a single (and rather minor) breach as being a breach of condition would be excessive and unreasonable.

THE IMPORTANCE OF THE TERM TO THE CONTRACT

If neither statute nor the parties adequately identify a term as a condition or warranty then the **6-027** court must decide this issue. In doing so the court will look to a number of factors, but the focus of its assessment will be to identify the relative importance of the term to the contract as whole.

The more important the term the more likely that the court will treat it as a condition. If the term is of less importance the court is more likely to treat this term as a warranty.

In assessing the relative importance of the term to the contract it is useful to consider two key cases, **Poussard v Spiers** (1875–76) L.R. 1 Q.B.D. 410 and **Bettini v Gye** (1875–76) L.R. 1 Q.B.D 183. These cases are quite similar on their facts (both concern contracts to perform in theatre productions); however the decisions are quite different.

In **Poussard v Spiers** (1876) 1 Q.BD. 410, a singer was contracted to perform in an opera. Owing to illness the singer missed the first week of the production, including the opening night. The court held that the obligation to perform on the opening night was a *condition* of the contract. The producers could therefore treat her contract of employment as coming to an end.

The facts of **Bettini v Gye** are similar except that the singer failed to attend a number of rehearsals. The court held that the obligation in the contract to attend rehearsals was a *warranty*. This breach simply gave the producers the right to sue for damages to represent their loss (whatever that might have been on the facts).

Hopefully, it is easy to see that an obligation to perform on the opening night (on which the reputation of the production will be made or broken) was of greater importance to the contract than the obligation to attend rehearsals. However, these cases also illustrate the fine line that divides an assessment of the importance of the term from an assessment as to the consequences of the breach. If the courts are to identify a term as a condition or a warranty then generally this decision should be taken by looking at the situation at the time the contract was formed. This of course means that the courts cannot be certain as to the effect a breach may have on the contract.

For these reasons the courts have adopted an alternative approach to the classification of contractual terms, the classification of a term as "innominate".

Innominate terms

6-028   If there is no express guidance in statute or by the parties and there is uncertainty or difficulty in assessing the importance of the term at the time the contract is formed, then an option for the court is to treat the term as being "innominate".

An innominate term is sometimes referred to as an "intermediate" term. This is because an innominate term is classed as *neither* a condition *nor* a warranty at the time the contract is formed. Instead, the court will classify the term upon breach. If the breach is serious and has the effect of depriving the innocent party of a substantial part of their bargain, the court will treat this breach as a breach of condition. If the breach is less serious, the court will treat this as a breach of warranty.

It is perhaps useful to think of an innominate term as a "floating" term. The term is in limbo between a condition and a warranty and the court will only classify the term upon the event of breach. Once the contract has been breached the court can assess the seriousness and the consequences of the breach and then decide whether to treat this as a breach of condition or a breach of warranty. Given the difficulties in assessing these issues at the time the contract is formed a default position in some cases will be to treat the term as innominate.

EXAMPLE OF AN INNOMINATE TERM

It is quite difficult to describe an innominate term. The best way to recognise an innominate term is to see one. The case of **Hongkong Fir Shipping Co Ltd v Kawasaki Kisen Kaisha Ltd** [1962] 2 Q.B. 26, was the first case where an innominate term was recognised. This case concerned the lease of a ship and the contract provided that the ship should "be in every way fitted for ordinary cargo service". The heart of the obligation was therefore to ensure that the ship was "seaworthy". This term was breached when the owners of the ship failed to provide an adequate crew to maintain and repair the ship. As a result, the ship was only at sea for a fraction of the first six months of the contract. The defendants sought to treat this as a breach of condition that discharged them of future obligations under the contract. The Court of Appeal held that there was breach of *warranty* and the breach therefore did not release the defendants from the contract.

6-029

Of course, there are many ways in which a ship could be rendered "unseaworthy". Such matters could range from something very serious indeed (such as a hole in the bottom of the ship's hull) to something very minor (a nail missing from a timber of the ship). It is unlikely that the parties intended *every* breach to have the effect of terminating the agreement. This was the problem for the Court of Appeal. If the term were classed as a *condition* then *every* breach would bring the contract to an end (irrespective of how minor the breach). If the term were classed as a *warranty* then a breach would *never* bring the contract to an end (irrespective of how serious the breach).

The courts therefore adopt a retrospective (or a "suck it and see") approach to such terms. They first identify the consequences and the seriousness of the breach and then look back to the term to classify it as either a condition or a warranty.

The approach of the courts to innominate terms can be summarised as follows:

- If the effect of the breach is to deprive the innocent party of a substantial part of their bargain then the court is more likely to treat the breach as a breach of condition that will bring the contract to an end.
- If the effect of the breach is to deprive the innocent party of only part of their bargain then the court is more likely to treat the term as a warranty giving rise to an action for damages.

THE ADVANTAGES OF CLASSIFYING A TERM AS INNOMINATE

6-030   There are a number of obvious advantages to the recognition of an innominate term. There is obvious flexibility; the court is not rigidly bound to a classification of a term upon formation of the contract (in ignorance of the actual consequences of the breach). This flexibility also allows the court to take account of the reasons why a party may be seeking to terminate the agreement. For example, in **Cehave NV v Bremer Handelgesellschaft mbH, (The Hansa Nord)** [1976] Q.B. 44, the purchaser of some animal feed argued that there had been a breach of condition due to the fact that a small proportion of the feed was damaged. The real reason why the claimants sought to terminate the agreement was that there had been a significant fall in the market value of the goods; the goods themselves remained satisfactory for their intended purpose.

THE DISADVANTAGES OF CLASSIFYING A TERM AS INNOMINATE

6-031   One of the key disadvantages of classifying a term as innominate is that it creates uncertainty for the parties. As the decision to classify a breach as either a breach of a condition or a warranty is taken *at the time of breach*, it makes it very difficult for the parties to regulate their conduct. Generally, the parties will be aware of their obligations under the contract and the effect of a breach of these obligations at the time the contract is made. With this in mind the parties then regulate their conduct accordingly. They are aware of what conduct will terminate the agreement and what conduct will simply result in a claim for damages. This also allows the parties to explore methods of risk allocation before the breach occurs. One party could claim that the breach was so serious that it ought to be classified as a breach of condition. The other party may argue that it is simply a breach of warranty. This has important consequences for the innocent party.

For example, an innocent party may argue that the other party has acted so as to breach a *condition* of the contract. As a result, the innocent party regards himself as being discharged of his obligations under the contract. However, if the court classifies the breach as a breach of *warranty* then the innocent party may have unwittingly committed a repudiatory breach of contract. This is despite the fact that there was initially no fault on behalf of the innocent party. These rather bizarre circles of events highlight one of the most obvious disadvantages of the recognition of a term as innominate.

Summary

1.   It is fundamental to be able to distinguish a term from a representation. Only a term will form a part of the contract and create legal obligations. A representation does not form part of the contract so the claimant will have to pursue another remedy (such as an action for misrepresentation) if this statement turns out to be false.

2. In order for a term to bind the parties it must also be incorporated into the contract. A term can be incorporated by signature, reasonable notice or by a previous course of dealings.

3. A term can be either express or implied. A term can be implied by the courts as a matter of fact to give effect to the intention of the parties or as a matter of law. Statutory provisions can also have the effect of implying terms into the contract (see the Sale of Goods Act 1979, for example).

4. Further, a term can be classed as either a condition or a warranty. A condition is a fundamental condition of a contract. A breach of a condition will go to the root of the contract and will bring the contract to an end. The innocent party will also be able to claim damages for breach of contract. A warranty is of less importance and as such a breach of a warranty will only give the innocent party the right to claim damages.

5. The courts have also recognised a third type of term referred to as an innominate term. At the time the contract is made an innominate term is classed as neither a condition nor a warranty. The court will decide whether to treat a breach of an innominate term as a breach of condition or warranty depending on the *seriousness of the breach*.

Key Cases Grid

Case	Court	Key Issues
Heilbut Symons & Co v Buckleton [1913]	House of Lords	In distinguishing between a term and a representation, the court will apply an objective test, using available evidence of what was said and done, to determine the intentions of the parties.
The Moorcock (1889)	Court of Appeal	An example of when the courts will apply a term into a contract as a matter of fact in order to give the agreement "business efficacy".
Shirlaw v Southern Foundries Ltd [1939]	Court of Appeal	The court may apply a term into a contract as a matter of fact to give effect to the intention of the parties if the clause is so obvious that it "goes without saying". The "officious bystander" test.

British Crane Hire Corp Ltd v Ipswich Plant Hire Ltd [1975]	Court of Appeal	The court may imply a term into a by custom. When parties are in the same industry and are of equal bargaining position then as a matter of habit, such terms should automatically be implied into the contract on the basis that both parties should be aware of them.
Poussard v Spiers (1876)	Queen's Bench Division	In identifying a term of as either a condition or warranty the court will look the relative importance of the term to the contract as whole. The more important the term the more likely that the court will treat it as a condition. The court held that the obligation to perform on the opening night was a *condition* of the contract.
Hongkong Fir Shipping Co Ltd v Kawasaki Kisen Kaisha Ltd [1962]	Court of Appeal	This case recognised the possibility of a term being classified as "innominate". The court will determine whether a breach shall be considered a breach condition or warranty depending on the *seriousness of that breach*.

End of Chapter Question

Rodney is a travelling salesman and sells printing supplies to clients of Ink-Jet Ltd. Hs contract of employment with Ink-Jet Ltd states that: "It shall be a condition of this agreement that the employee is required to visit at least three clients per week for fifty weeks of the year". Due to illness Rodney only manages to see two clients per week during April. When Ink-Jet Ltd discovers this they seek to terminate Rodney's contract of employment.

Advise Rodney.

Points of Answer

♦ The requirement to make a minimum number of visits would seem to be a term of the contract. In failing to make the visits as contracted, Rodney is technically in breach of contract.

♦ However, is the requirement to make a minimum number of visits a condition of the contract or a warranty?

♦ The contract clearly labels the term as a condition, but this will not be conclusive.

The court will look to the importance of the term in relation to the contract as a whole. See the approach of the **House of Lords in Schuler v Wickman**. If the term is classed as a condition then a breach will bring the contract to an end. This would seem a harsh consequence of failing to make a small number of visits for one month of the year.

♦ Perhaps this term could be best described as being innominate. Following the approach in **Hong Kong Fir** the court may look to the seriousness of the breach to determine whether it should be classed as breach of condition or warranty.

♦ In the circumstances, the breach would seem quite minor. The courts may therefore classify the breach as being one of warranty and as such may award damages for the loss suffered, but it would not entitle Ink-Jet Ltd to terminate the contract of employment.

◄ ....

Further Reading

Bojczuk, W. "When is a condition not a condition?" J.B.L. 1987, Sep, 353– 362.
    This article analyses the legal principles as to when a term will be classified as a condition of the contract, with particular attention to were the parties themselves provide that a term shall be a condition of their agreement.

Stone, R. and Cunnington, R. *Text, Cases and Materials on Contract Law* (London: Routledge-Cavendish, 2014), Chapter 6.

Treitel, G. *The Law of Contract*, 13th edn (London Sweet & Maxwell, 2011), Chapter 6.

Exclusion Clauses

7

CHAPTER OVERVIEW

In this chapter we:

- discuss the limitations on freedom of contract in light of the development of exclusion clauses

- explain the common law requirements of incorporation in relation to exclusion clauses

- explain the common law rules of construction

- consider and analyse the legislative responses to the use of exclusion clauses; The Unfair Contract Terms Act 1977 and the Unfair Terms in Consumer Contracts Regulations 1999

- consider proposals for reform contained within the Consumer Rights Bill 2013-14

Summary

Key Cases Grid

End of Chapter Question

Further Reading

Introduction

7-001 It is quite common practice for a party to include a term in the contract that seeks either to exclude or to limit their liability for breach of contract. At first glance it may seem strange that the courts are willing to entertain the existence of such clauses, given that their effect is to exclude or limit the liability of one party that may be in breach of their contractual obligations. However, as a contract is based on the principles of consent, provided the parties freely agreed to enter into the agreement and have freely accepted the terms of that agreement then the courts will be very reluctant to interfere with their bargain.

Given the self-regulatory nature of contract law, the principles of freedom of contract would appear to dictate that a party can enter into a contract with anybody they wish and on any terms they see fit. Therefore, if a party freely agrees to be bound by a clause in a contract which seeks to exclude or limit the liability of the other party, then the courts will be reluctant to intervene and regulate the agreement.

However, there are instances in which the courts will intervene and regulate such clauses, particularly where these clauses are used to exploit the relative bargaining strength of the parties or where such clauses are included in the party's standard terms of business.

Common law and statutory responses to exclusion clauses

7-002 There is an inevitable tension between exclusion clauses and freedom of contract. On the one hand the courts are reluctant to interfere with a freely negotiated bargain, but on the other the courts will seek to prevent one party from abusing this freedom by exploiting a stronger bargaining position. For example, there is nothing objectionable per se in the use of exclusion clauses. On the contrary, such clauses provide an invaluable mechanism by which business can allocate risk. For example, if losses are incurred by breach of an obligation then it is necessary to determine where liability for these losses falls. The use of exclusion clauses is one process by which the risk of loss may be allocated. As a result, the parties will be aware of where the risk will lie for breach of an obligation before such losses are incurred and the parties may take out appropriate insurance provisions to reflect this allocation of risk.

However, while exclusion clauses have a perfectly legitimate role to play in the sphere of contractual obligations, there is always the potential that a party may abuse their position with the introduction of such clauses. To this extent exclusion clauses may act as a form of consumer oppression. It is only relatively recently that the judiciary and Parliament have responded to regulate the operation of such clauses in the light of these concerns.

Restrictions have therefore been placed upon the use of exclusion clauses by the judiciary and Parliament.

1. There has been judicial intervention in the process of clause construction and interpretation.
2. Parliament has intervened, in the form of the Unfair Contract Terms Act 1977 (UCTA) and the Unfair Terms in Consumer Contracts Regulations 1999 (SI 1999/2083) (implementing EC Directive 93/13 on unfair terms in consumer contracts).

A three-stage approach to exclusion clauses

There are essentially three stages, or hurdles, that an exclusion clause must overcome before it will be binding on the parties.   **7-003**

1. The clause must be incorporated into the contract.
2. The clause must pass the test of "construction".
3. The clause must satisfy the relevant statutory provisions of the Unfair Contract Terms Act 1977 or the Unfair Terms in Consumer Contracts Regulations 1999.

In analysing the validity of exclusion clauses we will look first to the common law rules relating to incorporation and construction (the first two stages) and will then consider the legislative responses (the third stage).

Common law

At common law, if a party wishes to rely upon an exclusion clause, he or she must establish two things: **7-004**

1. that the clause has been incorporated into the contract; and
2. that upon true construction of the clause, it covers both the breach and the resulting loss or damage.

If these two stages are satisfied, only then will it be necessary to consider the effects of the relevant legislation.

Stage 1: incorporation

7-005 This may sound a relatively simple step, but in order for a clause to be binding on the parties it must first have been incorporated into the contract. If the clause is not incorporated then it will not bind the parties and it will have essentially failed at the first hurdle.

There are three primary methods by which a clause can be incorporated:

1. signature;
2. notice; and
3. previous course of dealings.

These methods are illustrated in Figure 7.1.

FIGURE 7.1 Incorporation of an exclusion clause

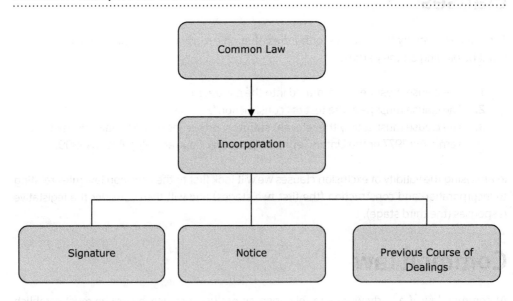

INCORPORATION BY SIGNATURE

This rule is applied quite strictly at common law; essentially, a party who signs a contractual document will be bound by the terms contained in the document. This is demonstrated in the case of **L'Estrange v F Graucob Ltd** [1934] 2 K.B. 394, in which the claimant took delivery of a defective cigarette vending machine. Upon delivery of the machine Mrs L'Estrange signed a sales agreement which, printed in very small (although just legible) print, contained a clause excluding liability for a defective product. When the claimant discovered the fault with the machine the defendants relied upon the clause in the sales agreement to absolve them of liability. The court held that the defendants could rely on the clause on the basis that Mrs L'Estrange's signature was unequivocal evidence of her assent to the terms of the agreement.

7-006

The fact that Mrs L'Estrange did not even read the document (so was unaware as to the existence of the clause) was not a relevant consideration for the court. As Scrutton L.J. commented:

> **"When a document containing contractual terms is signed, then in the absence of fraud or misrepresentation . . . the party signing it is bound, and it is wholly irrelevant whether he has read the document or not."**

This is a particularly harsh decision particularly in the light of the ordinary principles of offer and acceptance. If the agreement is to be viewed objectively, then it may seem quite unreasonable to hold a party to a contract that contains such onerous clauses as in **L'Estrange v Graucob**, where the party would have needed to go to great lengths in order to discover the existence of the clause because of the positioning and size of the print. However, in contrast, the decision in **L'Estrange v Graucob** does support the parol evidence rule, which states that a party should not be able to adduce oral evidence to challenge the content of a written document. In the court's opinion it would be undesirable to allow claimants to adduce evidence to contradict the substance of an agreement that they have freely entered into and signed.

There are situations, however, in which the courts will allow evidence to be adduced to challenge the validity of a signed document. This is particularly the case where the nature or content of the document has been misrepresented to the claimant. In **Curtis v Chemical Cleaning & Dyeing Co** [1951] 1 K.B. 805 the claimant took a dress to the defendants' shop to be cleaned. She was handed a slip of paper by the assistant headed "receipt", which she was asked to sign. When the claimant enquired as to the content of the "receipt" the assistant told the claimant that it excluded liability for specific damage, in particular damage to the beads and sequins with which her dress was trimmed. On the basis of this information the claimant signed the receipt.

In fact, the receipt contained a clause that sought to completely exclude liability for any type of loss or damage. When the dress was returned it had been stained and the claimant pursued an action for damages against the defendants. The Court of Appeal held that the defendants could not rely upon the exclusion clause as the claimant had been induced to sign the document by the assistant's innocent misrepresentation. In other words, because the assistant had created a false impression as to the content of the document, the defendants were not able to avail themselves of the relevant exclusion. As Denning L.J. observed:

> "By failing to draw attention to the width of the exemption clause, the assistant created the false impression that the exemption only related to the beads and sequins, and that it did not extend to the material of which the dress was made. It was done perfectly innocently, but nevertheless a false impression was created.

NOTICE

7-007 In the absence of a signature, notice will be the most common process of incorporating a clause into the contract. In fact, as there is no formal requirement that a contract be in a written form the ability to incorporate a term via notice will perhaps be of most relevance to everyday situations. For example, in **Parker v South East Railway Co** (1876–77) L.R. 2 C.P.D. 416, the claimant left his luggage at the defendants' cloakroom and was handed a ticket in return which contained written information. On the front of the ticket was printed the words "See back". On the back of the ticket it stated that the company would not be responsible for any item exceeding £10 in value. The same condition was also displayed in the cloakroom. The claimant's property (which was worth in excess of £10) was either lost or stolen and the claimant brought an action to recover the value of the lost property. The defendants denied liability on the basis of the exclusion clause.

The issue for the Court of Appeal was whether the defendants had taken sufficient steps to bring the clause to the attention of the claimant. In ordering a retrial the Court of Appeal made it clear that the defendants are only to take *reasonably sufficient* steps to bring the existence of the clause to the attention of the other party. As Mellish L.J. remarked:

> "The railway company must, however, take mankind as they find them, and if what they do is sufficient to inform people in general that the ticket contains conditions, I think that a particular plaintiff ought not to be in a better position than other persons on account of his exceptional ignorance or stupidity or carelessness. But if what the railway company do is not sufficient to convey to the minds of people in general that the ticket contains conditions, then they have received goods on deposit without obtaining the consent of the persons depositing them to the conditions limiting their liability.
>
> "I am of opinion, therefore, that the proper direction to leave to the jury in these cases is, that if the person receiving the ticket did not see or know that there was any writing on the ticket, he is not bound by the conditions; that if he knew there was writing, and knew or believed that the writing contained conditions, then he

is bound by the conditions; that if he knew there was writing on the ticket, but did not know or believe that the writing contained conditions, nevertheless he would be bound, if the delivering of the ticket to him in such a manner that he could see there was writing upon it, was, in the opinion of the jury, reasonable notice that the writing contained conditions."

There are a number of principles that we must now consider regarding the issue of notice.

1. Reasonable notice must be given as to the existence of the clause.
2. Reasonable notice must be given before or at the time the contract is made (but not after).

REASONABLE NOTICE MUST BE GIVEN AS TO THE EXISTENCE OF THE CLAUSE

Following the decision in **Parker v South East Railway** above it is clear that only reasonably sufficient notice, not actual notice, is required as to the existence of the clause. So, if reasonable steps are taken to draw the party's attention to the *existence* of the clause then whether that party is aware of the precise content is irrelevant. This principle is illustrated in the case of **Thompson v London Midland and Scottish Railway Co** [1930] 1 K.B. 41.

7-008

In **Thompson**, the claimant (who was illiterate) asked her niece to purchase a train ticket on her behalf. The ticket was for a special excursion fare and on the front of the ticket was printed "Excursion. For conditions see back". On the reverse of the ticket it stated that the ticket was issued "subject to the conditions in the defendant company's time tables and excursion bills". The timetable (which you had to purchase for sixpence) contained the following clause: "Excursion tickets . . . are issued subject to the general regulations and to the condition that the holders . . . shall have no rights of action against the company . . . in respect of . . . injury (fatal or otherwise) . . . however caused."

The claimant suffered personal injury when she stepped off the train at its destination, owing to the fact that the train was too long for the platform. The claimant brought an action for negligence against the train company as it should have warned her about disembarking from the train. Despite the rather elaborate scheme by which it was possible to view the conditions of the contract, the court nevertheless held that reasonable notice had been given as to the existence of the clause and as such the train company could rely on the clause in its defence.

Over to you. . .

Analyse the decision of the court in *Thompson v LMS Railway*. Can you think of relevant factors that were taken into account by the court in reaching the decision that the clause had been incorporated on the basis of reasonable notice?

The decision in **Thompson** may sound rather harsh given its particular facts (and incidentally, the judge over turned an earlier finding of the jury that the clause had not been incorporated), but the decision can again be linked to the relative principles of freedom of contract.

In **Thompson** even though the claimant was not actually aware of the relevant exclusion clause, there was (at least in theory) the possibility that Mrs Thompson (or someone on her behalf) could have enquired about the conditions under which the ticket was issued before deciding whether to contract. If she was not prepared to accept the relevant conditions then she could decide not to enter into the contract. However, if a party freely enters into a contract then the courts will be very reluctant to interfere with that agreement where there has been reasonable notice as to the existence of the clause. It is also important to note that the ticket purchased in Thompson was an "excursion" ticket. This was not a standard fare and was issued at a cheaper price. In the circumstances it would be reasonable to expect that such a ticket would be issued subject to more onerous restrictions.

REASONABLE NOTICE MUST BE GIVEN BEFORE OR AT THE TIME THE CONTRACT IS MADE (BUT NOT AFTER)

7-009 Not only must the party wishing to rely on the exclusion clause give reasonable notice as to the existence of the clause, but he must also give this notice before or at the time the contract is formed. The courts will not incorporate a term once the contract has been entered into. The timing of the notice is therefore vitally important in determining whether a clause has been validly incorporated.

In **Olley v Marlborough Court Ltd** [1949] 1 K.B. 532, a couple arrived at a hotel and paid for a week's accommodation in advance at the reception desk. They then proceeded to their room. In the room, behind the door, was displayed the following clause: "The proprietors will not hold themselves responsible for articles lost or stolen, unless handed to the manageress for safe custody. Valuables should be deposited for safe custody in a sealed package and a receipt obtained."

Owing to the negligence of the hotel, a stranger was able to obtain the key and stole a number of items from the couple's room (including some valuable fur coats). The Court of Appeal held that the clause excluding liability had not been incorporated into the contract. The contract had been made at the reception desk so as a result the notice displayed in the room came too late. The defendants could therefore not rely on the exclusion clause.

An interesting application of this principle can also be found in **Thornton v Shoe Lane Parking Ltd** [1971] 2 Q.B. 163. In this case Mr Thornton drove up to a ticket machine at an automated car park. The machine issued a ticket. On the front of the ticket it was stated that it was "issued subject to conditions". Mr Thornton took the ticket from the machine and proceeded inside the car park. There were several notices displayed next to the machine, one of which stated "cars parked at owner's risk". A further notice inside the car park stated that the owners of the car park would not be liable for personal injury suffered while on the premises. On returning to the car Mr Thornton suffered personal injury, which was as a result of the negligence of the owners. They sought to rely on the notices as excluding them from liability.

Lord Denning held that the contract was formed when the machine issued the ticket. As a result, the notice inside the car park came too late and again the clause was not validly incorporated. As to the notices displayed by the ticket machine, Lord Denning also held that given the unusual nature of the clause the notices were not sufficient to incorporate the clause. This reasoning can be understood by considering Denning's "red hand rule".

Over to you. . .

Contrast the decision in *Thornton* with that of *Thompson v LMS Railway*. In *Thornton* the court held that the contract was formed when the money was inserted into the ticket machine. The notice inside the car park therefore came too late. Surely, couldn't the same also be argued in Thompson; the contract in that case was formed when the ticket was purchased, so didn't the notice in the time-table also come too late? How can we reconcile these two cases?

UNUSUAL CLAUSES AND THE "RED HAND RULE"

The more unusual the clause or the more onerous in nature, the greater level of notice is required in order for the clause to be incorporated. In **J Spurling Ltd v Bradshaw** [1956] 1 W.L.R. 461 Denning L.J. suggested that some clauses:

7-010

> "would need to be printed in red ink on the face of the document with a red hand pointing to it before the notice could be held to be sufficient."

This is a suggestion that Lord Denning M.R. repeated in **Thornton v Shoe Lane Parking Ltd**, when interpreting a clause displayed on a sign outside a car park. We have already discussed the case of **Thornton** when assessing the requirement that notice must be given before the contract is formed. However, the Court of Appeal also had to decide whether a similar clause displayed before the contract was formed would be binding on the parties.

Lord Denning M.R. was of the opinion that the clause that sought to relieve the defendants from liability for personal injury suffered on the premises had not been validly incorporated into the contract. It was particularly unusual to exclude liability for personal injury in a contract for car parking. The unusual and onerous nature of the clause (onerous in that it excluded rights provided in statute by the Occupiers Liability Act 1957) required a greater level of notice to be given as to its existence and therefore was not incorporated into the contract.

NOTICE IN A CONTRACTUAL DOCUMENT

7-011   It is common that notice is given in a contractual document. If a party signs a document then he is generally bound by the terms contained within that document (**L'Estrange v Graucob**). However, there is a requirement that notice must be contained within a *contractual* document. Some documents, such as vouchers or receipts, may not be considered to be contractual documents for the purpose of incorporation. The courts apply an objective test to such documents. The key test is, would the reasonable man conclude that the document contained contractual terms and conditions?

In **Chapleton v Barry Urban DC** [1940] 1 K.B. 532, the plaintiff hired a deckchair from the defendant council. He was given a ticket which (among other things) stated the length of hire (three hours). The plaintiff put the ticket into his pocket without reading it. On the back of the ticket was printed the following clause: "The council will not be liable for any accident or damage arising from the hire of the chair". When the plaintiff sat on the deckchair the canvas gave way causing him to fall through the deckchair. The plaintiff sued the council for his personal injuries. The council sought to rely on the clause in the ticket as excluding it from liability.

The court held that the council could not rely on the clause to exclude it from liability as it had not been incorporated by a contractual document. The ticket was a mere voucher or receipt. It was not a document that the reasonable man would conclude contained contractual terms and conditions. The ticket may have been evidence of a contract, but it was not a contractual document itself. Therefore, reasonable notice had not been given as to the existence of the clause and the plaintiff could pursue his action for personal injury.

. . . .

Incorporation via a previous course of dealings

7-012   The court may be prepared to infer a clause based on the previous transactions between the parties. Even though there may not have been notice of the clause in the transaction in question, the court may still hold that the clause has been incorporated via a previous course of dealings between the parties. In other words, the party may not actually know about a clause in a particular transaction, but he is taken to know about its existence as notice of this clause has been given to him on his previous transactions.

There are, however, two requirements that must be met before the courts will infer a term based on a previous course of dealings:

1. There must be *sufficient* notice of the clause.
2. There must be *consistency* in the previous dealings.

THERE MUST BE *SUFFICIENT* NOTICE OF THE CLAUSE

In order to incorporate a term via a previous course of dealings there must have been a sufficient number of transactions between the parties. For example, in **Spurling v Bradshaw** [1956]
1 W.L.R. 461, the parties had previous dealings between them over many years. In this case the
defendant delivered eight barrels of orange juice to the plaintiff for storage. A few days later
the defendant received a "landing account" from the plaintiff (a confirmation that the goods
had been received). This document contained a clause excluding the plaintiffs from liability for
loss or damage to the goods. When the defendant went to collect the barrels he found that
they were either empty or so damaged that they were useless. When the defendant refused
to pay the storage charges the plaintiffs sued him for breach of contract. The defendant then
made a counterclaim arguing that the plaintiffs had been negligent.

The plaintiffs responded to the claim of negligence by relying on the exclusion clause in the
"landing account". This document had been sent to the defendant as part of the previous
transactions between the parties, but the defendant never read it. The court held that sufficient notice had been given of the clause based on their previous dealings. So, even though the
plaintiffs were found to have been negligent, they were protected by the clause in the landing
document which excluded them from liability.

Precisely *how many* transactions are required to incorporate a term via a previous course of
dealings is not entirely clear. In **Hollier v Rambler Motors (AMC) Ltd** [1972] 2 Q.B. 71, it was
held that "three or four occasions over the past five years" was not sufficient to incorporate a
term via a previous course of dealings.

THERE MUST BE *CONSISTENCY* IN THE PREVIOUS DEALINGS

If there is a course of dealings between the parties and they always contract in a particular way
but then depart from this in a particular transaction the courts may not incorporate the clause
on that occasion because of a lack of consistency in the transaction.

In **McCutcheon v David MacBrayne Ltd** [1964] 1 W.L.R. 125, the appellant entered into a contract with the respondent ferry company with which he had had previous dealings. The ferry
company agreed to ship the appellant's car from the Hebrides to the mainland. The appellant's
agent paid the shipping fee and was given a receipt of payment. The ferry sank because of the
negligence of the ferry company, completely destroying the appellant's car. When the appellant claimed damages for the value of the car the ferry company sought to rely on an exclusion
contained in their terms and conditions of carriage, to which the receipt made reference. The
appellant's agent did not read the receipt so was not aware of this fact. The terms and conditions of carriage also appeared on the walls of the ferry company's office.

In previous transactions between the parties the appellant had sometimes been asked to sign
a "risk note", which made reference to the exclusion. The agent was not asked to sign a "risk
note", on this occasion. The court held that the exclusion clause was not incorporated into the

contract. Even though there had been previous dealings between the parties, there was not a course of *consistent* dealings that would justify incorporating the clause.

Finally, it was held in **British Crane Hire Corp Ltd v Ipswich Plant Hire Ltd** [1975] Q.B. 303 that an oral contract between the parties contained an implied term that the contract would be subject to the standard terms of trade custom. There was a common understanding that standard terms of trade custom would apply to the contract despite the fact that the defendants never signed the document confirming this fact.

Stage 2: the clause must pass the test of "construction"

7-015   Once the clause is incorporated it must then pass the common law test of construction before the courts will give effect to the clause. When the courts "construe" a contractual term their intention is to give legal meaning to the ordinary words that are used. Sometimes the legal interpretation the courts arrive at bears little resemblance to the everyday meaning of such words. However, the tool of construction is used by the courts as a way of avoiding or limiting the strict effects of freedom of contract.

It may be that a party seeks to abuse their bargaining position and exclude liability for numerous types of loss or damage. The principle of freedom of contract would dictate that such exclusions are valid providing that the other party freely agreed to them. The courts have responded to such problems by developing strict rules of construction. These rules of construction can be seen as an underhand way of avoiding the unfairness that the principles of freedom of contract can produce

Lord Denning (in his last case) so dramatically stated in **George Mitchell (Chesterhall) Ltd v Finney Lock Seeds Ltd** [1983] QB 284:

> "Faced with this abuse of power—by the strong against the weak—by the use of small print conditions—the judges did what they could to put a curb upon it. They still had before them the idol, "freedom of contract". They still knelt down and worshipped it, but they concealed under their cloaks a secret weapon. They used it to stab the idol in the back. This weapon was called "the construction of the contract". They used it with great skill and ingenuity. They used it so as to depart from the natural meaning of the words of the exemption clause and to put upon them a strained and unnatural construction.

THE *CONTRA PROFERENTEM* RULE

7-016   The *contra proferentem* rule is the key method by which the courts will construe an exclusion clause. When the courts construe a clause *contra proferentem* they will interpret the clause *strictly* against the party wishing to rely on the clause. If there is any doubt or ambiguity in the phrases or the words used the courts will adopt an interpretation of that clause that is adverse to the party seeking to rely on it.

In **Houghton v Trafalgar Insurance Co Ltd** [1954] 1 Q.B. 247, a clause in an insurance contract sought to exclude liability for any accident when the car was carrying an "excessive load". The driver crashed his five-seater car when he was carrying six passengers. The insurance company refused to pay out on the policy as the vehicle was carrying an "excessive load" at the time of the accident. The court construed the clause *contra proferentem* and held that the phrase "excessive load" did not extend to passengers. If the insurance company had wished to exclude liability for accidents when carrying excessive *passengers* then it should have done so by the wording of its document.

There are two particular aspects of the *contra proferentem* rule that we will consider:

1. the *contra proferentem* rule and negligence;
2. the doctrine of fundamental breach:

FIGURE 7.2 **Overview of incorporation and construction**

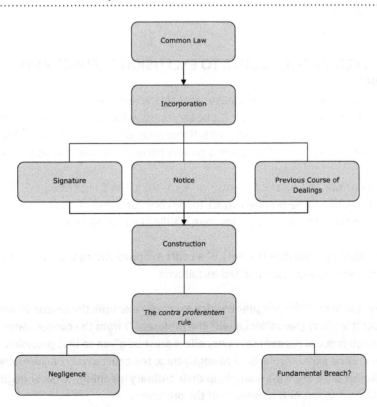

THE *CONTRA PROFERENTEM* RULE AND NEGLIGENCE

7-017 Although this book is obviously concerned with the law of contract, there are circumstances in which we will also have to consider other areas of law. The tort of negligence is particularly important in the context of exclusion clauses as it is very common for a party to try and exclude liability for both contractual (strict) liability and negligence liability.

THE DISTINCTION BETWEEN STRICT LIABILITY AND NEGLIGENCE LIABILITY

7-018 Contractual liability is said to be strict. In other words, the innocent party is not required to prove *fault* in order to bring an action for breach of contract. For example, in a contract for the sale of goods, if goods are delivered and they are not of satisfactory quality (in breach of a term implied under s.14 of the Sale of Goods Act 1979) then the innocent party does not need to prove that the seller was at fault breaching this term. The fact that the goods are not of satisfactory quality will be evidence of the breach and the seller will be strictly liable.

In contrast, liability in negligence requires the innocent party to prove fault. Negligence is a tortious action and is based on a failure by a party to meet a duty imposed by law to act *reasonably*. So, the innocent party will need to prove fault to bring an action for negligence; he will need to prove (on the balance of probabilities) that the defendant failed to conduct his actions with reasonable care and skill.

THE APPROACH OF THE COURTS TO EXCLUSION CLAUSES AND NEGLIGENCE

7-019 The courts adopt a strict approach to clauses that seek to exclude liability for negligence. One of the reasons for this approach is that it will be very unusual for a party to freely accept a clause exempting the other party from liability in negligence. Usually, these clauses will form part of a contract where an inequality of bargaining powers between the parties has been exploited.

Following the decision in **Canada Steamship Lines Ltd v The King** [1952] A.C. 192, it seems that the courts adopt a three-pronged attack to the construction of exclusion clauses that seek to exclude negligence. These three stages were clarified by Lord Morton:

> "Their Lordships think that the duty of a court in approaching the consideration of such clauses may be summarized as follows:
>
> 1. If the clause contains language which expressly exempts the person in whose favour it is made (hereafter called "the proferens") from the consequence of the negligence of his own servants, effect must be given to that provision.
> 2. If there is no express reference to negligence, the court must consider whether the words used are wide enough, in their ordinary meaning, to cover negligence on the part of the servants of the proferens.

3. **If the words used are wide enough for the above purpose, the court must then consider whether 'the head of damage may be based on some ground other than that of negligence'."**

We will now consider these three principles in more detail.

IF THE CLAUSE MAKES EXPRESS REFERENCE TO NEGLIGENCE

If the clause makes express reference to negligence the court will construct the clause as extending to negligence. However, as noted above, it is unusual in practice for there to be express mention of negligence in exclusion clauses. Unless there is an inequality of bargaining power a customer would be very reluctant indeed to accept such a clause.

7-020

IF THERE IS *NO* EXPRESS REFERENCE TO NEGLIGENCE

First, if the clause makes no express reference to negligence the court will have to decide whether the words used are *wide enough* to extend to negligence. Words that seek to exclude liability howsoever caused or "howsoever arising" may well be wide enough to cover both strict and negligence liability. Further clauses seeking to exclude "all liability whatsoever" would also be wide enough to extend to negligence. If the words used are not wide enough to extend to negligence then as a matter of construction the clause will not exclude such liability and it will be ineffective in relation to negligence liability.

7-021

Secondly, even if the words used are wide enough to extend to negligence, the type of restriction will be relevant in construing the clause. The courts adopt a more lenient approach to construction of clauses that seek merely to limit liability, rather than to exclude liability. This more lenient approach to limitation clauses was demonstrated in **Ailsa Craig Fishing Co Ltd v Malvern Fishing Co Ltd (The Strathallan)** [1983] 1 W.L.R. 964.

In this case the defendants agreed to provide security for boats moored in a harbour. Owing to the negligence of the defendants a boat belonging to the claimants sank and was totally destroyed. A clause in the contract sought to limit the liability of the defendants to £1,000. The claimants argued that this clause was ineffective as it only covered liability for the supply of services, but it did not apply when there had been a *total failure* to supply those services. This strict interpretation was rejected by the court. Upon a proper construction the clause did apply to the failure to provide services and was effective in limiting the defendants' liability to £1,000.

IS THERE LIABILITY OTHER THAN NEGLIGENCE?

Finally, when constructing clauses that seek to exclude liability for negligence, the courts distinguish between two situations:

7-022

1. where the *only basis* for liability is negligence;
2. where the party will be liable irrespective of negligence.

EXCLUSION OF NEGLIGENCE WHERE THE *ONLY BASIS* FOR LIABILITY IS NEGLIGENCE

7-023   If the only basis for liability is negligence then there is no need to make specific reference to negligence in the clause. In **Alderslade v Hendon Laundry Ltd** [1945] K.B. 189, the defendant laundry lost 10 linen handkerchiefs belonging to the claimant. The defendants sought to rely on a clause in the contract that limited their liability to 20 times the cost of laundering. The clause made no express mention of negligence.

The court held that the clause was effective in limiting the defendants' liability. In this case the defendants could only be liable as a result of negligence. Had the handkerchiefs been lost completely by accident, then the defendants would not be liable. However, in this case the defendants were only liable on the basis that they had failed to exercise reasonable care and skill when handling the claimant's property. As the only basis for liability was negligence the clause was constructed as applying to negligence even though there was no express reference to negligence in the clause.

However, even if the only basis of liability is in negligence, the words used in attempting to exclude liability must be clear and unambiguous. For example, in **Hollier v Rambler Motors**, it was held that a clause excluding liability for "damage caused by fire to customer's cars" was not effective as the words used did not make it clear that the garage would not be liable in the event of fire that was a result of its negligence. It is worth explaining this decision in a bit more detail to fully understand the reasoning of the court.

The facts of **Hollier** give a classic example of where the only basis of liability is negligence. Had a customer's car been damaged as a result of an *accidental* fire then the defendants would not have been liable for this damage—it was an accident and no liability would arise. However, if the fire was caused by the defendant's *negligence* then they would be liable for the loss caused. So, the only way in which the defendants would be liable is if they have been negligent. The clause on which the defendants sought to rely that they would not be liable for "damage caused by fire to customer's cars" was therefore ambiguous and circular. In other words, the clause was stating the obvious; it was simply telling customers that they will not be liable for loss or damage that was not their fault. The clause did not exclude liability for loss caused by fire as a result of their negligence and so the clause was ineffective and did not exclude the defendants' liability.

EXCLUSION OF NEGLIGENCE WHERE THE PARTY WILL BE LIABLE IRRESPECTIVE OF NEGLIGENCE

7-024   If there is a case of concurrent liability (where a party will be liable for both strict and negligence liability) then the court will construct the clause as extending *only* to the *non-negligence liability.* In **White v John Warwick & Co** [1953] 1 W.L.R. 1285, the plaintiff hired a bicycle from the defendants. When the plaintiff was riding the bicycle the saddle slipped, causing him personal injury. The defendants relied on a clause that stated: "Nothing in this agreement shall render the owners liable for any personal injury". The Court of Appeal held that the clause only extended to strict liability and would not cover liability as a result of the defendants' negligence in failing to adequately maintain the bicycle.

However, despite this strict approach, the courts again adopt a more flexible approach to clauses that seek to *limit* liability. For example, in **George Mitchell (Chesterhall) Ltd v Finney Lock Seeds Ltd** [1983] 2 A.C. 803, as the seller provided that he would replace or refund defective seeds the court was prepared to construct the relevant limitation as applying to both strict and negligence liability.

FUNDAMENTAL BREACH

The courts were hostile to clauses that sought to exclude liability for a breach of obligations   **7-025**
going to the root of the contract (a fundamental breach of contract). This hostility was particularly fierce before the enactment of the Unfair Contract Terms Act 1977, as the courts saw themselves as the last line of defence in relation to exclusion clauses and the tool of construction was their primary weapon.

For many years it was argued that there was a *rule of law* that prevented a party from excluding liability for a fundamental breach of contract. This approach was advocated by Denning L.J. in **Karsales (Harrow) v Wallis** [1956] 1 W.L.R. 936. Denning argued that a party who was guilty of a breach of obligations that went to the root of the contract cannot rely on any clause that seeks to exempt liability for the breach of those obligations.

Denning's reasoning was rejected (obiter) by the House of Lords in **Suisse Atlantique Société d'Armement SA v NV Rotterdamsche Kolen Centrale** [1967] 1 A.C. 361, but it was the decision in **Photo Production Ltd v Securicor Transport Ltd** [1980] A.C. 827 that was the final nail in the coffin for recognition of fundamental breach as a substantive rule of law.

If a party has been guilty of a breach of his obligations in a respect that goes to the very root of the contract, he cannot rely on the exempting clauses. In **Photo Production** the defendants were hired to secure a factory. One of the security guards lit a small fire to keep warm. This small fire developed into a bigger fire and eventually the whole factory was burnt to the ground. The defendants tried to rely on a clause that excluded them from liability in such cases. The House of Lords held that the clause was effective and reasonable in the circumstances.

The House of Lords made reference to relevant factors supporting this decision; the facts that the contract was between two businesses and that the price paid for the security services was very low indeed were relevant to whether the clause was effective. However, more importantly, the decision of the House of Lords makes it clear that the issue of fundamental breach is purely a matter of construction. It is not a rule of law that prevents a party from excluding liability in such cases; rather the courts will as a matter of construction decide whether the clause covers the liability in question. It could therefore be argued that the decision in **Photo Production** effectively closed the door to the courts refusing to enforce a clause on the grounds of a fundamental breach; what could be more fundamental than a security guard burning down the building he was hired to protect?

FIGURE 7.3 The three-stage approach to negligence following *Canada Steamship*

Stage	Yes	No
Stage 1 **Does the clause make express reference to negligence?**	**The clause will cover negligence**	**Go to Stage 2**
Stage 2 **Are the words wide enough to extend to negligence?**	**Go to Stage 3**	**The clause will be ineffective in relation to negligence**
Stage 3 **Is negligence the only basis of liability?**	**The clause will cover negligence**	**The clause will only extend to the *non-negligence* liability (unless the clause is a limitation clause—see *George Mitchell*)**

Stage 3: the clause must satisfy the relevant statutory provisions

Hear from the Author

Scan the QR Tag or follow the link below for an overview of the relevant statutory provisions.

uklawstudent.thomsonreuters.com/category/contract-fundamentals

7-026   The final hurdle the clause must overcome is that it must satisfy the relevant statutory provisions before it will be enforceable. There are a number of statutory provisions that govern exclusion clauses, but the two most important by far are:

1.   the Unfair Contract Terms Act 1977;
2.   the Unfair Terms in Consumer Contracts Regulations 1999.

Unfair Contract Terms Act 1977

Even though a clause has been validly incorporated into the contract and passed the relevant test of construction, the clause will still have to satisfy the provisions of the Unfair Contract Terms Act 1977 (hereafter, UCTA). It is somewhat misleading to think of UCTA as applying to "unfair contract terms" generally. In fact, UCTA is only concerned with exclusion or limitation clauses. Further, UCTA applies a test of *reasonableness* to such terms and is not truly concerned with whether such clauses are *fair* (but perhaps the title of an Act renamed the Unreasonable Exclusion and Limitations Clauses Act would not be quite as punchy).

7-027

OVERVIEW OF UCTA

The Unfair Contract Terms Act has two broad effects in relation to exclusion clauses. It renders some clauses automatically void, while others must pass the test of reasonableness.

7-028

The following is a list of the key sections that affect the validity of exclusion clauses:

- s.2: negligence liability;
- s.3: contractual liability;
- s.6: implied terms in contracts for the *sale* of goods and for hire purchase;
- s.7: implied terms in contracts for the *supply* of goods and services;
- s.8: terms excluding liability for misrepresentation; (this section will be considered further in Ch.8)
- s.11: the reasonableness test.

We shall consider these sections in more detail below, but initially we must define the scope of UCTA in relation to exclusion clauses.

The key to understanding the effect of UCTA (and exclusion clauses generally) is to first identify the type of liability in question. Firstly, the Act will only apply to "Business Liability" (s.3).

Once it has been established that the contract was formed in the "course of business", the precise type of liability needs to be identified.

Broadly, UCTA distinguishes between two types of liability:

(i)   Liability in negligence
(ii) Strict liability

Identifying the type of liability is fundamental to successfully navigating your way through the Act.

BUSINESS LIABILITY S.3

7-029 The majority of the sections in UCTA will only apply to business liability. The definition of "business" provided by s.14 is very wide indeed and includes, for example, professions and government departments. The key sections of UCTA will only apply if one party is dealing "in the course of business". However, the definition of "dealing as consumer" is also very wide and recognises both business-to-consumer contracts and business-to-business contracts. It is therefore possible for the business to deal as a consumer under UCTA.

"Dealing as consumer" is defined in s.12. This section provides that a party "deals as consumer" if he neither makes the contract "in the course of business" nor holds himself out as doing so. There are a number of important points that need to be made in relation to the definition provided in s.12. First, note that the definition of "deals as consumer" is expressed as a negative. If a party *does not* make the contract in the "course of business" then he *will* be *"dealing as consumer"*. Secondly, the phrase "deals as consumer" has been subsequently clarified by case law.

In **R&B Customs Brokers Co Ltd v United Dominions Trust Ltd** [1988] 1 W.L.R. 321, the plaintiffs (a freight and shipping company) purchased a car from the defendants for the use of the company director. The car developed a leaky roof and the company sought to reject the car and sue for breach of contract. The issue for the court was whether the plaintiffs were acting *in the course of business* or whether they were acting as *consumers* when they purchased the car. This distinction was important as the defendants sought to rely on a clause excluding them from liability for selling a product that was not of satisfactory quality. In other words, the defendants were trying to exclude a term that is implied under the Sale of Goods Act 1979. The ability to exclude this liability would depend on whether the plaintiffs were acting in the course of business or whether they were acting as consumers. Liability could not be excluded in relation to a consumer (see UCTA s.6).

The court held that the plaintiffs were acting as *consumers* and as such the defendants could not exclude their liability for selling a defective product. This is an interesting decision as it makes it clear that it is possible for a *business* to act as a *consumer* in some transactions. The Court of Appeal held that in order for a party to be *acting in the course of business* the transaction must have been "an integral part of that business". Applying this to the facts it is clear that the purchase of the car was *not* an integral part of the plaintiffs' business as a freight and shipping company. It was merely an *incidental* part of that business.

UCTA AND LIABILITY IN NEGLIGENCE

7-030 This is an aspect of contract law for which a basic appreciation of the law of tort is required. The basic elements of the tort of negligence require that:

1. the defendant owed the claimant a duty of care;
2. the defendant breached that duty; and
3. the breach of duty caused loss or damage to the claimant.

A party will breach their duty if they fail to act with reasonable care and skill. Therefore, in order to pursue an action for negligence the claimant is required to prove some fault on the part of the defendant.

If by a contractual term a party seeks to exclude liability for their negligence the term will have to satisfy the provisions of s.2 of UCTA.

NEGLIGENCE (S.2)

Once liability in negligence has been established it is then necessary to identify the type of loss that has been suffered. UCTA deploys a two-pronged attack in relation to negligence and distinguishes between two broad types of loss.

7-031

1. Section 2(1) applies where death or personal injury has been suffered as a result of negligence and states that liability for such loss *cannot* be excluded. Such clauses are therefore automatically void.
2. Section 2(2) applies to "other loss or damage" (loss or damage that is not death or personal injury) and states that such liability *can* be excluded but only insofar as the clause satisfies the test of *reasonableness*.

UCTA AND STRICT LIABILITY

A party may seek to exclude their strict contractual liability by use of an exclusion clause. The most common examples are when a seller or supplier of goods seeks to exclude their liability for breach of a term implied under the Sale of Goods Act 1979 or the Supply of Goods and Services Act 1982. This is referred to as strict liability as there is generally no need to establish fault in order to pursue legal action for breach of contract. For example, if defective goods are sold under a contract then the purchaser does not need to establish that the defect was due to the fault of the seller. The seller will be strictly liable for selling the defective goods (irrespective of fault). The ability of the party to limit their liability will depend on the distinction that UCTA draws between parties "dealing as consumer" and those dealing "otherwise" than as consumers.

7-032

CONTRACTS FOR THE SALE OF GOODS AND HIRE PURCHASE (S.6)

Section 6 of UCTA will apply when one party seeks to exclude their liability for breach of a term implied under the Sale of Goods Act 1979. A brief summary of these implied terms is found below:

7-033

FIGURE 7.4 **Summary of UCTA s.2 and liability for negligence**

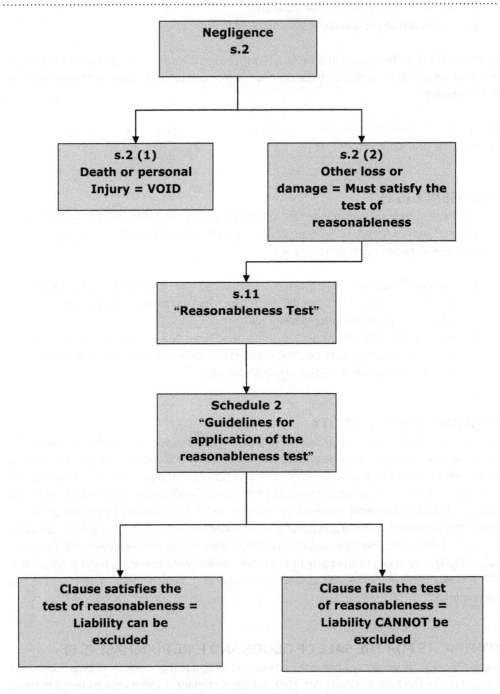

s.13: an implied term that goods must match their description;

s.14: an implied term that goods will be of satisfactory quality/fit for purpose;

s.15: an implied term when goods are sold by sample that the goods delivered will correspond with the sample.

THE ABILITY TO EXCLUDE LIABILITY UNDER S.6

The key to s.6 is to identify whether the party is "dealing as consumer".   **7-034**

> Under s.6(2) liability *cannot* be excluded for breach of implied terms as against a *consumer*.
> Unders.6(3) liability *can* be excluded as against a party dealing "otherwise than as consumer", providing the clause passes the test of *reasonableness*.

"DEALING AS CONSUMER"

As noted above, under s.12 a party will be "dealing as consumer" if he neither makes the con-   **7-035**
tract "in the course of business" nor holds himself out as doing so.

"IN THE COURSE OF BUSINESS"

The phrase "in the course of business" was interpreted in **R&B Customs Brokers Co Ltd v**   **7-036**
United Dominions Trust Ltd to mean that the transaction must be an *integral* part of that
business.

- If the transition was an integral part of the business it means that the party will be dealing "otherwise" than as a consumer and liability *can* be excluded for breach of an implied term insofar as it satisfies the test of reasonableness (s.6(3)).
- If the transaction was an incidental part of that business it means that the party will be dealing as a consumer and liability cannot be excluded for breach of an implied term above (s.6(2)).

THE ABILITY TO EXCLUDE LIABILITY UNDER S.7

Section 7 provides similar provisions to s.6 expect that s.7 applies to contracts for the supply   **7-037**
of goods and services. If goods are *sold* under a contract then s.6 will apply to that contract.
If goods are *supplied* under the contract and no title passes in those goods then s.7 will apply.
An application of s.7 may produce a similar result to the provisions of s.6, but UCTA draws a
distinction between these two broad types of contracts so technically it is necessary to follow a
slightly different route through UCTA.

- Under s.7(2) liability *cannot* be excluded for breach of the implied terms as against a *consumer*.
- Under s.7(3) liability *can* be excluded as against a party dealing otherwise than as a consumer, providing the clause passes the test of *reasonableness*.

FIGURE 7.5 **Summary of strict liability under UCTA s.6 and s.7**

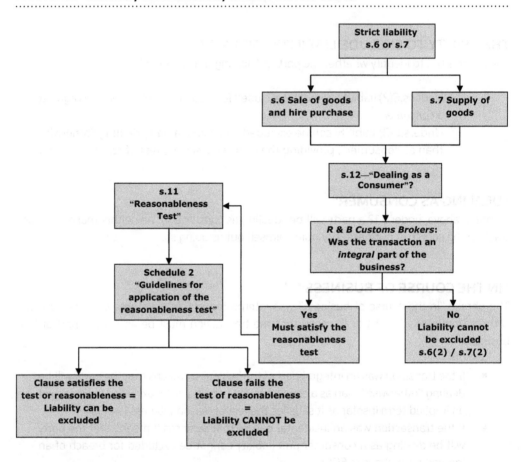

"THE REASONABLENESS TEST" (S.11)

7-038   If a clause is required to pass the test of reasonableness then the next stage is to consider s.11(1) of UCTA, which provides further guidance as to the elements of the reasonableness test. However, only a brief reading of this subsection will reveal a rather circular and unhelpful definition:

> "In relation to a contract term, the requirement of reasonableness for the purposes of this Part of this Act . . . is that the term shall have been a fair and reasonable one to be included having regard to the circumstances which were, or ought reasonably to have been, known to or in the contemplation of the parties when the contract was made."

Essentially this provides that a term shall be reasonable if it was reasonable in the circumstances (as students are often told, using the term you are defining as part of the definition is never good practice). That aside, there are some notable elements from this test that need to be considered. However, there are a few important aspects to note about the definition. First, s.11(5) makes it clear that the burden of proof in relation to the issue of reasonableness falls on the party seeking to rely on the clause. Secondly, s.11(2) also makes reference to Sch.2 to the Act which provides a number of "guidelines" for the application of the reasonableness test. Although these "guidelines" in Sch.2 are technically confined to an exclusion of liability under s.6 or s.7, the court will generally have regard to these guidelines when considering the issue of reasonableness (**Overseas Medical Supplies Ltd v Orient Transport Services Ltd** [1999] 2 Lloyd's Rep. 273). Finally, if the clause fails the test of reasonableness then the entire clause will fail. The courts will not sever the objectionable parts from the clause.

LIMITATION CLAUSES AND THE REASONABLENESS TEST (S.11(4))

In the same way that the courts adopt a more lenient approach to their construction of limitation clauses, s.11(4) of UCTA also provides more flexibility in respect of such clauses when applying the test of reasonableness.

7-039

In particular, the court should have regard to the following:

> (a)   the resources which he could expect to be available to him for the purpose of meeting the liability should it arise; and
> (b)   how far it was open to him to cover himself by insurance.

If a private individual is contracting with a large multinational company, for example, it is likely that the company would have the greater resources available to meet the liability in question. Further, the company may have also been able to guard against such loss by taking out insurance at minimal cost. If this is the case then the company may have more difficulty in arguing that the clause is reasonable in the circumstances. Of course, the converse reasoning applies. If the claimant could have taken out an increased level of insurance at minimal cost, then the balance may fall in favour of the defendant.

"GUIDELINES" FOR APPLICATION OF THE REASONABLENESS TEST (SCH.2)

In addition to s.11, Sch.2 to UCTA provides further guidance as to the application of the reasonableness test. Schedule 2 provides that when considering the issue of reasonableness, the court shall have regard to the following "guidelines":

7-040

(a) the strength of the bargaining positions of the parties relative to each other, taking into account (among other things) alternative means by which the customer's requirements could have been met;

(b) whether the customer received an inducement to agree to the term, or in accepting it had an opportunity of entering into a similar contract with other persons, but without having to accept a similar term;

(c) whether the customer knew or ought reasonably to have known of the existence and extent of the term (having regard, among other things, to any custom of the trade and any previous course of dealing between the parties);

(d) where the term excludes or restricts any relevant liability if some condition is not complied with, whether it was reasonable at the time of the contract to expect that compliance with that condition would be practicable;

(e) whether the goods were manufactured, processed or adapted to the special order of the customer.

REASONABLENESS AT COMMON LAW

7-041 The courts assess the issue of reasonableness by taking account of all the surrounding circumstances. The courts are not bound by the strict guidance under UCTA and can take into account different factors depending upon the nature of the transaction. For example, the court may look to particular trade custom or practice in deciding this issue of reasonableness. In **George Mitchell (Chesterhall) Ltd v Finney Lock Seeds Ltd** [1983] 2 A.C. 803, the defendants entered into a contract to supply cabbage seeds to the plaintiffs. The seeds were delivered to the plaintiffs along with an invoice. The invoice contained a clause that limited the defendant's liability to the contract price or to the price of replacing the seeds. The defendants delivered the wrong seeds and as a result the cabbages failed to grow properly and the whole crop had to be ploughed over. The price of the seeds was £201.60. The loss to the plaintiffs was over £61,000. The House of Lords held that the clause limiting the defendant's liability was unreasonable.

It is important to note that this case was decided before UCTA came into force. However, the court had to consider the issue of reasonableness under s.55(3) of the Sale of Goods Act 1979, which provides for a test very similar to the reasonableness test in s.11 of UCTA. There are a number of reasons why the clause was unreasonable. First, it was trade practice that suppliers of seeds would make voluntary payments in the case of defective seeds. These payments were evidence of the fact that to limit liability in this case was unreasonable. Secondly, the sellers could have insured against such risks without passing a significant increase in the price on to the consumer. In all the circumstances the clause was unreasonable.

A more recent interpretation of the reasonableness test can be found in **Watford Electronics Ltd v Sanderson CFL Ltd** [2001] EWCA Civ 317. In this case the defendants contracted to supply a software package to the claimant. The contract contained many different clauses that sought to limit the defendant's liability for loss that might arise under the contract. The software was defective and the claimants sued for their consequential loss (which ran into millions of pounds). The court held that the clause was reasonable in the circumstances.

An influential factor in this decision was that the agreement was between two large companies that were of equal bargaining position. In these cases the courts are going to be very reluctant to interfere with a freely negotiated agreement between the parties.

FIGURE 7.6 **Overview of UCTA**

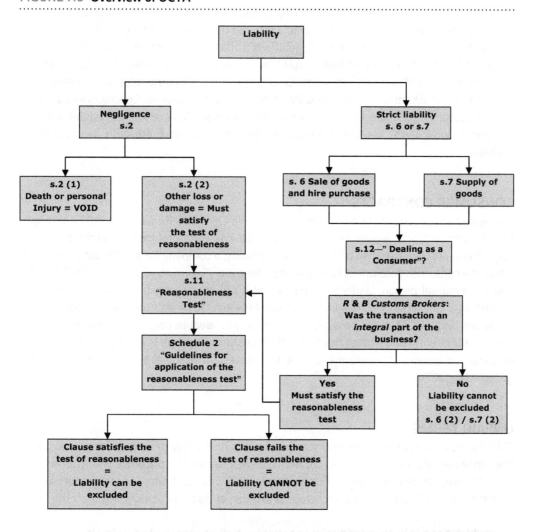

In consumer contracts the courts will be stricter in their assessment of the reasonableness test, especially when there is a clear inequality in the bargaining position of the parties. This was the case in **Smith v Eric S Bush** [1990] 1 A.C. 831, in which the court held that a clause in a mortgage application document that attempted to exclude the liability of the building society for inaccurate information provided by its surveyor did not satisfy the requirement of reasonableness.

The Unfair Terms in Consumer Contracts Regulations 1999

7-042   The Unfair Terms in Consumer Contracts Regulations 1999 implement the European Directive 93/13 on unfair terms in consumer contracts into our domestic legal system. Perhaps one of the most controversial aspects of the Regulations is that they did not amend or repeal UCTA. Instead, they provide an *additional* set of rules. In the UK we therefore have three bodies of law that now govern "unfair terms": the common law principles of incorporation and construction, the Unfair Contract Terms Act 1977 and the Unfair Terms in Consumer Contracts Regulations 1999. Unsurprisingly, there are obvious overlaps between UCTA and the Regulations and potentially unfair terms are at present subject to one *or both* of these quite separate legal regimes.

CONSUMER CONTRACTS

7-043   As the name suggests, the Unfair Terms in Consumer Contracts Regulations 1999 only apply to consumer contracts. A consumer is defined in reg.3 as a "natural person". In this sense the Regulations are narrower than UCTA. Most importantly, a company will not fall within the definition of a consumer. A company is a separate *legal* entity (**Salomon v Salomon** [1897] A.C.22) and not a natural person. Under the Regulations it will not be possible for a company to be dealing as a consumer. This is a key difference between UCTA and the Regulations. As you will recall, under UCTA it was possible for a company to "deal as consumer" if the transaction was not an "integral part of their business" (R&B Customs Brokers); the Regulations, however, only apply to business-to-consumer contracts. Business-to-business transactions will still be governed by UCTA.

UNFAIR TERMS

7-044   The Unfair Terms in Consumer Contracts Regulations 1999 apply to unfair terms generally. In this sense they are much wider than UCTA, which was really only concerned with clauses that sought to exclude or limit liability. Further, while UCTA imposed a test of reasonableness on such clauses, the Regulations subject clauses to a test of "fairness". Under reg.5 a term:

> **"which has not been individually negotiated shall be regarded as unfair if, contrary to the requirement of good faith, it causes a significant imbalance in the parties' rights and obligations arising under the contract, to the detriment of the consumer."**

THE REQUIREMENT OF "GOOD FAITH"

It is interesting that the Regulations subject a term to the test of "good faith". This aspect of the **7-045** Regulations reflects their European heritage, as the concept of "good faith" is something quite foreign to English lawyers (and most common law jurisdictions). The UK courts are quite happy to interpret and apply the concept of "reasonableness"; this is a concept that is familiar to almost all branches of domestic law. The concept of "good faith" is quite different. As Bingham L.J. observed in **Interfoto Picture Library Ltd v Stiletto Visual Programmes Ltd** [1989] Q.B. 433, the concept of good faith is altogether much wider than the requirement of reasonableness and can be difficult to pin down:

> **"In many civil law systems, and perhaps in most legal systems outside the common law world, the law of obligations recognises and enforces an overriding principle that in making and carrying out contracts parties should act in good faith. This does not simply mean that they should not deceive each other, a principle which any legal system must recognise; its effect is perhaps most aptly conveyed by such metaphorical colloquialisms as 'playing fair', 'coming clean' or 'putting one's cards face upwards on the table'. It is in essence a principle of fair and open dealing".**

Regulation 6 provides further guidance as to the requirement of "good faith" requiring that the term shall be assessed by: "taking" into account the nature of the goods or services for which the contract was concluded and by referring, at the time of conclusion of the contract, to all the circumstances attending the conclusion of the contract . . .".

Further, the Regulations also have guidance for the test of good faith in their very own Sch.2, which is very similar to the guidelines provided by Sch.2 to UCTA. This is interesting as two such similar tests, "good faith" and "reasonableness", are interpreted applying very similar criteria. Again, this gives rise to potential confusion as to the precise boundaries of these two separate legislative regimes.

The first case (and one of the few cases) to consider the application of the Regulations was the case of **Director General of Fair Trading v First National Bank Plc** [2000] Q.B. 672 (although this case actually concerned the 1994 version of the Regulations). This case concerned a specific term in a loan agreement that required interest to be paid on the debt despite the fact that judgment may have already been entered against the debtor. The Director General of Fair Trading applied to the court for an injunction to prevent the continued use of this clause.

The interesting aspect of this case is the manner in which the requirement of "good faith" was interpreted by the House of Lords. Its interpretation was focused on whether the clause caused a "significant imbalance" in the rights and obligations of the parties under the contract. On this analysis the clause was not "unfair" within the boundaries of the Regulations.

ENFORCEMENT OF THE REGULATIONS

7-046   Clauses that fall to be considered under the Regulations are referred to the Office of the Director General of Fair Trading. The Regulations therefore provide a public law remedy to a private law issue as it is the Office of Fair Trading that will ultimately decide whether a clause will be enforceable under the Regulations.

CORE TERMS

7-047   Under reg.6, core terms are excluded from the scrutiny of the Regulations. A core term is one that defines the subject matter of the contract. Such terms cannot be challenged under the Regulations, although the courts have faced difficulties in being able to identify these core terms. For example, it was argued that the clause in **Director General of Fair Trading v First National Bank** (above) was a core term (within the meaning of reg.6 and reg.3(2) of the 1994 Regulations) and as such could not be challenged on the grounds that it was unfair. The House of Lords held that the clause was not a core term and made it clear that the courts should adopt a cautious approach to such clauses as otherwise the breadth and application of the Regulations would be severely restricted.

Consumer Rights Bill 2013-14

7-048   This area of law is currently undergoing a significant period of review with proposals for reform contained within the Consumer Rights Bill 2013–14, the provisions of which are expected to become law during the 2014–15 Parliamentary session. At the time of writing, the Bill has completed its Committee Stage in the House of Commons.

The Consumer Rights Bill will impact on various aspects of Contract and Commercial Law, but this chapter is primarily concerned with the law relating to "Unfair Terms". The purpose of the Bill in this respect is to consolidate key consumer rights covering unfair terms in consumer contracts in one piece of legislation.

At present, the law relating to unfair terms is to be found in two separate pieces of legislation, the Unfair Contract Terms Act 1977 and the Unfair Terms in Consumer Contracts Regulations 1999.

The Unfair Contract Terms Act 1977 applies generally to the use of exclusion or limitation clauses and operates so as to render some clauses void and to subject others to a test of "reasonableness".

In contrast, the Unfair Terms in Consumer Contracts Regulations 1999 are concerned with the use of unfair terms generally (those terms that have not been individually negotiated), but are narrower in that they only apply to "consumer" contacts.

The Unfair Terms in Consumer Contracts Regulations 1999 did not repeal the Unfair Contract Terms Act 1977 and as such they provided an additional set of rules that regulated the use of unfair terms. For these reasons, the law relating to the control of unfair terms has been the focus of much review.

A report of the Law Commission report in 2005 highlighted that the two separate pieces of legislation have inconsistent and overlapping principles and as such further reform in this area was needed to simplify the current law. (http://lawcommision.justice.gov.uk/consultations/unfair_consumer_contracts.htm)

In 2012, the Law Commission again reviewed the existing legislation on unfair terms. The proposals are now reflected in the Consumer Rights Bill 2013-14.

Once (and if) in force, the subsequent Consumer Rights Act will repeal the Unfair Terms in Consumer Contracts Regulations 1999 completely.

The Unfair Contract Terms Act 1977 will be covered by the provisions of the new Consumer Rights Act, once (and if) in force.

....

FIGURE 7.7 **Application of Legislative Provisions in light of the Consumer Rights Bill 2013**

....

Contract	Legislative Provision
Contract between a "Trader" and a "Consumer" (a "consumer contract").	Consumer Rights Bill 2013
Contract between a Business and a Business	Unfair Contract Terms Act 1977
Contract between a Consumer and a Consumer	Unfair Contract Terms Act 1977

Overview of the Consumer Rights Bill 2013-14

7-049 Part 2 of the Bill concerns the use of unfair terms and seeks to clarify and consolidate the existing consumer legislation on unfair terms.

CONTRACTS AND NOTICES COVERED BY THE BILL – S.61

7-050 The provisions of the Bill will apply to **contracts** between a "trader" and a "consumer" (referred to as "consumer contracts" for the purposes of the Bill).

In addition, the provisions of the Bill will also apply to consumer **notices**. A consumer notice includes an announcement, whether or not in writing, and any other communication or purported communication, s.61(8), as long as it is reasonable to assume is intended to be read by a consumer, s.61(6). The explanatory notes to the Bill provide the example of a sign in a car park as such a consumer notice.

DEFINITION OF A "TRADER" AND A "CONSUMER" – S.2

7-051 A "trader" is defined by s.2(2) as "a person acting for purposes relating to that person's trade, business, craft or profession, whether acting personally or through another person acting in the trader's name or on the trader's behalf."

A "person" will include natural and legal persons. A registered company with separate legal personality (a legal person following the decision in **Salomon v Salomon** [1897] A.C.22) would therefore be a "person" for the purposes of the legislation.

A "consumer" is defined by s.2(3) as an individual acting for purposes that are wholly or mainly outside that individual's trade, business, craft or profession.

The definitions provided above mark a significant departure from those used under the Unfair Contract Term Act 1977. As the law stands, s.12 of the Unfair Contract Terms Act 1977 defines "dealing as a consumer" as a party that neither makes the contract "in the course of business" nor holds himself out as doing so. The phrase "in the course of business" was interpreted in light of the decision in **R&B Customs Brokers Co Ltd v United Dominions Trust Ltd** [1988] 1 W.L.R. 321, that required the transaction to be an "integral part of that business" in order for a party to be dealing "in the course of business."

The explanatory notes to the Bill provide a basic example of how the new definition of a consumer may apply to a particular scenario:

"The other main restriction on who is a consumer is that a consumer must be acting wholly or mainly outside their trade, business, craft or profession. This means, for example, that a person who works from home one day a week who buys a kettle and uses it on the days when working from home would still be a consumer.

Conversely, a sole trader that operates from a private dwelling who buys a printer of which 95% of the use is for the purposes of the business, is not likely to be held to be a consumer (and therefore the rights in this Part will not protect that sole trader but they would have to look to other legislation. For example, if the sole trader were buying goods, they would have to look to the SGA for protections about the quality of the goods)."

REQUIREMENT FOR CONTRACT TERMS AND NOTICES TO BE FAIR - S.62

An unfair term of a consumer contract (s.61 (1)) or an unfair consumer notice s.61(2)) is not binding on the consumer. The fact that the clause or notice is not binding on the consumer does not prevent the consumer from relying on the term or notice, s.62 (3). **7-052**

A term is unfair if, contrary to the requirement of good faith, if it causes a significant imbalance in the parties' rights and obligations under the contract to the detriment of the consumer, s.62 (4).

The same test applies to consumer notices, s.62 (6).

This test of "fairness" replicates that of reg. 5 of the Unfair Terms in Consumer Contracts Regulations 1999.

s.62 (5): Whether a **term** is fair is to be determined:

   (a) taking into account the nature of the subject matter of the contract, and
   (b) by reference to all the circumstances existing when the term was agreed and to all of the other terms of the contract or of any other contract on which it depends.

s,62 (7): Whether a **notice** is fair is to be determined:

   (a) taking into account the nature of the subject matter of the notice, and
   (b) by reference to all the circumstances existing when the rights or obligations to which it relates arose and to the terms of any other contract on which it depends.

CONTRACT TERMS WHICH MAY OR MUST BE REGARDED AS UNFAIR - S.63

7-053 This section makes reference to Schedule 2, which provides a "grey list" of terms which **may** be regarded as unfair. It should be noted that the list in Schedule 2 is not exhaustive and appearing on the list does not automatically render the term unfair. Rather, the list is to be used to assist the court when considering the application of the "fairness test" in s.62.

The content of Part 1 Schedule 2 of the Bill broadly reflects that of Schedule 2 of the Unfair Terms in Consumer Contracts Regulations 1999. Therefore, a term which has the effect of excluding or limiting a trader's liability in the event of the death or personal injury of the consumer may be regarded as unfair (Paragraph 1). Although, please note that this does not include a term that will be ineffective due to the operation of s.65, exclusion of liability for negligence (below).

However, the Consumer Rights Bill introduces three additional terms that may be regarded as unfair:

Paragraph 5 – A term that requires a consumer to pay a disproportionate amount if they decide not to continue with the contract may be regarded as unfair.

Paragraph 12 – A term that allows permits a trader to determine the subject matter of the contract after the contract has been agreed with the consumer may be regarded as unfair.

Paragraph 14 – A term that permits a trader to determine the prince under a contract, or a way to determine the price, after the contract has been formed may be regarded as unfair.

Finally, s.63 (6) provides that a term **must** be regarded as unfair if it has the effect of placing the burden of proof on the claimant in relation to compliance by a distance supplier with an obligation arising under the implementation of the Distance Marketing Directive 2002/65/EC.

EXCLUSION FROM ASSESSMENT OF FAIRNESS – S.64

7-054 This section provides certain terms that will be exempt from an assessment of fairness as stated in s.62. A term may not be assessed for fairness if it relates to:

- The main subject matter of the contract; or
- The appropriateness of the price

This exclusion will only apply if the term is "transparent and prominent", s.64(2). Therefore, if the clause relates to the main subject matter of the contract or to the appropriateness of the price, and it is **not** transparent and prominent then it **may** be subject to the test for fairness under s.62.

A **term** is "transparent" if it is expressed in plain and intelligible language and (in the case of a written term) is legible, s.64 (3).

A **consumer notice** is "transparent" if it expressed in plain intelligible language and is legible, s.68(2).

A term is "prominent" if it is brought to the consumer's attention in such a way that an average consumer would be aware of the term, s.64 (4). An "average consumer" means a consumer who is reasonably well-informed, observant and circumspect, s.64 (5).

An assessment of whether a clause is "prominent" has an inevitable overlap with the common law principles of incorporation. If a clause is not sufficiently clear and prominent, then it could be questioned whether sufficient notice has been given as to the existence of the clause for it be incorporated into the contract. See the approach in **Spurling v Bradshaw** and Denning's "Red Hand Rule".

If the clause is clear and transparent, then a clause relating to the appropriateness of the contract price or subject matter of the contract is exempt from an assessment of fairness. However, following the case of **Office of Fair Trading v Abbey National plc** [2009] UKSC 6 (a case interpreting Reg 6(2) under the Unfair Terms in Consumer Contracts Regulations 1999), it is clear if the term relates to an issue other than the amount paid, then the court may assess the fairness of the clause. The explanatory notes to the Bill provide an example. If a party enters into a contract with a catering company to provide a lunch and the contract contains a term that the party will pay £100 for a three course meal, the court cannot assess whether it is fair to pay £100. It can, however, consider other rights of the parties, such as the rights of the parties to cancel the contract, or when the contract price is due to be paid.

BAR ON EXCLUSION OR RESTRICTION OF NEGLIGENCE LIABILITY - S.65:
By operation of s.65(1):   7-055

"A trader cannot by a term of a contract or by a consumer notice exclude or restrict liability for death or personal injury resulting from negligence."

This replicates the operation of s.2(1) Unfair Contract Terms Act 1977, that also renders such clauses unenforceable, the provisions of which will continue to apply to business to business contacts.

A term seeking to exclude or restrict liability for other loss or damage (loss or damage that is not death or personal injury) will only be enforceable if the clause is fair, applying the test of fairness under s.62.

STATUTORY RIGHTS UNDER A GOODS CONTRACT.

7-056   A party may seek to exclude or restrict strict contractual liability by reference to a term in a contract.

Section 31 of the Consumer Rights Bill provides that a term of a contract to supply goods is **not binding** on the consumer to the extent that it would **exclude or restrict** the trader's liability arising under any of the following provisions:

- section 9 (goods to be of satisfactory quality);
- section 10 (goods to be fit for particular purpose);
- section 11 (goods to be as described);
- section 12 (other pre-contract information included in contract);
- section 13 (goods to match a sample);
- section 14 (goods to match a model seen or examined)

The operation of s.31 is relatively straightforward in that any attempt of a trader to exclude or restrict their liability as against a consumer for breach of any of the statutory implied terms above will not be binding on the parties.

The effect of s.31 Consumer Rights Bill corresponds with that of s.6 and s.7 of the Unfair Contract Terms Act 1977 (which will continue to apply to business to business contracts, as amended by the Bill). The Unfair Contract Terms Act 1977 will also continue to apply to consumer to consumer contracts s.6(4). Please see above for further guidance on the operation of the Unfair Contract Terms Act 1977 in relation to breach of these statutory implied terms in such contracts.

INSTALLATION AS PART OF CONFORMITY OF THE GOODS WITH THE CONTRACT- S.15

7-057   It is important to note the approach adopted in relation to goods that are both supplied and installed by a trader.

s.15 provides:

(1) Goods do not conform to a contract to supply goods if—
(a) installation of the goods forms part of the contract,
(b) the goods are installed by the trader or under the trader's responsibility, and
(c) the goods are installed incorrectly.

The effect of s.15 is to treat such a contract as one of goods for the purposes of the Bill. Therefore, if the installation is performed incorrectly (arising from negligence), then the negligence is treated as strict liability for the purposes of the Bill, meaning such a liability will be subject to s.31. Under s.31 such labiality cannot be exclude or limited.

STATUTORY RIGHTS UNDER A SERVICES CONTRACT

The Consumer Rights Bill implies various terms into a contract to supply a service: **7-058**

- section 49 (service to be performed with reasonable care and skill);
- section 50 (information about the trader or service to be binding);
- section 51 (reasonable price to be paid for a service);
- section 52 (service to be performed within a reasonable time);

If the trader seeks to **exclude** their liability for breach of an implied term that the service is to be performed with reasonable care and skill, s.57 (1) Consumer Rights Bill provides that such a clause **is not binding on the parties**.

Similarly, if the trader seeks to **exclude** their liability for breach of an implied term that information about the trader or service is binding, s.57(2) Consumer Rights Bill provides that such a clause **is not binding on the parties**.

However, if the trader seeks to **restrict** their liability for a breach of any of the implied terms above, s.57(3) Consumer Rights Bill provides that the clause is **not binding** if it prevents the consumer from recovering the **value of the contract price**. In other words, the consumer should always be entitled to a refund of the price of the service for breach of any of the implied terms above. If the trader seeks to restrict their liability to an amount that is less than the contract price, the clause will not be binding on the parties.

However, if the trader seeks to **restrict their liability to the price of the contract (or an amount in excess of the contract price)**, then such liability **may be limited**, providing the clause passes the test of **fairness** under s.62.

CONTRACT TERMS THAT MAY HAVE DIFFERENT MEANINGS - S.69

If a term in a consumer contract, or a consumer notice, could have different meanings, then **7-059**
meaning that is most favourable to the consumer is to prevail.

This approach reflects that adopted at common law in relation to the construction of the contract. At common law, the courts will construe a clause "contra proferentem," meaning that any ambiguity is interpreted harshly against the party seeking to rely on the clause.

FIGURE 7.8 **Summary of the Consumer Rights Bill 2013-14**

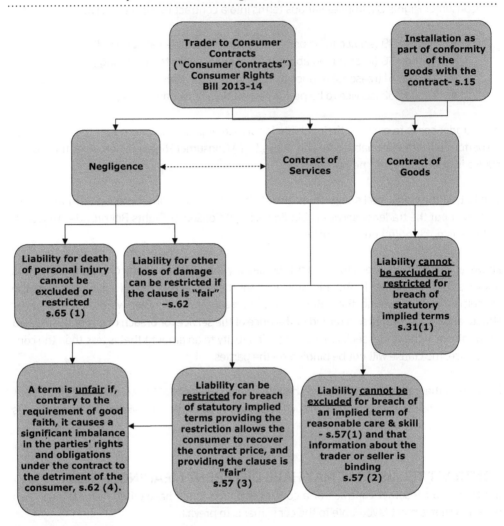

Trader to Consumer Contracts ("Consumer Contracts") Consumer Rights Bill 2013-14

Installation as part of conformity of the goods with the contract- s.15

Negligence

Contract of Services

Contract of Goods

Liability for death of personal injury cannot be excluded or restricted s.65 (1)

Liability for other loss of damage can be restricted if the clause is "fair" –s.62

Liability cannot be excluded or restricted for breach of statutory implied terms s.31(1)

A term is unfair if, contrary to the requirement of good faith, it causes a significant imbalance in the parties' rights and obligations under the contract to the detriment of the consumer, s.62 (4).

Liability can be restricted for breach of statutory implied terms providing the restriction allows the consumer to recover the contract price, and providing the clause is "fair" s.57 (3)

Liability cannot be excluded for breach of an implied term of reasonable care & skill - s.57(1) and that information about the trader or seller is binding s.57 (2)

Summary

1. In order for an exclusion clause to be binding it must first be incorporated into the contract. A clause can be incorporated via signature, notice or by a previous course of dealings.

2. Once incorporated the clause must then pass the common law test of construction. The process of construction is where the courts seek to give legal interpretation to the words that are used. The courts will interpret any ambiguity in the clause strictly against the party wishing to rely on it.

3. Finally, once the clause has passed the common law tests of incorporation and construction it must satisfy the legislative provisions of the Unfair Contract Terms Act 1977 and the Unfair Terms in Consumer Contracts Regulations 1999.

4. The Unfair Contract Terms Act 1977 has a two-pronged attack in relation to exclusion clauses. It renders some clauses automatically void while subjecting others to the test of "reasonableness".

5. The key to understanding UCTA is to identify the type of liability that is sought to be excluded.

6. Section 2 applies to negligence liability. Under s.2(1), liability for death or personal injury as a result of negligence cannot be excluded and a clause purporting to exclude such liability will be automatically void. Under s.2(2), a clause seeking to exclude liability for other loss or damage will be subjected to the test of "reasonableness".

7. Sections 6 and 7 apply to strict liability. If ownership rights in property pass under the contract (such as a contract for the sale of goods) then s.6 will apply. If no ownership rights pass under the contract (such as in a contract for hire) then s.7 will apply. Both sections draw a distinction between business and consumer contracts. Liability for breach of a term implied under the Sale of Goods Act 1979, or the Supply of Goods and Services Act 1982 cannot be excluded in a consumer contract. Such liability can be excluded in a business contract but only if the clause passes the test of reasonableness.

8. Section 12 provides a definition of "in the course of business", but following the decision in **R & B Customs Brokers** the transaction must be an integral part of the business before a contract has been made "in the course of business".

9. The reasonableness test is found in s.11 and is supplemented by further guidelines in Sch.2.

10. The Unfair Terms in Consumer Contracts Regulations 1999 only apply to consumer contracts and subject clauses to the test of "fairness". A clause will be unfair if it is contrary to the requirement of "good faith".

11. The following provides a summary of the provisions and impact of the Consumer Rights Bill 2013-14 which, **when in force**, will replace the current law in relation to "consumer contracts".

   Liability for death or personal injury as a result of negligence cannot be excluded or limited – s.65(1).

   Other loss of damage as a result negligence can be restricted, but only if the clause is "fair".

Under a contract of goods, liability cannot be excluded or limited for breach of stator implied terms – s.31(1)

In a contract of services, liability cannot be excluded for breach of an implied term of reasonable care and skill (s.57(1)) and that information about the trader or seller is binding (s.57(2)).

In a contract of services, liability can, however, be restricted for breach of statutory implied terms, providing that the restriction allows the consumer to recover the contract price, and providing the clause is fair – s.57(3).

A term is unfair if, contrary to the requirement of good faith, it causes a significant imbalance in the parties' rights and obligations under the contract to the detriment of the consumer – s.62(4).

Key Cases Grid

Case	Court	Key Issues
L'Estrange v F Graucob Ltd [1934]	King's Bench Division	Signature of a written document will bind a party to the terms of that document, regardless of whether the party has read the document of not.
Parker v South East Railway Co [1877]	Court of Appeal	In order to incorporate a term by notice, reasonable notice must be given as to existence of the clause. Note, there is no need the party to actually be aware of the clause providing reasonable steps were taken to bring the clause to the attention of the party.
Olley v Marlborough Court Ltd [1949]	Court of Appeal	Reasonable notice of the existence of the clause must be given before or at the time the contract is formed.
Spurling v Bradshaw [1956]	Court of Appeal	In relation to the issue of notice, the more unusual or onerous the clause, greater prominence needs to be given to the clause. Per Denning L.J.,the "Red Hand Rule: "[some clauses] would need to be printed in red ink on the face of the document, with a red hand pointing to it before the notice could be said to be sufficient."

Chapleton v Barry Urban DC [1940] 1 K.B. 532	Court of Appeal	For reasonable notice to be given in unsigned documents, it must be reasonable to expect the type of document to contain contractual terms.
McCutcheon v David MacBrayne Ltd [1964]	House of Lords	A clause may be incorporated on the basis of previous dealings, providing there have been sufficient and consistent transactions between the parties.
Canada Steamship Lines Ltd v The King [1952]	Privy Council (Canada)	This case outlines the three-stage approach to the construction of clauses that seek to exclude or restrict liability for negligence: 1. Does the clause make express reference to negligence? 2. If there is no express reference to negligence, are the words wide enough to cover negligence? 3. If the words used are wide enough for the above purpose, the court must then consider whether "the head of damage may be based on some ground other than that of negligence".

◄ ....

End of Chapter Question

John visits a local nightclub. He often visits this nightclub as it is one of the cheapest in the area. He pays £5 to enter the club and then takes his coat to the cloakroom attendant. John is then handed a document headed "receipt" and on the back is the following clause:

"The nightclub's liability for loss or damage to customer property, howsoever arising, is limited to the value of the entrance price only."

This clause also appears at the entrance to the nightclub.

Due to the carelessness of the cloakroom attendant, John's coat is mistakenly given out to another party. John discovers that his coat is missing and brings an action against the night-club to recover its full value (£120).

Advise the nightclub.

Points of Answer

The first issue is to consider the relevant principles at common law and whether the clause is incorporated into the contract.

A clause can be incorporated if reasonable notice is given as to the existence of the clause. Question whether the notice on the "receipt" would be sufficient. Firstly, it may come too late as the contract may have been formed when John pays his entrance fee (**Olley v Marlborough Court Hotel**). Also, question whether the document is one which a reasonable person would assume would contain terms and conditions (**Chapleton v Barry**).

The notices at the entrance may be sufficient provided they are sufficient prominent (apply Denning's "Red Hand Rule").

The clause may also be incorporated on the basis of previous dealings, given that John often visits the nightclub (**Spurling v Bradshaw**).

Next, consider whether the clause passes the relevant test of construction. Do the words used cover the liability in question?

The nightclubs are trying to limit their liability for negligence. Apply the three stages of **Canada Steamship** to decide whether the clause will cover negligent liability. Question whether the words are wide enough to cover negligence. Also, as negligence may be the only basis of liability, the court may construe it is as covering negligence (see the approach in **Alderslade**).

Finally, consider the provisions of the Unfair Contract Terms Act 1977. Negligence for "other loss or damage" can be limited under s.2 (2) providing the clause satisfies the test of reasonableness. Apply s.11 (1), s.11(4) (as this is a limitation clause) and the relevant "guidelines" in Sch.2 to determine this issue.

Note, that **once in force**, the provisions of the Consumer Rights Bill 2013-14 will apply to the contract between John and the nightclub as this will be a "consumer contract". The nightclub are able to restrict their liability for other loss or damage as a result of negligence, but only if the clause is "fair" applying the test in s.62.

Further Reading

For the latest information regarding the Consumer Rights Bill 2013-14, access the following link:

    http://services.parliament.uk/bills/2013-14/consumerrights.html

The Bill itself and the accompanying explanatory notes can be accessed at:

    http://services.parliament.uk/bills/2013-14/consumerrights/documents.html

Stone, R. and Cunnington, R. *Text, Cases and Materials on Contract Law* (London: Routledge-Cavendish, 2014), Chapter 7.

Treitel, G. *The Law of Contract*, 13th edn (London Sweet & Maxwell, 2011), Chapter 7.

Misrepresentation

8

CHAPTER OVERVIEW

In this chapter we:

- introduce misrepresentation and discuss the importance of distinguishing a term of the contract from a representation

- identify the key elements of an actionable misrepresentation

- distinguish between the different types of misrepresentation

- analyse the remedies for an actionable misrepresentation

- produce a structured approach to the issue of misrepresentation

Summary

Key Cases Grid

End of Chapter Question

Further Reading

Introduction

8-001   This chapter is concerned with the law relating to misrepresentation, which can be defined as a false statement of fact that induces the other party to enter into a contract. In other words, the law of misrepresentation seeks to provide a remedy for a party who has entered into a contract after relying upon a misleading pre-contractual statement. If successful, a claim for misrepresentation will render the contract *voidable* (not void).

Misrepresentation is an area that many students find difficult. There are several reasons for this, but one of the primary reasons is that the law of misrepresentation is found in a number of sources. The clear boundaries that usually separate contract law and the law of tort, for example, can become blurred in the context of the law of misrepresentation. For students who may not have studied contract law and tort concurrently it is often challenging to understand the foundations on which the law of misrepresentation is based. Further, the law of misrepresentation is a fusion of common law, equitable principles and statute law. Again, it is not easy to identify which of these sources of law is applicable in different situations.

That said, we will try and follow a clear and structured approach to the law of misrepresentation which should allow us to identify how all these different sources and bodies of law converge.

To achieve this we will adopt a four-stage approach:

1.   Distinguish a term of a contract from a representation.
2.   Identify an actionable misrepresentation.
3.   Differentiate between the different *types* of misrepresentation.
4.   Analyse the remedies for misrepresentation.

Stage 1: distinguishing a term from a representation

8-002   Not all pre-contractual statements will form part of the contract. If information is given or a promise made that is either false or never honoured, and the statement is incorporated as a term of the contract, then the appropriate cause of action will be for breach of contract. If a pre-contractual statement is not a term of the contract, but merely a representation, then the appropriate cause of action will be for *mis*representation. So, being able to identify which statements form part of the agreement (terms) and which do not (representations) is of fundamental importance, as this will dictate the relevant cause of action and the different remedies that are available to the innocent party.

Intention of the maker of the statement

In distinguishing between a term and a representation the court will seek to give effect to the intention of the parties. The task of the court is therefore to ascertain the intention of the maker of the statement. To assist the court a number of guiding factors or presumptions have been developed to which the court will refer when determining the issue of intention (**Heilbut, Symons & Co v Buckleton** [1913] A.C. 30). If the court decides that the maker of the statement intended that statement to form part of the agreement the court will treat that statement as a term of the contract.

8-003

As we discussed in connection with offer and acceptance, the issue of intention is assessed objectively. Of course, as we saw with offer and acceptance, an objective analysis of intention may well result in a conclusion that differs from what the parties actually intended. Similarly to the objective test of intention when distinguishing an offer from an invitation to treat, the courts use a number of guiding factors or presumptions to ascertain the intention of the maker of the statement. We shall now consider each in turn.

Has the statement been reduced to writing?

If the relevant statement has been reduced to writing there will be a greater presumption that it will form a term of the contract. What better evidence of the intention of the maker of the statement than it being contained in a written document? If this document is signed the parties will find it very difficult to argue that they didn't intend the contents of that document to form part of their agreement (**L'Estrange v F Graucob Ltd** [1934] 2 K.B. 394). The parties may try to introduce oral evidence that the content of the document does not reflect their true intentions at the time of entering into the agreement. The courts, however, will not be receptive to such claims. This is known as the "parol evidence" rule, which provides that where clear evidence of the parties' intentions is provided (such as a signed written document) then no further evidence in rebuttal should be accepted. The obligation imposed by, and the effect of, the parol evidence rule, is therefore to ensure that the written document containing the parties' agreement is presented in a very clear and precise manner so that no oral evidence of their intentions is required (nor will it generally be accepted).

8-004

This does not mean that an oral statement can never form a term of the contract. It is quite possible for parties to enter into a legally binding oral agreement and there is no strict requirement that this agreement be reduced to writing. However, the fact that an agreement has been reduced to writing will be a guiding factor for the courts in ascertaining the intention of the parties in relation to the term/representation distinction.

Does one party have specialist skill or knowledge?

If the party making a statement has specialist skill or knowledge and the other person relies upon this as a factor when entering into the contract, then the greater the presumption that such a statement will be a term of the contract.

8-005

In **Dick Bentley Productions Ltd v Harold Smith (Motors) Ltd** [1965] 1 W.L.R. 623 a car dealer stated that a car had done 20,000 miles. Relying upon this statement the plaintiff purchased the car for his wife. Almost immediately there were problems with the car and it was eventually discovered that the car had done nearer 100,000 miles. The plaintiff brought an action for breach of contract arguing that the statement as to the mileage was a term of the contract. The Court of Appeal held that, as the statement was made by a car dealer—a person with specialist knowledge of the motor industry who, as a result, was in a better position to find out the true mileage of the car—the statement regarding the mileage was indeed a term of the contract.

Compare this decision to that of **Oscar Chess v Williams** [1957] 1 W.L.R. 370, which is based on very similar facts. In **Oscar Chess**, a private seller described a car he had for sale as a "1948 Morris 10 saloon". In fact, it turned out to be a 1939 model and as a result was worth considerably less. The court held that the statement as to the car's age was a representation. The distinguishing factors here between **Oscar Chess** and **Dick Bentley** are that in **Oscar Chess** the private seller did not have any specialist skill or knowledge, nor was that relied upon by the purchaser. If anything, the purchasers in **Oscar Chess** (who were car dealers themselves) were in a better position than the private seller to discover the truth of the statement.

. . . .

Lapse of time

8-006   As the key test is that of intention and the relative importance that is given to pre-contractual statements, the courts will also look to the timing of the statement. The greater the lapse of time between a statement being made and the contract being entered into the greater the presumption that the statement will be a representation. The lapse of time between the statement being made and the final contract being agreed gives the courts an indication of the true intention of the parties and the relative importance that statement as an influential factor in entering into the contract.

Stage 2: identifying an actionable misrepresentation

8-007   As we have discussed, not all pre-contractual statements will give rise to an actionable misrepresentation. If a pre-contractual statement is a term of the agreement the appropriate cause of action will be for breach of contract. However, even if it has been decided that a pre-contractual statement is a representation, there are certain conditions that must be satisfied in order for an action in misrepresentation to succeed. An actionable misrepresentation is defined as a false statement of fact that induced the other party to enter into the contract.

Each of these elements must be present and we will break them down as follows:

1. a false statement;
2. a false statement of fact; and
3. a false statement of fact that induced the contract.

A false statement

It may sound quite straightforward to identify a false statement of fact. However, as we will see, these requirements have specific legal definitions which need to be considered.

8-008

First, as the law of misrepresentation is concerned with pre-contractual statements, we need to analyse what will amount to a "statement" for the purpose of an actionable misrepresentation. A "statement" carries a very wide legal definition that covers activities ranging from express words exchanged between the parties, to the conduct of the parties.

An interesting example of a statement being made by *conduct* can be found in **Spice Girls Ltd v Aprilia World Service BV** [2000] EMLR 478. In this case the defendants, who manufactured motorbikes and scooters, entered into a contract with a pop group, the Spice Girls, to sponsor their world tour. Before the contract was entered into, the Spice Girls attended a number of photo shoots and promotional events to advertise the defendants' products, although at that time the group knew that one of its members intended to leave. The group member intended to leave before the sponsorship deal with the defendants was due to expire.

The court held that the participation in the photo shoot amounted to a representation by conduct that the "claimant did not know, and had no reasonable ground to believe, that any of the group had an existing declared intention to leave the group before that date . . . [and that] the claimant had done nothing to correct that representation which was a continuing representation."

Of course, the claimants in the **Spice Girls** case never expressly stated that no member of the band intended to leave the group, but nevertheless their actions amounted to a representation as to that fact. So, if conduct would fall within the wide definition of a statement, a more interesting question is whether silence could ever constitute a "statement" for the purposes of misrepresentation.

Representation by silence

Given the self-regulatory nature of contract law it would seem contradictory if a representation could be made by silence, especially in light principle of "caveat emptor". This literally translates to "buyer beware". In other words, if the contracting party has not actively been misled then it will generally not be the responsibility of the court to ensure that the party has entered into a good bargain.

8-009

Notwithstanding the principle of caveat emptor, there are certain limited situations in which silence can form the basis of an actionable misrepresentation. As you will see, however, these situations are not truly examples of complete silence amounting to a false statement, they are more concerned with the situations in which a statement has been made and important information is withheld.

MISLEADING HALF-TRUTHS

8-010   In some situations a statement may be made with the intention of presenting a certain impression that is inherently false or misleading. For example, in **Nottingham Patent Brick & Tile Co v Butler** (1885–86) L.R. 16 Q.B.D. 778, a solicitor represented that he wasn't aware of any restrictive covenants relating to the property in question. This in essence was true. The solicitor was not aware of any restrictive convents, but this was due to the fact that the solicitor hadn't checked to see whether such covenants existed. In other words, the solicitor had only told half the story and as a result the contract was rescinded.

Hopefully you can see how the example of **Nottingham Patent Brick** illustrates how silence can form the basis of an actionable misrepresentation; that which was unsaid is just as important as the words spoken. In such cases the court will proceed on the basis that failing to disclose relevant information leads to an inference that the adverse facts affecting the statement are not true.

Similarly, in **Dimmock v Hallett** (1866–67) L.R. 2 Ch. App. 21 the vendor of a number of farms stated that the farms were currently let, which was true. However, the vendor failed to mention the fact that the tenants had given notice to quit. Again, this was considered to be a misleading half-truth giving rise to a misrepresentation.

CHANGE OF CIRCUMSTANCES

8-011   In this exception to the caveat emptor principle we will look at the obligations of disclosure imposed on the maker of a pre-contractual statement. Generally, there will be no positive obligation to disclose information. As stated above, the law of misrepresentation is more concerned with an active attempt to mislead rather than a failure to mention certain facts. So, the courts are more concerned with an active deception rather than imposing an obligation to tell the truth.

In **With v O'Flannagan** [1936] Ch. 575, during the negotiation for the sale of a medical practice, the vendor made a representation in January 1934 that the takings of the practice were £2,000 per annum. This at the time was true. However, when the contract of sale was signed in May 1934 the situation had changed. Owing to the illness of the vendor the business of the medical practice had fallen to almost nothing. When the purchasers discovered this fact they sought to rescind the contract on the basis of a misrepresentation. The court had to decide whether there was any obligation placed on the vendor to communicate the change in the circumstances of the business to the potential purchasers.

The court held that the statement regarding the takings of the business was a "continuing statement". The representation continued from the time it was made to the time the contract was formed and on this basis the vendor was under a duty to communicate the change of circumstances to the purchaser.

The approach of the courts in these situations is summed up quite nicely by Fry J. in **Davies v London and Provincial Marine Insurance Co.** (1878) L.R. 8 Ch. D. 469:

> **"If a statement has been made which is true at the time, but which during the course of the negotiations becomes untrue, then the person who knows it has become untrue is under an obligation to disclose to the other the change of circumstances."**

The decision in **With v O'Flannagan** highlights an interesting aspect of the courts' approach to misrepresentation and the inconsistency with which the courts approach this issue of silence. On the one hand, if there has been a false statement made then this should form the basis of an actionable misrepresentation regardless of whether the maker knew it to be false. On the other hand, however, when looking at silence and the caveat emptor rule, the requirement of knowledge becomes vitally important. In the context of a half-truth, the statement will form the basis of an actionable misrepresentation on the basis that the maker knows the basis of his statement is false when it is made. However, in the context of a change of circumstances, an actionable misrepresentation will only be found when the representor later becomes aware that the statement is false but takes no action to remedy this. With the focus now on the knowledge of the maker of the statement this appears to be inconsistent with the proposition above that an actionable misrepresentation be based purely on a false statement.

CONTRACTS UBERRIMAE FIDEI—"OF UTMOST GOOD FAITH"

Finally, the nature of the relationship between the parties may create an obligation to disclose relevant information regarding the contract, and failing to do so may give rise to an actionable misrepresentation. Where the nature of the contract is of "the utmost good faith" then stricter standards of disclosure will be imposed on the parties: a duty to provide a full picture of all relevant information, whether that information is specifically requested or not.

8-012

Perhaps the most practical examples of such contracts are contracts of insurance. As the insurance provider will need to assess the risk involved in providing an insurance policy, the insurer will require full disclosure of all the relevant factors when assessing that risk. If the applicant withholds or fails to mention key facts that impact upon this assessment, the insurer will not be in a position to fully calculate the risk to which it is exposing itself and the contract may be declared void.

An insurance provider cannot be expected to discover every fact that may be relevant to the insurance provision, nor may it even be possible for it to do so. In other words, it is the applicant who is in the better position to provide such information (or may be the *only* person capable of providing such information) so imposing a high standard of disclosure would seem justified in such contracts.

While a stricter duty of disclosure seems justified in insurance contracts the exact standard of this duty received the attention of the House of Lords in **Pan Atlantic Insurance Co Ltd v Pine Top Insurance Co Ltd** [1995] 1 A.C. 501. The key requirement is that the insured (and the insurer) must disclose material factors relating to the contract that would affect the decision of a "prudent insurer". In other words, if the prudent insurer would not have entered into the contract had the information been disclosed, the insurer can avoid the contract by reason of such a failure.

A false statement of fact

8-013 Once a false statement has been identified, the next stage is to identify whether that false statement contains a false statement of fact.

The fundamental principle here is that an action for misrepresentation must be based upon a false statement of fact. It is therefore necessary to identify as a matter of law what constitutes a statement of "fact" and then to distinguish this statement from statements that not will give rise to an actionable misrepresentation. A statement of opinion (false or not), for example, will not for the basis of an actionable misrepresentation in the law of contract.

DISTINGUISHING FACT FROM OPINION

8-014 It is often difficult to distinguish a statement of fact from one of opinion, but as noted above the distinction is fundamental in relation to forming the grounds of an actionable misrepresenta-tion. As we will see, the courts have developed a specific legal interpretation of the word "opin-ion". If this were otherwise then many individuals might find themselves bound by contracts after being misled on the basis that the representor phrased the statement as one of opinion or that they believed the statement to be true.

A classic example of the legal interpretation of the word "opinion" can be found in **Bisset v Wilkinson** [1927] A.C. 177, in which the seller of a plot of farm land represented that the land would hold 2,000 sheep. This statement turned out to be untrue, but the court held that the statement regarding the land's capacity was one of opinion and didn't give rise to an actionable misrepresentation.

It is interesting to compare this decision with that of **Smith v Land & House Property Corp** (1885) 28 Ch. D. 7, in which the plaintiffs stated in the particulars of a hotel they had up for sale that the hotel was let to a "most desirable tenant". In fact, the tenant was in arrears with the rent, a fact of which the plaintiffs were aware. So, the tenant was not as "desirable" as he was described. The purchasers argued that they would not have bought the hotel but for the statement in the particulars regarding the status of the tenant.

The court held that the description of the tenant as "most desirable" amounted to a false statement of fact which amounted to a misrepresentation. The reasoning in this case is on the basis that the plaintiff was directly aware of information that contradicted his statement about the tenant. His statement therefore contained an implied assertion that he knew of no information that rendered the tenant undesirable. The plaintiff had therefore made an implied statement that he knew of facts which justify his opinion. As the plaintiff did not have such facts to justify his opinion, this amounted to a false statement of fact for the purposes of misrepresentation.

Even if the plaintiff had said, "In my opinion, the property is let to a most desirable tenant", the conclusion would have been no different. As Bowen L.J. observed:

> "It is material to observe that it is often fallaciously assumed that a statement of opinion cannot involve the statement of a fact. In a case where the facts are equally well known to both parties, what one of them says to the other is frequently nothing but an expression of opinion. The statement of such opinion is in a sense a statement of a fact, about the condition of the man's own mind, but only of an irrelevant fact, for it is of no consequence what the opinion is. But if the facts are not equally known to both sides, then a statement of opinion by the one who knows the facts best involves very often a statement of a material fact, for he impliedly states that he knows facts which justify his opinion."

So, hopefully you can see how the effect of this legalistic interpretation of "fact" and "opinion" led to the conclusion that in **Bisset**, what would appear to be a statement of fact was actually intercepted as one of opinion and in **Smith**, what appeared to be a statement of opinion was actually one of fact.

Over to you. . .

In light of the discussion above, can you explain how we can reconcile the cases of *Bisset* and *Smith*? What factors did the court identify as relevant in distinguishing fact from opinion in these cases?

Firstly, in **Bisset** as neither the seller nor the purchaser had any experience of sheep farming, so neither of them was in better a position to know the truth of the statement regarding the land's capacity. This was not the case in **Smith** as the plaintiff had actual knowledge that contradicted his statement regarding the tenant. Secondly, as the statement by the seller in **Bisset** was made honestly, then the court should not infer that he knew the truth upon which the statement was based. This was not the case in **Smith**, where the plaintiff's statement was dishonest as it amounted to an implied assertion that he wasn't aware of any contradictory information.

As we have identified in **Smith**, if one party has particular skill or knowledge, which is relied upon by the other party, then the courts are more likely to treat a statement as being one of fact. However, this approach also overlaps with the distinction between a term and a representation discussed above. If a party with specialist skill or knowledge makes a statement, it is also more likely that the statement will become a term of the contract. This is on the basis that the maker of the statement represents that he has exercised his specialist skill or knowledge with reasonable care and skill in coming to his conclusion.

For example, in **Esso Petroleum Co Ltd v Mardon** [1976] Q.B. 801, a statement was made by one of Esso's servants that a proposed petrol station would have a throughput of 200,000 gallons. M relied on this statement and entered into a lease for the petrol station. Subsequently, the local council altered the planning permission for the station which meant that the size of the site was reduced and the throughput of the station was actually 78,000 gallons. When M eventually defaulted on the lease payments Esso brought an action to repossess the station. M's counterclaim was that Esso was liable for negligent misrepresentation and/or breach of warranty (a term of the contract).

You can probably see the difficulties facing M's counterclaim here. In order to form the basis of a misrepresentation, Esso's statement regarding the throughput must have been one of *fact*. At first glance it appears that such a statement would merely be one of *opinion* and therefore would neither form the basis of an actionable misrepresentation nor be a contractual term. However, the court held that the statement as to the throughput of the station was both a statement of fact and a term of the contract and on this basis damages were awarded to M for negligent misrepresentation and for breach of contract.

The reasoning behind this decision is again firmly rooted in the objective analysis of intention that is so familiar in contract law. First, although Esso never actually intended its statement to form part of the agreement (so as to be a term of the contract) an objective analysis would suggest differently. Secondly, although the statement as to throughput may initially sound like mere opinion, it actually contained a statement of fact—that the maker of the statement had exercised reasonable care and skill in forming that statement.

As Lord Denning observed:

"If a man, who has or professes to have special knowledge or skill, makes a representation by virtue thereof to another—be it advice, information or opinion—with the intention of inducing him to enter into a contract with him, he is under a duty to use reasonable care to see that the representation is correct, and that the advice, information or opinion is reliable. If he negligently gives unsound advice or misleading information or expresses an erroneous opinion, and thereby induces the other side to enter into a contract with him, he is liable in damages."

STATEMENTS OF LAW

Interestingly, for many years it was thought that a false statement of law could not form the basis of an actionable misrepresentation. At a basic level, the courts drew a very strict distinction between a statement of fact and one of law. As a statement of law was not one of fact, so it could not give rise to a misrepresentation. The only way in which a statement of law could be actionable would be if it were made fraudulently, following the principles in **Smith and Edgington v Fitzmaurice** (1885) L.R. 29 Ch. D. 459 (see below).

8-015

However, this strict distinction between fact and law gave rise to a number of unsatisfactory decisions. For example, in **Solle v Butcher** [1950] 1 K.B. 671 a statement that the Increase of Rent and Mortgage Interest (Restrictions) Act 1938 did not apply to a particular property was held to be a non-actionable statement of law. However, the distinction between a statement of law (the interpretation of a statute) and the application of the law (whether it applied to the property in question) is a very fine one indeed.

The House of Lords in **Kleinwort Benson Ltd v Lincoln City Council** [1999] 2 A.C. 349 finally laid to rest this unattractive distinction between fact and law and declared that a false statement of law could indeed be actionable. This reasoning was adopted by the High Court in **Pankhania v Hackney LBC** [2004] All E.R. (D) 205 (Jan).

STATEMENT OF FUTURE INTENTION

As with a statement of opinion, a statement of future intention will not form the basis of an actionable misrepresentation. Stating that you may act in a certain way in the future is not a statement of fact capable of supporting an action for misrepresentation. However, this rather general proposition is subject to a number of qualifications.

8-016

First, if the statement of future intention amounts to an express promise (I promise to pay when you deliver the subject matter of the contract) then this will form a term of the contract and will be actionable for breach of contract if that promise is not kept.

Secondly, as we have already seen from the case of **Spice Girls v Aprilia** there are ways in which certain actions can contain implied assertions of fact. The conduct of the group in that case amounted to an implied assertion as to their lack of knowledge regarding the group member's intention to leave. So, following on from this principle it is important to recognise that a statement as to the future can contain a statement of fact, but only when the maker of the statement does not genuinely believe the truth of its content.

In **Edgington v Fitzmaurice**, the plaintiff invested in a company and subscribed to a number of debentures after relying on false statements in the company prospectus. The prospectus stated that the money raised would be used to improve the business by renovating the company's buildings. In fact, the money was used to pay off the company's debts. The plaintiffs sought to recover the money that had been paid, on the grounds that such payment had been induced by a fraudulent misrepresentation.

The Court of Appeal accepted this argument and the plaintiffs were able to recover the money paid as a result of the defendant's fraud. In stating that the money would be used to refurbish the company's buildings, the directors of the company had misrepresented their state of mind.

As Bowen L.J. famously stated in **Edgington v Fitzmaurice** (1885) L.R. 29 Ch. D. 459:

> "There must be a misstatement of an existing fact: but the state of a man's mind is as much a fact as the state of his digestion. It is true that it is very difficult to prove what the state of a man's mind at a particular time is, but if it can be ascertained it is as much a fact as anything else. A misrepresentation as to the state of a man's mind is, therefore, a misstatement of fact."

The fundamental principle here is that a statement of future intention will only form the basis of an actionable misrepresentation when that statement is not genuinely held. As Bowen L.J. stated above, the state of a man's mind is a statement of fact. In other words, the false representation is as to the maker's state of mind. The maker represents that he is making the statement honestly (a statement of fact) so if the statement was actually made dishonestly then the maker has misrepresented a state of fact. It is this *false statement of fact* that will give rise to an actionable misrepresentation.

. . . .

A false statement of fact that induced the contract

8-017   The next element of an actionable misrepresentation is that the false statement of fact must have induced the other party to enter into the contract. In other words, the court will look to the importance placed upon the false statement by the representee and the extent to which this statement influenced his decision to enter into the contract. In the body of case law on this issue there was some confusion as to the precise test to be applied. However, it is possible to draw together the following principles:

1. the representation must have been *material* to the decision to enter into the contract; and
2. the representation must have actually been relied upon by the representee.

Note that this two-stage test and both stages must be satisfied in order for the representation to be actionable. However, as we will see, the boundaries between these two requirements are blurred at times.

THE REPRESENTATION MUST HAVE BEEN MATERIAL TO THE DECISION TO ENTER INTO THE CONTRACT

In order to establish that the representation induced the contract the first stage is to consider whether it was *material* to the decision to enter into the contract. The courts use an *objective* test to decide this issue. If the representation would have influenced the decision of a *reasonable person* to enter into the contract then the test of materiality will have been satisfied.

8-018

In **JEB Fasteners Ltd v Marks Bloom & Co** [1983] 1 All E.R. 583, the plaintiffs sought to purchase a company. The reason they wished to purchase the company was to secure the services of two of its directors. The plaintiffs were shown the company accounts, but these accounts were inaccurate because the accountants had been negligent in preparing the accounts. The plaintiffs' claim for misrepresentation was rejected. The inaccurate accounts had not induced the contract. The reason the plaintiffs purchased the company was to secure the services of the two directors. The decision to purchase the company was not induced by the inaccurate accounts.

To induce the contract the representation must have been material which is assessed objectively. However, what if the representee subjectively relies upon a statement that the reasonable person would not have considered as a relevant factor in entering into the contract? This issue was addressed in **Museprime Properties Ltd v Adhill Properties Ltd** (1991) 61 P. & C.R. 111. In this case a number of false statements were made during an auction for three properties. In particular, the auctioneer had stated that the rent reviews over the three properties could still be negotiated. This was false, as the rent reviews had been fixed. The purchasers brought an action for misrepresentation when they discovered the truth of these statements.

The defendants argued that it was unreasonable for the purchasers to have relied upon the statements, so it had not been established that the false statements were *material* to their decision to purchase the properties. The court held that even though it may have been unreasonable to have relied on the statements, the decision of the purchasers had *actually* been affected by the false statements. The purpose of the objective test was simply to determine what evidence the claimant must produce in order to satisfy the court that the representation was material to their decision to enter into the contract.

In other words, if the representation would have induced the reasonable man to enter into the contract then the court will infer that it was material to the representee. However, if it was *unreasonable* to have relied on the representation then the representee will have to produce evidence that it was actually material to his decision to contract. The issue of *reasonableness* therefore determines the burden of proof in relation to whether the representation was material to the representee's decision to enter into the contract.

THE REPRESENTATION MUST HAVE ACTUALLY BEEN RELIED UPON BY THE REPRESENTEE

8-019   The representation may have been material but it must also have been relied upon by the representee in order for it to be actionable. The courts apply a subjective test to this issue. An interesting example of this subjective approach is demonstrated in **Attwood v Small** (1838) 6 Cl. & Fin. 232. In this case, the plaintiffs made several false representations about the capacity of a mine. The respondents verified these statements with their own engineers who confirmed that they were accurate. On the basis of this information the respondents purchased the mine.

Several months after the sale the respondents discovered that the statements as to the capacity of the mine were false. The respondents sought to rescind the contract on the grounds of misrepresentation. The court held the plaintiff's statements had not induced the contract. The respondents had *not actually relied* on the statements of the plaintiffs; they had relied upon the statements of their own engineers.

Further, following **Redgrave v Hurd** (1881–82) L.R. 20 Ch. D.1, even if the innocent party has an opportunity to verify the accuracy of the statement, but nevertheless chooses not to take advantage of that opportunity, this will not necessarily prevent that party from seeking a remedy for misrepresentation. In this case the defendant entered into a contract to purchase a solicitor's firm from the plaintiff. The plaintiff made false statements regarding the profits of the practice. Had the defendant inspected the accounts, which he was invited to do, he would have discovered the true profits of the business.

The court held that the defendant could still bring an action for misrepresentation as the false statements regarding the profits had *actually* been relied upon by the defendant. The statements had therefore induced the contract. An invitation to verify will not prevent a successful action for misrepresentation. However, if the representee has acted unreasonably in declining to verify the statements this may amount to contributory negligence. A finding of contributory negligence will not prevent an action for misrepresentation, but it may reduce the amount of damages that are awarded, to reflect the fault of the representee.

Finally, the representee may have relied upon a number of facts in deciding whether to enter into the contract. In order for a representation to have induced the contract, it is not necessary that it was the *only* factor that induced the representee to enter into the contract. For example, you will recall in the case of **Edgington v Fitzmaurice** that the plaintiff entered into the contract due to a number of factors. The false statements made in the company prospectus and also the plaintiff's false assumption that he would be entitled to a share over company property induced him to enter into the contract. However, as the plaintiff's state of mind was affected by the representations (which, in part, was to blame for his decision to enter into the contract) the plaintiff was still able to pursue a successful action for misrepresentation.

Stage 3: what type of misrepresentation?

This is again a challenging element of misrepresentation, being able to distinguish between the different types of misrepresentation. This stage is crucial, as the distinction between the different types of misrepresentation will not only determine what the claimant must prove (and to what standard) in order to claim, but will also determine the remedies available to the claimant.

8-020

A further complication is added by the often confusing and sometimes contradictory terminology that the courts have adopted in describing the different types of misrepresentation. Generally speaking, the courts have recognised three different types of misrepresentation, namely fraudulent, negligent and innocent. These categories of misrepresentation are, however, founded on different bodies of law and to be able to distinguish between them it is necessary to have at least a basic understanding of these foundations.

An overview of the three main types of misrepresentation is provided in Figure 8.1. There are two broad categories of misrepresentation; misrepresentation at common law and misrepresentation: under the Misrepresentation Act 1967.

FIGURE 8.1 The three main types of misrepresentation

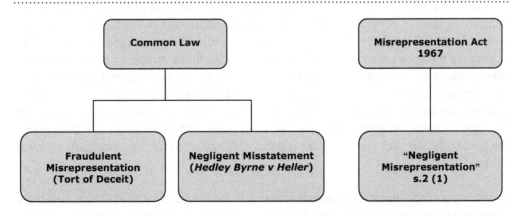

Fraudulent misrepresentation

8-021   As the title suggests, in order to be successful in an action for fraudulent misrepresentation, the claimant must establish fraud. An action for fraudulent misrepresentation is actually
founded on the tort of deceit, which is reflected in the relevant measure of damages awarded.
In terms of the degree of fault required on the part of the representor, fraud would appear
towards the very top of the hierarchy. This was demonstrated in the case of **Derry v Peek** (1889)
L.R. 14 App. Cas. 337, in which the test for fraud was clarified and required that the representation must have been made: (1) knowingly; or (2) without belief in its truth; or (3) recklessly,
careless whether it be true or false.

The key test is therefore that of honesty. If the representor makes a statement honestly (but
unreasonably) believing it to be true then it is unlikely that the test of fraud will have been
satisfied.

Negligent misrepresentation

8-022   This is perhaps the most confusing element of misrepresentation, which is partly a result of the
contradictory and misleading terminology mentioned above. While the courts are willing to
recognise a negligent misrepresentation it is not always clear on which foundations this action
is based. The development of "negligent" misrepresentation is directly linked to developments in the law of tort in relation to negligent misstatement and a statutory cause of action
under the Misrepresentation Act 1967. Confusingly, both of these are commonly referred to as
"negligent" misrepresentations. We will first focus on negligent misrepresentation at common
law—referred to as "negligent misstatement".

Negligent misstatement

8-023   As mentioned above, an action for negligent misrepresentation at common law is actually
founded on developments in relation to negligent misstatement in the law of tort and the
House of Lords decision in **Hedley Byrne & Co Ltd v Heller & Partners Ltd** [1964] A.C. 465.
In this case the appellants asked their bankers to enquire into a company's financial stability.
After conducting investigations into the other company, the bankers returned and stated that
the company was in a strong financial position. On the strength of this information the appellants entered into a contract with the company. Soon after, the company went into liquidation
resulting in substantial losses to the appellants. The appellants then brought an action against
the bank to recover such losses on the basis that they had relied upon the negligent advice of
the bank.

The House of Lords ultimately decided that the bank was not liable for its advice because there
was a disclaimer in the contract. When the bank provided the information it made it clear to the
appellants that it did so "without responsibility". Had it not been for this disclaimer the bank
would have been liable for its negligent advice on the grounds that the law will imply a duty

of care when a party with special skill provides information to a party who places trust in the accuracy of that information. In such situations the party providing the advice must know or ought to have known that the other party will place reliance upon this skill and judgment, and so must exercise reasonable care and skill when providing such advice.

It is therefore possible following from **Hedley Byrne** for a claimant to pursue an action for negligent misstatement where a duty of care arises based on the "special relationship" between the parties. Following developments in the law of tort, the scope for an action for negligent misstatement has been somewhat restricted. In particular, the decision of the House of Lords in **Caparo Industries Plc v Dickman** [1990] 2 A.C. 605, which introduced a further requirement as to "proximity" between the parties when assessing liability for negligent misstatement, makes it increasingly difficult to establish such a duty of care. So, while **Hedley Byrne** seemed to throw the door wide open to an action for negligent misstatement, the House of Lords in **Caparo** went some way to closing it by requiring sufficient proximity between the party giving advice and the party relying upon such advice, thereby limiting the potential number of individuals who may have a cause of action when relying upon such advice.

The scope of **Hedley Byrne** has been further restricted by legislative developments. As we will see, in the light of s.2 of the Misrepresentation Act 1967, the majority of claimants will now wish to pursue an action for negligent misrepresentation under the legislation, rather than at common law. That said, an action for negligent misstatement still has a number of advantages notwithstanding legislative developments. As we will see, only a false statement of fact will give rise to an actionable misrepresentation under the Misrepresentation Act 1967.

Over to you. . .

Given the enactment of the Misrepresentation Act 1967, can you identify any remaining advantages as to why a claimant may still wish to pursue an action for negligent misstatement in the law of tort?

It should be noted that the scope of negligent misstatement is much wider than that of the Misrepresentation Act. A claim in the tort of negligence can be brought in relation to both false statements of advice and *opinion*. In other words, liability for negligent advice will simply depend on a duty of care being breached between the person giving and the person receiving that advice.

The fundamental principle here is that an action for negligent misrepresentation at common law is based on the tortious action of negligent misstatement following the principles of **Hedley Byrne v Heller**. In order to succeed in an action for negligent misstatement, the claimant must establish a duty of care, based on sufficient proximity between the parties which is then breached if the party fails to exercise reasonable care and skill when providing advice.

Further, as an action for negligent misstatement follows these tortious principles, an action can be pursued for both a false statement of fact and/or opinion.

MISREPRESENTATION ACT 1967

8-024 Before the House of Lords in **Hedley Byrne** recognised the possibility of a negligent misrepresentation at common law, a claimant could only pursue an action for fraudulent or innocent misrepresentation. Perhaps rather unfortunately, Parliament reacted in 1967 by enacting the Misrepresentation Act, which sought to provide relief for negligent misrepresentation. The timing of this couldn't have been more ironic. After fraudulent misrepresentation was clarified by **Derry v Peek** in 1889, a claimant had been forced to wait many years for an actionable misrepresentation for negligence and then two came along at once.

It is, however, true to say that the majority of actions for an actionable misrepresentation will now be brought under the Misrepresentation Act 1967 (1967 Act). As we will see there are numerous advantages and reasons as to why a claimant would pursue an action under the 1967 Act rather than for fraudulent misrepresentation or negligent misstatement. Further, if successful the measure of damages for a misrepresentation under the 1967 Act is particularly generous in light of what the claimant is required to prove, which is demonstrated by s.2(1):

> **"Where a person has entered into a contract after a misrepresentation has been made to him by another party thereto and as a result thereof he has suffered loss, then, if the person making the misrepresentation would be liable to damages in respect thereof had the misrepresentation been made fraudulently, that person shall be so liable notwithstanding that the misrepresentation was not made fraudulently, unless he proves that he had reasonable ground to believe and did believe up to the time the contract was made the facts represented were true."**

This is a challenging and somewhat baffling section in relation to misrepresentation, although we shall now break down the various elements and focus on three key issues. First, what is the claimant required to prove in order to bring an action for misrepresentation? Secondly, what evidence can the defendant call as a defence to an actionable misrepresentation under the 1967 Act? Thirdly, how will damages be awarded for a misrepresentation under the 1967 Act?

WHAT IS THE CLAIMANT REQUIRED TO PROVE UNDER THE MISREPRESENTATION ACT 1967?

8-025 In order to succeed in an action for misrepresentation under the Misrepresentation 1967 Act, the claimant must simply prove (on the balance of probabilities) the elements of an actionable misrepresentation. In other words, all the claimant must establish is that a false statement of fact induced them to enter into the contract.

It is important to note that a misrepresentation under the 1967 Act is sometimes (and rather confusingly) referred to as an action for "negligent" misrepresentation. This causes confusion for students when trying to distinguish a "negligent misrepresentation" under the 1967 Act from a "negligent misstatement" at common law. However, as we will see, the elements for misrepresentation under the 1967 Act are significantly different from those of negligent misstatement.

The element of negligence is introduced by s.2(1), which operates so as to presume that all misrepresentations are made negligently. What is interesting is that at no point is the claimant required to prove negligence. As stated above, all that is required of the claimant is to establish the elements of an actionable misrepresentation, which by operation of s.2(1) will be presumed to be negligent unless the defendant is able to rebut this presumption. This leads us to the next issue.

WHAT EVIDENCE CAN THE DEFENDANT CALL AS A DEFENCE TO AN ACTIONABLE MISREPRESENTATION UNDER THE 1967 ACT?

Once the claimant has established the required elements of an actionable misrepresentation then the defendant will be required to prove a reasonable belief in the truth of that statement. The operation of s.2(1) therefore introduces a reverse burden of proof. If the defendant is not able to prove such a belief then the claimant will effectively be awarded a remedy for a negligent misrepresentation (without the claimant ever having to prove such negligence). In view of this it is rather misleading to refer to a misrepresentation under the 1967 Act as a "negligent misrepresentation", but perhaps the title of an "actionable misrepresentation for which the defendant is not able to prove a reasonable belief in its truth" is in truth not quite as punchy.

8-026

The courts have adopted a rather strict approach as to the requirement of "reasonable belief". In **Howard Marine & Dredging Co Ltd v A Ogden & Sons (Excavations) Ltd** [1978] Q.B. 574 a representation was made about the capacity of a barge that the claimants wished to hire. The defendants stated that the barge had a capacity of some 1,600 tonnes. In reaching this figure the defendants had relied upon an entry in the Lloyd's register which gave a similar capacity figure. However, the true capacity of the barge turned out to be around 1,000 tonnes and the claimants brought an action for misrepresentation under the Misrepresentation Act 1967. The defendants argued that they had a reasonable belief as to the truth of their statement regarding the barge's capacity as that statement was based on their recollection of the Lloyd's register. However, had the defendants checked the documentation that came with the barge (which they could have easily accessed), they would have discovered that the true capacity figure was much less than stated in the register. In other words, it was not reasonable for them to have relied on the figure in Lloyd's register (although it is difficult to think of a more authoritative source) and as a result the defendants had failed to discharge the burden in s.2(1) and were therefore liable for their negligent statement under the 1967 Act.

Even if the representor is able to discharge the burden under s.2(1) and prove a reasonable belief in the truth of his statement, this may not be the end of the story. It is highly likely in such cases that the representor will still be liable for an innocent misrepresentation.

DAMAGES UNDER THE MISREPRESENTATION ACT 1967 AND THE "FICTION OF FRAUD"

8-027   Not only is it misleading to talk of "negligence" in relation to s.2(1), but this section also makes reference to liability in fraud. Cast your mind back to the wording of wording of s.2(1), paying particular attention to the following extract:

> **"if the person making the misrepresentation would be liable to damages in respect thereof had the misrepresentation been made fraudulently, that person shall be so liable notwithstanding that the misrepresentation was not made fraudulently . . . "**

Over to you. . .

It is often said that the wording of s.2(1) creates a "fiction of fraud" in relation to the liability of the maker of the statement. In light of the wording of s.2(1) above can you identify why this is said to be the case?

The effect of s.2(1) is to create a "fiction of fraud". It states that the defendant shall be *so liable* notwithstanding that the misrepresentation was not made fraudulently. So to summarise, once the claimant has been able to establish an actionable misrepresentation, the burden then shifts to the defendant who must establish a reasonable belief in the truth of that statement. If the defendant cannot discharge this burden the claimant will be awarded damages *as if* that misrepresentation had been made fraudulently, but without the claimant ever having to establish fraud. As we will see, the measure of an award of damages for a fraudulent misrepresentation is particularly generous. Of course, under s.2(1) there is no requirement for the claimant to prove fraud (which is a difficult burden to discharge following **Derry v Peek**) but nevertheless the claimant will be awarded damages on the same basis as if the misrepresentation had been made fraudulently.

The cumulative effect of s.2(1) it is to produce a cause of action that is very attractive for any potential claimant and which is why the majority of claimants will be well advised to pursue an action under the Misrepresentation Act rather than for fraudulent or negligent misrepresentation at common law. First, the evidence the claimant needs to adduce in relation to a misrepresentation under the 1967 Act is very undemanding. The claimant must simply produce evidence to establish the basic elements of an actionable misrepresentation. Secondly, the burden will then shift on to the defendant, almost like a game of pass the parcel. The defendant will then have to produce evidence to establish a reasonable belief in the truth of the statement. Thirdly, if the defendant is unable to discharge the reverse burden (which as we have seen has been applied quite strictly by the courts) then the claimant will be awarded damages on the same basis as for a fraudulent misrepresentation but without having to discharge the onerous burden of proof required for fraud at common law.

The operation of s.2(1) is summarised Figure 8.2.

Hear from the Author

Scan the QR Tag or follow the link below for an overview of the operation of s.2(1) Misrepresentation Act 1967.

uklawstudent.thomsonreuters.com/category/contract-fundamentals

FIGURE 8.2 The operation of s.2(1) of the 1967 Act

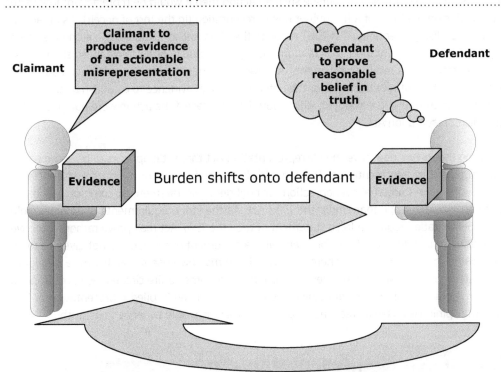

THE SCOPE OF FRAUDULENT OR NEGLIGENT MISREPRESENTATION AT COMMON LAW IN LIGHT OF THE MISREPRESENTATION ACT 1967

8-028   At first glance, it is difficult to see why a claimant would wish to pursue an action for fraudulent or negligent misrepresentation at common law, having regard to the Misrepresentation Act 1967. Given the minimal obligations imposed by the 1967 Act on the claimant in order to succeed in misrepresentation coupled with the generous award of damages under the Act it seems that the scope of other common law causes of action has been significantly limited.

Despite the powerful remedies that the Misrepresentation Act affords a claimant there are still instances in which a claimant may wish to pursue an action at common law for either fraud or negligence. This is particularly the case where a claimant must establish fraud as a requirement of establishing an actionable misrepresentation. For example, think back to the case of **Edgington v Fitzmaurice**.

As you may recall, this case concerned a statement of future intention (which would not usually form the basis of an actionable misrepresentation). In order for the statement of future intention to be actionable it would need to be established that the statement was made *fraudulently*. So, if a claimant were to pursue such an action then it would be more advantageous to pursue this on the basis of a fraudulent misrepresentation (in the tort of deceit). As an action under the Misrepresentation Act 1967 requires the claimant to establish the elements of an actionable misrepresentation, the claimant must prove fraud in order to establish such a misrepresentation. As a result, the elements of a fraudulent misrepresentation have already been established, but without the need for the defendant to call evidence to establish a reasonable belief in the truth of the statement, which would be the case if the action were pursued under the Misrepresentation Act.

So, even though we now have the Misrepresentation Act there still appears to be some scope for fraudulent misrepresentation. The same is also true of negligent misstatement following **Hedley Byrne**. As noted above, an action for negligent misstatement at common law has a potentially wider scope than under the 1967 Act. As the strict requirements of an actionable misrepresentation require a false statement of fact, the 1967 Act may prove rather restrictive in relation to a statement of opinion. Generally, a statement of opinion will not give rise to an actionable misrepresentation, whereas such opinion *may* give rise to liability for a negligent misstatement. However, this is where the argument becomes quite circular, as in most cases concerning a false statement of opinion there may also be an implied representation of fact that the opinion is based on reasonable grounds or a reasonable belief as to its truth.

. . . .

Innocent misrepresentation

8-029   Before developments in the law of tort in relation to negligent misstatement (**Hedley Byrne v Heller**), any misrepresentation that was not made fraudulently was considered to be an innocent misrepresentation. The primary remedy for an innocent misrepresentation is rescission. The scope for innocent misrepresentation has now been severely limited since the recognition of negligent misstatement and negligence under the 1967 Act. However, there are circumstances in which innocent misrepresentation will be of relevance. For example, if a claimant pursues an action under s.2(1) of the 1967 Act, and the other party is able to rebut the presumption of negligence, then the court can still award a remedy for innocent misrepresentation.

Stage 4: the remedies for misrepresentation

In our analysis of the Misrepresentation Act 1967 we have briefly looked at how damages will be awarded for such a misrepresentation having regard to the "fiction of fraud" introduced by s.2(1). We will revisit this area in more detail below but before doing so we will look at the other remedies available for misrepresentation and then analyse how these remedies differ between the different types of misrepresentation. As we will see, there is a wide range of remedies available for misrepresentation both at common law and in equity. Being able to identify when these remedies will be available and how they will affect the position of the parties can be difficult at times. For example, it may be the case that a claimant is entitled to a number of remedies flowing from a misrepresentation. Our task now is to try and understand how these remedies interact with one another.

8-030

Rescission

As the effect of misrepresentation is to render the contract voidable, then the contract will continue to bind the parties until the innocent party seeks to have the contract set aside (or avoided). Rescission is referred to as the primary remedy for misrepresentation and is generally available regardless of the type of misrepresentation that has occurred. The effect of an award of rescission is to put the parties back (so far as is possible) into the position they were in before they entered into the contract. The remedy of rescission is therefore one way in which the innocent party can seek to have the contract set aside as a result of an actionable misrepresentation. If goods have passed under the contract then these goods are to be returned. If money has passed in exchange for those goods then the money must also be returned.

8-031

Bars to rescission

As rescission is an equitable remedy, it is not available to the claimant as of right. Indeed, there are a number of situations in which the claimant may lose their right to rescind the contract. These are commonly referred to as the "bars to rescission" and we shall consider each in turn.

8-032

AFFIRMATION

8-033   If the claimant is taken to have affirmed the contract then he will lose the right to rescind the contract. In some situations it may not be apparent to the claimant that they have entered into a contract on the basis of a misrepresentation. Evidence of such a misrepresentation may only become available at a later date. However, once it has been discovered that the contract was entered into as a result of a misrepresentation, the claimant should take action to remedy the situation (such as seeking to rescind the contract). If the claimant does not take such corrective action on discovering the misrepresentation then the courts may decide that the claimant has affirmed the contract and has therefore lost the right to rescind.

A typical example can be found in the case of **Long v Lloyd** [1958] 2 All E.R. 402. In this case the claimant purchased a lorry from the defendant, which was described as being in "exceptional" and "first-class condition". After travelling only a few miles the lorry broke down. The claimant accepted the defendant's offer to repair the lorry and continued to use it before it broke down again. When the claimant sought to rescind the contract the court refused to grant such a remedy on the basis that the claimant had affirmed the contract. The first time the lorry broke down the claimant discovered that the lorry was not at all in "exceptional condition" but nevertheless agreed to accept the lorry in light of the repairs offered by the defendant.

LAPSE OF TIME

8-034   As we have seen in relation to affirmation above, the courts can be quite strict in their decision to deny the remedy of rescission. They adopt a similar approach when assessing the lapse of time between the misrepresentation and its discovery by the claimant. For example, in **Leaf v International Galleries** [1950] 2 K.B. 86, where a claimant purchased a painting following a representation that it was by the famous artist Constable, the claimant was unable to rescind the contract when it was discovered some five years later that the painting was not in fact by Constable.

This may seem quite a harsh decision particularly taking into account the fact that the claimant only found out that the painting was not by Constable when he took the item to sell at auction. This, it could be argued, is a different scenario from cases such as **Long v Lloyd**, above, where the claimant discovered the truth of the statement but decided to accept the goods anyway. In **Leaf** the claimant took steps to rescind the contract as soon as he was aware of the misrepresentation (albeit five years later). However, as Denning L.J. observed in **Leaf**:

> **"Assuming that a contract for the sale of goods may be rescinded in a proper case for innocent misrepresentation, the claim is barred in this case for the self-same reason as a right to reject is barred. The buyer has accepted the picture. He had ample opportunity for examination in the first few days after he had bought it. Then was the time to see if the condition or representation was fulfilled. Yet he has kept it all this time. Five years, have elapsed without any notice of rejection. In my judgment he cannot now claim to rescind."**

So, in cases where the claimant discovers the truth the clock will start ticking at that point and if the claimant fails to take remedial action once aware of the truth, rescission may be barred on the basis that he has affirmed the contract. However, if the claimant does not discover the truth for a considerable amount of time, but had ample opportunity to discover the truth at an earlier date, then the clock will start ticking from the time that he could have discovered the truth and he will be denied rescission on the basis of a lapse of time.

This bar to rescission therefore seems quite difficult to justify in view of the distinction above. If the parties have acted innocently and honestly then it seems particularly unjust if that innocent party is unable to rescind the contract when the truth is discovered because of a lapse of time. On the other hand, it could be equally unjust to allow a party to revisit an agreement that they were quite content with for many years after discovering the misrepresentation. It seems that the courts have to draw the line somewhere and following Lord Denning's analysis in **Leaf** it seems that a strict limitation of days or weeks (rather than years) is to be imposed in such cases.

IMPOSSIBILITY OF RESCISSION

One of the fundamental guiding principles of rescission is that of *restitutio in integrum*.   **8-035**
Translated, this Latin maxim requires that the parties be put back into their pre-contractual positions. However, this will not be possible in all cases, especially where goods that have passed under a contract have either perished or been destroyed. In these situations it may be impossible to restore the parties to their pre-contractual positions, so the remedy of rescission is not available. This will almost inevitably be the case if one of the parties has consumed the goods that passed under the contract.

A classic (and somewhat amusing) example is given by Crompton J. in **Clarke v Dickson** (1858) 120 E.R. 463; El. Bl. & El. 148, in which he draws an analogy with the sale of a cake. If you enter into a contract to purchase a cake as a result of a misrepresentation then the remedy is quite simple, you can give the cake back. However, if you have eaten the cake then it is not possible to return both parties to their pre-contractual state. In other words, you can't have your cake and eat it.

The cake example in **Clarke** is quite easy to appreciate. If the goods have been consumed or destroyed then complete rescission is impossible. A more difficult problem arises when the goods have not been completely destroyed or consumed, but rather have altered in either condition or value.

For example, in **Erlanger v New Sombrero Phosphate Co** (1877–78) L.R.3 App. Cas. 1218, a case that concerned the purchase of a phosphate mine, when the purchasers sought to rescind the contract the House of Lords had to consider whether such rescission was possible. The purchaser had already extracted a quantity of phosphate from the mine, which had in turn reduced the value of the mine. The conclusion of the House of Lords was to require the purchaser to make a payment in view of the profit he had made, but which also reflected the mine's decline in value.

Erlanger also demonstrates the more lenient approach taken by the courts of equity in relation to rescission. As an amount of phosphate had already been extracted from the mine then, technically, complete rescission was impossible. It was not possible to restore both parties to their pre-contractual positions. Notwithstanding this, if the courts can, so far as is just, restore the parties to such a position (by ordering a payment, for example) then even a case such as **Erlanger** will succeed in obtaining an order of rescission being granted.

THIRD-PARTY RIGHTS

8-036 Finally, the courts will be very reluctant to grant rescission where to do so would affect the rights of a third party. It can be quite common for a third party innocently to acquire rights under a contract that was initially induced as a result of a misrepresentation. It may be that the representee only becomes aware of the misrepresentation once he has sold the goods to a third-party. In such cases the courts may regard the third party rights as a justification to deny an award of rescission if to make the award would disturb those third-party rights.

This final bar to rescission can be seen as a kind of amalgamation of the lapse of time and impossibility bars above. For example, if a claimant only discovers the truth of the misrepresentation following a significant lapse of time, at which point the goods have been passed to a third party, then rescission is likely to be barred on the basis of the lapse of time and the courts' reluctance to affect the rights of the third party who acquired the property. Secondly, if goods have passed to a third party then it may be impossible to rescind the contract on the basis that the third party cannot be found and the goods cannot be traced. However, there also seem to be further policy considerations at work here. Even if the goods can be traced to the third party, as a matter of policy the courts will still be reluctant to interfere with the rights of that third party where he has innocently acquired such rights.

A particular problem, however, arises where the goods may have been obtained as a result of mistaken identity (unilateral mistake). The effect of unilateral mistake as to identity is to render the contract void (see **Shogun Finance Ltd v Hudson** [2004] 1 A.C. 919). If the contract is void for mistake then it is impossible for a third party to acquire ownership rights under the contract. As a result, any property that has passed can be returned to the original owner who relinquished the goods by reason of mistake.

The fundamental principle here is that the remedy of rescission is generally available for all types of misrepresentation. However, as rescission is an equitable remedy it will not always be available as of right. The claimant may lose the right to rescind the contract based on his own conduct (affirmation), a lapse of time, impossibility of rescission or if to do so would interfere with the rights of a third party. What is interesting is the potential overlap between these different "bars" to rescission and in particular their harsh application at common law.

Damages for misrepresentation

As we have seen, rescission is the primary remedy for misrepresentation and will be available for all types of misrepresentation, subject to the relevant bars. Damages are also available for a misrepresentation, although the measure and basis of their award will differ depending on the *type* of misrepresentation. This is the final issue we need to consider in relation to misrepresentation and will bring together all the issues above. We have looked at what evidence the claimant is required to adduce to establish an actionable misrepresentation and how the different requirements of each type of misrepresentation are met. Finally, we shall analyse how damages will be awarded for the different types of misrepresentation. For each type of misrepresentation we will focus on the measure of an award of damages and the relevant tests of remoteness of damage.

8-037

Damages for fraudulent misrepresentation

As we have discussed above, the standard of proof required of the claimant is very high in relation to fraud. The key test from **Derry v Peek** is that of dishonesty, which the claimant must prove in order to pursue an action for fraudulent misrepresentation. However, once this standard has been met the damages awarded for a fraudulent misrepresentation can be very generous.

8-038

First, as to the measure of damages for fraudulent misrepresentation, it is clear following the case of **Doyle v Olby (Ironmongers) Ltd** [1969] 2 Q.B. 158 that damages for a fraudulent misrepresentation are to be awarded on the tortious basis. In other words, the compensatory aim of an award of damages for fraudulent misrepresentation is to put the claimant into the position he would have been in had the misrepresentation not been made. This is different from the contractual measure of damages, which would have the effect of putting the claimant into the position he would have been in had the misrepresentation been true. This statement is not too controversial given that an action for fraudulent misrepresentation is based in the tort of deceit, so it seems logical that damages should be awarded on the same tortious principles. However, what is more controversial is the relevant test of remoteness of damage for fraudulent misrepresentation.

We will embark upon a more detailed analysis of remoteness of damage in Ch.14, but put simply the test of remoteness places a limitation on the amount of damages that can be recovered *in law*, irrespective that the loss may have *in fact* been caused by the defendant. Again, as fraudulent misrepresentation is an action in the tort of deceit, it would seem logical that the tortious test of remoteness should apply. The tortious test of remoteness states that a claimant can only recover damages for such loss that was "reasonably foreseeable". However, following **Doyle v Olby (Ironmongers) Ltd**, an award of damages for fraudulent misrepresentation will not be subject to such a test. In other words, the claimant is able to recover "all consequential loss" as a result of a fraudulent misrepresentation. In effect, this removes the remoteness test for a fraudulent misrepresentation (which is much wider than the "reasonable forseeability" test that is usually applied in tort) with the consequence that the claimant may well be able to recover more damages than would have been available applying the strict tortious principles.

It may seem strange that an award of damages for fraud should not be subject to the same tortious principles on which it is based. However, the justification for such an approach is high-lighted in Lord Denning's judgment in **Doyle v Olby**:

> **"In fraud, the defendant has been guilty of a deliberate wrong by inducing the plaintiff to act to his detriment. The object of damages is to compensate the plaintiff for all the loss he has suffered, so far, again, as money can do it . . . The defendant is bound to make reparation for all the actual damages directly flowing from the fraudulent inducement. The person who has been defrauded is entitled to say:**
>
> **'I would not have entered into this bargain at all but for your representation. Owing to your fraud, I have not only lost all the money I paid you, but, what is more, I have been put to a large amount of extra expense as well and suffered this or that extra damages.'**
>
> **All such damages can be recovered: and it does not lie in the mouth of the fraudulent person to say that they could not reasonably have been foreseen."**

Essentially, Denning is saying that since the defendant induced the other party to enter into a contract by deliberately misleading them, the defendant cannot turn round and claim that they should only be liable for damages that were "reasonably foreseeable". So, not only does the lack of remoteness test go hand in hand with the high standard required for fraud, but it also recognises the relevant fault and blameworthiness of the defendant when such damages are awarded (although whether this should be the case is more contentious given that it departs from the usual principles of an award of damages).

So, the measure of damages for fraudulent misrepresentation is calculated on the tortious basis (as if the misrepresentation had not been made). Conceptually, this can be difficult to distinguish from the contractual measure (as if the statement had been true). However, a useful example can be found in **East v Maurer** [1991] 2 All E.R. 733. In this case the defendant owned two hairdressing salons in the same area. During the sale of one of these salons the defendant represented that he would not work at a rival salon in the same area. On the basis of this statement the claimants purchased one of the salons. They ran the business for a short period but were unable to make a profit as their business was reducing rapidly. They later discovered that the defendant, despite his representation, was working at his other salon in direct competition with the claimants. The claimants then brought proceedings against the defendant for deceit.

The Court of Appeal held that damages should be awarded not only for the actual loss to the business but also for the loss of profit that could reasonably have been anticipated. So, in seeking to put the claimants back into the position they would have been in had the misrepresentation not been made, the court found the defendant liable not only for the loss to the claimants' business but also for the profit that the claimants *might* have made had they purchased another hairdressing business for a similar sum.

The next issue is that of remoteness of damage. As stated above, the court in **Doyle v Olby** clarified that there was no test of remoteness for an award of damages for fraudulent misrepresentation. In practice this means that the claimant is able to recover all consequential loss as a result of that fraud. The House of Lords applied this principle in **Smith New Court Securities Ltd v Scrimgeour Vickers (Asset Management) Ltd** [1997] A.C. 254 where the claimants were induced to purchase company shares as a result of a fraudulent misrepresentation. The defendants represented that two other bidders were interested in purchasing the shares and as a result the claimants paid a higher price. They finally purchased the shares for 82¼p each, after increasing their initial bid from 78p each as a result of the misrepresentation. In total the claimants purchased just over £23 million of shares at the price of 82¼ p per share.

The shares dropped in value owing to a fraud that was perpetrated against the company. The claimants sold the shares at this reduced value resulting in a loss of around £11 million. The defendants argued that they should only be liable for the difference between the 78p and 84¼p purchase price per share. Their argument was based on the fact that the claimants would have been prepared to pay 78p had it not been for the misrepresentation, so they should only be liable for the loss caused by their fraud. This would have resulted in the defendants being liable for a sum of around £1.2 million. However, the House of Lords held that the defendants were liable for the difference between the price paid and the amount subsequently realised on sale, which came to about £12 million. This award represented the consequential loss suffered by the claimants. The claimants would not have purchased the shares for 78p per share as this figure was not acceptable to the defendants. Accordingly, the claimants were awarded damages for the loss that flowed directly from the acquisition of the shares.

Damages for negligent misstatement

8-039   As mentioned above, an action for negligent misrepresentation at common law is based on the principles of negligent misstatement from **Hedley Byrne v Heller**. As a result, the appropriate measure of damages is naturally based on the tortious principles (to put the claimant into the position he would have been in had the misrepresentation not been made). This relationship with tort, however, has further consequences for the claimant.

First, the damages that a claimant is able to recover as a result of a negligent misstatement are limited by the tortious test of remoteness. In **Overseas Tankship (UK) Ltd v Morts Dock & Engineering Co (The Wagon Mound)** [1961] A.C. 388, it was confirmed that a claimant may only recover the damages that were "reasonably foreseeable" as a result of such negligence. Applying the same test of remoteness, a claimant in negligent misstatement may only recover damages that the defendant could "reasonably foresee" would flow from the misrepresentation.

Further, in the same way that an award of damages in tort may be reduced based on contributory negligence following the Law Reform (Contributory Negligence) Act 1945, the case of **Gran Gelato Ltd v Richcliff Group Ltd** [1992] Ch. 560 confirms that damages for negligent misstatement will also be subject to such a reduction having regard to the contributory negligence of the claimant.

Damages under the Misrepresentation Act 1967 s.2(1)

8-040   As has been discussed above, the operation of s.2(1) of the 1967 Act provides a very powerful cause of action for claimants. Not only does this section impose a rather low burden of proof on the claimant (who must simply adduce evidence of an actionable misrepresentation) but, once that burden is discharged, if the defendant is not able to prove a reasonable belief in the truth of that statement, then the "fiction of fraud" in s.2(1) operates so as to award the claimant damages on the same basis as if the statement had been made fraudulently.

In this respect it is misleading to refer to an action under the 1967 Act as either negligent or fraudulent. It is misleading as the claimant at no point is required to prove the negligence of the defendant. Further, the claimant, if successful under s.2(1), will be awarded damages on the same basis as would be the case if the statement had been made fraudulently, again without ever having to prove such fraud.

A further issue is the relevant measure of damages under s.2(1). Despite some confusion from cases such as **Watts v Spence** [1976] Ch.165, it is clear from **Sharneyford Supplies Ltd v Edge** [1987] Ch.305 that the appropriate measure of damages under s.2(1) is the tortious measure (to put the claimant into the position he would have been in had the misrepresentation not been made). This was confirmed by the Court of Appeal in **Royscot Trust Ltd v Rogerson** [1991] 2 Q.B. 297, which held that for assessment of an award of damages under s.2(1) the appropriate measure is the same as for fraudulent misrepresentation. So, even if the loss was unforeseeable, such loss will still be recoverable pursuant to the generous measure of damages under s.2(1).

Finally, given the "fiction of fraud" created by s.2(1) it is also the case that the principles of contributory negligence do not apply to an award of damages under s.2(1), therefore mirroring the position in the tort of deceit (**Alliance & Leicester Building Society v Edgestop Ltd** [1994] 2 All E.R. 38). However, following the decision in **Gran Gelato Ltd v Richcliff** it appears that the principles of contributory negligence may apply where there is concurrent liability in negligence and under the Misrepresentation Act 1967. This could lead to the peculiar situation in which the claimant will be seeking to pursue an action under the 1967 Act whereas the defendant will actually be arguing that he has breached a duty of care in order to activate the principles of contributory negligence as a partial defence to such negligence.

The fundamental principle here is that an award of damages under s.2(1) Misrepresentation Act 1967 will be awarded on the same basis as an action for fraud in the tort of deceit. This is due to the so called "fiction of fraud" introduced by this section. The wording of s.2 (1) and in particular the words "so liable" have been interpreted so as to treat the representor as if he actually perpetrated fraud (without the representee ever having to prove such fraud). These words "so liable" also have the effect that damages will be awarded on the same tortious measure as for fraud, and that there is no test of remoteness of damages for an award under s.2(1)—the representee is able to claim "all consequential loss".

Figure 8.3 outlines the difference between the types of misrepresentation and gives a summary of how the damages differ for each type of misrepresentation.

FIGURE 8.3 **Summary of types of misrepresentation and damages available**

Type of misrepresentation	What must the claimant prove?	What damages are recoverable?
Fraudulent misrepresentation (tort of deceit)	That the false statement was made knowing it was false, or with reckless disregard for its truth (*Derry v Peek*)	Damages are awarded on the tortious measure ("out of pocket loss"); and "all consequential loss" is recoverable (no test of remoteness of damage— *Smith and New Court Securities Ltd v Scrimgeour Vickers*)
Negligent misrepresentation (tort of negligent misstatement)	Claimant to establish a duty of care, breach and that such breach caused the loss or damage in question (*Hedley Byrne v Heller*)	damages are awarded on the tortious measure ("out of pocket loss"); but only loss that is "reasonably foreseeable" will be recoverable (the remoteness test in tort)
Negligent misrepresentation (1967 Act s.2)	Claimant *only* need establish an actionable misrepresentation (a false statement of fact that induced the contract); then the burden shifts to the maker of the statement who must prove a reasonable belief in its truth. If this burden is not discharged the claimant will be awarded damages for misrepresentation under the 1967 Act.	"The fiction of fraud": damages awarded on the same basis as for fraudulent misrepresentation: Damages are awarded on the tortious measure ("out of pocket loss"); and "all consequential loss" is recoverable (no test of remoteness of damage)

Damages under the Misrepresentation Act 1967 s.2(2)

8-041 As the effect of misrepresentation is to render the contract voidable, the innocent party may seek to avoid the contract via the remedy of rescission. However, the effects of rescinding the contract can be quite serious. As the court is essentially declaring the contract void by rescinding the contract, the court will be reluctant to take this step especially when compensation would provide an adequate remedy. To this extent s.2(2) allows the court to award damages in lieu (in place of, or instead of) rescission.

The wording of s.2(2) is as follows:

> "Where a person has entered into a contract after a misrepresentation has been made to him otherwise than fraudulently, and he would be entitled, by reason of the misrepresentation, to rescind the contract, then, if it is claimed, in any proceedings arising out of the contract, that the contract ought to be or has been rescinded, the court or arbitrator may declare the contract subsisting and award damages in lieu of rescission, if of opinion that it would be equitable to do so, having regard to the nature of the misrepresentation and the loss that would be caused by it if the contract were upheld, as well as to the loss that rescission would cause to the other party."

In other words, instead of rescinding a contract following a non-fraudulent misrepresentation, the court at its discretion may award damages in place of rescission. As the wording of s.2(2) is phrased in terms of "in lieu of rescission" then it would seem logical that this remedy goes hand in hand with the ability of the claimant to rescind the contract. If the right to rescind is lost then logically it should follow that the court is no longer able to award such damages "in lieu" of rescission. The precise boundaries of s.2(2) are therefore not particularly clear and there has been some confusion as to the relationship between s.2(2) and the ability to rescind the contract.

In **Thomas Witter Ltd v TBP Industries Ltd** [1996] 2 All E.R. 573 the court considered whether an award of damages under s.2(2) was dependent upon the right to rescind being available. Upon a literal interpretation it would seem particularly clear, that in order to award damages in place of rescission, the ability to rescind the contract must be present. However, the court decided that to interpret s.2(2) in this way would be too restrictive and could lead to the possibility that the innocent party be left with no remedy at all. With that in mind the court declared that the ability to award damages in lieu of rescission does not depend upon the right to rescind being available at the time a claim for damages is considered. Rather, the ability to rescind the contract must have been available to the party in the past, but not necessarily at the time the court has to consider an award of damages under s.2(2).

If the right to rescind has been lost, for example because the contract has been affirmed, then it seems particularly generous to award damages in place of a remedy that is no longer available owing to the actions of the innocent party. On the other hand, if s.2(2) were interpreted literally so that the ability to award damages is only available while the right to rescind is available, this could have particularly harsh consequences for the innocent party who may have lost the right to rescind, for example, because of a lapse of time. Of course, the difficulty in calculating what damages will be awarded in cases where the right to rescind has been lost could give weight to the argument that the right to rescind must still be available in order for the court to consider the application of s.2(2).

This position was adopted by the High Court in **Zanzibar v British Aerospace (Lancaster House) Ltd** [2000] 1 W.L.R. 2333, in which it was decided that in order for damages under s.2(2) to be awarded, the right to rescind must subsist at the time the case reaches court. This seems to be the most logical conclusion given the difficulties in assessing damages if the right to rescind has been lost at the time the case finally reaches court.

Exclusion of liability for misrepresentation

8-042   It is possible for a party to include a clause in the contract that seeks to limit or exclude liability for misrepresentation. It may sound strange that a party is able to exclude liability under a contract for their pre-contractual statements as it is usually the case that a party will seek to limit or exclude their liability for their future actions, rather than to exclude their pre-contractual behaviour. However, this is again the inevitable tension that arises between such clauses and freedom of contract.

The ability to limit or exclude liability for misrepresentation is governed by s.3 of the Misrepresentation Act 1967 (as amended by s.8 of the Unfair Contract Terms Act 1977) and provides that:

If a contract contains a term which would exclude or restrict—

(a) any liability to which a party to a contract may be subject by reason of any mis-representation made by him before the contract was made; or

(b) any remedy available to another party to the contract by reason of such a mis-representation, that term shall be of no effect except in so far as it satisfies the requirement of reasonableness as stated in section 11(1) of the Unfair Contract Terms Act 1977; and it is for those claiming that the term satisfies that require-ment to show that it does.

Therefore in relation to a clause excluding liability for misrepresentation the position is the same as that in the majority of other such clauses: the clause must pass the test of reasonableness. The reasonableness test in s.11 of the Unfair Contract Terms Act 1977 will apply to clauses exclud-ing misrepresentation in the same way as it applies in relation to any other type of exclusion clause. Similarly, the courts will also adopt a strict approach in the way in which they construe such clauses. Just as very clear and precise words are required to exclude negligence, so will equal precision be required in relation to misrepresentation. Words such as "Liability for any pre-contractual misrepresentation will be excluded" will suffice (see **Thomas Whitter Ltd v TBP Industries Ltd** [1996] 2 All E.R. 573).

Please note, that once the provisions of the Consumer Rights Bill 2013–14 are in force, s.3 Misrepresentation Act 1967 will no longer apply to "consumer contracts". Under the Consumer Rights Bill 2013–14, a term in a consumer contract that seeks to exclude or restrict liability for misrepresentation will only be binding on the parties if the clause is "fair", applying the test in s.62 Consumer Rights Bill 2013–14.

A structured approach to misrepresentation

One of the most difficult aspects of misrepresentation is being able to identify the key issues. The four-stage approach adopted in this chapter is summarised Figure 8.4.

8-043

Hear from the Author

Scan the QR Tag or follow the link below for an overview of the key issues and suggested structure in relation to the topic of misrepresentation.

uklawstudent.thomsonreuters.com/category/contract-fundamentals

FIGURE 8.4 **Overview of misrepresentation**

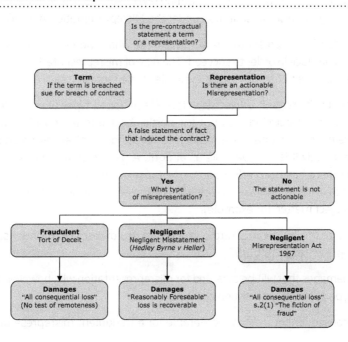

Summary

1. Misrepresentation is concerned with false pre-contractual statements and the effect of an actionable misrepresentation is to render the contract voidable.

2. It is important to distinguish a term of a contract from a representation. A term forms part of the contract and the innocent party may be able to pursue an action for breach of contract if a term of that contract is not met. The distinction between a term and a representation is based primarily on the intentions of the parties, although the courts use a number of guiding factors to assist them with this distinction.

3. If the statement is a representation then the next stage is to consider whether the statement is *actionable* for misrepresentation. An actionable misrepresentation is defined as a *false statement of fact that induced the other party to enter into the contract*.

4. Only a false statement of *fact* will be actionable for misrepresentation. Generally, a statement of opinion or future intention will not be actionable (unless made fraudulently).

5. If a statement is actionable for misrepresentation then it is important to identify the type of misrepresentation. There are three broad types of misrepresentation:

   (a) Fraudulent misrepresentation, which is an action in the tort of deceit;
   (b) Negligent misstatement at common law (**Hedley Byrne v Heller**); and
   (c) Negligent misrepresentation under the Misrepresentation Act 1967.

6. The type of misrepresentation will determine what evidence the representee will have to produce in order to succeed. The type of misrepresentation will also determine the extent of the remedies available to the representee.

7. Generally, the remedy of rescission is available for all types of misrepresentation. The effect of rescission is to put the parties back into the position they were in before the contract had been made. However, note that as rescission is an equitable remedy it is not available as of right. A party can lose the right to rescind where there has been affirmation, or a lapse of time, or where rescission would affect third-party rights or if rescission is impossible (because of the destruction of the subject matter, for example).

8. Note that the court can award damages "in lieu of rescission" under s.2(2) of the Misrepresentation Act 1967.

9. The damages that will be awarded for misrepresentation will, however, depend on the type of misrepresentation claimed.

10. "All consequential loss" is recoverable for a fraudulent misrepresentation. Loss

that is "reasonably foreseeable" is recoverable for a negligent misstatement. "All consequential loss" is also recoverable for a negligent misrepresentation under the Misrepresentation Act 1967, owing to the "fiction of fraud" introduced by s.2(1).

11. Finally, s.2(1) of the Misrepresentation Act 1967 is partially favourable to the claimant. It imposes a low burden of proof on the claimant (the claimant only needs to prove the elements of an actionable misrepresentation). The burden then shifts on to the defendant who must prove a reasonable belief in the truth of his statement. If the defendant cannot do so, the claimant will be awarded the favourable damages under s.2(1). Even if the defendant is able to rebut the presumption of negligence, the claimant may still be awarded remedies for an innocent misrepresentation.

Key Cases Grid

Case	Court	Key Issues
Bisset v Wilkinson [1927]	**Privy Council (New Zealand)**	A statement regarding the capacity of a price of land to graze sheep was held to be a statement of opinion and not actionable for misrepresentation, as neither party was in better a position to know the truth of the statement.
Smith v Land & House Property Corp (1885)	**Court of Appeal**	When one party is in the stronger position to know the truth of the statement, a statement of belief may contain an implied statement that they knew of facts which justify their opinion.
Edgington v Fitzmaurice (1885)	**Court of Appeal**	A statement of future intention is generally not actionable for misrepresentation, unless it is made fraudulently. In such cases the maker of the statement may have misrepresented their state of mind. Per Bowen L.J: "the state of a man's mind is as much a fact as the state of his digestion. It is true that it is very difficult to prove what the state of a man's mind at a particular time is, but if it can be ascertained it is as much a fact as anything else. A misrepresentation as to the state of a man's mind is, therefore, a misstatement of fact."

With v O'Flannagan [1936]	Court of Appeal	A statement of fact must be true when made and must also be true at the time the contract is formed. The court will treat the statement as being a continuing statement for these purposes and a failure to disclose a relevant change of circumstances may therefore form the basis of a misrepresentation.
JEB Fasteners Ltd v Marks Bloom & Co [1983]	Court of Appeal	The false statement of fact must induce the contract. It must be material to the decision of the other party to enter into the contract. If the party would have entered into the contract regardless, or they entering in the contract for different reasons (such as securing the services of the company directors, as in this case) then the false statement of fact will not be actionable for misrepresentation.
Doyle v Olby (Ironmongers) Ltd [1969]	Court of Appeal	In an action for fraudulent misrepresentation, damages are assessed applying the tortious measure. Damages will be awarded so as to put the claimant into the position they would have been in had the misrepresentation not been made. Further, in actions for fraud, the usual test of remoteness of damage will not apply. As Denning observed: "All such damages can be recovered: and it does not lie in the mouth of the fraudulent person to say that they could not reasonably have been foreseen." Note the significance of this approach in light of the "fiction of fraud" introduce by s.2 (1) Misrepresentation Act 1967.

End of Chapter Question

Ryan wishes to purchase a used Aston Martin car and visits a specialist dealer. He sees a model he likes and negotiates to purchase the car. As part of the negotiations the sales representative tells Ryan that the car is in excellent working order and that he believed the gearbox has just undergone a major service. In fact, the gearbox had not been serviced and was slowly leaking transmission fluid. Ryan decides not to purchase the car that day as he wants to look at some other models before purchasing.

Two months later Ryan returns to the dealership and purchases the car. He starts to drive back home but within twenty minutes of leaving the dealership the gearbox malfunctions leaving Ryan unable to drive the car. Ryan calls a recovery service and returns the car to the dealership. The dealership offers to fix the gearbox and Ryan accepts. Three months after the repairs the gearbox explodes causing significant damage to underside of the car and the engine.

Advise Ryan.

Points to answer

♦ The first issue is to determine whether the statements relating to the condition of the car and the gearbox are terms of the contract or representations.

♦ There is no evidence that the statements were reduced to writing and note the lapse of two months between the statements being made and the purchase. Compare the cases of **Dick Bentley** and **Oscar Chess**. The dealership may have specialist skill and knowledge but without knowing more about Ryan it is not clear whether he placed any reliance on this information.

♦ If the statements are representations then are they actionable for misrepresentation?

♦ A misrepresentation is a false statement of fact that induced another to enter into a contract. The statement regarding the gearbox may be a statement of opinion and therefore not actionable following **Bisset v Wilkinson**. However, by saying that he believed the gearbox had been serviced, the sales representative may have made an implied assertion of fact following the approach in **Smith v Land & House Property Corp** (he implied that he had reasonable grounds on which to make that statement).

♦ If the statement is actionable for misrepresentation then consider what type of misrepresentation has been made; was it fraudulent, negligent, or actionable under s.2(1) Misrepresentation Act 1967?

♦ Under s.2(1) Ryan need only prove that the statement was actionable, then it would be up to the sales representative to prove that he had a reasonable belief in the truth of his statement.

♦ In relation to remedies, question whether Ryan is able to rescind the contract. Affirmation and lapse of time are relevant here.

♦ Explain the award of damages and the "fiction of fraud" under s.2(1) in considering what loss Ryan will be able to recover.

Further Reading

Poole, J and Devenney, J. "Reforming damages for misrepresentation: the case for coherent aims and principles."

This article examines the basis on which damages are awarded for misrepresentation, with particular attention to s.2(1) Misrepresentation Act 1967 and the "fiction of fraud".

Stone, R. and Cunnington, R. *Text, Cases and Materials on Contract Law* (London: Routledge-Cavendish, 2014), Chapter 8

Treitel, G. *The Law of Contract*, 13th edn (London Sweet & Maxwell, 2011), Chapter 9.

Mistake

9

CHAPTER OVERVIEW

In this chapter we:

- **consider the effect of mistake on the enforceability of the agreement**
- **identify the different types of mistake**
- **discuss common mistake as to the existence of the subject matter (res extincta)**
- **discuss common mistake as to title (res sua)**
- **analyse the relevant principles of mistake as to quality**
- **analyse the relevant principles of unilateral mistake as to identity and the House of Lords decision in *Shogun Finance v Hudson***

Summary

Key Cases Grid

End of Chapter Question

Further Reading

Introduction

9-001   The law of mistake is concerned with the enforceability of agreements and is described as a "vitiating factor" in relation to the contract. If the court identifies an operative mistake then the effect will be to render the contract void for mistake.

The effect of mistake at common law is to render the contract *void*. A declaration that the contract is void is essentially a declaration that no contract ever existed between the parties. This is fundamentally different to a *voidable* contract. A voidable contract will continue to bind the parties to their obligations until such time as the contract is voidable or completed.

The distinction between a void and voidable contract has particular consequences for third parties who acquire property following an operative mistake. If the original contract between the seller and purchaser is void for mistake then any subsequent transfer of property will also be void. As a result the purchaser will not have acquired any title in the property to pass to the third party. Even though the third party would have bought the property in good faith from the purchaser, the third party will be required to return the property back to original seller. This rather harsh consequence is summarised by the Latin maxim *nemo dat quod non habet* (you cannot transfer ownership of property which you do not own).

The potentially harsh consequences that the operation of mistake can have on third parties is one reason for the courts' reluctance to recognise mistake as vitiating an agreement between the parties. Further, and more importantly, the role of the courts is to give effect to the agreement of the parties. If, objectively, the parties have formed an agreement then the courts will seek to enforce such an agreement, thereby giving effect to the intention of the parties. The courts are not concerned whether one party has entered into a bad or disadvantageous bargain. Providing that the parties freely entered into the agreement then the courts will be very reluctant to interfere with the resulting contract.

The boundaries of mistake

9-002   Defining the boundaries of mistake is not an easy task. A party could argue "mistake" in a number of ways: a mistake as to the price of an item, a mistake as to the subject matter of the contract or even whether he would have entered into a contract had he known about a particular fact in relation to the contract. However, whether the courts will recognise these mistakes as *operative* is a different matter. Only an operative mistake in law will have the effect of vitiating the agreement.

For many years there has also been tension in the relationship between mistake at common law and in equity. For the most part this tension has been resolved by the decision in **Great Peace Shipping Ltd v Tsavliris Salvage (International) Ltd** [2003] Q.B. 679 in which the

Court of Appeal severely limited the application of mistake in equity. Therefore, the focus of this chapter will be primarily on mistake at common law.

Identifying the type of mistake

The first stage in approaching an issue of mistake is to identify the type of mistake in question. This again can be quite difficult as judges, authors and commentators have developed many weird and wonderful ways of describing and classifying the different types of mistake. For the purposes of this book, however, we are concerned with two categories of mistake:

9-003

1. common mistake;
2. agreement mistake.

. . . .

Common mistake

A common mistake is concerned with situations in which both parties make the same mistake as to some fundamental element of the contract.

9-004

Broadly, there are two situations that will give rise to a common mistake:

1. a mistake as to the existence of the subject matter of the contract (*Res extincta*);
2. a mistake as to title (*res sua*).

MISTAKE AS TO THE EXISTENCE OF THE SUBJECT MATTER OF THE CONTRACT—*RES EXTINCTA*

The principle of *res extincta* is concerned with situations in which the parties enter into a contract in the mistaken belief that the subject matter of the contract exists. If, at the time of entering into the contract, the subject matter no longer exists then the contract will be void for common mistake (this position is also contained in statutory form in the Sale of Goods Act 1979 s.6). This is referred to as common mistake as *both parties* have made the *same* mistake, a mistake as to the existence of the subject matter.

9-005

DESTRUCTION OF THE SUBJECT MATTER

If the subject matter of the contract exists before the contract is entered into but at some time before the contract is formed the subject matter is destroyed, then again the principle of *res extincta* will have the effect of rendering the contract void.

9-006

A simple example of these principles in action can be seen in **Couturier v Hastie** (1856) H.L. Cas. 673. In this case the parties had agreed to sell and purchase some corn. Unknown to either party, before the contract was formed the corn started to perish and was sold on by the captain of the delivery vessel. The fact that the corn was not then provided under the contract of sale was sufficient justification for releasing the defendants from their obligations to pay for the corn.

Interestingly, while the decision of **Couturier** was effectively to recognise that the contract was void because of the parties' mistaken belief as to the subject matter, the *reasoning* of the court was not based on the issue of mistake at all. In fact, the reasoning was primarily focused on the fact that the failure to supply goods under a contract of sale was due to the destruction of the corn. To this extent it is perhaps more accurate to explain the decision based on a total failure of consideration.

Further, it is important to note that the courts will be concerned with the status of the subject matter at the time the agreement is formed. The mistake as to the existence of the subject matter must occur *before* the contract is formed. If the mistake occurs after the formation of the contract then the contract will be frustrated by the destruction of that subject matter (see **Taylor v Caldwell** at p.317).

It is interesting to compare the decision of **Couturier** with that of **McRae v Commonwealth Disposals Commission** (1951) 84 C.L.R. 377. This case concerned the tender for purchase of a sunken oil tanker that was stated as lying in a particular location on the "Jourmand Reef". In fact, neither the tanker nor the reef existed. The plaintiffs successfully bid for the right to salvage the tanker. When they arrived at the described location and found that the tanker did not exist they brought an action for breach of contract against the defendants and sought to recover the expenses they had incurred in putting together the salvage voyage. The plaintiffs argued that the contract was void for mistake as the subject matter of the contract did not exist.

The court held that the contract was not void for mistake, but damages were awarded for breach of contract. The defendants had warranted that the tanker existed and that it could be found at a particular location. When this turned out to be false the plaintiffs were entitled to damages to represent the defendant's breach of promise.

MISTAKE AS TO TITLE—*RES SUA*

9-007   The principles of *res sua* will operate to render the contract void and will arise where a party has mistakenly purchased his own property. Now, it may sound rather implausible that a party would mistakenly purchase property that he already owns, but there are a number of examples where exactly that has happened. In **Cooper v Phibbs** (1867) L.R. 2 H.L. 149, a nephew entered into a contract with one of his uncle's daughters to lease a fishery. Unknown to both parties, the nephew had already acquired ownership rights in the fishery and therefore the daughter had no title to transfer: the nephew had mistakenly purchased a lease for property that he already owned.

The court granted rescission in this case to reflect the mistake, but later in **Bell v Lever Bros** Lord Atkin explained that the decision was also correct in relation to a claim of *res sua* with the effect that the contract would be declared void for common mistake.

COMMON MISTAKE AS TO QUALITY

An interesting aspect of common mistake is whether a mistake as to the *quality* of what is being contracted for could ever render the contract void. This issue was considered by the House of Lords in **Bell v Lever Brothers Ltd** [1932] AC 161. Here the defendant company had entered into an agreement with one of its directors (Bell) that he was to remain director for a fixed period of time. Before the expiration of the agreement the company restructured and as such sought to terminate the contract of employment with Bell. In order to terminate the agreement the company paid Bell £50,000. However, after the payment had been made the company discovered that Bell had been involved in contracts that conflicted with the interest of the company and that would have justified the company terminating his contract of employment without the need for any payment. The company therefore sought to recover the payments that they had made in the mistaken belief that Bell was entitled to compensation for the termination of his employment.

9-008

The essence of the argument here relates to the quality of what was being contracted for. The company argued that a contract under which no compensation was payable was essentially different from a contract under which £50,000 was payable. The House of Lords rejected this argument and held that the contract was not void for mistake.

The fundamental principle concerning mistake as to quality is summarised by Lord Atkin in **Bell v Level Brothers**:

> **"In such a case, a mistake will not affect assent unless it is the mistake of both parties and is as to the existence of some quality which makes the thing without quality essentially different from the thing as it was believed to be."**

Applying this reasoning to the facts of **Bell** itself, it can be seen that the nature of the agreement was to terminate Bell's employment with the company. The fact that the company had to pay £50,000 to do this (as opposed to nothing had they discovered Bell's conduct earlier) had not rendered the contract essentially different from what the parties believed it to be. The nature of the contract was to terminate Bell's employment and that is what was provided by the contract.

There are many problems following the decision in **Bell v Lever Brothers**, most notably the difficulty in applying the relevant principles to subsequent cases. In fact, it could be disputed whether the door to an argument for mistake as to quality was effectively shut by the House of

Lords in **Bell**. For example, if a contract under which £50,000 is payable is not *essentially different* from a contract under which no compensation is payable then perhaps the bar has been raised to an almost unattainable level regarding mistake as to quality.

The very restrictive approach to mistake as to quality is further illustrated in Lord Atkin's obiter comments in **Bell** where he gives numerous hypothetical examples of events that would not render the contract void for mistake as to quality. Perhaps the following statement is the most controversial:

> "A buys a picture from B: both A and B believe it to be a work of an old master, and a high price is paid. It turns out to be a modern copy. A has no remedy in the absence of representation or warranty."

Again, it is difficult to think of what could be more important or fundamental when considering an issue of quality, but such a mistake would not render the contract void for mistake. Further authority for this position can be found in **Leaf v International Galleries** [1950] 2 K.B. 86. The plaintiff purchased a painting believing it to be by Constable. Some time later he discovered that it was not by Constable at all. The plaintiff brought an action for misrepresentation so any references to mistake as to quality were strictly obiter. Nevertheless, approving **Bell v Lever Brothers**, the Court of Appeal held that the contract would not have been void for mistake. Of course, there may be other remedies in the law of misrepresentation in such cases, but again, it appears that the scope of an argument for mistake as to quality has been severely restricted by the decisions in **Bell** and **Leaf**.

Despite the very clear statements in these cases that a mistake as to, for example, the authenticity of an item, will not render the contract void for mistake, the *reasoning* is less clear. Lord Atkin's reasoning seems to be very simplistic and restrictive. If we take the painting example above, he would argue that the contract is simply for the purchase of a painting. If the painting is provided (despite the fact that it is not by the artist both parties believed it to be) then the lack of that quality has not rendered the contract *essentially different*. The contract was for the purchase of that particular painting and that was what was received under the contract.

However, Treitel argues that **Bell** and **Leaf** were wrongly decided. If we take the painting example above, an individual purchases what both parties believe to be a genuine Rembrandt and a high price is paid to reflect this fact. If you were to ask the purchaser what he has just bought he may well reply "A Rembrandt". In this case it would be difficult to bring this response within the reasoning of Lord Atkin. The contract was not simply for the purchase of a painting, but for the particular quality that painting had (the fact that it was a Rembrandt). If the painting then turns out to be a modern copy Treitel would argue that the contract is void for mistake as to quality.

ASSOCIATED JAPANESE BANK V CREDIT DU NORD

The problems following the decisions in **Bell** and **Leaf** and the uncertainty surrounding mistake as to quality were further addressed in **Associated Japanese Bank (International) Ltd v Credit du Nord SA** [1989] 1 W.L.R. 255. This case concerned two banks. The plaintiff bank agreed to purchase four engineering machines from Mr Bennett (a rogue/fraudster) and then to lease the machines back to him. The bank required a guarantor for the purchase price (some £1 million). The defendant bank agreed to act as the guarantor. When the purchase took place and Mr Bennett received the £1 million purchase price, Mr Bennett then disappeared and consequently never paid for the lease of the machines. The plaintiff bank sought to enforce the guarantee against the defendant bank.

9-009

The defendant bank argued that the contract for the guarantee was void for mistake. However, in order to succeed, the bank would have to distinguish its claim from one of *res extincta*. An argument based on the fact that the machine never existed would have been of little benefit to the defendant bank following **McRae v Commonwealth Disposals Commission**. As Mr Bennett had warranted that the machines existed, which was untrue, then the appropriate remedy would be to award the bank damages for breach of contract (of course, this would have been of little help if Mr Bennett could not be traced).

Rather, the defendant bank framed its argument as one of mistake as to the quality of the contract. In other words, the nature of the contract (a guarantee) was *essentially different* from what the bank believed it to have been. Whether the machines existed did not affect the nature of the contract, but rather the fact that the machines did not exist affected the *obligations* created by the contract of guarantee. As Steyn J. observed:

> **"For both parties the guarantee of obligations under a lease with non-existent machines was essentially different from a guarantee of a lease with four machines which both parties at the time of the contract believed to exist. The guarantee is an accessory contract. The non-existence of the subject matter of the principal contract is therefore of fundamental importance."**

Following this analysis the court held that the contract was void for mistake as to quality.

THE LIMITED ACCEPTANCE OF MISTAKE AS TO QUALITY

The case of **Associated Japanese Bank v Credit du Nord** is a very rare example of the court being prepared to accept a plea of mistake as to quality. In fact, the key test of essential *difference* identified in **Bell v Lever Brothers** which appeared to introduce a very wide flexible test for such mistakes has found a very strict and rigid application by the courts (as illustrated in cases such as **Leaf v International Galleries**). Interestingly, courts in other jurisdictions have been prepared to accept mistake as to quality as rendering the contract void.

9-010

Despite the acceptance of such mistakes in other commonwealth jurisdictions, there have been few examples in the domestic courts. One of the rare examples can be found in **Nicholson and Venn v Smith-Marriott** (1947) 177 L.T. 189, in which the court considered that a mistake as to the "authenticity" of some napkins described as belonging to Charles I could render the contract void when it was discovered that they were in fact from the Georgian period. The difference in the periods had rendered the contract *essentially different*. However, these statements are strictly obiter so any thoughts that the test in **Bell v Lever Brothers** had finally found a more flexible application are perhaps somewhat premature.

Agreement mistakes

9-011   The next broad category of mistake is referred to as "agreement mistakes". As with a common mistake there must be a fundamental mistake, but the mistake in question relates to a *fundamental element of the agreement* between the parties. The effect is to render the contract void as the parties never actually agreed on a fundamental element of the contract. To this extent it is perhaps more useful to think of the effect of an agreement mistake as to *negative* the agreement. Again, the objective test of intention is important here in determining the fact of agreement.

As an "agreement mistake" is primarily concerned with the fact of whether the parties have formed a complete agreement, in reality the courts play a limited role in regulating the agreement. In the majority of cases the parties themselves will realise if there has been some fundamental mistake as to their agreement. In such cases the parties can then remedy this problem by a further agreement or can simply decide to contract elsewhere on different terms. However, once the matter has been referred to the courts, the courts must then examine the elements of the agreement in deciding how to give effect to the objective intentions of the parties.

The broad category of "agreement mistakes" can be split into two sub-categories:

1.   Mutual mistake; and
2.   Unilateral mistake.

It is now important to distinguish between these two sub-categories.

MUTUAL MISTAKE

9-012   A mutual mistake arises when both parties make a fundamental mistake as to the contract, but the parties make a *different* mistake. As the parties are mistaken as to different issues it is appropriate to describe the parties as being at cross-purposes with one another. A mutual mistake therefore goes to the heart of offer and acceptance and the courts will again use an objective test in determining whether the contract is binding. If there is sufficient ambiguity as to the fact of agreement the effect will be to negative any perceived agreement between the parties.

In **Raffles v Wichelhaus** (1864) 2 Hurl. & C. 906, the defendants agreed to purchase a consignment of cotton from the plaintiffs. The cotton was to be carried by the cargo ship *Peerless*, which sailed from Bombay. However, this seemingly straightforward agreement resulted in some fundamental confusion between the parties. There were two ships by the name *Peerless* that sailed from Bombay. One ship sailed in October and the other sailed in December. The plaintiff had offered the cotton on the basis that it would be carried by the *Peerless* that sailed in December. The defendant accepted under the mistaken belief that the cotton would be delivered by the *Peerless* that sailed in October.

The court held that this was a fundamental mistake by both parties and as such was sufficient to negative the agreement. There was sufficient ambiguity as to which ship was to deliver the cotton and therefore the parties never formed an agreement as to a fundamental element of the contract.

It is interesting to compare this decision in **Raffles v Wichelhaus** with that of **Smith v Hughes** (1870–71) L.R. 6 Q.B. 597. In this case the plaintiff agreed to sell oats to the defendant. The defendant intended to feed these oats to his racehorse. The plaintiff supplied the defendant with a sample of oats and the next day the defendant agreed to purchase a large order of the oats that were supplied. The defendant then refused to accept the oats claiming that the oats were *new* and that he had intended to buy *old* oats. The plaintiff never warranted that the oats were old, but the price agreed was quite high for new oats.

The defendant's argument of mistake was rejected and the contract was binding. Although, subjectively, the defendant had not intended to purchase new oats, objectively there was sufficient evidence that the parties had formed an agreement. The defendant agreed to purchase the oats from the sample provided by the plaintiff and those oats were supplied under the contract.

The difference between the decisions in **Raffles** and **Smith** can therefore be explained by applying the simple objective test of intention to the agreement. In **Raffles** the ambiguity of identity of the vessels meant that neither party formed an agreement as to a fundamental element of the contract. In Smith, however, the agreement was quite clear: the contract was for the purchase of the oats supplied by the sample. The ambiguity between "new" or "old" oats was not sufficient to negative this agreement.

WHO CAUSED THE MISTAKE?

If the mistake in question was due to the actions or the fault of the other party then the courts will be reluctant to apply the objective principles of agreement and hold the parties to the contract. In **Scriven Bros & Co v Hindley & Co** [1913] 3 K.B. 564, the defendant mistakenly purchased a quantity of tow at an auction. He thought he was bidding for hemp, which was more valuable than tow (a fibrous material used to manufacture clothes). As a result the defendant ended up paying a higher price than would have been expected for the tow.

9-013

The confusion over the different lots was caused by the actions of the auctioneers. When the lots were unloaded off the cargo vessel they were both labelled with the same shipping mark (despite the fact that these two different commodities would not usually have carried the same mark). The auction catalogue simply identified the two lots by their shipping number. The defendant then inspected one of the lots carrying that number which happened to be a bale of hemp. However, at the auction he bid on the lot of tow. When the defendant discovered this mistake he refused to pay for the tow.

The court held that there was no agreement between the parties. As the mistake had been caused by the auctioneer's negligence in failing to distinguish the two different lots, the court was prepared to ignore the fact that the parties had objectively formed an agreement to sell and purchase tow. The contract was therefore void for mistake.

Unilateral mistake

9-014   A unilateral mistake arises when only one party to the contract is mistaken. Despite the fact that objectively the parties may have formed an agreement, the courts will again be prepared to disregard this objective analysis if it becomes clear that one party was aware of the other's mistake. The courts will not enforce an agreement where one party has taken advantage of the other's mistake. As a result the courts will declare such a contract void for unilateral mistake.

The courts have recognised that a unilateral mistake can generally arise in two broad circumstances:

1. A unilateral mistake as to a term of the contract; and
2. A unilateral mistake as to identity.

However, the courts have approached the above circumstances in a sometimes contradictory and controversial manner.

UNILATERAL MISTAKE AS TO A TERM OF THE CONTRACT

9-015   In order for a unilateral mistake as to a term of the contract to be operative, the court requires that the other party was aware of such a mistake. In **Hartog v Colin & Shields** [1939] 3 All E.R. 566, the purchaser of some hare skins took advantage of the seller's mistake that the goods were to be sold at a price per pound. The intention of the seller was to sell the skins at a price per *piece*, in accordance with standard trade custom and practice. The court held that there was no contract between the parties. The mistake in question was as to a term of the contract (a price per pound instead of a price per piece) and the purchaser was aware of this mistake. In these circumstances the courts will not allow a party to "snap up" an offer where one party realises that there has been a mistake as to the terms of that offer.

UNILATERAL MISTAKE AS TO IDENTITY

Again, mistaken identity is referred to as a unilateral mistake as one party is aware of the other's mistake. Usually such a mistake will be instigated by a fraudster or rogue who will then seek to exploit this mistake to his or her advantage. The effect of a unilateral mistake as to identity will be to render the contract void.

9-016

THE IMPORTANCE OF A CONTRACT BEING DECLARED *VOID* FOR MISTAKE AS TO IDENTITY

The distinction between *void* and *voidable* contracts is of particular importance in the context of mistaken identity. Most of the cases we will consider revolve around a rogue who conceals his true identity in order for the other party to accept a worthless cheque for payment of goods. Before this fraud is discovered the goods are sold on to a third party. When the worthless cheque bounces the original owner of the goods will then seek to recover the items that have been obtained fraudulently. The rogue will have disappeared so the position of the third party depends upon whether the contract was void or voidable.

9-017

The original owner of the goods may claim fraudulent misrepresentation. However, the effect of a successful claim of misrepresentation will be to render the contract *voidable*. In the majority of cases the fraud does not come to light until the cheque has bounced and the goods have been sold on to a third party. If the contract is not avoided before the goods are sold to the third party then the third party will acquire title in those goods.

However, a successful claim of mistake will render the contract void. This means that no contract existed between the original owner and the rogue and as a result the rogue could not have transferred any title in those goods to the third party. The third party, despite the fact that he may have purchased the property in good faith from the rogue, will be required to return the goods to the original owner. The third party will then have to pursue an action against the rogue for a breach of an implied term as to title under s.12 of the Sale of Goods Act 1979. In reality this will provide little remedy for the third party as in the majority of cases the rogue cannot be traced so it is not possible to sue him for breach of contract.

The consequences of the distinction between a voidable and a void contract are summarised in Figures 9.1 and 9.2.

Hear from the Author

Scan the QR Tag or follow the link below for an overview of the distinction between a void and voidable contract and why this distinction is important in determining which party may bear the loss of any fraud under the contract.

uklawstudent.thomsonreuters.com/category/contract-fundamentals

FIGURE 9.1 A *voidable* contract

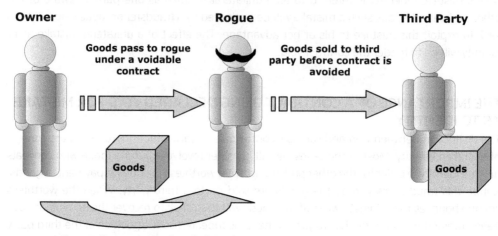

Owner

Rogue

Third Party

Goods pass to rogue under a voidable contract

Goods sold to third party before contract is avoided

Goods

Goods

Owner discovers the fraud after goods are sold to third party.   If rogue cannot be found the loss will lie with <u>the owner</u>

FIGURE 9.2 A *void* contract

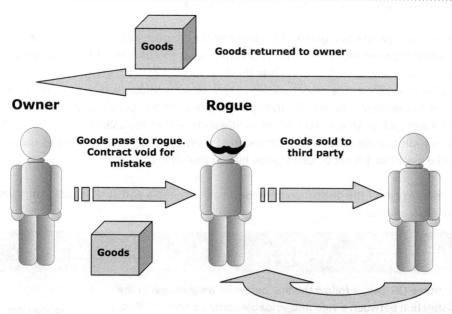

Goods returned to owner

Goods

Owner

Rogue

Goods pass to rogue. Contract void for mistake

Goods sold to third party

Goods

Breach of s.12 Sale of Goods Act 1979. If rogue cannot be found the loss will lie with the <u>third party</u>

IDENTITY MUST BE OF FUNDAMENTAL IMPORTANCE

In order for a contract to be void for mistake as to identity, it must be established that the issue **9-018** of identity was of fundamental importance to the parties. In deciding this issue the courts have developed a number of "presumptions". These presumptions depend on whether the contract is in the form of a written document or is concluded face-to-face between the parties. Further, as you will see, the courts also draw an uneasy distinction between a mistake as to identity (which, if of fundamental importance, will render the contract void) and a mistake as to the *attributes* of an individual (which will not render the contract void for mistake).

MISTAKE AS TO IDENTIFY AND WRITTEN CONTRACTS (CONTRACTS INTER ABSENTES)

When a contract is in written form, the courts apply the strong presumption that the contract **9-019** is between the parties named in the document. If one of the parties turns out to be someone other than the person named in the document, then the contract will be void for mistake.

In **Cundy v Lindsay** (1877–78) L.R.3 App. Cas. 459, an individual named Blenkarn (a rogue) entered into a contract to purchase some handkerchiefs from the plaintiff. Blenkarn gave his address as Wood Street, Cheapside. The plaintiffs believed that they were entering into a contract with a reputable firm (Blenkiron), which was also based in Wood Street. Blenkarn took advantage of the plaintiffs' mistake by signing the correspondence in a way that made it look like the plaintiffs were actually dealing with Blenkiron.

When Blenkarn obtained the goods he sold them on to the defendants who purchased them in good faith. The House of Lords held that the contract was void for mistake. The plaintiffs only intended to contract with the firm named in the document (Blenkiron). As Lord Cairns explains:

> **"Their minds never for an instant of time rested upon him [Blenkarn], and as between him and them there was no consensus of mind which could lead to any agreement or contract whatsoever."**

Again, this left the defendants in a difficult position. They faced an action in the tort of conversion and had to return the goods to the plaintiffs. The plaintiffs then had to recover their loss from Blenkarn.

A MISTAKE AS TO *IDENTITY* OR A MISTAKE AS TO *ATTRIBUTES*?

The decision in **Cundy v Lindsay** is a good illustration of the approach the courts take in rela- **9-020** tion to written documents. As the only information available to the parties is the information contained in the document there is a strong presumption that you only intended to contract with the party named in that document. However, this is not an absolute rule, merely a presumption. This presumption can be rebutted by evidence that the issue of identity was not of fundamental importance to the parties. Perhaps rather unhelpfully, the courts distinguish between a mistake as to identity which can render the contract void and a mistake as to attributes, which may render the contract voidable.

In **King's Norton Metal Co v Edridge Merrett & Co** (1897) 14 T.L.R. 98, a rogue (Wallis) represented that he was acting as a business called "Hallam & Co". In reality, there was no such business and the company was a complete fabrication. The plaintiffs entered into a contract with Hallam & Co to supply goods which the company was to pay for on credit. The goods that were received were sold on to an innocent third party (the defendants). In an action to recover the goods from the defendants the plaintiffs claimed that the contract between themselves and Hallam & Co was void for mistake as to identity. They claimed they that only intended to contract with the party named in the written document (Hallam & Co) and not with Mr Wallis.

The court rejected this argument on the basis that *identity* was not of fundamental importance to the parties. The plaintiffs were mistaken as to the *creditworthiness* of the party named in the document. The mistake as to creditworthiness of the party (the ability to pay for the goods) was a mistake as to the *attributes* of the party and therefore the contract was not void for mistake as to identity (although the contract was voidable on the facts).

This distinction between a mistake as to *identity* and a mistake as to *attributes* has found a stricter application in contracts that are concluded face-to-face between the parties.

FACE-TO-FACE CONTRACTS (CONTRACTS *INTER PRAESENTES*)

9-021   When dealing face-to-face there is a strong presumption that you intend to deal with the individual in front of you. For this reason it will be very difficult indeed to argue that identity is of fundamental importance. With a written contract the only way to identify the party is by means of the information stated in the document itself; however, when the contract is concluded face-to-face, you enter into a contract with a person that you can identify via sight and sound and there is little scope for mistake about that. It is for this reason that the courts have rarely accepted a claim of mistake of identity when the parties are dealing face-to-face.

The strong presumption in relation to face-to-face contracts is illustrated by **Phillips v Brooks Ltd** [1919] 2 K.B. 243. A rogue entered a jewellery shop and stated that he was "Sir George Bullough" and gave his address as St James's Square. The shop owner checked this information in the directory and confirmed that a Sir George lived at the address provided. The jeweller then allowed the rogue to depart with a ring in exchange for a worthless cheque. The ring was subsequently sold on to a third party and the jeweller sought to recover the ring from this third party when the cheque bounced.

The court held that the contract was not void for mistake. The jeweller had entered into a contract with the individual before him in the shop. The *identity* of that individual was not of fundamental importance to the jeweller, the jeweller was only concerned with the individual's ability to pay for the ring (an *attribute*).

A similar approach was adopted in **Lewis v Averay** [1972] 1 Q.B. 198. The scenario is very familiar in that a rogue pretended to be someone else in order to obtain property in return for a worthless cheque. In this case the rogue impersonated the famous television actor Richard Greene (of Robin Hood fame) in order to purchase a car from the plaintiff. Despite this information the plaintiff was still reluctant to accept a cheque that the rogue had completed in the name of "R Green". To pursue the plaintiff (and to complete the fraud), the rogue then produced a Pinewood Studios identity card that contained a photograph of the rogue and which was issued to "Richard Green". The plaintiff then accepted the cheque and allowed the rogue to take the car. The cheque inevitably bounced, by which time the car had been sold on to an innocent third party (the defendant).

The court refused the plaintiff leave to recover the car from the defendant. The plaintiff had not established that identity was of fundamental importance and as such had failed to rebut the presumption applied by the courts in face-to-face contracts. Again, the mistake was merely as to an attribute of the individual (his creditworthiness) and not as to his identity.

REBUTTING THE STRONG PRESUMPTION IN FACE-TO-FACE CONTRACTS

The crux of the problem is that when goods are advertised or available for sale to the general public it is always going to be difficult to argue that identity is of fundamental importance to the parties. The primary concern for the seller will be the purchaser's ability to pay for the item in question. Following **Phillips** and **Lewis** it is clear that a mistake as to the ability of a party to pay (a mistake as to creditworthiness) is a mistake as to that party's attributes, which will not render the contract void for mistake.

9-022

However, it is possible for a claimant to rebut this presumption. For example, if it is the claimant who approaches the rogue with the proposal of a contract then it will be easier to establish that identity was of fundamental importance; the claimant was only prepared to contract with that individual and no one else. For example, in **Hardman v Booth** (1863) 1 Hurl. & C. 803, the plaintiff intended to contract with a firm, "Thomas Gandell & Sons". The plaintiff approached a member of the family, Edward Gandell, believing that Edward was acting as a representative of the firm. In fact, Edward was acting in a personal capacity and the resulting contract was between the plaintiff and Edward. The court held that the contract was void for mistake. The identity of the other party was of fundamental importance to the plaintiffs, who only ever intended to contract with the firm and not an individual (Edward).

MISTAKEN IDENTITY AND THE EFFECT ON THE CONTRACT

9-023   Of course, in **Lewis v Averay** the contract was voidable for misrepresentation, but as the contract had not been avoided before the car was sold to the third party, the loss rested with the plaintiff. This decision also raises one of the most contentious issues regarding mistake— the effect that an operative mistake should have on the contract in these situations. As a consequence of such fraud there are usually two innocent parties: the seller who has been defrauded of his property and the innocent third party who bought the property in good faith from the rogue.

If the contract is void, this favours the third party who will have acquired title in the goods. If the contract is voidable, the seller has the ability to avoid the contract before the goods are sold on and thus can rescind the contract. Lord Denning in **Lewis v Averay** suggested that the appropriate effect in such cases should be to render the contract *voidable* for mistake. However, given the restricted interpretation of "identity" following cases such as **Lewis v Averay** and **Phillips v Brooks**, with the courts making a strict distinction between mistakes as to identity and mistakes as to attributes, this approach has not found favour with the courts.

THE DECISION IN INGRAM V LITTLE

9-024   Despite the criticisms of **Phillips v Brooks** and **Lewis v Averay**, a more problematic decision regarding mistake as to identity is that of **Ingram v Little** [1961] 1 Q.B. 31. Again, the scenario is familiar, but the decision is very surprising. Here the rogue persuaded two elderly ladies to part with their car in exchange for a worthless cheque. Initially the women were reluctant to accept a cheque and insisted that payment be in cash. The rogue then gave the women his name and address, which they checked against a telephone directory. The directory revealed that a person of that name lived at the address provided. On the basis of this information the women accepted the cheque and the rogue left with the car.

The Court of Appeal held that the contract was void for mistake. Therefore, the court was willing to accept that identity was of fundamental importance to the parties. However, this decision is very difficult to reconcile with that of cases such as **Phillips v Brooks** and **Lewis v Averay**. It would seem that the mistake in **Ingram** was exactly the same; the women were again merely mistaken as to the *creditworthiness* of the individual (an attribute) and therefore the contract should not have been declared void. In fact, it is perhaps easier to argue that the *only* fact the women were concerned with was the ability of the individual to pay, which is why they were initially reluctant to accept a cheque.

Further, it is difficult to see how the women demonstrated that it was the issue of *identity* that was of fundamental importance to them. There is little to distinguish their rather minimal efforts to verify the identity of the rogue from the efforts of the jeweller in **Phillips v Brooks**. Despite these obvious problems the Court of Appeal found in favour of the elderly ladies.

EXPLAINING THE DECISION IN *INGRAM V LITTLE*

As mentioned above, it is very difficult to reconcile the decision in **Ingram v Little** with **Phillips v Brooks** and **Lewis v Averay**. The reasoning of the Court of Appeal in Ingram appears to be based on an analysis of offer and acceptance. The court held that the women directed their offer of sale towards the individual that the rogue was impersonating (a Mr Hutchinson). As the rogue was not Mr Hutchinson, he could not accept that offer. The contract was therefore void.

9-025

However, this reasoning becomes rather circular and indeed fails to address the fact that *identity* must have been of fundamental importance. The offer could only have been accepted by Mr Hutchinson if identity was of fundamental importance and it is submitted that this requirement was not established on the facts of the case.

Given the problems with the decision in **Ingram** it is not surprising that the court in **Lewis v Averay** doubted the correctness of this decision. In fact, Devlin L.J. (dissenting) concluded that the contract in Ingram should not be void for mistake, stating that:

> "There was nothing to rebut the ordinary presumption that the first plaintiff was addressing her acceptance to the person to whom she was speaking . . . In the present case, the rogue's identity was immaterial. His credit-worthiness was material, for the plaintiffs were really concerned with his credit-worthiness, not with his identity, but credit-worthiness in relation to a contract was not a basic fact, and a mistake about it did not vitiate a contract."

In the light of these irregularities perhaps the best way to approach **Ingram** is to recognise that there are underlying policy considerations also at work (the desire of the court to protect the innocent and vulnerable old ladies) and to recognise the decision as somewhat of an anomaly given the particular facts.

The House of Lords decision in *Shogun Finance v Hudson*

The most recent and authoritative decision on mistake can be found in the House of Lords decision in **Shogun Finance Ltd v Hudson** [2004] 1 A.C.919. The facts are quite complex and for this reason an outline of the case is set out in Figure 9.3. In this case a rogue entered a Mitsubishi dealer and identified himself as Mr Durlabh Patel. He selected a car and the dealer agreed to sell on hire purchase. Mr Patel produced a stolen driving licence belonging to the real Mr Patel as proof of his identity. The dealer completed the application form and the rogue signed the application in the name of "Durlabh Patel". The dealer then faxed the application form along with the driving licence to Shogun Finance.

9-026

Shogun Finance completed the necessary credit checks and approved the application. The rogue then paid a 10 per cent deposit to the dealer and was allowed to drive the car away. The car was subsequently sold to Mr Hudson. The cheque used to pay for part of the deposit bounced and Shogun Finance brought an action against Mr Hudson to recover the car.

In his defence Mr Hudson tried to avail himself of the protection of s.27 of the Hire Purchase Act 1964 by arguing that the rogue was a debtor under the finance agreement and therefore Mr Hudson had acquired title to the car. The Court of Appeal rejected this argument and held that the contract was between the finance company and the person named in the written document. As the document was signed in the name of "Mr Patel", only the "real" Mr Patel was a debtor under the agreement. Of course, the court was not going to hold the real Mr Patel liable given the rogue's fraud in using his stolen driving licence and imitating his signature. Mr Hudson then appealed to the House of Lords.

The House of Lords dismissed the appeal by a majority of three to two (Lords Nicholls and Millett dissenting). Again, the House focused on the form of the contract in question. As the contract was in writing the House applied the principles from **Cundy v Lindsay** (1877–78) L.R.3 App. Cas. 459 and **Hector v Lyons** (1989) 58 P. & C.R. 156, that the contract was between the finance company and the person named in the written document (Mr Patel). As the real Mr Patel had not entered into the finance agreement, the contract was void for mistake as to identity.

FIGURE 9.3 *Shogan Finance v Hudson*

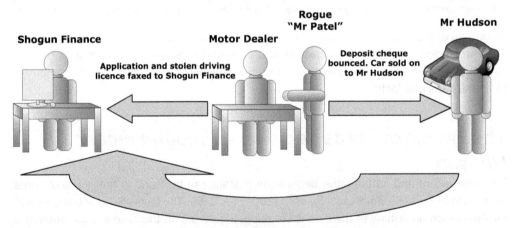

Shogun Finance v Hudson

Contract void for mistaken identity. The car (or the value thereof) to be returned to Shogun Finance.

This decision had particularly harsh consequences for Mr Hudson. As the contract was void for mistake, Mr Hudson was not a debtor under s.27 of the Hire Purchase Act 1964 and was therefore liable to return the car (or the value thereof) to Shogun Finance. This is despite the fact that he purchased the car in good faith from the rogue. Given the effect of the decision for Mr Hudson, it is interesting to compare the reasoning of the majority with that of the minority in assessing the merits of this decision.

THE MAJORITY DECISION

■ Lord Hobhouse

The reasoning of Lord Hobhouse was firmly based on the fact that a written document was used to identify the parties. The written document identified Mr Patel so Shogun Finance only intended to enter into a contract with the party named in that document. As the rogue was not Mr Patel, the contract was void for mistaken identity. Lord Hobhouse was of the opinion that identity was of *fundamental importance* to Shogun Finance as they used this information to check the credit rating of the applicant and to assist them in deciding whether to enter into a credit agreement with the applicant.

9-027

Mr Hudson argued that the car dealer in the showroom was an agent of Shogun Finance and as such the face-to-face principles from **Phillips v Brooks** and **Lewis v Averay** should apply. The face-to-face principles create a strong presumption that a party intends to deal with the individual in front of him. This would mean that the car dealer would have intended to deal with the "rogue" (not Mr Patel) and the "rogue" would therefore be a debtor under the Hire Purchase Act and Mr Hudson would be able to keep the car.

Lord Hobhouse rejected the agency argument on the following grounds:

> **"The rule that other evidence may not be adduced to contradict the provisions of a contract contained in a written document is fundamental to the mercantile law of this country; the bargain is the document; the certainty of the contract depends on it."**

Lord Hobhouse therefore relied on the parol evidence rule, which states that it is not possible to call further evidence to contradict the content of a written document. Again, the focus was purely on the written document. The use of a written document to identify the parties meant that identity was presumed to be of fundamental importance following **Cundy v Lindsay**. Mr Husdon was prevented from calling additional evidence to establish the existence of an agency relationship and the contract was void for mistake.

■ Lord Walker and Lord Phillips

Again, Lord Walker and Lord Phillips gave weight to the fact that a written document was used to identify the parties. They reaffirmed the distinction between contracts made face-to-face and contracts concluded in a written document (not face-to-face). As a written document was

9-028

used to identify Mr Patel, the only information on which the finance company had to base their decision was the information provided in the document. The document identified Mr Patel, so the contract was void for mistake as the finance company did not enter into a contract with Mr Patel.

Lord Phillips also made reference to the principles of offer and acceptance to support this conclusion.

> "Where there is an issue as to whether two persons have reached an agreement, the one with the other, the courts have tended to adopt the same approach to resolving that issue as they adopt when considering whether there has been agreement as to the terms of the contract. The court asks the question whether each *intended*, or must be deemed to have *intended*, to contract with the other."

Applying these principles, Shogun Finance only *intended* to deal with Mr Patel (the party named in the written document). However, the offer came from the "rogue". As a result there was no contract between the finance company and the "rogue", so the rogue was not a debtor for the purposes of the Hire Purchase Act.

Lord Phillips recognised that in face-to-face contracts a party *intends* to deal with the party in front of him. However, again, Lord Phillips decided that as a written document was used to identify the parties there could be no doubt as to the finance company's *intention*; they *intended* to deal only with the person named in the written document (Mr Patel). Therefore, **Cundy v Lindsay** remains the leading authority on this point as was approved by the majority.

THE MINORITY VIEW

9-029   Lord Nicholls and Lord Millett disagreed with the majority and held that the strict distinction between written documents and the face-to-face principles should be disregarded. To distinguish between parties identified in written documents and parties identified face-to-face would have no discernible effect on the outcome of the case. As Lord Nicholls observed:

> "Some time was taken up in this case with arguments on whether the dealer was an agent for the finance company and for what purposes. This was in an endeavour to bring the case within the 'face-to-face' principle. The need for such singularly sterile arguments underlines the practical absurdity of a principle bounded in this way. The practical reality is that in the instant case the presence or absence of a representative of the finance company in the dealer's showroom made no difference to the course of events. Had an authorised representative of the finance company been present no doubt he would have inspected the driving licence himself and himself obtained the information needed by his company. As

> it was, a copy of the licence, together with the necessary information, were faxed to the finance company. I can see no sensible basis on which these different modes of communication should affect the outcome of this case. I would set aside the orders of the assistant recorder and the Court of Appeal, and dismiss this action. Mr Hudson acquired a good title to the car under section 27 of the 1964 Act."

The minority therefore argued that **Cundy v Lindsay** should not be followed and that the distinction between written documents and contracts concluded face-to-face should only have an effect on the way in which the contract is enforced. The effect of the fraud should render the contract *voidable*, but not void.

Over to you. . .

Reflect on the dissenting speeches of Lord Nicholls and Lord Millet. They argue that there should be no logical distinction between cases formed face-to-face or those contracts formed at a distance. Do you agree with their approach? What advantages could you identify by following their reasoning?

There is certainly merit in this line of reasoning. Whether the contract is face-to-face or at a distance the issue remains the same. In both cases a party intends to deal with the party he is addressing, whether face-to-face or in a written document. In the case of a written document the party intends to deal with the individual signing the document, and not strictly the person named in the document. For this reason it seems that an application of **Cundy v Lindsay** would then lead to an absurd result. If the strict distinction between face-to-face and written documents were maintained, then a contract would be void for mistake as to identity when the fraudster uses a written document to perpetrate his fraud, whereas the contract would be voidable (usually for misrepresentation) if the fraud is perpetrated face-to-face. This poses an interesting question: why should the position of an innocent third party be determined by the method by which the rogue chooses to perpetrate his fraud?

Perhaps a better way to allocate loss would be to focus on the issue of fault. This would be the preferred approach of the minority. For example, in **Shogun** there were two innocent parties, but one "more innocent" than the other. The finance company had allowed the fraud to be perpetrated and had agreed to release property without full payment after conducting very minimal checks to verify the identity of the rouge (a similar scenario to that in **Phillips v Brooks**). In this case the risk should lie with the party that is more at fault (Shogun Finance) rather than Mr Hudson who purchased the car in good faith from a fraudster. The suggestion that the fraud renders the contract voidable in such cases would certainly seem to be the preferable approach.

THE CONSEQUENCES OF THE DECISION IN *SHOGUN FINANCE V HUDSON*

9-030   Despite the attractive reasoning of the minority in Shogun Finance, the unattractive decision remains. The courts are still prepared to draw an uneasy distinction between those contracts concluded in a written document or those concluded face-to-face. The majority of the House of Lords were prepared to approve **Cundy v Lindsay** despite the fact that there is little discernible logic in distinguishing between these different types of contract. For example, what if a "rogue" were to perpetrate a similar fraud, but instead of doing so face-to-face he did so over the telephone? Applying the minority reasoning of Lord Nicholls and Lord Millett, it would seem to make little difference. There would still be a contract, between the parties, but the "rogue's" fraud would have the effect of rendering the contract *voidable*. Applying the reasoning of the majority to this example is more difficult as telephone communication does not clearly fit with the strict face-to-face/written document distinction.

Documents signed by mistake (non est factum)

9-031   Finally, the courts may exceptionally release a party from a contract where the party has signed a document by mistake. In such cases the claimant will make a plea of non est factum (which approximately translates as "it is not my deed").

In order to plead successfully non est factum, the claimant must establish that the contract they signed was fundamentally different from what they believed it to have been. Further, the claimant must not have been careless in signing the document.

These requirements are demonstrated in **Saunders v Anglia Building Society** [1971] A.C. 1004. Here, an elderly widow intended to transfer ownership of her property to her nephew who would, in return, allow her to live in the property. The nephew intended to use the property as security for a loan. A friend and adviser of the nephew presented the widow with a document which he told her was to transfer the property to the nephew. Actually, the document transferred ownership of the property to the friend. The widow was not aware of this fact as she had broken her glasses and therefore signed the document without reading it.

The court rejected her claim of non est factum on two grounds. First, the document was not fundamentally different from what the widow believed it to have been. The nature of the document was for the transfer of her property (albeit to a different party). Secondly, the widow had been careless in signing the document without reading it. As a result of the decision in **Saunders**, the scope of non est factum has been severely limited. However, there have been occasions in which it has been pleaded successfully (see **Lloyds Bank Plc v Waterhouse** [1991] Fam. Law 23).

Summary

1. An operative mistake will render the contract void. This has potentially harsh consequences for a third party who purchases property in good faith in ignorance of any initial operative mistake.

2. There are two broad categories of mistake, common mistake and "agreement mistakes". A common mistake arises where both parties make the same mistake as to some fundamental element of the contract. A common mistake can arise in relation to the existence of the subject matter of the contract (*res extincta*) or a mistake as to title (*res sua*).

3. The courts have adopted a very restrictive approach in relation to claims of common mistake as to quality. Following **Bell v Lever Brothers**, for a common mistake as to quality to be operative the lack of quality must render the contract "essentially different" from what it was believed to have been.

4. Agreement mistakes go to the heart of offer and acceptance and will have the effect of negativing the agreement between the parties. An agreement mistake can be mutual (where the two parties make different mistakes) or unilateral (where only one party is mistaken).

5. For a unilateral mistake as to identity to render the agreement void it must be established that identity is of fundamental importance. In determining this issue the courts use a number of presumptions depending on the way in which the contract is formed.

6. If the contract is concluded at a distance and is contained in a written document, then there is a strong presumption that the claimant only intended to deal with the person named in that document. If the party named in the document is not the party the claimant believed he was contracting with, then the contract may be void for mistake.

7. If the contract is concluded face-to-face then there is a strong presumption that you intend to contract with the person in front of you. In these cases it will be very difficult to rebut this presumption and if it is not rebutted the contract will only be voidable (usually for misrepresentation).

8. Finally, if a contract is signed by mistake then the principle of non est factum may release the innocent party from the contract. However, the document must be of a different nature from what the party believed it to have been and the party must not have been careless in signing the document.

Key Cases Grid

Case	Court	Key Issue
Bell v Lever Brothers Ltd [1932]	House of Lords	The House of Lords recognised that a common mistake as to quality could potentially render a contract void. Per Lord Atkin: "In such a case, a mistake will not affect assent unless it is the mistake of both parties and is as to the existence of some quality which makes the thing without quality essentially different from the thing as it was believed to be."
Cundy v Lindsay (1878)	House of Lords	This case concerns a unilateral mistake as to identify and establishes that in contracts not formed face-to-face, there is a strong presumption that the parties only intend to deal with those persons identified in the written document.
Phillips v Brooks Ltd [1919]	King's Bench Division	In contracts concluded face-to-face, there is a strong presumption that the parties intend to contract with those they identify as stood in front of them. The identity of the contracting party must be of fundamental importance. A mistake as to the creditworthiness of an individual (a mistake as to an attribute), will not be sufficient to render a contract void for unilateral mistake as to identify.
Shogun Finance Ltd v Hudson [2004]	House of Lords	The House of Lords confirmed the (rather artificial) distinction between those contracts formed face-to face and those not formed face-to-face. The House of Lords rejected the agency argument advanced by the defendant and following Cundy v Lindsay held that as the contract was reduced to writing, the presumption was that the Claimants only ever intended to deal with party named in the contractual document. The contract was therefore void for mistake when it was discovered that the contract was not with Mr Patel. In particular, note the dissenting speeches in Shogun and the proposal that cases of mistake should simply render all contracts voidable, rather than void and thus providing further enhanced protection for innocent 3rd parties in such cases.

| Saunders v Anglia Building Society [1971] A.C. 1004 | House of Lords | In exceptional cases, a party who has signed a document by mistake may be released from the contract following a successful plea of non-est factum ("it is not my deed").
The document signed must be fundamentally different from what the party believe it to be and the party must not have been careless in signing the document. |

End of Chapter Question

Vinnie enters a jewellery shop intending to purchase a Rolex watch. He agrees to purchase a watch and the shop owner asks that Vinnie pays in cash. Vinnie then produces a "Musicians Union" card displaying his picture and says that he is the famous international recording artist David Hasseltoff. The shop owner agrees to accept the cheque providing that Vinnie signs a written document providing details of his address and bank details. Several days later the cheque bounces. The shop owner traces the watch by using its serial number and brings an action against John to recover the watch. John purchased the watch from Vinnie in good faith.

Advise John.

Points of Answer

♦ This is an example of a unilateral mistake as to identify. If operative, the mistake can render the contract void. If the mistake is not operative then the contract may only be voidable for misrepresentation. This distinction between a void and voidable contract will determine whether the shop owner is able to recover the watch from John.

♦ Consider whether the face-to-face or non face-to-face principles will apply to this contract.

♦ In order to be operative, the shop keeper will need to establish that Vinnie's identity was of fundamental importance. Compare and contrast the decisions of **Philips v Brooks, Lewis v Averay** and **Ingram v Little** in relation to the face-to- face principles.

♦ However, in light of the House of Lords decision in **Shogun Finance v Hudson** it seems that the written document will be of most significance. Applying **Cundy v Lindsay** the court may decide that the shopkeeper only intended to deal with the party named in the document (David Hasseltoff) and as such the contract may be void for mistake.

♦ If the contract is void then John will have to return the watch (or the value thereof) to the shop owner as he acquired no ownership rights in the watch.

Further Reading

Elliott, C. "No Justice for Innocent Purchasers of Dishonestly Obtained Goods: Shogun Finance v Hudson", [2004] J.B.L. 381

> A critical account of the House of Lords decision in Shogun Finance v Hudson and how the differing approaches of the majority and the minority in considering the rights and interests of the innocent parties under the contract.

Chandler, A. Devenney, J and Poole, J. "Common mistake: theoretical justification and remedial inflexibility."J.B.L. 2004, Jan, 34–58

> This article explore the origins and development of the law relating to common mistake, with particular analysis of Great Peace Shipping Ltd v Tsavliris Salvage (International) Ltd [2002] and Bell v Lever Brothers Ltd [1932].

Stone, R. and Cunnington, R. *Text, Cases and Materials on Contract Law* (London: Routledge-Cavendish, 2014), Chapter 8

Treitel, G. *The Law of Contract*, 13th edn (London Sweet & Maxwell, 2011), Chapter 9.

Duress and Undue Influence

10

CHAPTER OVERVIEW

In this chapter we:

● **discuss the relevant principles of duress, focusing in particular on the principles of economic duress**

● **distinguish duress from undue influence**

● **analyse the different categories of undue influence**

● **analyse the ways in which the court will presume influence between two contracting parties**

● **consider the issues relating to undue influence and third parties.**

Summary

Key Cases Grid

End of Chapter Question

Further Reading

Introduction

10-001 As with mistakes, discussed in the previous chapter, the operation of duress may vitiate an agreement between the parties. Simply, duress extends to situations in which a party has been forced to act in a particular way as a result of illegitimate pressure. You may be familiar with the concept of duress from everyday situations and when most people think of duress they associate the word with threats of physical force or violence to a person or his friends or family. Such conduct may of course have criminal law sanctions over and above any contractual issues that arise. However, even this very basic concept of duress based on threats of violence or physical force translates across into the law of contract.

A person may enter into a contract on the basis that he or she has been threatened with physical consequences if they do not enter into a particular agreement. The scope of such threats in a finding of duress will be considered below in more detail. However, even this simple example raises a number of fundamental issues. First, what effect will such threats have on the validity of any resulting agreement? If a party acted in a particular way as a result of improper pressure, does this necessarily mean that they were incapable of forming an agreement? If the parties reached an agreement (albeit as a result of improper pressure) will the courts intervene to assess the validity of such an agreement? Secondly, identifying the effect that these threats have on the individual can be difficult. An individual might make quite an innocuous threat or statement which then has an exaggerated effect on the conduct of the other contracting party. The maker of the statement could then find that the agreement is challenged on the basis of duress. Whether an objective or subjective assessment of duress should be applied will of course have a dramatic effect on the validity of any agreements that are challenged on such grounds.

There are also further issues when assessing duress in the sphere of contract law. While it is entirely possible that an individual may claim that they entered into a contract as a result of threats of violence or physical force, a more complicated problem arises where those threats fall short of violence. For example, a party may enter into a contract on the basis of improper *commercial* or *economic* pressure exercised by the other party. This is a particular problem in the light of the principles of freedom of contract.

Given the self-regulatory nature of contract law the courts are faced with a difficult task when having to consider the scope of economic duress. Distinguishing between *legitimate* economic pressure which can act as a vital negotiating tool and which also provides the foundations of which freedom of contract is based, and distinguishing between illegitimate threats which can render the contract voidable, can be a difficult.

Further there are number of problems when assessing the operation of duress. First, as questioned earlier, does the fact that a party acted in a particular way as a result of improper pressure mean that they were incapable of forming an agreement? Of course, a party is quite capable of forming an agreement even when doing so under duress. In other words, the party suffering as a result of duress may not have had their free will sapped away so that they are simply acting under the command of the party exercising such pressure. Rather, the courts will have to address the more complex issues that arise where a party is subjectively capable of forming an agreement but that agreement should be challenged on more wide-ranging policy grounds due to the operation of duress.

Threats of physical force or violence

Although the primary focus of this chapter will be on illegitimate commercial pressure, the coercion of a contracting party by threats of physical force or violence also has a role to play outside the scope of the criminal law. As mentioned above, it is possible for a party to claim that they entered into an agreement on the basis of such threats. In assessing the scope of threats of physical force or violence within contract law it is necessary to separate the vital elements. First, the threats must be *sufficient* to amount to duress. In other words, not all threats will automatically amount to duress. An assessment of what threats will enable a contract to be set aside on the basis of duress needs to be conducted. Secondly, if the threats are sufficient to amount to duress, then it will need to be considered what effect these threats had on the individual when entering into the contract. In other words, what standard is required at law before it can be said that a defendant suffered duress? Thirdly, there must be a causal link between the threats and the resulting actions of the claimant (the individual claiming duress).

10-002

These requirements can be simply summarised as a two-limb test, all of which must be satisfied in order for a claimant successfully to plead duress:

1. was the nature of the threats sufficient to amount to duress? If so
2. what effect did such threats have on the claimant?

We will consider each of these limbs in turn.

Was the nature of the threat sufficient to amount to duress?

It is the case that not all threats are capable of giving rise to duress. However, in assessing this requirement of duress the courts have focused on the need for some kind of illegitimate (as in *illegal*) behaviour. Once it has been established that the conduct of the defendant constituted of some kind of illegal act then the courts are apparently prepared to set the resulting agreement aside. The degree of illegality also appears to be very wide indeed. The courts are not only concerned with illegal criminal acts, as behaviour falling short of criminal conduct (such as a tort) may amount to conduct sufficient to give rise to duress. In assessing the operation of duress the first step is therefore to consider the requirement of illegitimate conduct on behalf of the defendant.

10-003

In **Barton v Armstrong** [1976] A.C. 104 the claimant sought to set aside an agreement by which he was required to purchase the defendant's interest in a company after the defendant had threatened that he would have the claimant murdered if the claimant did not go through with the transaction. The Privy Council (unsurprisingly) set the contract aside on the basis of duress. The decision in **Barton** itself is uncontroversial; the threat of death was sufficient for the plea of duress to succeed. Given that the touchstone for duress appears to be that of illegitimate conduct on behalf of the defendant then this would apparently narrow the importance of the conduct of the claimant in such cases. There remains some uncertainty as to the precise effect that the defendant's actions must have on the claimant.

Effect of the threats on the claimant

10-004   As mentioned in the introductory paragraphs it is possible for an individual to enter into a contract voluntarily, albeit reluctantly, on the basis of the defendant's conduct. The dichotomy for the courts has been to distinguish the situation where a voluntary act is induced as a result of improper pressure from the situation where the acts of the defendant result in the claimant entering into a contract involuntarily. This has always been a difficult distinction to draw and is not a distinction that is unique to contract law. The criminal law courts have also wrestled with this distinction in deciding whether the defence of duress will be available to a defendant.

It is perhaps useful to draw an analogy with the criminal law in assessing the necessary effect that such threats have on the claimant. In particular, we will see how the criminal law has addressed this tension and difficulty in distinguishing between a voluntary and an involuntary act of the party coerced. In the criminal law case of DPP for **Northern Ireland v Lynch** [1975] A.C. 653, the House of Lords was willing to accept that in order for the defence of duress to be available it is not necessary that the threats operated so as to "overbear the will" of the defendant. In other words, the House of Lords recognised that even in the most extreme situations an individual may still be faced with a choice. It may be that only one option is realistically available, but nevertheless they may have to choose the lesser of two evils.

In the principles relating to contract law there has been more hesitation to accept this position and the authorities have instead still referred to the need for the claimant's will to be "overborne". This causes difficulties as it would seem that the claim of duress will only be available where the claimant acts involuntarily as a result of the coercion of the defendant. This is contradictory as not all the cases in which duress was found to be actionable have been concerned with a claimant who was acting as a complete automaton as a result of the defendant's threats. Indeed, it is questionable whether the threat in **Barton** itself could be said to have "overborne the will" of the claimant so that he was acting completely involuntarily.

So, we seem to have come somewhat full circle. Despite the consistent requirement that the will of the claimant be "overborne" by the actions of the defendant, this requirement seems to have been observed more in form than substance. Rather, the key test appears to be that of *illegitimate behaviour* of the defendant.

Economic duress

We have so far discussed duress in the context of a physical threat of force or violence. However, these types of threat are quite rare in contract law. It is more likely that the nature of the threat in question will be a threat to *breach a contract*. These types of threat are capable of amounting to "economic duress". As we will see, the courts have been rather slow in developing legal principles to govern these types of threat. Early attempts to recognise economic duress were made in cases such as **Stilk v Myrick**, but these fell short of declaring economic duress as a general principle of law.

There are a number of reasons why the courts have been slow in developing specific legal principles that recognise economic duress, but one of the underlying problems is the inevitable tension between principles of economic duress and the principles of freedom of contract.

One of the key issues in relation to economic duress is again trying to define its boundaries. The principles of freedom of contract recognise the use of legitimate economic pressure which can be a useful and lawful bargaining tool. However, the use of illegitimate pressure may amount to duress. This requires the courts to distinguish between a *legitimate* and an *illegitimate* threat.

The courts recognised that threats to *goods* could amount to economic duress (**Skeate v Beale** (1840) 11 Ad. & El. 983), but this still fell short of recognising an accepted doctrine of economic duress.

· ·

The development of economic duress

It was not until the decision in **Occidental Worldwide Investment Corp v Skibs A/S Avanti (The Siboen and The Sibotre)** [1976] 1 Lloyd's Rep. 293, that the courts started to develop a clearer doctrine of economic duress. In this case the plaintiffs had chartered two ships from the defendants. The plaintiffs threatened that they would go bankrupt if the defendants refused to renegotiate the charter agreement. In fact, the plaintiffs were not on the verge of insolvency. The plaintiffs were quite solvent and they were seeking to exploit a recession in the shipping industry to their advantage. The defendants agreed to renegotiate the charter agreement as it would have been very difficult for them to charter the vessels to anyone else given the recession. The defendants then changed their minds and sought to bring the agreement to an end on the basis that the plaintiffs had exerted improper pressure in procuring the renegotiation. The plaintiffs sued for breach of contract.

The court held that as the contract had been renegotiated as a result of the plaintiff's *fraud* then the agreement could be set aside. Interestingly, in his judgment Kerr J. seemed

10-005

10-006

to accept that a threat to *breach a contract* could amount to economic duress. However, the defendant's claim of economic duress failed on the facts. Kerr J. held that the defendant's will had not been "overborne by compulsion" so as to bring the contract to an end for duress.

Following Kerr J.'s judgment it seemed that the court was moving towards a more recognised doctrine of economic duress. Kerr J. recognised the possibility of a claim of economic duress, although it failed on the particular facts of the case. The door to accepting economic duress as a reason for avoiding a contract was opened by Kerr J., but this still fell short of recognising economic duress of as a full-blown legal doctrine.

However, an important step towards recognising a general doctrine of economic duress came with the decision in **North Ocean Shipping Co v Hyundai Construction Co (The Atlantic Baron)** [1979] Q.B. 705. In this case the defendants had contracted to build an oil tanker for the plaintiffs. A price was agreed and it was also agreed that the plaintiffs were to pay in instalments. The US dollar collapsed and the defendants demanded that the plaintiffs made an additional payment of 10 per cent to reflect this drop in value. The defendants threatened that they would not complete the tanker if the plaintiffs did not make this additional payment. The plaintiffs agreed to make this additional payment as they needed the tanker to meet a charter. Sometime after taking delivery of the tanker the plaintiffs challenged the extra payment on the grounds of economic duress.

The court held that the plaintiffs could not recover the extra payments owing to their delay in bringing the action (eight months). Their delay had demonstrated that they had accepted (affirmed) the contract. However, had the claim been brought sooner, the court was prepared to recognise that the actions of the defendants *would* have amounted to economic duress. The court held that the defendants' threat to break the contract had no *legal justification*.

Again, we have the recognition of a claim of economic duress, but on the particular facts of the case it was not actually available to the plaintiffs. This was again the case in **Pao On v Lau Yiu Long** [1980] A.C. 614. Here the claimants threatened to breach their contract unless the defendants agreed to guarantee the loss of the claimants in their performance of the contract. The court again rejected a claim of economic duress. The reason for this decision was that there was an alternative legal remedy available to the defendants. The defendants could have claimed specific performance to compel the plaintiffs to meet their contractual obligations.

The decision in **Pao On** is important for two reasons. First, it provides further recognition of a general doctrine of economic duress. Secondly, Lord Scarman outlined a number of criteria that should be taken into account when deciding whether economic duress is available on the facts of a particular case. He expressed these as follows:

"In determining whether there was a coercion of will such that there was no true consent, it is material to inquire whether the person alleged to have been coerced did or did not protest; whether, at the time he was allegedly coerced into making the contract, he did or did not have an alternative course open to him such as an adequate legal remedy; whether he was independently advised; and whether after entering the contract he took steps to avoid it. All these matters are relevant in determining whether he acted voluntarily or not".

These criteria can be summarised as follows:

1. Did the person alleged to have been coerced protest at the time?
2. Was there any realistic alternative available to the coerced person, such as an adequate legal remedy?
3. Was the person coerced independently advised?
4. Did the person coerced take steps to avoid the contract?

The decision in **The Atlantic Baron**, for example, can be explained on the basis of the second criterion; there was an adequate legal remedy of specific performance that the plaintiff could have pursued.

■ Did the party coerced have any realistic alternative?

10-007

Lord Scarman's four criteria above are useful in distinguishing *legitimate* from *illegitimate* pressure. However, it seems that the second criterion has been elevated above the others in terms of the weight that the courts attach to this. This is demonstrated by the decision in **Atlas Express Ltd v Kafco (Importers and Distributors) Ltd** [1989] Q.B. 833. Kafco entered into a contract with Woolworths. The carriage company (Atlas) had underestimated the size of the order to the extent that it became commercially unviable for them. They demanded more money or they would not make the deliveries. Kafco agreed to make the extra payment (although they admitted that they felt "over a barrel"). The court held that actions of Atlas amounted to economic duress. As a result, Kafco was not bound to make the extra payment.

The court attached considerable weight to the fact that Kafco had no *realistic alternative* but to promise the extra payment. There was no adequate legal remedy available to Kafco. It would have been pointless for Kafco to have claimed damages or specific performance. First, a claim of specific performance would have involved going to the court (a lengthy process) and the goods needed to be delivered urgently in order to avoid breaching their contract with Woolworths. Secondly, damages would not have provided an adequate remedy. The damages they would have recovered would come nowhere near compensating them for the loss of the business relationship with Woolworths that would inevitably result if the goods were delivered late.

Economic duress and a lawful act

10-008 In addition to the useful guidance provided in **Pao On**, Lord Scarman also recognised that a *lawful* act could give rise to a claim of economic duress. In other words, the threat must be *illegitimate*, but a *lawful* act could amount to illegitimate pressure.

In **CTN Cash & Carry Ltd v Gallagher Ltd** [1994] 4 All E.R. 714, the claimant entered into a contract with the defendant to purchase cigarettes. However, by mistake, the defendants delivered the cigarettes to the wrong address. The cigarettes were then stolen by a third party. The defendants demanded payment for the cigarettes and threatened that they would withdraw the claimant's credit facility if the payment was not made.

The court held that there was no economic duress on the facts of the case as the threat to withdraw the credit facility had been made in "good faith"; the defendants honestly believed that the cigarettes were at the claimant's risk. However, if this threat had not been made in good faith, the court was prepared to find that a lawful act (withdrawing credit) could amount to economic duress. Again, the door was opened (albeit slightly) to the possibility of economic duress by a lawful act.

Further recognition of lawful act duress can be found in the more recent decision of **Progress Bulk Carriers Limited v Tube City IMS LLC** [2012] EWHC 273 (Comm).

The defendants had a contract to sell scrap metal to the buyers. The defendants needed to transport the consignment to China and entered into a contract with the claimants to charter a vessel. The defendants made clear that they required a particular vessel as stipulated by the buyers. Unknown to the defendants, the claimants chartered the vessel to another party. This constituted a repudiatory breach of contract. When this was discovered by the defendants, the claimants offered a substitute vessel and also offered to compensate the defendant for any damages suffered.

The defendants proposed the substitute vessel to the buyers, but in the meantime the price of scrap metal was falling and the defendants were incurring additional storage cost due to the delay. The buyers accepted the substitute vessel but on the understanding that they would receive a reduction in the contract price from the defendants due to the delay. The claimants then refused to provide the vessel unless the defendants agreed to waive all of their claims against the claimants. Under protest, the defendants agreed to waive their claims in order to avoid greater losses caused by any further delay. The claim in this case concerned whether the defendant's agreement to waive their claim of damages (a settlement) was enforceable.

The court held that the defendant's agreement to waive their claim of damages had been procured by *illegitimate* pressure and was not enforceable. The claimant's demand for the defendants to waive their claim of damages was not in itself unlawful (as the promise to provide the subsequent vessel and to compensate the defendants was not strictly binding), but it was viewed as *illegitimate* in light of the repudiatory breach of contract. Their actions amounted to "lulling the defendants into a false sense of security" whilst "quietly manoeuvring them into a corner", leaving the defendants with no alternative but to agree to waive their claim. This case therefore provides that lawful, but unethical, acts may constitute *illegitimate* pressure for the purposes of duress.

Undue influence

It is often difficult to distinguish undue influence from duress. Both doctrines are concerned with the exercise of improper pressure, but the doctrines are founded on very different principles. The doctrine of economic duress is founded on common law principles and operates where a party has made an illegitimate threat. The effect is to vitiate consent and render the contract voidable. The doctrine of undue influence is an equitable doctrine but will also operate so as to render a contract voidable as a result of one party exploiting a relationship that exists between the parties.

10-009

> ## Over to you. . .
>
> **Claims of duress and/or undue influence may arise from very similar facts given that both are both concerned with improper conduct that results in a party entering into a contract. Can you think of how a claim of duress may differ from one of undue influence?**

Initially, we can distinguish the doctrine of duress from undue influence on the basis that the doctrine of duress is concerned with threats that are made from one party to the other. The doctrine of undue influence on the other hand is concerned with the nature of the relationship between the parties which is exploited to the advantage of one party or is based on a relationship that has the potential to be exploited.

The difficulty surrounding undue influence is in identifying the type of relationship that can give rise to a finding of undue influence. As we will see, the law has developed over the years so as to categorise the nature of the relationships that may give rise to undue influence, but the precise basis and justification for relieving a party from liability as a result of undue influence has only recently been clarified.

Categories of undue influence

The starting point is to consider what categories of relationships will give rise to undue influence. **In Bank of Credit and Commerce International SA v Aboody** [1990] 1 Q.B. 923, the Court of Appeal identified two distinct "classes" of undue influence. Although **Aboody** has subsequently been overruled by **CIBC Mortgages Plc v Pitt** [1994] 1 A.C. 200, the House of Lords in **Barclays Bank Plc v O'Brien** [1994] 1 A.C. 180, confirmed the "classes" of undue influence established in **Aboody**.

10-010

These categories are as follows:

1. Class 1: actual undue influence;
2. Class 2: presumed undue influence:
   - Class 2A: a recognised relationship that automatically gives rise to a presumption of undue influence;
   - Class 2B: relationships from which undue influence should be presumed.

A singular concept of undue influence?

10-011   Following **Barclays Bank Plc v O'Brien** there was some obvious confusion as to whether "actual" undue influence and "presumed" undue influence were actually just a way of describing two different situations in which undue influence may arise or whether they were in fact operated as two separate entities. For example, if a claimant were to successfully argue "actual" undue influence (Class 1) this would be based on the fact that the claimant was able to prove that such undue influence had been exerted (albeit on the balance of probabilities). However, if the claimant failed to adduce sufficient evidence to prove "actual" undue influence then the claimant could still rely upon a "presumption" of undue influence: a presumption based on a recognised relationship (Class 2A) or due to the fact that the relationship is one from which undue influence should be presumed (Class 2B).

If this distinction is correct then it seems that the courts are relieving the individual claiming undue influence from liability based on two contrasting justifications. First, it seems that an individual will be relieved from liability for "actual" undue influence (Class 1) on the basis that the other party exercising influence has done so improperly. This is different from the justification for relieving an individual from liability due to "presumed" undue influence (Class 2). The justification for relieving a party from liability in relation to Class 2 is either that the nature of the relationship automatically gave rise to a presumption of undue influence (Class 2A) so as to affect the consent of the complainant, or that the relationship is one from which undue influence should be presumed (Class 2B) so as to affect the consent of the complainant.

So, it is difficult to say, following the above classifications, that undue influence is a singular concept that can arise in different situations. It is perhaps more accurate to say that the courts were willing to relieve an individual from liability on the basis of undue influence based on different and competing justifications.

"Presumed" undue influence and Royal Bank of Scotland v Etridge (No. 2)

10-012   The confusion and distinction between these different classes of undue influence now needs to be evaluated in the light of the House of Lords decision in **Royal Bank of Scotland Plc v Etridge (No.2)** [2002] 2 A.C. 773. In this case the House of Lords confirmed that the "presumption" of undue influence is an *evidential* issue. In so deciding the House of Lords made it clear that there is only a single concept of undue influence, but the way in which the undue influence can be *proved* may vary. In other words, the House of Lords clarified that there is an evidential process that needs to be followed. The sole question for the court remains: did one party exercise undue influence? The way in which the court answers that question will be based upon the evidence presented before the court.

To this extent, the broad "categories" of undue influence identified in **Aboody** remain. The courts are prepared to accept *evidence* of actual or presumed undue influence in forming a conclusion as to whether such influence was exerted by one party. However, one important modification needs to be analysed.

As the House of Lords in **Etridge (No.2)** confirmed that the "presumption" of undue influence is an *evidential* issue, then the way in which such undue influence is proved must be in accordance with the correct evidential process.

Therefore, post-**Etridge**, in relation to "presumed" undue influence, the courts are prepared to accept that a recognised relationship (the old Class 2A) will automatically give rise to an *evidential presumption of influence*. This is an important modification, as previously under the old Class 2A undue influence from **Aboody**, the position of the courts was to accept that a recognised relationship gave an automatic presumption of undue influence. Now, the position is that a recognised relationship will give rise to a presumption, but only as to *influence* (and not undue influence). Once it is established that the relationship between the parties falls into one of the recognised categories, this presumption cannot be rebutted by the other party. In order for that presumption of *influence* to become a finding of *undue* influence, the court will need to be satisfied that one party exploited the nature of the relationship. Such exploitation can be established as a matter of evidence, for example, the nature of the transaction may be one that calls for explanation (see below).

If the nature of the relationship does not automatically give rise to a presumption of influence (the old Class 2B), then the claimant will need to adduce evidence that the relationship is one from which influence should be presumed. Once this has been established the court will then look at the nature of the transaction in deciding whether a presumption of *undue* influence arises. Once a presumption of undue influence is established then it will be for the other party to rebut this presumption by adducing evidence that he did not exercise such undue influence. If the other party is unable to rebut this presumption of undue influence then the court will make a finding of undue influence.

We will now consider how these modified categories of undue influence operate in equity.

Actual undue influence

10-013   In order to successfully claim actual undue influence then (unsurprisingly) the claimant must prove that the other party exercised such undue influence in relation to the transaction concerned. In the light of **Etridge (No.2)** it may seem unlikely that an individual would wish to pursue an action for actual undue influence. Given that a presumption of influence can arise based on a recognised relationship, or on the basis of a relationship from which influence should be presumed, then it may be asked why an individual would wish to go to such lengths as proving actual undue influence. Even in the light of the modified presumptions, there are still occasions when an individual may wish to prove actual undue influence. For example, if you are able to prove actual undue influence then it circumvents the other party trying to rebut a presumption should it arrive.

It could be argued that an action for actual undue influence is advantageous as it can operate in relation to a one-off transaction. In other words, the claimant will not need to prove a long-standing relationship between the parties before the court will accept that undue influence was exerted by one party over the other. The problem with this argument is that the courts may find it difficult to distinguish undue influence from duress in such situations. It should be borne in mind that the cases that we will now consider in relation to actual undue influence have all been based on an existing and prolonged relationship between the parties.

In **Bank of Credit and Commerce International SA v Aboody** [1990] 1 Q.B. 923, the liabilities of a family-run company, of which the husband and wife were directors and shareholders, were secured by three charges over the wife's house. When the business finally collapsed and the bank sought to enforce the charges against the wife's property, the wife challenged the validity of the charges on the basis that they had been obtained as a result of the actual undue influence of the husband.

Mrs Aboody was able to prove that the guarantees were signed as a result of actual undue influence. On the facts of the case it was not particularly difficult to prove such actual undue influence. The marriage between Mr and Mrs Aboody was an arranged marriage, with Mr Aboody some 20 years her senior and Mrs Aboody placed all her trust and confidence in her husband. When the guarantees were signed, and in the presence of the solicitor who was advising Mrs Aboody about the consequences of signing the documents, Mr Aboody burst into the office and shouted: "Why the hell don't you get on with what you are paid to do and witness her signature?" Mrs Aboody, who at that stage was reduced to tears, then signed the guarantees.

The Court of Appeal in **Aboody** clarified what an individual claiming actual undue influence must prove:

"(i) Leaving aside manifest disadvantage, a person relying on a plea of actual undue influence must show that (a) the other party to the transaction (or someone who induced the transaction for his own benefit) had the capacity to influence the complainant, (b) the influence was exercised, (c) its exercise was undue, and (d) its exercise brought about the transaction."

An interesting hang-over effect from **Aboody** and the earlier decision of **National Westminster Bank Plc v Morgan** [1985] A.C. 686 is the apparent requirement for a "manifest disadvantage". This requirement could of course lead to the conclusion that a party who may actually have been subjected to undue influence, which more often than not will involve fraudulent activity, may not be relieved from liability if the nature of the transaction was not of a "manifest disadvantage" to the claimant. The need for a "manifest disadvantage" was, however, finally laid to rest by **CIBC Mortgages Plc v Pitt** [1994] 1 A.C. 200, which overruled **Aboody** and confirms that such a disadvantage is not an ingredient of the doctrine of undue influence (whether actual or presumed).

"Presumed" undue influence

Remember, in light of the decision of the House of Lords in **Royal Bank of Scotland Plc v Etridge (No 2)** [2002] 2 AC 773, it is no longer correct to talk of a presumption of undue influence. Rather, as a matter of evidence, a presumption of influence may arise out of the nature of the relationship between the parties, as a result of a transaction which calls for explanation, which cannot then be rebutted by the other party as to establish that the coerced party entered into that transaction freely.   **10-014**

While we will still refer to the broad categories of relationships that may give rise to a presumption of influence, the primary question for the court will be to determine, in the light of the evidence adduced, whether undue influence was exercised by one party over the other.

■ A relationship that automatically gives rise to a presumption of influence

If a claimant is able to bring himself within one of the recognised categories of relationship then a presumption of influence will automatically be raised. This category would previously have been labelled as Class 2A following the principles established in **Aboody**. However, note the important modification—a recognised relationship only gives rise to a presumption of influence. We will examine the circumstances in which that presumption of influence becomes a finding of undue influence below.   **10-015**

■ The recognised relationships

There are lists of relationships that the courts will recognise as automatically giving rise to a presumption of influence. Such relationships are all based on trust and confidence so it is not controversial that such relationships should automatically raise a presumption of influence. Examples include doctor and patient, solicitor and client, parent and child.   **10-016**

Perhaps one of the most famous examples of such a relationship based on trust and confidence can be found in the case of **Allcard v Skinner** (1887) 36 Ch. D. 145. Mrs Allcard had joined a spiritual sisterhood and bound herself to observe the rules of poverty, chastity and obedience required by the sisterhood. The rule of poverty required members to give up all their property to the poor, their family or the sisterhood. Shortly after becoming a member Mrs Allcard transferred her property to the sisterhood. Mrs Allcard subsequently left the sisterhood and tried to argue that the transfer was made as a result of undue influence exercised by the leader and Lady Superior.

Although Mrs Allcard's claim failed on the basis that she had failed to bring her action within the required time, the Court of Appeal was prepared to recognise that such a relationship automatically gave rise to a presumption of undue influence. Such a presumption seems to arise from the equitable principles on which the doctrine of undue influence is based. As Bowen L.J. commented:

> ". . . it seems to me that, although this power of perfect disposition remains in the donor under circumstances like the present, it is plain that equity will not allow a person who exercises or enjoys a dominant religious influence over another to benefit directly or indirectly by the gifts which the donor makes under or in consequence of such influence, unless it is shown that the donor, at the time of making the gift, was allowed full and free opportunity for counsel and advice outside—the means of considering his or her worldly position and exercising an independent will about it. This is not a limitation placed on the action of the donor; it is a fetter placed upon the conscience of the recipient of the gift, and one which arises out of public policy and fair play."

Husband and wife

10-017   Perhaps the most notable omission from this list of recognised relationships is that of husband and wife. The courts have refused to recognise this as a relationship that automatically gives rise to a presumption of influence.

> ## Over to you. . .
>
> **Can you think of any justifications as to why the relationship between husband and wife should not automatically give rise to a presumption of influence?**

In **Midland Bank Plc v Shephard** [1998] 3 All E.R. 17, the husband arranged for his overdraft to be transferred to the joint account held by him and his wife. Unknown to the wife, the transfer document stated that she would also be liable on the joint account for any loan or overdraft. The husband then drew on the overdraft but shortly afterwards, the husband became insolvent. The bank then obtained judgment for the outstanding amount and sought to enforce this against the wife. The wife sought to be relieved from liability on the basis that her signature authorising the opening of the joint account had been obtained as a result of undue influence.

In dismissing the wife's appeal Neil L.J. relied upon the obiter of Dillon L.J. in **Kings North Trust Ltd v Bell** [1986] 1 All E.R. 423 in which he stated that:

> "There is no presumption of law that a transaction between husband and wife for the husband's benefit was procured by undue influence on the part of the husband and there is no rule that such a transaction cannot be upheld unless the wife is shown to have had independent advice."

Following **Shephard**, it is clear that the relationship of husband and wife does not automatically give rise to a presumption of undue influence. However, this does not mean that transactions entered into in such relationships cannot be challenged on other grounds. For example, in **Barclays Bank v Kennedy** (1989) 21 H.L.R. 132, the Court of Appeal was prepared to accept that the husband can be an agent of the bank when seeking the signature of the wife to guarantee the husband's overdraft. As Purchas L.J. observed:

> "Although *Midland Bank plc v Shephard* confirms that the law does not presume undue influence arising out of the confidential relationship between husband and wife, this does not mean that those who are seeking to obtain the consent of the wife to an agreement, which is manifestly to her disadvantage, are entitled to divest themselves of vicarious responsibility for the conduct of the husband, when they are content to leave it to him to obtain that consent and when it is established by the evidence that he did obtain her consent by deceit or undue influence."

This has ramifications for lenders in that they may face a claim of negligence should undue influence be proven to exist between a husband and wife on the basis that the husband was acting as their agent when securing the signature for such a guarantee.

◼ A relationship that gives rise to a presumption of influence

10-018

If the relationship between the parties does not fall within one of the recognised relationships, then the court will have to consider whether the nature of the relationship between the parties is such that influence should be presumed. This will fall within the old Class 2B category. It may sound like a subtle distinction between the old Class 2A and Class 2B, but the nature of the presumption is fundamentally different. Remember, once the court is satisfied that the relationship is one which automatically gives rise to a presumption of influence then this presumption is irrebuttable. However, if the nature of the relationship does not automatically give rise to such a presumption then any presumption of influence that follows can be rebutted by the other party.

■ When will a presumption of influence arise?

10-019   Although the relationship between the parties will not automatically give rise to a presumption of influence, the claimant can adduce evidence to show that such influence should be presumed. Following principles similar to those in **Allcard v Skinner**, the claimant must prove that the relationship was in fact based on trust and confidence so as to give rise to a presumption. It is into this "category" of influence that the relationship between husband and wife will now fall.

If we recall the facts of **Bank of Credit and Commerce International SA v Aboody** [1990] 1 Q.B. 923, it is difficult to see how such a relationship would not give rise to a presumption of influence, particularly in view of the fact that the wife placed her total trust and confidence in her husband.

Further, Lord Browne-Wilkinson in **Barclay's Bank v O'Brien** [1994] 1 A.C. 180 appeared to accept such a conclusion (although referring to the old "classes" of undue influence) when he said:

> "Although there is no Class 2(A) presumption of undue influence as between husband and wife, it should be emphasised that in any particular case a wife may well be able to demonstrate that de facto she did leave decisions on financial affairs to her husband thereby bringing herself within Class 2(B) i.e. that the relationship between husband and wife in the particular case was such that the wife reposed confidence and trust in her husband in relation to their financial affairs and therefore undue influence is to be presumed. Thus, in those cases which still occur where the wife relies in all financial matters on her husband and simply does what he suggests, a presumption of undue influence within Class 2(B) can be established solely from the proof of such trust and confidence without proof of actual undue influence."

In **Lloyds Bank Ltd v Bundy** [1975] Q.B. 326, the defendant, an elderly farmer, granted a charge over his farm to secure the business debts of his only son. When the son required further security the assistant manager of the bank delivered the papers to the defendant's house for him to sign and advised that the defendant sign the documents. The defendant had banked at the same branch for many years and placed trust and confidence in the advice of the manager and signed the documents guaranteeing his son's debts. The defendant gave evidence to the effect that he "always trusted" the manager and "simply sat back and did what they said". Eventually the son's business collapsed and the bank sought possession of the defendant's property.

The Court of Appeal relieved the defendant from liability on the basis that a presumption of undue influence had arisen out of the nature of the relationship of trust and confidence and such a presumption had not been rebutted by the other party as the bank manger did not advise the defendant to seek independent advice.

In allowing the appeal Lord Denning M.R. stated:

> "English law gives relief to one who, without independent advice, enters into a contract upon terms that are very unfair, or transfers property for a consideration which is grossly inadequate, when his bargaining power is grievously impaired because of his needs or desires, or his ignorance or infirmity, coupled with undue influences or pressures brought to bear on him by or for the benefit of the other."

However, in **National Westminster Bank Plc v Morgan** [1985] A.C. 686, the House of Lords was not prepared to relieve the wife from liability after signing a charge over the matrimonial home on the grounds that the nature of the relationship (again, bank and customer) was not one of trust and confidence so as to give rise to a presumption of undue influence. The House of Lords held that the relationship between the parties had never gone beyond the normal business relationship of banker and customer and that the transaction had not been disadvantageous to the wife.

■ The requirement of a "manifest disadvantage"

The decision in **Morgan** is a good example of how the courts approach relationships that do not automatically give rise to a presumption of influence, but the principles from **Morgan** should be treated with some caution. Following the cases of **Aboody** and **Morgan** it appeared to be a requirement that, in order for a presumption of undue influence to arise, the nature of the transaction must be a "manifest disadvantage" to the wife. This requirement was problematic for a number of reasons. Perhaps most importantly, the requirement that the transaction be a "manifest disadvantage" failed to recognise that a wife, in granting a charge over the matrimonial home, may be acting quite properly and there is certainly nothing dubious about her actions. Granting such a charge will certainly be disadvantageous to the wife, but in reality the matrimonial home will be the only asset that could be used to secure such business debts.

10-020

This issue was finally tackled by the House of Lords in **Etridge (No.2)** in which it held that a "manifest disadvantage" was not a requirement in raising a presumption of influence. The fact that a transaction is manifestly disadvantageous to one party may well be very strong evidence of the fact that any influence exercised may have been *undue* in nature, but it is not a strict requirement in order for a presumption of influence to be raised.

Interestingly, the House of Lords in **Etridge (No.2)** appeared to favour the rather archaic statement of Lindley L.J. in **Allcard v Skinner** [1887] L.R. 36 Ch. D. 145:

> "Where a gift is made to a person standing in a confidential relation to the donor, the Court will not set aside the gift if of a small amount simply on the ground that the donor had no independent advice. In such a case, some proof of the exercise of the influence of the donee must be given. The mere existence of such influence is not enough in such a case . . . But if the gift is so large as not to be reasonably accounted for on the ground of friendship, relationship, charity, or other ordinary motives on which ordinary men act, the burden is upon the donee to support the gift."

This approach is certainly favourable to the requirement of a "manifest disadvantage" and allows the court to look at many factors in deciding whether a presumption of influence arises.

So, the key issue for the court decide will be to whether the transaction is one that *calls for explanation*.

■ When does a presumption of influence become a finding of undue influence?

10-021   There will be an automatic presumption of influence if the relationship falls within one of the recognised categories (Class 2A). Alternatively, a presumption of influence will arise if the nature of the relationship is such that it gives rise to a presumption of influence (Class 2B). However, following the decision in **Etridge**, it is clear that only a presumption of *influence* arises at this stage. If the transaction is one that "calls for explanation" (cannot readily be explained by the nature of the relationship) then there will be a presumption of *undue influence*. It will then be for the party alleged to have exercised such influence to rebut this presumption. The party will have to prove that he did not exercise such undue influence. If he cannot rebut this presumption then the court will make a *finding of undue influence*. The contract will then be *voidable* for such undue influence.

FIGURE 10.1 **Summary of presumed undue influence**

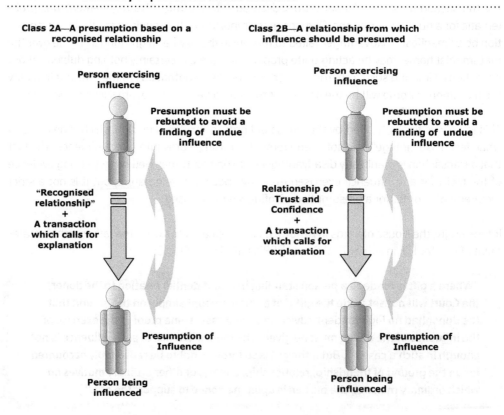

Undue influence and third parties

A particular problem arises for lenders when there is a relationship between the surety and debtor. In such situations the contract of surety may have been obtained as a result of undue influence being exercised over the surety by the debtor. The question is to what extent the contract between the bank and the surety will be affected by the actions of a third party to that contract (the debtor).

10-022

The answer to this question lies in the doctrine of notice. There may be situations in which the bank will have *actual* notice of the undue influence between the debtor and the surety. This could easily arise, for example, if the bank manager delivers the documents to the home of the surety and witnesses the actions of the debtor in obtaining the signature for the guarantee. A more difficult issue is that of *constructive* notice. Constructive notice will arise when the bank ought to have known about the exercise of undue influence based on the nature of the relationship and the resulting transaction.

This issue was tackled by the House of Lords in **Barclays Bank v O'Brien** [1994] 1 A.C. 180. The facts are not particularly unusual in that Mr O'Brien persuaded Mrs O'Brien to guarantee the husband's overdraft by granting a charge over the matrimonial home. The branch manager had requested that the bank ensured that Mrs O'Brien was fully aware of the nature of the transaction and that she sought legal advice. This request was not met and the wife signed the deed following the husband's representation that the guarantee was to the value of £60,000. In fact the guarantee was to the value of £130,000. When the husband exceeded the overdraft the bank sought to enforce the charge.

The House of Lords was prepared to relieve the wife from liability on the basis that the bank was deemed to have constructive notice of the undue influence between the husband and the wife.

An overview of the issues in relation to third party cases are illustrated in Figure 10.2.

Hear from the Author

Scan the QR Tag or follow the link below for an overview fo the legal principles relating to undue influence and third parties.

uklawstudent.thomsonreuters.com/category/contract-fundamentals

In order for the bank to be fixed with constructive notice there is a two-stage process that will be followed by the courts:

10-023

1. Stage 1: is the bank "put on inquiry" as to undue influence?

2. Stage 2: if the bank is "put on inquiry" what steps must it take to avoid constructive notice?

■ Stage 1: is the bank "put on inquiry"?

10-024 The House of Lords in **O'Brien** held that the bank is *put on inquiry* when a wife offers to stand surety for her husband's debts where:

1. the transaction is on its face not to the financial advantage of the wife; and

2. there is a substantial risk in transactions of that kind that, in procuring the wife to act as surety, the husband has committed a legal or equitable wrong that entitles the wife to set aside the transaction.

....

FIGURE 10.2 **Third-Party cases and undue influence**

....

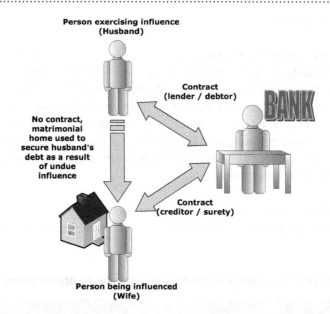

Once the creditor is put on inquiry the creditor must take "reasonable steps" in order to avoid constructive notice of such undue influence. These "reasonable steps" include advising the wife as to the true nature and extent of the transaction and advising the wife to seek independent legal advice before signing the guarantee. Such advice could be given at a private meeting between the bank and the wife.

The difficulty with such cases is setting the minimum standard that will act as a trigger so as to put the bank on inquiry. The courts wrestled in trying to identify this minimum standard, but the key test was precisely formulated by Lord Nicholls in **Royal Bank of Scotland Plc v Etridge (No.2)** [2002] 2 A.C. 773:

"If a bank is not to be required to evaluate the extent to which its customer has influence over a proposed guarantor, the only practical way forward is to regard banks as 'put on inquiry' in every case where the relationship between the surety and the debtor is non-commercial. The creditor must always take reasonable steps to bring home to the individual guarantor the risks he is running by standing as surety."

Over to you. . .

Consider the relationship between husband and wife and how the principles outlined above in *Etridge* would apply to such cases.

It now follows that the bank will automatically be put on inquiry when the nature of the relationship between the parties is "non-commercial". So, in a case involving a wife standing as surety for the debts of her husband, the bank will automatically be put on inquiry as to the possibility of undue influence. Once put on inquiry the bank must then take certain steps in order to avoid being fixed with constructive notice of undue influence.

■ Stage 2: when put on inquiry what steps must the bank take to avoid *notice* of undue influence?

Despite the decision of the House of Lords in **Barclays Bank v O'Brien** [1994] 1 A.C. 180, there remained some uncertainty as to the precise steps that a lender should take after being put on inquiry so as to avoid constructive notice of undue influence. Arranging a private meeting between the bank and the surety is certainly a first step, but of course this would not relieve the bank from liability if it were to give negligent or misleading advice in such a meeting. As a result, the preferred approach is for the bank to advise the surety to seek independent legal advice. This course of action has many advantages for the bank, but primarily the bank will be able to assume that the solicitor provided adequate and accurate legal advice (**Banco Exterior Internacional v Mann** (1995) 27 H.L.R. 329). The bank will not have to ensure that the legal advice was complete or conducted properly. In such situations the bank will simply rely on written confirmation of the solicitor that the surety received legal advice.

10-025

The facts that will give rise to notice and the steps the bank should take to avoid being fixed with constructive notice are summarised in Figure 10.3.

FIGURE 10.3 **Notice and constructive notice of undue influence**

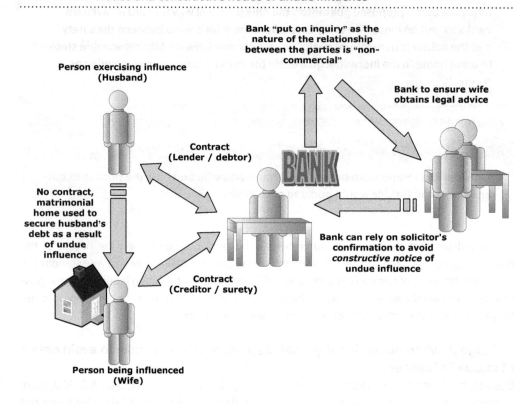

Summary

Duress

1. Duress involves the threat of physical force or violence to the person. The effect of duress is to render the contract *voidable*.

2. It is important to distinguish threats of physical force or violence from economic duress. The nature of the threat in economic duress is usually a threat to breach a contract.

3. The courts must distinguish between legitimate commercial pressure (which will not amount to economic duress) and *illegitimate* commercial pressure that will amount to economic duress.

4. The key test is whether the person coerced had any *realistic alternative* (**Atlas Express v Kafco**) but to accede to the threat.

5. Finally, following **CTN Cash & Carry**, it is possible that a lawful threat may amount to illegitimate pressure and therefore economic duress.

Undue Influence

1. Undue influence differs from duress in that it is the nature of the relationship (rather than the threat) that is important to the validity of the contract.

2. There are different categories of undue influence:

    (a) Class 1: actual undue influence;
    (b) Class 2: presumed undue influence:
    (c) Class 2A: a recognised relationship that automatically gives rise to a presumption of undue influence;
    (d) Class 2B: relationships from which undue influence should be presumed.

3. In relation to "presumed" undue influence it is important to take account of the decision of the House of Lords in **Etridge (No.2)**. If the relationship falls within one of the recognised categories then there will be an automatic presumption of *influence* (Class 2A). This will become a presumption of *undue influence* if the nature of the transaction is one that calls for explanation.

4. If the relationship does not fall within one of the recognised categories then it will need to be established that there is a relationship of trust and confidence between the parties (Class 2B). This presumption of *influence* will become a presumption of *undue influence* if the nature of the transaction is one that calls for explanation.

5. Once there is a presumption of undue influence, that presumption will have to be rebutted by the part alleged to have exercised undue influence. If the presumption is not rebutted the court will make a finding of undue influence and the contract will be voidable.

6. In relation to third-party cases, the doctrine of notice is fundamental. If a party is deemed to have constructive notice of undue influence then the contract will again be declared voidable.

7. A bank will be "put on notice" as to the possibility of undue influence if the nature of the relationship between the other contracting parties is "non-commercial".

8. Once the bank has been put on notice it must take reasonable steps to avoid being fixed with constructive notice. This will usually involve making sure that the party guaranteeing the debt receives independent legal advice.

Key Cases Grid

Case	Court	Key Issues
Pao On v Lau Yiu Long [1980]	Privy Council (Hong Kong)	This cases provides relevant guidelines that assist in distinguishing legitimate from illegitimate commercial pressure. 1. Did the person alleged to have been coerced protest at the time? 2. Was there any realistic alternative available to the coerced person, such as an adequate legal remedy? 3. Was the person coerced independently advised? 4. Did the person coerced take steps to avoid the contract?
Atlas Express Ltd v Kafco (Importers and Distributors) Ltd [1989]	Queen's Bench Division	A useful application of the *Pao On* criteria which highlights the significant weight that will be attached to whether the party cohered had "any realistic alternative", such as a adequate legal remedy.
Allcard v Skinner (1887)	Court of Appeal	The relationship of religious advisor and disciple provides an example of a recognised relationship for the purposes of undue influence. Further, in terms of determining the existence of undue influence, the court will have regard to the nature of the transaction between the parties. Per Lindley L.J: ". . . if the gift is so large as not to be reasonably accounted for on the ground of friendship, relationship, charity, or other ordinary motives on which ordinary men act, the burden is upon the donee to support the gift."
Royal Bank of Scotland Plc v Etridge (No.2) [2002]	House of Lords	In cases involving undue influence exercised by a 3rd party, the issue of notice will determine whether such contracts are enforceable. When the relationship between a party acting as surety and the debtor is non-commercial, the lender will be put on inquiry. Once put on inquiry, the lender must take reasonable steps to avoid having constructive notice of any such undue influence. The reasonable steps identified in this case are for the lender to ensure that the surety receives independent advice before entering into the contract.

End of Chapter Question

Bob, a builder, enters into a contract with Sara. Bob agrees to construct a conservatory for Sara by July, 1 for a contract price of £10,000. Bob completes the work on time and issues Sara with an invoice for £10,000. Sara then tells Bob that she will not pay the full amount and hands over a cheque for £4,000. Bob reluctantly accepts as he is in severe financial difficulties and needs all the money he can get in order to pay an overdue invoice to one of his suppliers.

Two weeks later Bob claims the outstanding £6,000 from Sara. Bob has evidence that Sara was aware of his financial difficulties when she refused to pay the full amount due under the contract.

Advise Bob.

Points of Answer

- ◆ Consider whether Sara's threat to breach the contract amounts to economic duress.
- ◆ The Sibeon is authority for the fact that an illegitimate threat to breach a contract can amount to economic duress. The facts of this case are also very similar to that of **D & C Builders v Rees**. While we have discussed this case in the context of estoppel, the court held that by exploiting the financial difficulties of the other party the contract was voidable for duress.
- ◆ State and apply Lord Scarman's guidelines in **Pao On** in relation to a claim of duress. Note the importance of whether Bob had an "alternative course open to him such as an adequate legal remedy?"
- ◆ Following the case of **Atlas Express v Kafco**, question whether pursuing legal action would have been a realistic alternative for Bob given the urgent need to meet the outstanding invoice.

Further Reading

Macdonald, E. "Duress by threatened breach of contract". J.B.L. 1989, Nov, 460–473

This article provides an analysis of when a threat to breach a contract may constitute duress in light of the decision in Atlas Exprfess v Kafco.

Stone, R. and Cunnington, R. *Text, Cases and Materials on Contract Law* (London: Routledge-Cavendish, 2014), Chapter 10 (Duress), Chapter 11 (Undue Influence)

Treitel, G. *The Law of Contract*, 13th edn (London Sweet & Maxwell, 2011), Chapter 10.

Illegality

CHAPTER OVERVIEW

In this chapter we:

- **introduce the situations in which the courts may refuse to enforce an agreement between the parties due to issues of illegality or public policy**

- **discuss statutory provisions as to the legality of a contract**

- **discuss the common law principles in relation to legality**

- **analyse the use of contractual terms in restraint of trade**

Summary

Key Cases Grid

End of Chapter Question

Further Reading

Introduction

11-001 Despite the general theme of party freedom that flows through contract law, there may be situations where the courts will refuse to enforce an agreement. The parties may have formed a valid agreement and that agreement may be supported by consideration, which is the key test of enforceability at common law. However, despite this fact the courts will be reluctant to enforce an agreement that is contrary to the law or contrary to public policy.

It is important to consider the word *illegality* in its wider sense. In this context illegality extends further than contrary to the law of contract. A criminal act (a public wrong) or a civil wrong (such as the commission of a tort) may justify the court in refusing to enforce a subsequent agreement.

Even if the contract is not strictly *illegal* in its broad sense, the court may still refuse to enforce a contract on the basis of public policy. There are again many aspects to the phrase *public policy* and of course this concept changes over time. However, at the heart of it will be the need to protect the public interest. Therefore, contracts to commit a crime will not be enforced by the courts (**Bigos v Bousted** [1951] 1 All E.R. 92). The courts may refuse to enforce an agreement to prevent vexatious and persistent claims (**Hamilton v Al Fayed** [2002] EWCA Civ 665).

Illegality and performance

11-002 It is important to distinguish between contracts that are in themselves illegal and contracts that *become* illegal in the way that they are performed.

Examples of contracts that are illegal in themselves are not too difficult to identify. If the contracts creates obligations that are illegal to perform (such as the commission of a criminal offence) then the courts will not enforce the contract. However, some contracts may have been formed quite legally but will then *become* illegal in the way that they are performed. What is interesting is differing approach of the courts when considering the *validity* of these contracts.

On the one hand it would seem harsh to penalise both parties when only one party is at fault. On the other it would seem right that the courts should not enforce obligations following an illegal act.

The courts seem to have adopted two approaches to the validity of such contracts.

1. The illegal act renders the obligations under the contract unenforceable; or
2. The illegal act does not affect the obligations under the contract, but the wrong-doer will be punished for his illegal act.

The illegal act renders the obligations under the contract unenforceable

In **Anderson Ltd v Daniel** [1924] 1 K.B. 138, it was a statutory requirement that the seller of artificial fertiliser provides a statement of its chemical content on the sales invoice. The seller failed to do so in breach of the statute. The court held that the agreement was not enforceable. This therefore released the purchaser from his obligation to pay for the fertiliser.

11-003

The illegal act does not affect the obligations under the contract, but the wrongdoer will be punished for his illegal act

In **St John Shipping Corp v Joseph Rank Ltd** [1957] 1 Q.B. 267, the carrier of goods overloaded his ship (an offence under the Merchant Shipping Act (Safety and Land Conventions) 1932). The purchaser argued that the contract had been performed illegally and that this released him from the obligation to pay for the goods. The court disagreed and held that although the carrier would be punished for a breach of the Act, this did not affect the obligation of the purchaser to pay for the goods.

11-004

Following these two cases it seems that there is a general question that the court will ask in assessing the validity of the contract: what was the aim or the purpose of the legislation? Was the aim of the legislation to punish the illegal act or to invalidate the agreement?

1. If the aim of the legislation was to invalidate such agreements then the obligations will not be enforced (**Anderson Ltd v Daniel**).
2. If the aim of the legislation was to punish the wrongdoer then the parties will be bound to their contractual obligations (**St John Shipping Corp v Joseph Rank Ltd**).

Contracts illegal under statute

Identifying contracts that are illegal under statute is not difficult. Parliament has expressly declared what types of contracts are illegal and unenforceable. Examples of such contracts are as follows.

11-005

Competition Act 1998

The Competition Act 1998 seeks to target agreements that have the effect of restricting, preventing or distorting trade. The effect will be that such contracts are unenforceable at law. However, considerable power rests with the Office of Fair Trading to decide whether such agreements are enforceable, rather than the courts assessing this fact.

11-006

Wagering contracts

11-007 Wagering contracts are controlled by s.18 of the Gaming Act 1845, which states:

> "All contracts or agreements, whether by parole or in writing, by way of gaming or wagering, shall be null and void; and no suit shall be brought or maintained in any court and law or equity for recovering any sum of money or valuable thing alleged to be won on any wager, or which shall have been deposited in the hands of any person to abide the event on which any wager shall have been made . . ."

The effect of the 1845 Act is to render the contract void. It is perhaps inaccurate to describe such contracts as *illegal*. Such contracts may have been legally formed, but will be rendered void and unenforceable by the Act.

This now needs to be read in the light of the Gambling Act 2005. Apart from a few powers delegated to the Gambling Commission to declare wagering contracts void, the effect of the 2005 Act is that a contract should not be declared automatically void simply on the grounds that it is a contract of wager.

Breach of statutory requirements

11-008 Legislation may impose restrictions upon the enforceability of some types of contract unless specific requirements are met. For example, in **Re Mahmoud and Ispahani** [1921] 2 K.B. 716, the Seeds, Oils and Fats Order 1919 required that *both* the seller *and* purchaser of linseed oil must hold a licence. Despite the fact that the buyer misled the seller and said that he had a licence (when he did not) the court refused to enforce the agreement as it was contrary to the legislation.

Contracts illegal at common law

11-009 The courts will refuse to enforce some contracts at common law on the grounds that they are contrary to public policy or morality. However, defining the precise boundaries of *public policy* is very difficult indeed. There are no strict rules that govern such issues; rather the courts proceed on the basis that there are some common values held by society. If the effect of a contract is such as to breach these common values then the courts will not enforce the contract as it would be against the public good.

Public policy and immorality

11-010 Some matters of public policy are not too controversial. For example, most people would agree that it would be immoral to allow a criminal to benefit from his crime under a contract.

For this reason such contracts will be void (**Beresford v Royal Insurance Co Ltd** [1937] 2 K.B. 197).

The courts have for hundreds of years also accepted that the commission of a *civil* wrong could render the contract unenforceable at common law. This was the case in **Allen v Rescous** (1677) 2 Lev. 174, where the civil wrong was to commit an assault.

The courts have also recognised further types of contracts that will be unenforceable at common law as being contrary to public policy or morality.

SEXUALLY IMMORAL CONTRACTS

Unsurprisingly, the majority of the case law in the area of immorality relates to the provision of sexual acts or services. For example, a contract for the hire of a carriage for the purpose of prostitution was held to be contrary to public policy in **Pearce v Brooks** (1865–66) L.R. 1 Ex. 213.

11-011

An interesting argument was advanced in **Armhouse Lee Ltd v Chappell**, The Times, August 7, 1996. In this case the defendants advertised their "sex line" services in the plaintiff's magazines. When the plaintiff sought payment the defendants' refused on the grounds of illegality. They argued that such advertisements were immoral and that the contract was not enforceable. The court disagreed and held the defendants liable under the contract.

Morality, particularly sexual morality, changes over time. To declare contracts invalid on the basis of outdated beliefs would not achieve the aim of giving effect to the common values of society. The courts recognise this and there have been a number of recent cases that illustrate the more lenient approach of the courts to the issue of sexual immorality.

One of the most extreme examples of this approach can be found in **Sutton v Mischon de Reya** [2003] EWHC 3166. The contract in this case was for a "slavery agreement" to be drafted between the slave and his sexual master. The court accepted that in principle such agreements were not contrary to public policy.

CONTRACTS THAT CHALLENGE THE SANCTITY OF MARRIAGE

Any contract that has the effect of challenging the sanctity of marriage will be unenforceable on the grounds of public policy. It used to be the case that an agreement to marry created direct contractual obligations. This is no longer the case since the enactment of the Law Reform (Miscellaneous Provisions) Act 1970. However, it is still the case that a party cannot be *prevented* from marrying. If a contract seeks to impose such a restriction then the contract will be void and unenforceable.

11-012

Further, a one-sided promise to marry a person (and no one else) with the further promise to pay compensation if this does not happen will also be void (**Lowe v Peers** (1768) 4 Burr. 2225).

Practices such as "marriage brokering" will also fall within this category of illegality. In these cases a fee is paid in return for a person being introduced to potential suitors. A party will not be able enforce the contract if their expectations under the contract are not met. Again, such contracts are contrary to public policy (**Hermann v Charlesworth** [1905] 2 K.B. 123).

Finally, a contract of separation that is formed whilst the marriage subsists will also be void. This poses interesting questions in relation to prenuptial agreements. These agreements are formed before marriage and seek to allocate and divide marital assets should the couple separate. Prenuptial agreements are also void as contravening public policy. This is surprising given that these agreements are becoming increasingly popular in modern (and celebrity!) marriages. The recent approach of the courts has been to take account of (but not to enforce) these agreements when dividing marital assets (**X v X (Y and Z intervening)**) [2002] 1 F.L.R. 508).

CONTRACTS THAT SEEK TO CHALLENGE THE JURISDICTION OF THE COURT

11-013   The nature of contract law is generally self-regulatory. Only if a dispute arises is the matter referred to the court. The court then has the jurisdiction to resolve this dispute. However, a contract that seeks to oust the jurisdiction that the courts have over contractual disputes will be void. A challenge to the jurisdiction of the court can arise if one party agrees not to pursue a prosecution in return for payment (**Keir v Leeman** (1846) 6 Q.B. 308).

It is quite common for commercial contracts to contain an "arbitration clause". When a matter is referred to arbitration the dispute between the parties is resolved by an appointed third party, not the court. At first glance these clauses would appear to conflict with public policy. However, such clauses are usually valid. The aggrieved party will ultimately have a right of appeal to the courts, thereby maintaining the supremacy of the court (**Scott v Avery** (1855) 5 H.L. Cas. 811). Should an arbitration clause seek to oust this right then the clause may well be declared void as being contrary to public policy.

Illegality and restraint of trade

11-014   Freedom of contract gives the parties exceptional freedom to agree to any terms they wish. However, with this freedom comes the potential for abuse. There is always the risk that a party may seek to abuse the principles of freedom of contract as a method of restraining trade. In this context restraint of trade could mean that an individual is prevented from working for another employer or is prevented from working in a particular industry.

THE GENERAL RULE

11-015   Clauses that seek to restrain business activity do not just apply to individuals. A company has a separate legal personality and contractual capacity following the decision in **Salomon v Salomon** [1897] A.C. 22, and may undertake not to compete with the business interests of another company. For these reasons the general approach of the courts has been to treat restraint of trade clauses as being void for being contrary to public policy.

EXCEPTIONS TO THE GENERAL RULE

While restraint of trade clauses are prima facie unenforceable, the courts have accepted that such clauses may be enforceable provided that they are *reasonable*. The nature of the restriction must be reasonable and the clause must also be reasonable in terms of public policy.

11-016

The leading case on this issue is **Nordenfelt v Maxim Nordenfelt Guns & Ammunition Co Ltd** [1894] A.C. 535.

In this case it had been agreed that **Nordenfelt** "would not make guns or ammunition anywhere in the world, and would not compete with Maxim in any way for a period of 25 years".

Lord MacNaghten stated the current state of the law regarding restraint of trade clauses:

> "The true view at the present time I think, is this: The public have an interest in every person's carrying on his trade freely: so has the individual. All interference with individual liberty of action in trading, and all restraints of trade of themselves, if there is nothing more, are contrary to public policy, and therefore void. That is the general rule. But there are exceptions: restraints of trade and interference with individual liberty of action may be justified by the special circumstances of a particular case. It is a sufficient justification, and indeed it is the only justification, if the restriction is reasonable—reasonable, that is, in reference to the interests of the parties concerned and reasonable in reference to the interests of the public, so framed and so guarded as to afford adequate protection to the party in whose favour it is imposed, while at the same time it is in no way injurious to the public."

THE RESTRAINT MUST BE REASONABLE

It is possible to distil Lord MacNaghten's comments in Nordenfelt into two key principles that represent the approach of the courts to restraint of trade clauses:

11-017

- **(i)** The clause must be reasonable in relation to the protection of the parties
- **(ii)** The clause must be reasonable as regards public policy

THE CLAUSE MUST BE REASONABLE IN RELATION TO THE PROTECTION OF THE PARTIES

In order to be effective, a clause in restraint of trade must be reasonable in the way that it relates to the parties. The courts have recognised a limited number of interests that need

11-018

protection. Restraint of trade clauses can be used to protect these "legitimate interests", but the clause must be reasonable to achieve this aim.

The House of Lords in **Herbert Morris Ltd v Saxelby** [1916] 1 A.C. 688, recognised two legitimate interests that can be protected by use of a restraint of trade clause:

1. the goodwill in the sale of a business; and
2. trade secrets.

Even though a clause may seek to protect one of these interests, it must be reasonable in the way it achieves this. The issue of reasonableness will depend on the facts of the case and a number of guidelines have been developed by the courts.

THE CLAUSE MUST BE REASONABLE AS REGARDS PUBLIC POLICY

11-019   Once it has been established that the clause is seeking to protect a legitimate interest, it must also be reasonable in terms of public policy. This is very rarely argued, but there are a few limited examples of clauses that were declared void as being unreasonable having regard to public policy. For example, in **Wyatt v Kreglinger** [1933] 1 K.B. 793, a contract contained a clause which restrained the claimant from working in the wool industry for life. The court held that this restriction offended public policy and was not enforceable. It is difficult to see precisely what principle of policy was offended in this case, but restriction of the supply of skilled labour when such labour was in short supply is one of the arguments put forward.

GUIDING FACTORS IN ASSESSING REASONABLENESS

11-020   Once it has been established that the clause is reasonable in that it seeks to protect a legitimate interest and that it does not offend public policy, the courts will look to further guiding factors in assessing whether the clause is reasonable and therefore enforceable.

1. **The nature of the *interest* that is being protected**
   The court will assess whether there is a legitimate interest that one party is seeking to protect. In cases involving trade secrets the courts adopt a more lenient approach to restraint of trade clauses. For example, in **Forster v Suggett** (1918) 35 T.L.R. 87, it was held that a five-year restriction to protect trade secrets in relation to the glass- blowing industry was reasonable in the circumstances.

2. **The duration of the restriction**
   The longer the duration of the restriction, the more likely it is to be unreasonable. However, the court may have to look at the interest being protected alongside the duration in deciding the issue of reasonableness. This was the case in **Fitch v Dewes** [1921] 2 A.C. 158, in which a clause of unlimited duration that pre-

vented a solicitor from working within seven miles of Tamworth was held to be reasonable.

3. **The extent of the restriction**

The extent of the restriction encompasses many elements. These include the extent of activities being restrained and the geographical extent of the restriction. For example, if a company has a limited business interest in a specific geographical location then it would be unreasonable for that company to impose a restriction preventing a competing party from operating in a business sector that does not conflict with these interests. In Nordenfelt however, a munitions manufacturer sold his business and agreed not to compete against the worldwide business interests of the purchaser for 25 years. The court held that a worldwide restriction *was* reasonable as it reflected the multinational business interests of the company.

EXCLUSIVE SERVICE AGREEMENTS

It is possible that an individual will undertake to work exclusively for one party. This is referred to an exclusive service agreement and the courts have adopted different approaches to such clauses depending on the nature of the restriction.   **11-021**

In **A Schroeder Music Publishing Co Ltd v Macaulay** [1974] 1 W.L.R. 1308, Macaulay, a 21-year-old unknown songwriter, entered into an exclusive agreement with Schroeder Music Publishing. The agreement was for five years and required Macaulay to assign the worldwide copyright in all his songs to Schroeder. There was a further clause in the agreement that if royalties from the sale of Macaulay's material exceeded £5,000 then Schroeder had the option to renew the contract and that Schroeder could terminate the agreement at any time with one month notice. Schroeder did not promise that it would release any of the material produced by Macaulay during the course of the agreement.

These restrictions were very harsh indeed and had the effect of preventing Macaulay working for anyone else while at the same time Schroeder did not guarantee that it would release any material at all. If Schroeder refused to release material then how was Macaulay supposed to make a living? Unsurprisingly, the court held that the clause was unduly restrictive. Such a one-sided agreement was contrary to public policy and was void.

However, it is interesting to contrast **Schroeder** with the decision in **Panayiotou v Sony Music Entertainment (UK) Ltd** [1994] 2 W.L.R. 241. The history of this case is very long so it is useful to highlight some of the relevant background facts. This case concerned the successful 1980s pop group, Wham. The band members, George Michael and Ridgeley were in dispute with their record company over their contract. They eventually reached a compromise agreement in 1984 when they entered into a contract with CBS. George Michael then became a successful solo artist and again renegotiated his contract with CBS (a record company that was later pur-chased by Sony). In 1990 a further negotiation of the contract took place, which gave George Michael very favourable terms indeed in exchange for his commitment to produce music exclu-sively for Sony. Owing to artistic differences George Michael wanted to develop his own solo career further and sought to be released from his contract with Sony.

The court held that it would be contrary to public policy to allow George Michael to be released from his contract. George Michael had entered into free and favourable renegotiations, with full legal advice, with the result that this contract did not amount to restraint of trade. Although Sony could not compel George Michael to produce music for them, they could prevent him working for another record label—which largely explains George Michael's disappeared from the charts in the mid-1990s (once bitten, twice shy, perhaps?).

Over to you. . .

Compare the two cases of *Schroeder* and *Panayiotou*. **What factors can you iden-tify as relevant in distinguishing these cases?**

Contrasting this case with **Schroeder** it is clear, for example, that a free renegotiation to the party's financial advantage is different from an unduly restrictive one-sided bargain as in **Schroeder**.

CONSTRUCTION OF THE CONTRACT

11-022   When assessing restraint of trade clauses, the courts will also adopt different tests of construc-tion in determining whether the clause is legally enforceable. However, there appear to be two different methods of construction that have been developed by the courts, with no clear guid-ance as to which approach should be adopted in each case.

THE LITERAL APPROACH

11-023   As the name suggests, by the literal approach the courts will interpret the clause using the ordinary meaning of the words used. The courts will not reformulate the agreement between the parties and will adopt a strict and literal interpretation of the words used. The literal approach to construction is demonstrated in **JA Mont (UK) Ltd v Mills** [1993] I.R.L.R. 172.

The defendant was a managing director of a paper tissue company. The company was taken over and the defendant was made redundant. As part of his redundancy the company agreed to pay him a severance fee if the defendant agreed not to work for any other paper tissue com-pany for one year.

At first instance the restriction was upheld as the court was of the opinion that the defendant may have used confidential information if he were allowed to work for another company in the paper tissue industry. However, the Court of Appeal held that the restriction was unenforceable. The only legitimate interest that could be protected in this case was the use of confidential information. The restriction imposed by the company did not express this and the court refused to investigate whether the company had actually intended to phrase the restriction in this manner. On a literal interpretation the clause did not seek to protect a legitimate interest. The only effect of the restriction was to prevent the defendant from seeking employment in the paper tissue industry, which was contrary to public policy.

THE FLEXIBLE APPROACH

In the flexible approach the courts will look beyond the actual words used and attempt to give effect to what the parties intended to achieve by the words used. An example of this approach can be seen in **Littlewoods Organisation v Harris** [1977] 1 W.L.R. 1472. The defendant was employed by the claimant company to work on the company's mail order catalogue. Between them Littlewoods and another company, GUS, controlled two-thirds of the mail order business in the UK. GUS had worldwide business interests, but the business of Littlewoods was confined to the UK. There was a clause in the defendant's contract that prevented him from working for GUS or any of its subsidiaries worldwide within 12 months of leaving Littlewoods.

11-024

On a literal interpretation, the clause was too wide and would be unenforceable. Littlewoods did not have any business interests outside the UK and its activity in the UK was confined to the mail order sector so it was not necessary to protect these interests in this way. However, the court adopted a more flexible approach when interpreting the clause. The court interpreted the clause as restricting the defendant from seeking employment for 12 months within the UK mail order sector. This must have been the intention of the claimants to protect their relevant business interests.

Over to you. . .

In relation to construction of such clauses can you identify any problems with the approach adopted by the court in *Littlewoods*?

The problem comes in reconciling these two approaches. As the Court of Appeal identified in **Hanover Insurance Brokers Ltd v Schapiro** [1994] I.R.L.R. 82, further guidance is required as to which approach is to be preferred in each case. As it stands, the courts have a wide discretion as to which rules to apply when construing the restriction. It may be possible for the courts to reverse engineer their decisions; they can form their conclusion as to the validity of the clause and then adopt the appropriate method of construction that will support this conclusion.

SEVERANCE

11-025   Rather than declaring the illegal term void and unenforceable, the court may choose to sever (or remove) the objectionable term from the contract. The courts can sever a term in any illegal contract, but it is in assessing restraint of trade clauses that severance has been most widely used. There are, however, a number of restrictions that limit the court's ability to sever an objectionable term:

- The application of the "blue pencil" test; and
- Severance must not alter the nature of the contract.

THE "BLUE PENCIL" TEST

11-026   Imagine that you had a blue pencil and were able to strike out the objectionable terms. This is the approach the courts take with objectionable terms. If the objectionable term can be struck out leaving behind a valid contract then the courts may opt to do this rather than declaring the entire restriction void for illegality. However, the courts adopt a strict approach and will only sever a term in this way if it can be completely removed without any need to rewrite or alter the contract. After the term has been removed the contract must still be readable and intelligible. If the removal of the term means that the contract no longer makes sense then the courts will not sever the term.

A classic example of the blue pencil test can be found in **Goldsoll v Goldman** [1915] 1 Ch. 292. In this case the plaintiff and the defendants were both in the business of selling imitation jewellery in London. The defendant sold his business to the plaintiff and the defendant undertook that he:

> **"would not for the period of two years either solely or jointly with or as agent or employee for any other person or persons or company directly or indirectly carry on or be engaged concerned or interested in or render services (gratuitously or otherwise) to the business of a vendor of or dealer in real or imitation jewellery in the county of London or any part of the United Kingdom of Great Britain and Ireland and the Isle of Man or in France, the United States, Russia, or Spain, or within twenty-five miles of Potsdamerstrasse, Berlin, or St. Stefans Kirche, Vienna."**

First, the clause was unreasonably wide in area. The plaintiff only had business interests in the UK so there was no need to restrict the defendant from selling jewellery in the other countries listed. The terms were severed so as to limit the restriction to the UK and the Isle of Man.

Secondly, the clause was unreasonably wide in preventing the defendant from selling real jewellery. Again, the plaintiff was only in the business of selling *imitation jewellery* so the restriction on selling "real" jewellery could be severed.

Applying the blue pencil test the clause would now read that the defendant:

> "would not for the period of two years either solely or jointly with or as agent or employee for any other person or persons or company directly or indirectly carry on or be engaged concerned or interested in or render services (gratuitously or otherwise) to the business of a vendor of or dealer in ~~real or~~ imitation jewellery in the county of London or any part of the United Kingdom of Great Britain and Ireland and the Isle of Man ~~or in France, the United States, Russia, or Spain, or within twenty-five miles of Potsdamerstrasse, Berlin, or St. Stefans Kirche, Vienna.~~"

SEVERANCE MUST NOT ALTER THE NATURE OF THE CONTRACT

11-027

As we have noted, the courts adopt a strict approach to the blue pencil test. Even if it is possible to sever the objectionable terms in this way, there is a further restriction that severance of the objectionable part must not alter the nature of the contract.

In **Attwood v Lamont** [1920] 3 K.B. 571, the defendant was employed as a draper, tailor and general outfitter at a London department store. The defendant agreed not to work within 10 miles of Kidderminster in "the trade or business of a tailor, dressmaker, general draper, milliner, hatter, haberdasher, gentlemen's, ladies' or children's outfitter". In breach of this restriction the defendant worked as a tailor within the restricted area and the plaintiff sought to enforce the clause that restricted him from working in that area.

The court held that the clause was unreasonably wide and was void for illegality. The purpose of the restriction was to protect the plaintiff's entire business so it was not possible to sever all the objectionable restrictions. If the court had limited the restriction simply to the profession of a tailor this would have altered the nature of the contract. The defendant's promise was not to compete against the business of the plaintiff and the restriction could not be broken down into smaller chunks that were capable of being severed.

Summary

1. A contract can be void and unenforceable under statute or at common law for illegality.

2. At common law the courts assess whether the clause in question is contrary to public policy. There are many examples provided above of contracts that are contrary to public policy, but one of the most controversial is the use of restraint of trade clauses.

3. Restraint of trade clauses are prima facie void as being contrary to public policy. However, there are limited circumstances in which a restraint of clause can be valid:

(a) the clause must be reasonable in relation to the protection of the parties;

(b) the clause must be reasonable as regards public policy.

4. First, the clause must be needed to protect a legitimate interest. Protecting trade secrets and business "goodwill" are key examples.

5. Once it has been established that there is an interest worthy of protection, the clause must be reasonable in protecting that interest. In assessing whether the clause is reasonable the courts will look to the nature of the restraint including its length and geographical restriction.

6. The courts adopt both literal and flexible interpretations to restraint of trade clauses and can also sever objectionable parts of the contract to make it enforceable. When severing such terms the removal of term should leave behind a coherent contract (the blue pencil test) and severance of the objectionable term must not alter the nature of the contract.

Key Cases Grid

Case	Court	Key Issues
Nordenfelt v Maxim Nordenfelt Guns & Ammunition Co Ltd [1894]	House of Lords	This case concerned the use of a restraint of trade clause. In determining whether such clauses are enforceable: (i) The clause must be reasonable in relation to the protection of the parties (ii) The clause must be reasonable as regards public policy
A Schroeder Music Publishing Co Ltd v Macaulay [1974]	House of Lords	An exclusive service agreement in this case as held to be void as such a one-sided agreement was contrary to public policy.
Littlewoods Organisation v Harris [1977]	Court of Appeal	This case illustrates a flexible approach to the interpretation of the contract that seeks to give effect to the intention of the claimants to protect their relevant business interests.

Goldsoll v Goldman [1915]	Court of Appeal	Rather than declaring the illegal term void and unenforceable, the court may choose to sever (or remove) the objectionable term from the contract. Severance must not alter the nature of the contract (Attwood v Lamont [1920] 3 K.B. 571)

End of Chapter Question

Sam works in the research and development unit of Soda-Pop Ltd, a large soft drink manufacturer. Soda-Pop Ltd manufacture and supply soft drinks to restaurants in the south of England, but are also looking to developing business opportunities in central England. Sam's contract of employment contains the following clause:

> **"Following termination of this contract of employment the employee shall not hold a position relating to the development of soft drinks for any other company located in south, central and northern England, for a period of five years."**

Sam has been offered a job as a marketing executive by Fizz Ltd, a rival drinks manufacturer. Soda-Pop Ltd is seeking to enforce the above clause.

Advise Sam.

Points of Answer

♦ Following the decision in **Nordenfelt**, contracts which are contrary to public policy are prima facie void.

♦ However, clauses in restraint of trade may be enforceable providing they are seeking to protect a legitimate interest and are reasonable in order to protect the interests of the parties.

♦ The case of **Herbert Morris** recognised that restraint of trade in order to protect company trade secrets could be a legitimate interest worthy of protection. As Sam works in the research and development unit he may well have access to confidential information as to the production of the Soda-Pop Ltd's products.

♦ The further requirement is that the clause must be reasonable in seeking to protect this interest. See the case **Foster v Suggett** in relation to five year restriction in order to protect trade secrets.

♦ However, question the extent of the restriction. Firstly, as Sam has been offered a position as a marketing executive would this create an opportunity to exploit his knowledge of any trade secrets? Also, note the geographical restriction. As Soda-Pop Ltd only have business interests in southern and central England then is it reasonable to extend the restriction to northern England?

♦ Consider the approach in Goldsoll and application of the "blue pencil" test. Reference to northern England, for example, could be struck from the clause without alternating the nature of the contract.

Further Reading

Stanton, M. "Absorption or sterilisation? Restraint of trade in the music industry." Ent. L.R. 1995, 6(4), 123–126.

An account of the law relating to restraint of trade in light of the decision in Panayiotou v Sony Music Entertainment (UK) Ltd [1994]

Stone, R. and Cunnington, R. Text, Cases and Materials on Contract Law (London: Routledge-Cavendish, 2014), Chapter 13.

Treitel, G. The Law of Contract, 13th edn (London Sweet & Maxwell, 2011), Chapter 11.

Discharge of Obligations: agreement, performance and breach

12

CHAPTER OVERVIEW

In this chapter we:

- **introduce the ways in which obligations can be discharged under the contract**

- **discuss how the parties can discharge their obligations by agreement**

- **consider a bilateral and unilateral discharge of obligations by agreement**

- **consider discharge by partial and substantial performance of the contract**

- **discuss discharge of obligations by breach of the contract**

Summary

Key Cases Grid

Further Reading

Introduction

12-001   A contract is a legally binding agreement: an agreement brings the contract into existence and an agreement can bring the contract to an end. We have already looked at ways of forming and enforcing the agreement, but the next few chapters are concerned with discharge of obligations under the contract. When parties are discharged from their obligations under the contract they are no longer required to meet the terms of the agreement.

There are a number of ways in which parties can be discharged from their obligations under a contract.

1.   The parties can *agree* that obligations are discharged.
2.   The parties can *perform* all their obligations under the contract.
3.   The parties may *breach* their obligations under the contract.

Finally, the doctrine of frustration can also discharge the parties from their obligations under the contract. Discharge by frustration will be considered in the next chapter.

Discharge by agreement

12-002   Obligations can be discharged under a contract and the contract brought to an end if both parties agree to do this. The parties will form a separate agreement to bring the contract to an end. This agreement must also be supported by consideration to be legally enforceable. The requirement of consideration is important as it will prevent one party from going back on their agreement and arguing that the other party is in breach of (the original) contract for failing to meet their obligations under that contract.

As an agreement to discharge obligations under a contract must be supported by consideration, it is important to distinguish between bilateral and unilateral discharges. A bilateral discharge is where both parties receive the benefit of the discharge. A unilateral discharge is where only one party (usually the promisee) receives the benefit of the discharge.

Bilateral discharge

12-003   If both parties wish to receive the benefit of the discharge then the agreement to discharge those obligations must be supported by consideration. Usually, if both parties are in agreement to bring the contract to an end it will not be difficult to identify the valuable consideration supporting the agreement to discharge. However, particular problems arise when the parties are seeking to *vary* the terms of their existing agreement.

A variation will inevitably have the effect of discharging some obligations under the contract, but may leave others unaltered. We have already discussed the problems of consideration in relation to variation of agreements in our discussion of **Stilk v Myrick** and **Williams v Roffey**. In **Williams**, the court was prepared to accept that an agreement to vary obligations under the contract was binding even though the other party did not *strictly* provide anything further in terms of consideration to support that agreement. It therefore seems that the doctrine of promissory estoppel may have an increased role to play in such cases, where an agreement to discharge may be binding if reliance is placed on that promise, despite the lack of strict consideration.

Unilateral discharge

If only one party seeks the benefit of the discharge then, again, that party will need to provide consideration to support an agreement to release him from obligations under the contract. In such cases one party has usually performed all the obligations required of him under the contract (the promisor) and will then agree to discharge the other party from performing his obligations (the promisee). This creates difficulties for the requirement of consideration. If the promisee has not fully performed his obligations under the contract it is difficult to see how he has provided any consideration to support the promise of discharge. Therefore, the common approach is that such agreements are not enforceable. So again, it would seem that the doctrine of promissory estoppel will have an important role to play in such agreements that are not strictly supported by valid consideration.

12-004

Discharge by performance

When a party has performed his obligations he will be discharged from those obligations under the contract. There can be difficulties in identifying the required level of performance to discharge obligations. For example, in a unilateral contract the act of acceptance will be by performing the required acts under the contract. The precise point at which acceptance becomes effective and performance complete is not always clear.

12-005

Performance must be precise and exact

There is a rule that performance of obligations under a contract must be precise and exact. Only if the party fulfils the precise obligations under the contract will he be discharged from these obligations. If the party fails to meet his precise obligations under the contract he may be in breach of contract. The distinction between performance and breach can be very subtle at times.

12-006

In **FW Moore & Co Ltd v Landauer & Co** [1921] 2 K.B. 519, a contract for the purchase of fruit required that 3,000 tins of fruit be delivered in cases of 30 tins. The correct number of tins was delivered (3,000 in total) but half of the cases delivered contained 24 tins. The court held that there had not been a full and complete performance of the contract. The contract required cases of 30 tins to be delivered and this obligation had not been performed by delivering some cases of 24 tins and some cases of 30 tins. The purchaser therefore had the right to reject the whole delivery and refuse to pay for the goods.

The requirement that performance be precise and exact has found a particularly harsh application in contracts for the sale of goods. In relation to contracts for services, the courts have developed a slightly more flexible approach but the requirement for precise and exact performance has still produced some quite severe decisions.

In **Cutter v Powell** (1795) 6 Term Rep. 320, the defendant promised to pay Cutter 30 guineas if Cutter agreed to act as second mate on the defendant's vessel. The ship was sailing from Jamaica to Liverpool, but about 20 days short of Liverpool, Cutter died. His widow brought an action to recover a proportion of the 30 guineas. She claimed that Cutter had substantially performed his obligations under the contract so she was entitled to a proportionate amount of the 30 guineas. The court rejected this argument and her claim was dismissed. Cutter had not performed the obligations required of him under the contract. Only upon arriving in Liverpool would the contract have been discharged by performance.

Over to you. . .

The decision in *Cutter v Powell* may, initially, appear quite harsh. Can you think of how this decision could be justified in light of the particular facts?

It should be noted that the agreed lump sum of 30 guineas was a large sum indeed for such contracts. The court held that Cutter ran the risk that he may be entitled to nothing at all under the contract as the reward for performance was so great. Unfortunately for Cutter, his risk did not pay off.

Construction of the contract

12-007   When assessing the issue of performance under a contract, the courts will construe the contract to determine whether there is the need for a complete or a substantial performance in order for contractual obligations to be discharged.

Severable obligations

12-008   A way of avoiding the potentially harsh consequences of cases such as **Cutter v Powell** will be for the courts to sever (or divide) the obligations under the contract. Rather than treating the contract as one big chunk, it may be possible to divide the overall obligations into smaller obligations. This process of severing obligations is most common in relation to contracts of employment. To treat the obligations under a contract of employment as one continuing obligation may be particularly unfair. If an annual salary was only payable once the final day's work in that year had been completed, and the employee failed to come to work on that final day, then strictly, the employer would be entitled to refuse payment for the whole year. In these cases, the courts would divide the obligations into smaller chunks, usually weekly or monthly and the employee would be entitled to payment to reflect his level of performance.

Partial performance

If the obligations under the contract have been *substantially* performed then the court may construe a failure to perform the outstanding obligations as giving rise to a breach of warranty. If there has only been a *partial* performance of the contract then the court may construe this as a breach of condition. It may be that one party will argue that their partial performance was accepted by the other party, thereby releasing them of their obligations under the contract. However, the courts will look to whether the parties had a free choice to accept this partial performance.

12-009

In **Sumpter v Hedges** [1898] 1 Q.B. 673, the claimant had only performed part of a building contract before ceasing work and leaving the site. This left the defendants to complete the outstanding work themselves using the materials left behind by the claimant. The court held that the claimant was entitled to the cost of the materials used by the defendants, but not for the work that had been performed. As the defendants had a choice to use the materials to complete the work the claimant was able to recover the value of these materials. However, the defendants had no choice but to continue the work after the claimant had left the site, so the claimant was not able to claim for the value of the work that he had partially completed.

Substantial performance

The courts may construe the contract as requiring only a substantial performance to discharge obligations. This does not mean that a party will not be liable for failing to meet all the obligations under the contract, rather that the contract will be construed as entitling the innocent party to sue for damages in respect of those obligations left unperformed. The courts will treat a substantial performance in the same way as a breach of warranty under a contract. A breach of warranty will simply entitle the innocent party to claim damages.

12-010

For example, in **Dakin & Co Ltd v Lee** [1916] 1 K.B. 566, there was a contract to repair a house. The contract price was £1,500. A number of discrepancies arose between what was contracted for and what was provided under the contract. The contract required that the underpinning of the walls would be four feet. In fact the claimants only underpinned the walls to the depth of two feet. Instead of using five-inch thick columns to support the window, only four-inch columns were used. Despite these discrepancies, the Court of Appeal held that the builders had substantially performed their obligations under the contract and were entitled to payment. The builders were to be paid the £1,500 minus the cost of remedying the defects (£80).

In **Hoenig v Isaacs** [1952] 2 All E.R. 176, the plaintiff contracted to refurbish the defendant's flat. The work was completed but the defendant refused to pay, arguing that the work was not of a satisfactory quality. As a result, the defendant argued that he was not obliged to pay for the work as the plaintiff had not performed his obligations under the contract. The Court of Appeal held that as the plaintiff had substantially performed his obligations under the contract the defendant was not released from his obligation to pay for the work completed. The defects with the work were very minor and inexpensive to correct so the court therefore approached the breach in a similar way to a breach of warranty. This gave the defendant the right to claim damages for the breach, which were relatively minor (the difference between the contract price and the cost to remedy the defects).

In contrast, in **Bolton v Mahadeva** [1972] 1 W.L.R. 1009, a contractor agreed with the defendant to install a central heating system. The contract price was £560. After the work had been completed the central heating system was found to be inadequate; it could not heat the house satisfactorily and it gave off fumes. It would cost £174 to remedy these defects. The contractor then brought an action for the contract price minus the cost of the remedial work (£560-£174 = a claim for £386). The court held that the contractor was not entitled to this payment as he had not substantially performed his obligations under the contract.

The case of **Bolton** illustrates the difficulties if the courts are prepared to accept substantial performance as an exception to the rule that performance must be complete and precise. It is not always easy to distinguish between a "substantial performance" and a performance that falls short of providing what was bargained for. For example, work being "substantially performed" (as in **Hoenig**) will be of little use if that work is of such low quality that it is almost worthless (as in **Bolton**). The decision of the court to recognise a "substantial performance" will therefore hinge on the facts of the particular case, making it difficult to draw firm conclusions as to when this is likely to happen.

Prevention of performance

12-011   Generally, there must be a full and complete performance in order to discharge a party from his obligations under a contract. If one party is prevented from performing their obligations under the contract owing to the actions of the other party, then that party may be able to recover money on a quantum meruit basis (money had for work done).

In **Planche v Colbourn** (1831) 8 Bing. 14, the plaintiff contracted to write a book (the subject matter was, out of interest, costumes and ancient armour). The plaintiff was entitled to payment of £100 due upon completion of the book. The publishers then abandoned the series in which the book was to appear. The court awarded the plaintiff £50 on a *quantum meruit basis.*

This amount represented the work he had undertaken in partial performance but was unable to complete because of the decision of the publishers to abandon the series.

Discharge by breach

A breach of contract will entitle the innocent party to claim an appropriate remedy for the breach. The innocent party may claim damages, may seek specific performance, or may attempt to terminate the agreement. The precise effect of the breach will depend on whether there has been a breach that goes to the root of the contract (a breach of condition) and will repudiate the agreement or a less significant breach (a breach of warranty) that simply gives the innocent party the right to claim damages. It may be useful to refer back to Ch.6 to remind yourself how the courts distinguish between these different types of terms. Also, remember that a breach of an innominate term may be classed as a breach of condition or a breach of warranty depending on the seriousness of the breach.

12-012

However, a breach in itself will not terminate the agreement. First, to terminate an agreement the breach must have been a breach of condition. Secondly, the innocent party has to accept this breach. In **Heyman v Darwins Ltd** [1942] A.C. 356, the court was of the opinion that acceptance of the breach had to be expressly communicated to the defaulting party. This was doubted in **Vitol SA v Norelf Ltd (The Santa Clara)** [1996] A.C. 800 when the court held that the need for communication of the acceptance of a breach was not strictly necessary. On the other hand, it is doubtful that complete inactivity by the innocent party will be effective, so in the majority of cases express communication will be the most obvious way to accept the breach.

A further point to note is that the innocent party has the *choice* to accept the breach. In most cases the innocent party will simply accept the breach and sue for breach of contract. However, following the decision in **Photo Production v Securicor** [1980] A.C. 827, it is clear that the innocent party can elect not to terminate the agreement following a breach of condition. The party can choose to continue with the contract and sue for damages for the defendant's breach. As the innocent party has the freedom to choose whether to accept the breach, a particular problem arises in relation to an anticipatory breach.

Anticipatory breach

An anticipatory breach arises where one party indicates that he will not be able to meet his obligations under the contract *before* the contract is completed. For example, the builders contracted to refurbish a house may expressly state that they will not be completing their obligations under the contract. In this case the innocent party will not have to wait until the date for performance has passed. The claimants can treat the builder's actions as an anticipatory breach of contract.

12-013

In **Hochster v De La Tour** (1853) 2 El. & Bl. 678, the defendant employed the claimant as a courier. The claimant was to accompany the defendant on his international tour which began on June 1. On May 11 the defendant wrote to the claimant stating that the claimant's services were no longer needed. This is a classic example of an anticipatory breach. The claimant did not have to wait until June 1 to bring an action for breach of contract. The claimant could treat the notice on May 11 as an anticipatory breach and bring an action at that point.

Once the innocent party has been given notice of an anticipatory breach then an action for breach of contract can be brought at that point. However, if there is a delay in accepting the breach, the innocent party may lose the right to sue for breach of contract. In **Avery v Bowden** (1855) 5 El. & Bl. 714, the defendants charted the plaintiffs ship to sail to Odessa and to load cargo at the port within 45 days. When the ship arrived there was no cargo to collect. The defendants contacted the plaintiffs and told them that there was no hope of the cargo arriving and instructed them to leave Odessa. The plaintiffs, however, remained in Odessa in that hope that the cargo would arrive. In the meantime the Crimean War broke out, which made it illegal to perform the contract as the port of Odessa was considered to be the port of an enemy.

The plaintiffs then sought to bring the contract to an end arguing that the defendants' notice that the goods would not arrive was an anticipatory breach. The court held that the plaintiffs affirmed the contract by remaining in Odessa despite the defendants' instructions to leave. As the contract had been affirmed the plaintiffs had lost the right to sue under the contract. This decision had a further sting in the tail, as the outbreak of war also frustrated the contract (see Ch.13 for a discussion as to the effects of frustration on the contract).

Summary

1. If obligations under a contract are discharged then the effect is to release the parties of those obligations under the contract. The remedies available will depend on the manner in which those obligations were discharged.

2. Obligations can be discharged by agreement. The agreement to discharge obligations under a contract will be treated as a separate agreement and generally must be supported by consideration to be enforceable.

3. Obligations can also be discharged by performance. If all the primary obligations under a contract have been performed then the contract will no longer bind the parties to those obligations under the contract. The general rule is that performance must be complete and precise. Therefore, the courts may treat a *partial* performance of a contract as being a breach of condition that will repudiate the agreement. However, a *substantial* performance may be treated as a breach of warranty giving the right to claim damages.

4. Finally, obligations can be discharged by breach. The innocent party can accept the breach and sue for breach of contract or he may elect to continue to perform under the contract. In the case of an anticipatory breach the innocent party must again accept the breach in order to avoid a finding that he has affirmed the contract and therefore lost the right to sue under the contract.

Key Cases Grid

Case	Court	Key Issue
Cutter v Powell (1795)	Court of King's Bench	Illustrates the, sometimes harsh requirement, that performance of obligations under a contract must be precise and exact.
Planche v Colbourn (1831)	Court of King's Bench	Generally, there must be full and complete performance in order to discharge the contractual obligation. However. If one party is prevented from performing due to the actions of the other party, then the court may award money on a quantum meruit basis (money had for work done).
Hochster v De La Tour (1853)	Court of Queen's Bench	An example of anticipatory, when one party indicates that he will not be able to meet his obligations under the contract *before* the contract is completed.

Further Reading

Stone, R. and Cunnington, R. *Text, Cases and Materials on Contract Law* (London: Routledge-Cavendish, 2014), Chapter 14.

Treitel, G. *The Law of Contract*, 13th edn (London Sweet & Maxwell, 2011), Chapter 17.

Frustration

13

CHAPTER OVERVIEW

In this chapter we:

- **introduce how obligations under a contract can be discharged due to the doctrine of frustration**
- **discuss the development of the doctrine of frustration**
- **analyse the events which may frustrate a contract; destruction of the subject matter and non-occurrence of an event**
- **analyse and contrast the key authorities as to whether the non-occurrence of an event can frustrate the contract**
- **consider the effect of frustration at common law in relation to contractual obligations**
- **analyse the provisions of the Law Reform (Frustrated Contracts) Act 1943**

Summary

Key Cases Grid

End of Chapter Question

Further Reading

Introduction

13-001 The previous chapter was concerned with situations in which obligations under a contract can be discharged, with the focus being on performance, agreement and breach. We will now focus on the doctrine of frustration, which is the final way in which obligations under a contract can be discharged.

A contract will be described as "frustrated" where, after the contract has been formed, an event occurs that is beyond the control of both parties and that has the effect of making the obligations under the contract impossible to perform or radically alters the nature of the obligations.

The doctrine of frustration is fascinating as it finds its roots in a number of archaic and over-lapping principles. Trying to reconcile and apply these principles, however, is not an easy task. Perhaps rather appropriately (or ironically?), students often find the doctrine of frustration difficult to grasp, particularly when trying to analyse the effects of the modern doctrine on the contract in question. With this in mind we shall briefly look at the foundations of the law of frustration before embarking upon a more detailed analysis of *how* the doctrine of frustration affects the obligations of each party under the contract.

Hear from the Author

Scan the QR Tag or follow the link below for an introduction to the principles of frustration.

uklawstudent.thomsonreuters.com/category/contract-fundamentals

Outline and development of the doctrine of frustration

13-002 If a party fails to meet his or her obligations under a contract then the innocent party will be able to pursue an action for breach of contract. However, as mentioned above, the doctrine of frustration is concerned with events that occur *after* the contract has been formed so that it is then impossible (or illegal) to perform those obligations under the contract. To some extent the doctrine of frustration excuses a potential breach of contract on the basis that neither party is at fault in failing to meet these obligations owing to an event that is beyond their control. However, this has not always been the case and as we shall see the modern doctrine of frustration is quite removed from its archaic founding principles.

THE DOCTRINE OF "ABSOLUTE OBLIGATIONS"

The starting point in the development of the law of frustration is the common law doctrine referred to as the doctrine of "absolute obligations". Quite simply, this doctrine provided that the obligations under a contract are absolute. The courts would therefore not be prepared to discharge (or excuse) a failure to meet contractual obligations under a contract. The fact that an event occurred after the contract had been formed that made it impossible to perform such obligations was irrelevant.

13-003

This doctrine is quite harshly demonstrated in the case of **Paradine v Jane** (1674) Aleyn 26 in which even the outbreak of war did not affect the obligations under a lease for a plot of land.

At first glance it may appear difficult to justify the doctrine of absolute obligations given the potentially harsh consequences that follow. However, such an approach is in line with a strict interpretation of freedom of contract. If the parties had intended to avoid the consequences of an event (such as the outbreak of war) then the parties should have provided measures to avoid this event in the contractual document. If the parties did not provide for such events in the contract then the courts would not intervene to discharge them from those obligations to which they have freely agreed.

In fact, particularly in maritime and shipping contracts, it has been common practice for the parties to outline the obligations and liabilities before the contract is formed. This means that each party is aware of their liabilities and obligations up front and can take out insurance previsions to protect them in the event of breach. Clauses were inserted into the contract, referred to as force majeure clauses, which had the further effect of excusing liability for an event which otherwise would result in a breach of contract. For example, a natural disaster such as a hurricane may make it impossible for a vessel to deliver its cargo by the agreed deadline, but such an event and the liability that flows would usually be provided for in the contract. The courts would then give effect to the terms that the parties had agreed when deciding the issue of liability.

THE LIMITATIONS ON "ABSOLUTE OBLIGATIONS"

As we have seen, the very strict application of the doctrine of absolute obligations meant that the courts would only excuse where the parties had provided for such an event in the contract. However, a turning point in the development of the doctrine of frustration comes with the decision in **Taylor v Caldwell** (1863) 3 B. & S. 826. In this case the plaintiffs hired a music hall from the defendants for four nights to stage a number of performances. Before the first performance took place the music hall was destroyed in an accidental fire. The destruction of the music hall was something that was beyond the control of either party, but the court had to decide whether the defendants were liable for breach of contract as it was no longer possible for them to meet their obligations to the plaintiffs.

13-004

Strictly, if the court were to apply the doctrine of absolute obligations then the defendants would be liable for breach of contract by failing to provide the music hall for four nights as agreed. However, Blackburn J. made it clear that the doctrine of absolute obligations only applied where one party had explicitly accepted to bear the risk of such an event occurring. For example, if the defendants in **Taylor v Caldwell** had agreed to provide the music hall for four nights, irrespective of the risk, then the courts might have held them to their absolute obligations. However, as neither party had explicitly made such a promise then the court was prepared to approach the obligations in a more flexible way. It is at this point that we start to see the birth of the modern doctrine of frustration with the courts beginning to recognise a limitation to the theory of absolute obligations in the form of an implied-term approach to contractual obligations.

THE IMPLIED-TERM THEORY OF FRUSTRATION

13-005   The decision in **Taylor v Caldwell** marked an important step in the development of the law of frustration. Until this decision the courts adopted a very strict application of the doctrine of absolute obligations and were not prepared to excuse a breach of contract unless measures to avoid the risk were provided for in the contract. However, Blackburn J. in **Taylor v Caldwell** approached the issue of contractual obligations based on a theory of "implied terms". For example, using the facts of **Taylor v Caldwell** as illustration, both parties would have intended that the music hall being in existence would be an implied term of the contract. So, the court was prepared to give effect to this implied term with the result that when the music hall was destroyed the parties were discharged (or excused) from their obligations to perform under the contract.

The approach of the court in **Taylor v Caldwell** may seem odd in light of the principles of freedom of contract. One of the founding principles is that the courts are reluctant to interfere with a contract that has been freely negotiated by the parties. However, with the development of the "implied-term" theory of contractual obligations, the courts would seem to be doing just that, rewriting the agreement to include elements that were never agreed by the parties. However, such an approach was justified by Blackburn J in **Taylor v Caldwell** on the grounds that the parties should be excused from performance based on their presumed intention. This has some merit in that it avoids the parties having to draft unnecessarily long contractual documents that account for all potential possibilities and risks.

THE SHIFT IN THE *CONSTRUCTION* OF OBLIGATIONS

13-006   While the implied-term theory of obligations proved satisfactory in cases such as **Taylor v Caldwell** it was not possible in every case to identify an implied term to excuse a breach. However, the courts were still prepared to accept the possibility of excuse (or frustration) in the absence of an implied term. The courts shifted their attention from implied obligations and focused on their *construction* of the obligations under the contract. In other words, when the court interprets the obligations under the contract it will look at any express terms, any implied terms, and also at the nature of the contract itself—including all the surrounding circumstances.

Such an approach was first developed by the House of Lords in **Davis Contractors Ltd v Fareham Urban DC** [1956] A.C. 696. As Lord Radcliffe observed in that case:

> **"It would be simpler to say at the outset that frustration occurs whenever the law recognises that without default of either party a contractual obligation has become incapable of being performed because the circumstances in which performance is called for would render it a thing radically different from that which was undertaken by the contract."**

So, if performance is impossible, or in the circumstances performance of those obligations is radically different from that which was contracted for then the courts will excuse a breach of those obligations (and will discharge the parties from their obligations) owing to the contract being frustrated.

What events can frustrate a contract?

There are many events that can frustrate a contract and we will look at many examples from case law. However, the same fundamental principles are present in relation to all these events. A frustrating event must occur after the contract has been formed, the event must be beyond the control of both parties and the effect of must be to make the obligations under the contract impossible to perform, or to render those obligations "radically different" from those which were contracted for.

13-007

Destruction of the subject matter

If the subject matter of the contract is destroyed this will potentially frustrate the contract. This is also linked to the fundamental principle that such destruction will make obligations under the contract impossible to perform. A classic example comes from the case of **Taylor v Caldwell** (1863) 3 B. & S. 826, in which the destruction of the music hall by fire meant that it was no longer possible to hold the performances that were contracted for. The destruction of the subject matter in this case had therefore frustrated the contract between the parties.

13-008

Non-occurrence of an event

If a contract is dependent upon an event taking place then will the non-occurrence of that event frustrate the contract? This is perhaps the most interesting (and controversial) aspect of

13-009

the law of frustration and as we will see the following principles are somewhat contradictory and thus difficult to reconcile. However, we will try to distil the fundamental principles from the relevant case law to arrive at some conclusions regarding the non-occurrence of an event.

THE CORONATION CASES

13-010 Interestingly, the leading principles relating to the non-occurrence of an event arise out of the same broad facts, the coronation of Edward VII. In **Krell v Henry** [1903] 2 K.B. 740, the defendant hired a flat in Pall Mall from the plaintiff. The flat had a particularly good view of the King's coronation procession that was due to pass through Pall Mall. The defendant paid a deposit for the room with the remainder due upon leaving the flat. However, the King was taken ill and the coronation procession never took place. The plaintiff then brought an action against the defendant claiming the amount due for the hiring of the flat.

The Court of Appeal held that the cancellation of the coronation procession had frustrated the contract for the hire of the flat. The reasoning of the Court of Appeal was expressed by Vaughan Williams L.J. who pronounced that that the occurrence of the event—the coronation procession taking place—was the "foundation of the contract". As a result, the defendant was not required to pay the remainder due under the contract as this obligation had been discharged by the frustrating event.

It is interesting to compare the decision in **Krell v Henry** with that of **Herne Bay Steam Boat Co v Hutton** [1903] 2 K.B. 683, not only because they are based on very similar facts but also because these cases were heard within a few days of each other and were also heard by the same panel of judges in the Court of Appeal. The case of **Herne Bay Steam Boat Co** was again concerned with events surrounding the coronation of Edward VII, but in this case the defendants hired a steam boat from the plaintiffs. They intended to sail the boat round the bay and to watch a naval review that the King was due to conduct. The naval fleet had gathered in the bay but because of the King's illness the review itself was cancelled. The plaintiffs then brought an action claiming the balance due for the hiring of the steam boat.

Interestingly, the Court of Appeal held that the cancellation of the naval review did not frustrate the contract between the plaintiff and defendant. The review taking place was not the "foundation of the contract" so the defendant was liable to pay the outstanding balance.

RECONCILING *KRELL* WITH *HERNE BAY STEAM BOAT COMPANY*

13-011 The decisions in **Krell v Henry and Herne Bay Steam Boat Co** seem very difficult to reconcile. Indeed, it seems amazing that two cases with such similar facts, heard at almost the same time (and by the same judges) were decided so differently regarding frustration. These two cases also create real difficulties for students when applying the relevant principles and when embarking upon the tricky task of identifying the "foundation" of the contract.

A starting point is to consider the opinion of Stirling L.J. in **Herne Bay** who argues that the naval review was not the foundation of the contract as the cancellation of the review did not totally defeat the purpose of the contract of hire:

> "The fleet was there, and passengers might have been found willing to go round it. It is true that in the event which happened the object of the voyage became limited, but, in my opinion, that was the risk of the defendant whose venture the taking the passengers was."

Over to you. . .

Stirling L.J. argued that the contract in *Herne Bay* was not frustrated as it was still possible to perform part of the contract—the fleet was still there so there was still some value left in the agreement. However, can you think of any criticisms of this approach in light of the facts of both *Herne Bay* and *Krell*?

The fact that the fleet was still there and that the passengers could still enjoy the voyage by steaming round the fleet meant that there was still some value left in the contract. This analysis, however, fails to adequately explain the differences between **Krell** and **Herne Bay**. For example, if this analysis were applied to **Krell** then it could be argued that there was still some value present in the contract for the hiring of the room, despite the cancellation of the procession. The defendant could still enjoy the room, could use the room as he wished for the remainder of the period of hire, so there was still some quality left in the contract.

Further, what if the fleet had sailed away in **Herne Bay** so that it was no longer possible for the passengers to enjoy this aspect of the voyage? Would the contract then be frustrated since all the value in the contract had been lost? Even if the fleet had sailed away, it is still highly unlikely that this would frustrate the contract for the hiring of the boat (the reasoning for which we will now gather from the decision of Vaughan Williams L.J.) so the approach of Stirling L.J. is best viewed merely as a starting point in reconciling these two cases.

Vaughan Williams L.J. in **Krell v Henry** provides some further and slightly more robust justification for the decision by using a hypothetical example of a contract for the hire of a taxi:

> "It would follow that if a cabman was engaged to take someone to Epsom on Derby Day at a suitable enhanced price for such a journey . . . both parties to the contract would be discharged in the contingency of the race at Epsom for some reason becoming impossible; but I do not think this follows, for I do not think that in the cab case the happening of the race would be the foundation of the contract . . . No doubt the purpose of the engager would be to go to see

the Derby, and the price would be proportionately high; but the cab had no special qualifications for the purpose which led to the selection of the cab for this particular occasion. Any other cab would have done as well."

There are two key elements to take from this interesting, if somewhat unusual, example. First, Vaughan Williams L.J. places emphasis on the quality of what is being contracted for, as did Stirling LJ. However, Vaughan Williams L.J. is focused on the quality of the subject matter in question, rather than looking at the commercial nature of the contract as a whole. The cab in his example has no particular quality that separated it from any other cab. So, applying this analysis to the cases of **Krell v Henry** and **Herne Bay Steam Boat Co v Hutton**, it can be argued that the steam boat in the **Herne Bay** case had no particular quality that distinguished it from any other boat, unlike the hiring of the room in **Krell** which had a particularly good view of the procession route.

Secondly, when trying to assess the "foundation of the contract" it is necessary to look at this issue from the perspective of *both* parties. As Vaughan Williams L.J. observes in his example, the race taking place may have been the reason why the taxi was hired from the perspective of the passenger, but the race taking place would not be the foundation of the contract so far as the cabdriver is concerned. The happening of the race is therefore not the foundation of the contract from the perspective of both parties so the non-occurrence of that event will not frustrate the contract for the hire of the taxi.

There are again, however, problems with both approaches of Vaughan Williams L.J. First, it is difficult to argue that the room in **Krell** had any particular quality that separated it from any other room that overlooked the procession route. All these rooms would have had an equally good view, so in fact any room along the route would have done just as well. Secondly, Vaughan Williams L.J.'s reference to "a suitably enhanced price" in his cab example is not particularly helpful. Indeed, this approach would suggest that the happening of the event (the race taking place) may well have been the foundation of the contract from the perspective of the cabdriver as well as the passenger so that its cancellation would frustrate the contract (despite Vaughan Williams L.J.'s conclusion that it would not be frustrated).

Finally, in reaching his decision in **Krell**, Vaughan Williams L.J. did so by applying the implied-term theory of frustration (or excuse) as developed in **Taylor v Caldwell** (1863) 3 B. & S. 826. It was never expressly agreed between the parties that the procession taking place formed part of the contract, but the court was nevertheless prepared to imply such a term based on the fact that both parties would assume that the event taking place was fundamental to the contract. For example, the room was a private apartment and was only hired on the occasion in question because of the particularly good view it gave of the King's procession route. Given the shift in emphasis towards the construction of the contract and the move away from the implied-term theory it makes it even more difficult for the principles from **Krell** to survive within the modern law of the doctrine of frustration.

Criticisms of the approaches in **Krell** and **Herne** aside, the fundamental principle (and the preferable way of reconciling these cases) is to focus on the "foundation of the contract" by looking at this issue from the perspective of both parties.

The fact that the room was only let out for the occasion of the King's coronation and for the particular view the room had of the procession route (and a suitably high price was charged) demonstrated that the procession taking place was the foundation of the contract so far as both parties were concerned. The non-occurrence of this event therefore frustrated the contract.

In contrast, in **Herne** the naval review taking place was not the foundation of the contract so far as the boat company were concerned, so the non-occurrence of the event did not frustrate the contract.

. . . .

Illegality

So far we have approached the issue of frustration in the context of impossibility: an event beyond the control of either party that makes the obligations under the contract impossible to perform. However, there are events that can nevertheless frustrate the contract with it still being technically possible to perform those obligations. Illegality is an example of such an event. After the contract has been formed an event may occur that makes it illegal to continue performing obligations under the contract.

13-012

Such an event is often described as radically altering the obligations under the contract, which is justification for excusing a failure to meet those obligations. Strictly, however, in the majority of cases the obligations under the contract have not changed, they remain the same but rather the surrounding circumstances have now altered the level of performance. So perhaps it is better to explain such frustrating events in these contracts on the basis that the parties undertook to perform a lawful act (as a requirement of enforceability of the agreement) which has subsequently been rendered unlawful by an event beyond the control of either party. The *nature* of the agreement has been radically altered and as such the courts will not insist upon performance of those obligations.

It is first necessary to recognise that such illegality can arise in a number of ways. Usually, this will be as a result of the actions of the prevailing government. For example in **Metropolitan Water Board v Dick Kerr & Co Ltd** [1918] A.C. 119, a contract to build a reservoir was frustrated when the Ministry of Munitions (in an attempt to free resources during wartime) declared it illegal to continue with its construction.

However, in **FA Tamplin Steamship Co Ltd v Anglo-Mexican Petroleum Products Co Ltd** [1916] 2 A.C. 397, when a vessel that was leased for a period of five years to carry petroleum products was requisitioned by the government to be used as a troop ship, the contract was not frustrated by such government intervention. Although the vessel could not be used for commercial purposes while requisitioned by the government, it was still possible that for a period of the five-year lease the vessel could have been used in such a way. The contract had therefore not been radically altered by the actions of the government.

The outbreak of war itself can frustrate a contract. In **Avery v Bowden** (1855) 5 El. & Bl. 714, the contract for the lease of a cargo vessel was frustrated by the outbreak of the Crimean War, as it became illegal to unload cargo at the vessel's destination, Odessa, which was considered to be the port of an enemy at the time.

Non-availability of the parties owing to death or illness

13-013   If one of the parties to the contract is unavailable owing to death or illness then this again can frustrate the contract. Perhaps not too controversially, the death of one of the parties will frustrate the contract, especially so if performance of the contract can only be undertaken by that individual (**Hall v Wright** (1859) 120 E.R. 695). Many of the cases in this area have been concerned with the effect on a service contract (a contract of employment) of death or illness.

In **Condor v The Barron Knights Ltd** [1966] 1 W.L.R. 87, the plaintiff, the drummer in a comedy musical group was employed to perform seven nights per week. One evening he collapsed and was eventually admitted to a mental hospital following a mental breakdown. The medical opinion was that in order to avoid further breakdowns the drummer should perform no more than four nights per week. On hearing this news the band terminated the contract of employment between themselves and the drummer. The court held that as the drummer was unable to meet his obligations because of illness the contract of employment had been breached and the drummer's action for wrongful dismissal therefore failed.

Frustration and leases

13-014   If a party holds a lease over property, the individual has been conferred rights in relation to that property—in the context of contract law the rights will be to use that property for commercial or residential purposes. Following the case of **National Carriers Ltd v Panalpina Ltd** [1981] A.C. 675, it is clear that a lease can be frustrated. However, it has been quite rare for this to occur. The court will look to relevant factors to determine whether a lease should be frustrated by an intervening event. Particularly, the court will look to how long the lease has to run. The longer the lease, the less likely it is that the court will decide that it has been frustrated. The reasoning is quite clear as the court will be reluctant to declare a contract frustrated when there are still many years left to run on the lease. The case of **Panalpina** itself provides a good example. In this case the local council closed the road giving access to a warehouse that was subject to a lease. The road closure meant that the warehouse would have restricted access for about 18 months. The court refused to accept that the lease had been frustrated by the closure of the road as the lease over the warehouse was for a total of

10 years. A greater level of interference with the rights of the leaseholder was required, rather than a disruption for a mere 18 months.

Limitations on the doctrine of frustration

As has been made clear, a contract will be frustrated by an event that is beyond the control of either party. In such cases the courts will relieve the parties from their obligations under the contract and excuse a breach of those obligations that will inevitably follow. It is therefore important to recognise that there is always a fine line between frustration and breach of contract. For this reason there are a number of limitations placed upon the doctrine of frustration so that the courts will refuse to excuse a breach of contract.

13-015

Self-induced frustration

If the supervening event is within the control of one of the parties, then the courts will not discharge the parties' obligations and the innocent party will be able to pursue an action for breach of contract. This is referred to as self-induced frustration as one party is responsible for bringing about the event that has the effect of making the obligations under the contract impossible to perform, or rendering them radically different from those that were contracted for. As we will see, the courts have adopted a particularly harsh application and interpretation of self-induced frustration.

13-016

In **Maritime National Fish Ltd v Ocean Trawlers Ltd** [1935] A.C. 524 the defendants chartered five fishing vessels, which they intended to use to perform "otter trawls" (a technique that allowed for a wider span at the mouth of the net and hence increasing the size of the haul). One of the vessels was chartered from the plaintiffs. In order to fish using "otter trawls" it was necessary to obtain a licence from the Minister of Fisheries. The applications were made but only three licences were granted. The defendants allocated the licences to three vessels, but not to the vessel chartered from the plaintiffs. The defendants then claimed that the charter between themselves and the plaintiffs had been frustrated as the plaintiffs were unable to meet the obligations under the charter owing to the lack of the trawling licence.

This claim of frustration was rejected. The defendants were free to allocate the licences as they wished and as they actively decided not to allocate a licence to the plaintiffs' vessel then the impossibility of performance was self-induced and did not frustrate the charter agreement.

A further and even harsher example of the courts' approach to self-induced frustration can be seen in the case of **J Lauritzen AS v Wijsmuller BV (The Super Servant Two)** [1990] 1 Lloyd's Rep. 1. Here, the defendants agreed to deliver some drilling equipment that belonged to the claimants. The defendants had two vessels that were capable of transporting the equipment from Japan to Rotterdam: *Super Servant One* and *Super Servant Two*. The defendants decided to assign *Super Servant Two* to transport the equipment. Before the equipment was transported, *Super Servant Two* sank. The defendants then claimed that the sinking of *Super Servant Two* (an event beyond their control) had frustrated the contract to transport the equipment.

Surprisingly, the court held that the sinking of *Super Servant Two* had not frustrated the contract. The court decided that the inability of the defendants to transport the drilling equipment was due to their decision in the way the vessels were allocated. It was their decision to allocate *Super Servant Two*, rather than *Super Servant One* to transport the equipment. As this decision was something within the control of the defendants, the impossibility of performance was self-induced by their actions.

Allocation of risk and frustration

13-017 Of course, it was always possible that the defendants could have provided for such risk in **Super Servant Two**. Particularly in maritime contracts it is commonplace for the parties to include a force majeure clause in the contract that will make it clear where such risks of the voyage will lie. Therefore, while the decision in **Super Servant Two** provides a particularly harsh example of the limitations of the doctrine of frustration, it also provides clarification that it is the issue of construction that will be of most importance in deciding whether such breaches should be excused. If upon a construction of the contract it is possible for the court to allocate the risk of the supervening event then the court will see this as a preferable alternative to the doctrine of frustration.

Further, the courts are prepared to imply terms into the contract as a mechanism for allocating risk, which is what happened in the case of **Jackson v Union Marine Insurance Co Ltd** (1974–75) L.R. 10 C.P. 125. Here, the contract was for the charter of a ship to sail from Liverpool to San Francisco, stopping on the way at Newport to upload some cargo. After leaving Liverpool the ship ran aground and as a result never made it to Newport. While the contract did not provide a time limit as to when the delivery of cargo should be made, the contract did contain a clause stating that all "dangers and accidents of navigation excepted". In interpreting the clause the court was prepared to imply a term into the contract that performance should take place within a "reasonable time". Therefore the jury decided that the contract had been frustrated as it would be some eight months before the ship could be repaired and ready to sail.

A radical change of obligations is required; mere delay will not suffice

13-018 It is important to note that simply because the obligations have become more expensive or more time consuming to perform, this will not in itself frustrate the contract. In **Tsakiroglou and Co Ltd v Noblee Thorl GmbH** [1962] A.C. 93, a vessel was contracted to deliver cargo from the Sudan to Hamburg. The vessel was forced to take a longer route following the closure of the Suez

Canal. This route took the vessel round the Cape of Good Hope, which took over twice as long as the original route, inevitably increasing the expense for the shippers. The closure of the Suez Canal was held not to frustrate the contract. Even though the time and expense had increased, the fundamental obligations under the contract had not been radically altered by the closure.

The effect of frustration on the contract

We have looked at ways in which a contract can be frustrated. The more difficult task is to assess the effect frustration will have on the obligations under the frustrated contract. Simply, the effect of frustration will be to relieve the parties of their obligations under the contract. However, identifying precisely what obligations will be discharged and the consequences that flow from this finding will form the basis of the remainder of this chapter. As we will see, both common law and statute provide for the effects of frustration upon contractual obligations, but neither provides a completely satisfactory (nor completely comprehensible) solution. There is a trade-off between the clarity (but harshness) of the common law and the complexity (but fairness) under statute.

13-019

. . . .

The position at common law

At common law the effect of frustration on the contract was rather clear and unsophisticated. The effect of a frustrating event was to relieve the parties of those obligations that fell to be performed after the frustrating event. Those obligations that arose before the frustrating event were unaffected. In other words, the "loss lies where it falls".

13-020

There is merit in this approach in that it certainly simplifies the position of the parties under a frustrated contract. However, as we will see, this simplistic approach also gave rise to some very harsh and unjust conclusions.

In **Appleby v Myers** (1866–67) L.R. 2 C.P. 651, the plaintiffs contracted to erect machinery on the defendant's premises and to repair the machinery for two years. Payment for this work was due upon completion of the contract. During the performance of the contract the defendant's premises and the machinery were destroyed by an accidental fire. The court decided that this event had frustrated the contract and as a result both parties were relieved of obligations arising after this frustrating event. However, as the obligation to pay arose after the frustrating event, the defendants had no obligation to pay the plaintiffs for the work that had been completed. This future obligation of the defendants had been discharged by the frustrating event. The plaintiffs were therefore entitled to nothing at all for the work they had performed before the frustrating event.

Similarly, in **Chandler v Webster** [1904] 1 K.B. 493, a case arising out of the same coronation facts as in **Krell v Henry**, the claimant hired a room to watch the coronation procession of

Edward VII. As the parade was cancelled because of the King's illness the contract for hire was frustrated. However, the court had to decide what effect this event would have on the obligations under the contract. The price of the room was £141, which was payable in advance. The claimant actually paid £100 before the procession was cancelled. As the obligation to pay for the room in full had arisen before the frustrating event, the claimant could not recover the £100 already paid, and also was required to pay the outstanding balance of £41. An outline of this case can be seen in Figure 13.1.

FIGURE 13.1 *Chandler v Webster*

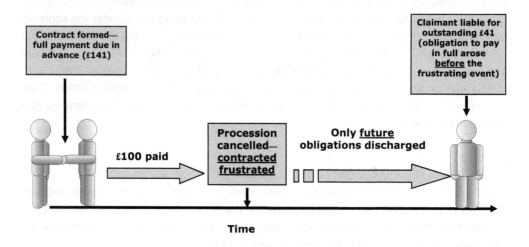

THE HARSH EFFECTS OF THE COMMON LAW RULES

13-021   Not only are the decisions of cases such as **Appleby v Myers** and **Chandler v Webster** particularly harsh on their facts, but they are also disconnected from logic. For example, in **Krell v Henry**, as the obligation to pay for the room arose after the frustrating event (upon vacating the room), the effect of such frustration was to relieve the defendant from any obligation to pay for the room which he had enjoyed during the course of the hire period. However, as the obligation to pay in full in **Chandler** arose before the frustrating event, the claimant was still required to pay the full amount even though the contract might have been deprived of all its value because of the frustrating event. It is odd that a debtor under a contract should actually be in a better position than a person who has paid in full.

Surely, the courts should seek to approach the obligations of the parties under a frustrated contract by taking into account not just *when* the obligations arose, but also the *nature* of those obligations and the effect that a frustrating event will have on the position of *both parties*.

A TOTAL FAILURE OF CONSIDERATION

These cases now have to be evaluated in light of the decision of the House of Lords in **Fibrosa**   **13-022**
Spolka Akcyjna v Fairbairn Lawson Combe Barbour Ltd (The Fibrosa) [1943] A.C. 32 the
respondents, an English company, agreed to sell machinery to the appellants, a Polish company, for £4,800. The appellants paid £1,000 in advance as agreed under the contract. The
contract between the parties was then frustrated by the outbreak of the Second World War.
The appellants sought to recover the £1,000 payment but the respondents refused as they had
already incurred considerable expenses in partial performance of the contract.

The House of Lords decided that the appellants were able to recover the £1,000 already
paid under the contract because of a "total failure of consideration". The appellants had not
received any of the performance promised from their bargain before the frustrating event so
were able to recover the £1,000 payment in an action for "money had and received" (a quasi-
contractual remedy based on the principles of restitution). An outline of the **Fibrosa** case can
be found at Figure 13.2.

FIGURE 13.2 *The Fibrosa*

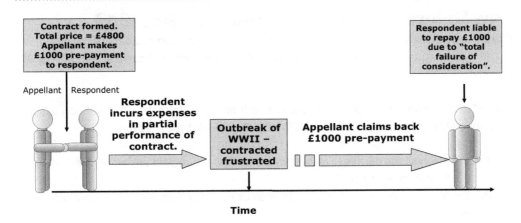

While the decision of the House of Lords in **The Fibrosa** goes some way to remedying the
harsh effect of frustration at common law demonstrated in **Appleby v Myers** and **Chandler v
Webster**, the underlying problems remain the same. The effect of the decision in **Fibrosa** is to
reverse the allocation of risk between the parties. Pre-**Fibrosa** the risk would lie with the party
making the pre-payment before the frustrating event. However, following the decision in
Fibrosa it now seems that such risk will lie with the party receiving the pre-payment.

If the parties freely agreed that a pre-payment was due, then the underlying purpose of such
a payment will be to allow the recipient to use this to absorb the costs of partial performance
under the agreement. To this extent, the decision in **Fibrosa** appears to contradict the freedom
of the parties to allocate risk between themselves and also ignores the commercial reality of
such agreements.

SOME UNRESOLVED PROBLEMS FOLLOWING THE *FIBROSA*

13-023 Despite the efforts of the House of Lords in **The Fibrosa** to remedy the harsh position at common law, there are still a number of substantial problems that remain. First, as demonstrated on the facts of **The Fibrosa** itself, the position at common law failed to recognise the position of a *recipient* of a pre-payment who may have incurred expenses in partial performance of the contract. In such cases the recipient will not be able to offset any of these expenses under the contract and will in fact receive no award at all to recognise their partial performance.

Further, if the appropriate remedy for a claimant in this situation is to pursue an action based on a "total failure of consideration" then this will only be successful where the claimant has received no part of the bargain whatsoever. If the claimant receives even the merest glimmer of what was contracted for then such an action will fail.

To this extent, the decision of the House of Lords in **The Fibrosa** certainly cannot be seen as a complete solution to the harshness of the rules at common law.

Law Reform (Frustrated Contracts) Act 1943

13-024 If cases such as **Appleby v Myers** and **Chandler v Webster** were symptomatic of the problems at common law then the Law Reform (Frustrated Contracts) Act 1943 can be seen as a partial remedy.

The 1943 Act provides a two-pronged approach to frustrated contracts and the effects of such an event on the obligations of the parties. Briefly, the 1943 Act provides for:

1. the ability of the parties to recover where there is a sum *paid* or *payable before* the frustrating event (s.1(2));
2. the ability to recover for *benefits conferred* by *partial performance* of the contract (s.1(3)).

We will consider each provision in turn.

ABILITY TO RECOVER WHERE THERE IS A SUM PAID OR PAYABLE BEFORE THE FRUSTRATING EVENT (S.1 (2))

13-025 Following the strict application of the common law principles, if the obligation to pay in full arose before the frustrating event and a pre-payment is made under a contract that was then frustrated, then that pre-payment will not be recoverable. Further, as the obligation to pay in full arose before the frustrating event, the entire balance (minus the pre-payment) will still be due to be paid. The 1943 Act s.1(2) sought to remedy this position.

Section 1(2) reads as follows:

> **"All sums paid or payable to any party in pursuance of the contract before the time when the parties were so discharged (in this Act referred to as 'the time of discharge') shall, in the case of sums so paid, be recoverable from him as money received by him for the use of the party by whom the sums were paid, and, in the case of sums so payable, cease to be so payable:**
>
> **Provided that, if the party to whom the sums were so paid or payable incurred expenses before the time of discharge in, or for the purpose of, the performance of the contract, the court may, if it considers it just to do so having regard to all the circumstances of the case, allow him to retain or, as the case may be, recover the whole or any part of the sums so paid or payable, not being an amount in excess of the expenses so incurred."**

The drafting of s.1(2) is certainly not a model of clarity and it is primarily for this reason why many students struggle when applying the effects of s.1(2). However, the basics effects of s.1(2) can be summarised as follows:

1. Money paid under a frustrated contract is repaid.
2. Money payable (money owed) under a frustrated contract ceases to be payable (is no longer owed).
3. A party who receives a pre-payment, or was due such a payment before the frustrating event, can offset any expenses incurred by partial performance against the amount paid, or the amount payable.

The effect of s.1(2) is to depart from the harsh application following **Chandler v Webster**. This provides a remedy for one of the lingering problems from **The Fibrosa**, whereby receiving a partial benefit under the contract would have precluded an action based on a "total failure of consideration" (see above at p.330).

In order for a party to be able to offset his expenses against the amount paid or payable, the court must consider that it is just for him to do so, having regard to all the circumstances of the case.

In **Gamerco SA v ICM/Fair Warning (Agency) Ltd** [1995] 1 W.L.R. 1226, the plaintiffs, a Spanish music promoter, agreed with the defendants, an agency who had undertaken to organise the tour of the rock group Guns N' Roses, to promote the group's concert in Madrid. The contract was frustrated when the stadium's safety permit was withdrawn and no alternative venue could be found. The plaintiffs had made a pre-payment of $412,000 to the defendants and had also incurred $400,000 in expenses. The defendants had also incurred expenses in preparing for the concert.

The court allowed the plaintiffs to recover the full amount of their pre-payment under s.1(2) ($412,000) and refused to allow the defendants to offset any of their expenses incurred in preparation for the concert. In reaching this decision, Garland J. had to decide how the discretion provided by s.1(2) should operate and in doing so he also rejected the arguments of "total retention" and "equal division" as the appropriate means of allocating the loss. Thus, Garland J. made it clear that the proviso to s.1(2), which can operate to allow a party to off-set their expenses incurred by partial performance, has to be balanced against the loss of the plaintiff. As the defendants' loss was relatively low compared to the loss faced by the plaintiffs, the court refused to apply the proviso to s.1(2) to the loss of the defendants. The operation of s.1(2) is illustrated in Figure 13.3.

FIGURE 13.3 **The operation of s.1(2) of the 1943 Act**

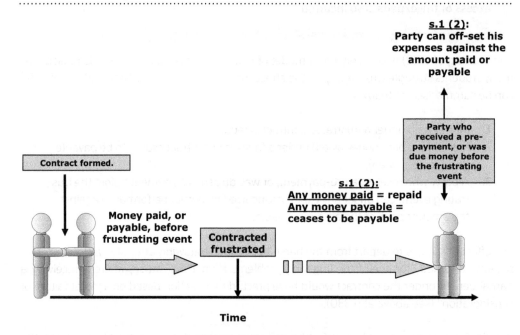

THE ABILITY TO RECOVER FOR BENEFITS CONFERRED BY PARTIAL PERFORMANCE OF THE CONTRACT (S.1 (3))

13-026   Section 1(3) allows a party to recover the value of any benefit that has been conferred on the other party by their partial performance of a frustrated contract. Again, the operation of s.1(3) marks a significant departure from the harsh position at common law, especially in the situations where payment is due in full at the end of the contract. As you will recall from the case of **Appleby v Myers** (1866–67) L.R. 2 C.P. 651, if a frustrating event occurs before the obligation to pay arises, then a party who may have incurred significant expenses in their partial performance will not be entitled to any payment at all. Further, s.1(2) will not provide a remedy here as this section only applies where money is paid, or is payable, *before* the frustrating event.

The wording of s.1(3) is as follows:

> "Where any party to the contract has, by reason of anything done by any other party thereto in, or for the purpose of, the performance of the contract, obtained a valuable benefit (other than a payment of money to which the last foregoing subsection applies) before the time of discharge, there shall be recoverable from him by the said other party such sum (if any), not exceeding the value of the said benefit to the party obtaining it, as the court considers just, having regard to all the circumstances of the case and, in particular,—
>
> (a) the amount of any expenses incurred before the time of discharge by the benefited party in, or for the purpose of, the performance of the contract, including any sums paid or payable by him to any other party in pursuance of the contract and retained or recoverable by that party under the last foregoing subsection, and
> (b) the effect, in relation to the said benefit, of the circumstances giving rise to the frustration of the contract."

Again, this is a long and complex section to understand and apply. Simply, however, s.1(3) provides some relief in situations like **Appleby v Myers**, by allowing a party to recover *up to* the value of the benefit that has been conferred by their partial performance. However, the ability to recover is again at the discretion of the court, after considering whether it would be *just* having regard to all the circumstances. A two-stage approach is suggested.

A TWO-STAGE APPROACH TO THE APPLICATION OF S.1(3)

In applying s.1 (3) the courts embark upon a two-stage process. First, it is necessary for the court to identify and value the "benefit" that has been conferred by partial performance of the contract. Secondly, the court will then decide upon the "just sum" to be awarded.

13-027

Each stage will now be considered in turn.

STAGE 1: CALCULATION OF THE "VALUABLE BENEFIT" UNDER S.1(3)

The first difficulty with s.1(3) is identifying the value of the benefit that has been conferred by partial performance. Following the case of **BP Exploration Co (Libya) Ltd v Hunt (No.2)** [1983] 2 A.C. 352 and the opinion of Robert Goff J. in the High Court (which was affirmed by the House of Lords) the value of the benefit is to be calculated as an "end product". Importantly, this "end product" is valued *after* the frustrating event. The value of the benefit that is conferred sets the maximum amount that can be awarded under s.1(3). Note that the approach of Robert Goff J. is controversial as it does seem inconsistent with the wording of s.1(3) itself.

13-028

Further, in some cases it may be difficult to calculate the "valuable benefit", particularly where the contract is solely for the provision of a service that does not result in an "end product". In such cases the court can assess the value of the service itself.

STAGE 2: THE AWARD OF THE "JUST SUM" UNDER S.1(3)

13-029   Secondly, the court must calculate the "just sum" to be awarded. Again, the "just sum" cannot exceed the value of the benefit identified in stage 1.

BP V HUNT (NO.2) [1983] 2 A.C. 352

13-030   Both stages 1 and 2 are illustrated in the case of **BP v Hunt (No.2)**. Here, the defendants had been granted an oil concession by the Libyan Government. They entered into an agreement with BP who were to assess the potential of the oil field and develop the field for the production of oil in return for a share of the confession (referred to as a "farm-in" agreement). Oil production began but some four years into the agreement the contract was frustrated when the Libyan Government nationalised the plaintiff's oil concession. Both parties received some compensation from the Libyan Government, but the amount did not reflect the expenses that both parties had incurred during the performance of the contract.

The court held that the value of any benefit conferred by BP should be calculated as an "end product". In other words, BP could not recover for their actual expenses in performing the contract (which amounted to some $98 million). However, as an "end product", the value of the benefit conferred was the value of the oil that Hunt had received plus the compensation from the Libyan Government. This gave a valuable benefit of $85 million.

The "just sum", however, is calculated by assessing the services that had been provided by BP, minus the amount that they were able to recover for the oil produced. This gave a "just sum" of $35 million. No further deductions were required as this figure was substantially less than the benefit conferred on **Hunt** ($85 millon).

Unfortunately, the facts of **BP v Hunt** are notoriously difficult to comprehend without any particular knowledge of the industry in question. Perhaps a more straightforward way to approach the application of s.1(3) is to use the facts of **Taylor v Caldwell** (1863) 3 B. & S. 826, as a guide. As you will recall, this case concerned the hiring of a music hall for a number of concerts. Before the first performance could take place the music hall was destroyed by fire. Let us consider the position if the contract had been for a total of five performances and that the music hall had burnt down after three performances had taken place. Further, let us also consider the position if full payment had been due at the end of the contract (after the frustrating event).

First, s.1(2) would be of no help here as no money was paid, or payable, before the frustrating event. So, we must consider the application of s.1(3). The fact that three performances have taken place will have conferred a valuable benefit on the defendants. As the valuable benefit is calculated as an "end product", the maximum that the claimant can recover under s.1(3) will be the value of the three performances that have taken place. The operation of s.1(3) is illustrated in Figure 13.4.

FIGURE 13.4 **The operation of s.1(3) of the 1943 Act**

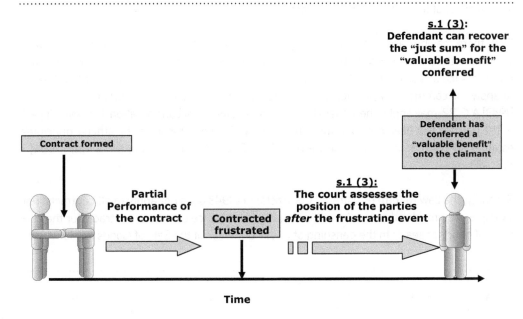

THE EFFECT OF S.1(3) ON *APPLEBY V MYERS*

There is one final problem to consider in the application of s.1(3). As you will recall, the "valuable benefit" under this section is to be calculated as an "end product". However, what will be the position if the benefit is destroyed by the frustrating event? This is precisely what happened in **Appleby v Myers**: the frustrating event, the accidental fire, not only destroyed the defendants' premises, but also the machinery that had been erected by the claimants.

It is not entirely clear how s.1(3) operates in such cases. Following a strict interpretation of Robert Goff J.'s assessment of the valuable benefit, the court is to assess this value as an "end product". If the frustrating event destroys the end product then of course there is nothing for the court to value. This would have the rather unjust consequence that the claimant would have no remedy under the 1943 Act and therefore would be in the same position at common law that the Act sought to remedy.

To this extent, it appears that there is a potential role for the common law position. This is also true of the position following **The Fibrosa**.

13-031

LAW REFORM (FRUSTRATED CONTRACTS) ACT 1943 AND THE SCOPE FOR THE COMMON LAW EFFECT OF FRUSTRATION

13-032 Given the enhanced flexibility of the Law Reform (Frustrated Contracts) Act 1943, it may be thought that there is little or no scope for the operation of the harsher common law principles. In the majority of cases this will indeed be the case. However, there are a number of limited circumstances in which the courts will have to revert to the common law principles when assessing the effect of frustration on the contract.

First, there may be cases where no money was paid, or payable, before the frustrating event and where the partial performance of that contract has not conferred a benefit on the other party. In such a case neither s.1(2) nor s.1(3) will have any application, so the courts will have to apply the common law principles. The more lenient approach of the courts in **The Fibrosa** [1943] A.C. 32, may apply where there has been a total failure of consideration. However, if part of the bargain has been provided then the courts will have to resort to the stricter principles established in **Appleby v Myers** [1866–67] L.R. 2 C.P. 651 and **Chandler v Webster** [1904] 1 K.B. 493.

Secondly, the Law Reform (Frustrated Contracts) Act 1943 does not apply to all contracts. For example, s.2 provides that the Act will not apply to insurance contracts, contracts for the carriage of goods at sea or to the perishing of goods under s.7 of the Sale of Goods Act 1979.

Summary

1. The doctrine of frustration is concerned with events that occur after the contract has been formed and are beyond the control of both parties. The effect must be to render the contract impossible to perform or to radically alter the obligations under the contract. The broad effect of frustration will be to relieve the parties of their obligations under the contract.

2. At common law the effect of a frustrating event is to relieve the parties of those obligations that are due to be performed *after* the frustrating event. Obligations that arise *before* the frustrating event are unaffected. This has the potential to operate in a harsh manner, particularly where one party has made a pre- payment before the frustrating event or has incurred expenses by their partial performance of the contract.

3. Following the case of **The Fibrosa**, the common law made limited allowances for the recovery of expenses incurred by partial performance under a frustrated contract, but only where there had been a "total failure of consideration". If the claimant received even the smallest amount of what was contracted for then the strict common law effects of frustration would apply to the contract.

4. Under statute, the Law Reform (Frustrated Contracts) Act 1943 provides some partial relief to the harsh position at common law. Under s.1(2) of the 1943 Act, the court has discretion to allow a claimant to offset his expenses against the amount paid or payable before the frustrating event (**Gamerco SA v ICM/Fair Warning (Agency) Ltd**).

5. Under s.1(3) of the 1943 Act, the court has discretion to allow a claimant to recover a "just sum" for the valuable benefit that has been conferred by their partial performance of a contract. The value of the benefit conferred will be assessed as an "end product" (**BP v Hunt (No.2)**)

Key Cases Grid

Case	Court	Key Issue
Taylor v Caldwell (1863)	Court of King's Bench	An important decision that limited the application of the doctrine of absolute obligations. The destruction of the subject matter in this case frustrated the contract and the obligations of the parties were discharged.
Krell v Henry [1903]	Court of Appeal	The non-occurrence of an event can frustrate the contract, providing that event is the foundation of the contract so far as both parties are concerned. Contrast with Herne Bay Steam Boat Co v Hutton [1903].
Maritime National Fish Ltd v Ocean Trawlers Ltd [1935]	Privy Council (Canada)	If the supervening event is within the control of one of the parties, then may amount to self-induced frustration, which will not discharge the parties' obligations under the contract.
Appleby v Myers (1867)	Court of Exchequer Chamber	At common law, the effect of frustration is that the "loss lies where is falls". Only future obligations are discharged under the contract.
Gamerco SA v ICM/Fair Warning (Agency) Ltd [1995]	Queen's Bench Division	Under s.1(2) Law Reform (Frustrated Contracts) Act 1943, the court has a discretion to allow a party who has incurred expenses in the partial performance of a contract, to off-set their expenses against money paid or so payable

		before the frustrating event, an amount which is limited to the actual expenses incurred. Under s.1(2) Law Reform (Frustrated Contracts) Act 1943, the court has a discretion to allow a party who has incurred expenses in the partial performance of a contract, to off-set their expenses against money paid or so payable before the frustrating event, an amount which is limited to the actual expenses incurred.
Bp v Hunt (No.2) [1983]	House of Lords	When assessing its discretion to award a "just sum" under s.1(3) Law Reform (Frustrated Contracts) Act 1943, the court will value the relevant benefit as an "end product".

End of Chapter Question

Prince Williamson announces his engagement and confirms that his Royal Wedding will take place on, 10 August. Following the wedding ceremony there will be a parade through the centre of London. Harry, an enthusiastic Royalist, enters into a contract with Charles to rent a private apartment that has a particularly good view of the parade route. The contract price is £1,000 of which £400 is payable on arrival and the remaining £600 upon departure. Charles goes to great lengths to ensure that the room is prepared for Harry's arrival including the installation of a flat screen TV to allow Harry to watch the wedding ceremony.

Unfortunately, on the morning of 10th August, Prince Williamson is taken ill and the wedding ceremony and the parade are cancelled. Harry has already checked into the apartment and is refusing to pay the outstanding £600 due under the contract. Harry also seeks to recover the £400 he paid upon his arrival.

Advise the parties.

Points of Answer
♦ Has the cancellation of the event frustrated the contract for the hiring of the room? Compare and contrast the reasoning in **Krell** and **Herne** Bay. Was the event at the *foundation of the contract* so far as both parties were concerned?
♦ If the contract is frustrated then what effect will this frustration have on the obligations of the parties?
♦ At common law only *future* obligations are discharged (**Appleby v Myers**). The obligation to pay the outstanding £600 would therefore be discharged as this

was an obligation that arose after the frustrating event. However, the obligation to pay the £400 upon arrival arose before the frustrating event so would not be discharged at common law.

♦ Contrast the common law position with the operation of the Law Reform (Frustrated Contracts) Act 1943.

♦ Under s.1(2) any money paid under the contract (£400) is due to be paid back to Harry. Any money owed (£600) ceases to be owed. This will be subject to the court's discretion to allow Charles to offset his expenses against the amount paid before the frustrating event (see **Gamerco v Fair Warning (Agency)**). The expense he incurred in preparing the room can be taken into account under s.1 (2).

◄ ....

Further Reading

Clark, P. "Frustration, Restitution and the Law Reform (Frustrated Contracts) Act 1943" L.M.C.L.Q. [1996] 170

An analysis of Gamerco SA v ICM / Fair Warning (Agency) Ltd and how expenditure incurred up to time of frustration should be apportioned.

Stone, R. and Cunnington, R. *Text, Cases and Materials on Contract Law* (London: Routledge-Cavendish, 2014), Chapter 12.

Treitel, G. *The Law of Contract*, 13th edn (London Sweet & Maxwell, 2011), Chapter 19.

Damages

14

CHAPTER OVERVIEW

In this chapter we:

- **explain how the courts assess and award damages for breach of contract**

- **consider the limitations to an award of damages; remoteness of damage and the rule in *Hadley v Baxendale***

- **analyse the decision and obiter in *Parsons v Uttley* as to the award of damages**

- **discuss the relevant measure for an award of damages in contract**

- **explain the relevant principles in relation to liquidated damages**

- **discuss the requirement to mitigate loss under a contract**

Summary

Key Cases Grid

End of Chapter Question

Further Reading

Introduction

14-001 If a party fails to meet their obligations under the contract then the innocent party will be able to pursue an action for damages to compensate them for their loss. The aim of an award of damages is therefore to compensate the innocent party for their loss, rather than to punish the other party for breaching the contract.

The primary role of the court is to preserve the self regulatory nature of contract, rather than to act as an arbitrary force in allocating retribution. The reason why the courts hold individuals to their bargains is due to that fact that both parties freely entered into their agreement. The courts, so far as possible, will endeavour to ensure that this agreement is honoured and will award damages to compensate the innocent party when this fails.

The compensatory aim of an award of damages in contract law is to put the innocent party (as far as possible) into the position he would have been in had the contract not been breached. An award of damages in contract is described as being "forward" looking in that it seeks to protect the expectation of the innocent party under the contract. What would the innocent party have expected to receive under the contract? The courts will then compensate the innocent party for any loss of this expectation.

Limitations on an award of damages

14-002 There are a number of factors that can limit an award of damages for breach of contract. The most important of these is the principle of remoteness of damage. The principle of remoteness determines what damages will be recoverable following a breach. Losses that are "too remote" from the breach of contract will not be recoverable. However, the principles of remoteness of damage have been questioned and modified by the courts over the years and it is necessary to trace this development to fully understand this key limitation on an award of damages.

Remoteness of damage

14-003 Even though the innocent party may suffer loss as a result of a breach of contract, that party will not be able to claim for all the losses that flowed from that breach of contract. Even though such loss may have *in fact* been caused by the breach of contract, as a matter of *law* there are limitations upon the amount of damages that are recoverable for breach of contract. This limitation is referred to as the test of "remoteness of damage". The courts will not allow a party to recover losses that are too remote from the breach of contract.

Imagine, for example, if you enter into a contract to purchase a classic car from a car dealer. You agree a price of £10,000. However, you know that a collector is looking for this particular car to complete his collection and is willing to pay you £100,000 for the car. The car dealer knows nothing of this. The dealer then breaches the contract and fails to deliver the car. Had the contract not had been breached you would have sold the car on to make a profit of £90,000. Will the dealer be liable for this £90,000 loss?

The short answer is no, on the basis that this loss is too remote. The car dealer would not have reasonably contemplated a loss of £90,000 following his breach of contract; he would only have contemplated a loss of £10,000. This is why the principles of remoteness are so important; they act to protect the party in breach from unusual loss that may have *in fact* been caused by the breach but will be "too remote" as the loss could not have been contemplated as a result of the breach.

HADLEY V BAXENDALE

The contractual test of remoteness was established in **Hadley v Baxendale** (1854) 9 Ex.341. The plaintiffs owned a flour mill and contracted with the defendants to deliver a replacement crankshaft after the plaintiffs' crankshaft had broken. The contract was breached when the defendants failed to deliver the shaft within a reasonable time. The plaintiffs brought an action claiming the loss of profit whilst the mill was inoperable. The court clarified the relevant test of remoteness of damage in contract law:

14-004

> "Where two parties have made a contract which one of them has broken, the damages which the other party ought to receive in respect of such breach of contract should be such as may fairly and reasonably be considered either arising naturally, i.e., according to the usual course of things, from such breach of contract itself, or such as may reasonably be supposed to have been in the contemplation of both parties, at the time they made the contract, as the probable result of the breach of it."

■ The two limbs of *Hadley v Baxendale*

On the facts of **Hadley v Baxendale** the plaintiffs were unable to recover any loss from the breach of contract. The loss was not a natural consequence of the breach, as such loss would not arise according to the usual course of things. It was common practice for mills to keep a spare crankshaft to cover for such instances. Nor did the defendants reasonably contemplate the loss, as they did not know that the mill was unable to operate without the replacement shaft. On this basis the loss was too remote and therefore irrecoverable.

14-005

While the facts of **Hadley v Baxendale** are slightly unusual in relation to the loss suffered—not everyone can claim to be familiar with the trade practices of a mill—this is exactly the point that we can take from this case. The first limb of **Hadley v Baxendale** concerns loss that arises naturally from the breach. This will usually be uncontroversial as the straightforward principles of causation apply. However, the second limb of **Hadley v Baxendale** is concerned with loss that was reasonably contemplated by *both parties* at *the time the contract was entered into*. In order for such loss to be recoverable, the court will have to assess the level of knowledge of both parties. If one party seeks to pass the risk of particular damage (which does not naturally arise from the breach) then express communication must be made to the other party of this risk. Only in these circumstances can it be said that the other party would "reasonably contemplate" such loss.

Two limbs or a single test?

14-006 While the principles of remoteness stated in **Hadley v Baxendale** are conceptually quite straightforward, there remained some unresolved issues as to how these principles are to be applied to the particular types of loss. The root of the problem is that there appear to be two distinct limbs to the rule of remoteness: loss that was a natural consequence of the breach, *OR*, loss that was reasonably contemplated. By introducing the word, *"OR"*, the question remained as to whether the court in **Hadley v Baxendale** had developed two distinct tests of remoteness, or are these to be considered as one single test of remoteness?

The court sought to address this problem in **Victoria Laundry (Windsor) Ltd v Newman Industries** [1949] 2 K.B. 528. In this case the plaintiffs owned and ran a laundry business. They contracted with the defendants who were to supply a boiler. The plaintiffs required the boiler by a specific date to allow them to meet a number of dyeing contracts they had obtained from the Royal Navy (although they did not communicate this fact to the defendants). The defendants delivered the boiler late and the plaintiffs claimed damages for breach of contract.

The Court of Appeal held that the ordinary business loss the plaintiffs incurred by the late delivery was recoverable, as such loss was a natural consequence of the breach. However, the loss of the dyeing contracts was not recoverable. This loss did not arise naturally from the breach, nor was it reasonably contemplated by the defendants as they had no knowledge of the existence of such contracts.

It is perhaps useful to distil this decision into the ability to recover the type of loss in question:

1. *Normal loss* will be recoverable as it arises naturally from the breach.
2. *Abnormal loss* will only be recoverable if it was reasonably contemplated by both parties at the time the contract was made.

To this extent it not particularly helpful to speak of two separate limbs of remoteness of damage from **Hadley v Baxendale** as in reality they are one and the same thing. The primary focus is whether the loss was "reasonably contemplated" by both parties. As the reasonable person will as a matter of course always contemplate the normal loss flowing from the breach, this loss will always be recoverable. However, in order for abnormal loss to be recoverable it must be established that it was in the reasonable contemplation of both parties at the time the contract was formed. Therefore, in order for abnormal loss to be recoverable the knowledge of the both parties will be the key to determining whether the loss is too remote.

While it is perhaps no longer correct to speak of two separate limbs of the test of remoteness, when it comes to applying the test it is still useful to distinguish between the different types of loss. The distinction between normal and abnormal loss makes it very easy to establish whether such loss will be recoverable. The only particular difficulty comes in relation to abnormal loss when the relevant knowledge of the parties has to be taken into account.

■ The "degree of likelihood" required in contract and the relationship with the law of tort

Just because a party may be aware of the possibility of a particular type of loss, is this sufficient for it to be said that such loss was in the "reasonable contemplation" of the party? In order to answer this question it is necessary to analyse the *level* of knowledge (or the degree of likelihood) that is required in relation to the type of loss in question. In fact, following the decision in **Victoria Laundry** there was some distinct confusion as to the appropriate test in general to be applied in contract law. Asquith L.J. suggested that:

14-007

> **"In cases of breach of contract the aggrieved party is only entitled to recover such part of the loss actually resulting as was at the time of the contract *reasonably foreseeable* as liable to result from the breach." [Emphasis added]**

This is a very strange observation indeed, as the test of "reasonable foreseeability" is the test of remoteness of damage in the law of tort. As we will see, not only are the compensatory aims of an award of damages in tort different from those of contract law, but the test of "reasonable foreseeability" is generally accepted as a wider and more generous assessment of damages than the contractual test of "reasonable contemplation".

THE HERON II

Whilst the obiter of Asquith L.J. in **Victoria Laundry** demonstrates the confusion as to the relevant test of remoteness of damage in contract, the position was finally clarified by the House of Lords in **Koufos v C Czarnikow Ltd, (The Heron II)** [1969] 1 A.C. 350. In this case the plaintiffs chartered a ship to deliver a consignment of sugar. The ship-owners knew that the plaintiffs were sugar merchants and that they intended to sell the sugar immediately upon arrival. The delivery of sugar was late arriving at its destination, and as a result the value of the sugar was lower because of a fall in the sugar market at the destination. The plaintiffs sought to recover damages for this fall in value.

14-008

The House of Lords applied **Hadley v Baxendale** (albeit in its modified form) and held that the loss of the fall in value was recoverable. In other words, such loss should have been reasonably contemplated by the defendants at the time the contract was formed. However, there is still confusion as to the precise standard that is required, and how this is different from the test in tort.

If we look at the decision in **The Heron II** it is possible to draw some general conclusions as to the precise standard (although none of the Law Lords made this test explicitly clear). First, it is clear that there is a higher degree of likelihood required in contract in order for such loss to be recoverable. For example, the tortious test of "reasonable foreseeability" would allow a claimant to recover loss where there was only a "slight possibility" that such loss would be suffered as a result of the breach of duty. Even though the possibility that such loss would be suffered is slight, the loss may still be reasonably foreseeable and thus recoverable. However, in contract law, in order for loss to be recoverable it must have been a "serious possibility" that the loss would have resulted from the breach of contract. Applying these principles to the facts of The Heron II, there was a serious possibility, that the market price might fall at the time that the contract was formed, and such loss should therefore have been in the reasonable contemplation of the defendants.

Therefore, the tests of remoteness in contract and tort and the varying degrees of likelihood can be summarised as follows:

1. Tort = reasonably foreseeable—*slight possibility* that loss would be suffered by the breach of duty.
2. Contract = reasonable contemplation—*serious possibility* that loss would be suffered as a result of the breach of contract.

The result of these two different tests of remoteness in contract and tort is that loss that may be recoverable in the law of tort may be too remote in contract because of the higher degree of likelihood that is required in contract.

JUSTIFICATION FOR THE DIFFERING TESTS OF REMOTENESS

14-009   It has been established that the test of remoteness in contract provides a stricter test than that in the law of tort. The result is that damages that are recoverable in tort may be too remote in contract. In understanding why this is the case it is important to recognise that the relationship between the parties in contract and tort is quite different. This is a point that Lord Reid emphasises in **The Heron II** [1969] 1 A.C. 350:

> "In contract, if one party wishes to protect himself against a risk which to the other party would appear unusual, he can direct the other party's attention to it before the contract is made, and I need not stop to consider in what circumstances the other party will then be held to have accepted responsibility in that event. But in tort there is no opportunity for the injured party to protect himself in that way, and the tortfeasor cannot reasonably complain if he has to pay for some very unusual but nevertheless foreseeable damage which results from his wrongdoing."

A party has a free choice whether or not to enter into a contract and also has the ability to communicate, or allocate, any unusual loss before the contract is formed. However, in the majority of tortious claims this will not be possible. There is generally no freedom to accept the wrong that has been committed or to allocate such risk before the wrong occurs. For example, if a claimant is injured in an accident by the negligent driving of the defendant, then the claimant has no opportunity to communicate any unusual loss he may suffer to the defendant before the accident occurred. As such it would make sense to apply the wider test of remoteness to such loss, with the claimant being able to claim loss that was reasonably foreseeable as a result of the defendant's breach of duty.

While the House of Lords in **The Heron II** confirmed that the appropriate test in contract law is the stricter test of "reasonable contemplation", there remains some debate as to whether this should be the test in contract and also debate as to the precise relationship between the tests in contract and tort.

PARSONS V UTTLEY

In **Parsons (Livestock) Ltd v Uttley Ingham & Co Ltd** [1978] Q.B. 791, the Court of Appeal considered the relationship between the contractual and tortious tests of remoteness and whether such a distinction could be justified in all cases. In **Parsons**, the defendants were contracted to install a food hopper which was to dispense "pig nuts" to feed the claimant's herd of pigs. In breach of contract the defendants installed the hopper with inadequate ventilation causing the pig nuts to go mouldy. The pigs then ate the mouldy nuts and as a result a total of 254 top grade pigs died from a rare intestinal disease that developed from eating the mouldy nuts.

14-010

The claimant brought an action for breach of contract claiming for two types of loss. First, damages for loss of the pigs that had died. Secondly, damages for the loss of future profits he would have made on the sale of those pigs. The Court of Appeal held that the loss of the pigs was recoverable, but the loss of future profit was too remote. The decision in Parsons in itself is not too controversial, but the different routes taken by the judges to come to this decision require further analysis.

◾ The majority decision—Scarman and Orr L.JJ.

Scarman L.J. (with whom Orr L.JJ. agreed) held that the loss of the pigs was recoverable as the *type* of harm was reasonably contemplated by the defendants. So long as the *type* of harm was reasonably contemplated (in this case, physical harm), then it was not necessary that the *extent* of that harm was contemplated. The defendants would have contemplated the *serious possibility* that feeding mouldy nuts to the pigs would result in some physical harm. They may not have contemplated that the pigs would have developed a rare intestinal disease, but this relates to the *extent* of the harm, which is irrelevant.

14-011

Scarman L.J. also held that the loss of profit on those pigs (pure economic loss) was not recoverable. However, no explanation was offered as to why this was the case. A further problem emerges from Scarman L.J.'s decision. At first it seems consistent with the decision of the House of Lords in **The Heron II**: reference to the *type* of loss being a *serious possibility* suggests that the stricter contractual test of remoteness applies to the loss of the pigs. However, Scarman L.J. then concludes that the remoteness tests in contract and tort are the same. This conclusion is inconsistent with the opinion of Lord Reid in **The Heron II**.

■ The minority decision—Lord Denning M.R.

14-012   Although Lord Denning's reasoning was not accepted by Scarman and Orr L.JJ., it provides an interesting analysis of the differing contractual and tortious tests of remoteness. In particular, Denning questions whether the current distinction between contract and tort is justified. He argues that it should be the *type of loss* suffered that should determine the test of remoteness, rather than the cause of action (whether the action is for breach of contract or in the law of tort).

Therefore, in addressing the first type of loss, the loss of the pigs, Lord Denning identified this type of loss as "physical harm". In order to recover for physical harm Denning argued that such loss must have been "reasonably foreseeable" as a result of the breach. As the physical harm to the pigs was *reasonably foreseeable* the loss of the pigs was recoverable.

In addressing the second type of loss, the loss of future profits, Lord Denning identified this type of loss as "economic harm". In order to recover for economic harm Denning argued that such loss must have been "reasonably contemplated" by the defendants at the time the contract was made. Such loss was not recoverable in this case as it was not in the *reasonable contemplation* of the defendants.

A summary of Lord Denning's reasoning is as follows:

1.   Loss of pigs = physical harm = was such loss "reasonably foreseeable": the wider, tortious test of remoteness applies.
2.   Loss of future profits = economic harm = was such loss in the "reasonable contemplation of both parties": the stricter, contractual test of remoteness applies.

The reasoning of Lord Denning is difficult to reconcile with **Hadley v Baxendale, Victoria Laundry (Windsor) Ltd v Newman** and **The Heron II** [1969] 1 A.C. 350, which all confirm that the appropriate test of remoteness in contract law is that of "reasonable contemplation". Indeed, the House of Lords in **Jackson v Royal Bank of Scotland** [2005] UKHL 3 recently confirmed that the appropriate test in contract law is whether the type of loss was *reasonably contemplated* at the time the contract was formed. As the action in **Parsons** was for breach of contract, how could Lord Denning justify applying the tortious test of "reasonable foreseeability" to the loss of the pigs?

Lord Denning explained that all these cases were concerned with economic loss, which justified applying the stricter contractual test of remoteness. However, as the claim for the loss of the pigs was for physical loss, it was not appropriate to apply this test and as such the wider tortious test should apply.

Justification for Lord Denning's reasoning

In **Parsons**, Denning argued that it should be the type of loss suffered that should determine 14-013
the test of remoteness and not whether the claimant decides to frame his action in contract or
in tort. He gives the following example to support his argument:

> "Yet another class of case is where a hospital authority renders medical services
> in contract to a paying patient and gratuitously to another patient without any
> contract. The paying patient can sue in contract for negligence. The poor patient
> can sue in tort. The test of remoteness should be the same whether the hospital
> authorities are sued in contract or in tort."

Over to you. . .

Reflecting on Denning's example above, do you agree with this approach? Can
you identify any advantages to Denning's proposal compared to the traditional
approach of identifying whether the cause of action rests in contract or tort

There is certainly merit in this argument. In this hospital example above the claimant will have
suffered the same loss so why should different tests of remoteness potentially affect the amount
of damages that should be recovered? Surely, the court should seek to compensate the claimant for his loss and not be distracted between the artificial distinction between contract and tort.

FIGURE 14.1 Summary of the reasoning in *Parsons v Uttley*

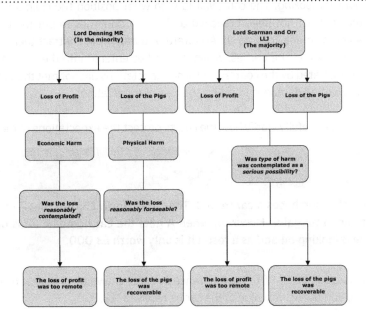

TRANSFIELD SHIPPING INC V MERCATOR SHIPPING INC

14-014 The rule in **Hadley v Baxendale** has recently been revisited by the House of Lords in the case of **Transfield Shipping Inc (Appellants) v Mercator Shipping Inc (Respondents)** [2008] UKHL 48. This case provides an interesting overview as to interpretation and application of the relevant principles of remoteness. In this case the House of Lords declared that the limits of liability should be decided by making reference to responsibilities that the parties had assumed. Whether a loss was of the type that arose out of the ordinary course of things may in exceptional cases depend on whether the defendants had assumed the responsibility for that loss. This marks a significant change of emphasis as to the application of the principles of remoteness. However, that said, identifying a clear ratio is difficult as the Lords adopt differing approaches in order to arrive at a unanimous decision.

It is perhaps too early to determine whether the "assumption of responsibility" test adopted by the House in Transfield will evolve into a general principle of remoteness. The few cases that have considered this issue would suggest not. The first instance decision of **Sylvia Shipping Co Limited v Progress Bulk Carriers Limited** [2010] EWHC 542 indicates that the assumption of responsibility approach would be limited to exceptional cases turning on their particular facts.

The compensatory aim of an award of damages in contract

14-015 The compensatory aim of an award of damages in contract is to put the innocent party into the position he would have been in had the contract not been breached. In this sense, contractual damages are *forward looking*. The court will look to what position the claimant *would* have been in had the contract not been breached and award damages to put the claimant into this position, so far as money can do so. An award of damages in contract therefore protects the expectation interest of the parties. When the parties entered into the agreement certain expectations were created by the contract. If those expectations are not met then the court will remedy this by awarding damages to reflect the loss of expectation.

An example should hopefully clarify how the courts protect the expectations of the parties.

Over to you. . .

Suppose that A purchases a car from B. The car is worth £5,000, but A only pays £4,000 (a good bargain). However, when A gets the car home he finds out that the engine is leaking oil and as a result it is only worth £3,000.

A's *expectation* loss will be £2,000: the difference between the value of the car he expected to receive (£5,000) and the *actual* value of the car he received (£3,000).

Assessing the expectation interest

The usual position is that an award of damages in contract law will seek to protect the expectation interest of the parties. In most cases this will mean that the award will be the difference between the value of what was *expected* and the value of what was *provided* under the contract. In order to award damages on this basis the courts must be able to identify and put a figure on the "value" of such loss. The courts generally identify that value by looking at the "market price".

THE MARKET PRICE

If the breach of contract is in relation to the sale of goods then the position is quite straightforward. If the seller is in breach of contract by failing to deliver goods under the contract then the purchaser will be able to claim any difference between the contract price and the "market price" of those goods. This is provided by s.51(3) of the Sale of Goods Act 1979.

However, there are a number of problems that may arise. First, the market price may be less than the contract price (in which case the reliance interest may be the appropriate measure of damages). Secondly, what if there is no "market price" by which to measure the loss? The latter can easily be the case in relation to bespoke items or items made to order. In these cases the courts will still try to identify a market price but they will do so based on their own assessment. However, the figure that the court arrives at will to some extent be a "stab in the dark".

"THE COST OF THE CURE"

The court can also award damages to reflect the "cost of the cure". This may be attractive to the claimant in some cases, as the cost of remedying the breach may exceed the relevant market value. The courts have, however, demonstrated an obvious reluctance to award damages on this basis, especially when to do so would be *disproportionate*.

An interesting example of this approach can be found in the US case of **Jacob & Youngs v Kent** (1921) N.Y. 239. The plaintiffs stated that a particular type of pipe should be used for the plumbing of a newly constructed house. The defendants used a different type of pipe (although it was of the same quality). The court refused to award the plaintiffs the cost of the cure, which would have meant ripping out all the pipes and replacing them with the type specified in the contract. This would have been a disproportionate response in the circumstances. Instead, the court awarded the plaintiffs damages to reflect the difference in value of the pipes, which on the facts was almost nothing at all.

RUXLEY ELECTRONICS & CONSTRUCTION LTD V FORSYTH

The House of Lords also had to consider a similar issue in **Ruxley Electronics & Construction Ltd v Forsyth** [1996] 1 A.C. 344. In this case, Ruxley entered into a contract with Forsyth to construct a swimming pool in his garden. The contract price was £17,797. Forsyth stipulated that the swimming pool must be six feet six inches deep as he wished to use the pool for diving. When the pool was completed it was found only to be six feet in places, most notably in the area used for diving. The cost of ripping out the pool and reinstalling it to the specified depth would have been £21,560.

The Court of Appeal held that the full £21,560, the cost of the cure, should be awarded, despite the fact that the pool was still perfectly suitable for diving. The Court of Appeal also awarded Forsyth £2,500 to reflect his loss of amenity (non-pecuniary loss to reflect his loss of enjoyment). Ruxley appealed.

Over to you. . .

Imagine you were sitting in the House of Lords and were to hear this appeal. What factors would you take into account in reaching your decision as to the appropriate award of damages in this case

The House of Lords reversed the decision of the Court of Appeal and Forsyth only recovered damages for his loss of amenity. To award the cost of the cure in this case would be unreasonable and disproportionate. **Jacob & Youngs v Kent** was considered on this issue. The minor discrepancy in depth had no obvious effect on the *usability* of the pool and did not justify awarding the cost of the cure.

Speculative loss and the expectation interest

14-020   Sometimes it can be very difficult to assess the claimant's loss. This is especially so when the claimant is seeking to recover for loss of opportunity following the breach of contract. Such loss is speculative and the court will have the difficult task of almost guessing what position the claimant would have been in had the contract not been breached. Despite the difficulties in quantifying speculative loss, in limited situations the courts will attempt to place a value on this loss.

LOSS OF OPPORTUNITY

14-021   An example of when the courts will award expectation damages for speculative loss arises in relation to the loss of an opportunity. Of course, if the breach of contract deprives the claimant of an opportunity they would otherwise have had, the courts will have a difficult time in quantifying this loss. However, despite these problems, the courts have awarded damages for loss of an opportunity.

In **Chaplin v Hicks** [1911] 2 K.B. 786, the defendant (a theatrical agent) agreed that he would allow the claimant to audition along with 49 other women for the opportunity of being selected as one of the 12 successful women that he would employ. In breach of this agreement the defendant refused to allow the claimant to audition. As a result she was not one of the women selected for employment. The claimant sued the defendant for breach of contract and claimed damages for the loss of her opportunity to audition. The defendant argued that she should only be awarded nominal damages (if anything at all) as even if she had auditioned there was only a one in four chance that she would have been successful. The court awarded the claimant £100 (a very large award indeed) to represent her loss of opportunity.

THE RELIANCE INTEREST

Although the primary measure of damages in contract law will be to protect the expectation interest, it may be possible for the claimant to recover damages based on the reliance interest. It is important to recognise the difference in an award of damages between the expectation and reliance interest. The amount of compensation may be more favourable or more restrictive depending on the particular facts of the case. Any advice that is given to the party as to which measure of damages to pursue should hopefully take account of these differences.

14-022

The basis of an award of damages on the reliance interest is to put the parties into the position they would have been in had the wrong not been committed. This measure of damages is backward looking. The court does not seek to compensate the parties for a loss of expectation, but rather seeks to put them back into the position they were in before entering into the contract. Let us apply this to our car example:

Over to you. . .

Suppose that A purchases a car from B. The car is worth £5,000, but A only pays £4,000 (a good bargain). However, when A gets the car home he finds out that the engine is leaking oil and as a result it is only worth £3,000.

A's *reliance* loss will be £1,000. A expended £4,000 on a car that was only worth £3,000. The court will award damages to represent this wasted expenditure.

THE RELIANCE INTEREST AND SPECULATIVE DAMAGES

Even though the courts will seek to place a value on some speculative losses (see damages for loss of opportunity above), there are some situations in which the expectation loss is too speculative to quantify. In these cases the courts cannot make an award of damages on the expectation interest but may be able to make an award on the reliance interest. As you will recall the reliance interest is *backward looking* and seeks to put the claimant into the position they would have been in had they not entered into the contract. If the expectation losses are too speculative then this may be the only way to compensate the claimant for their loss.

14-023

In **Anglia Television Ltd v Reed** [1972] 1 Q.B. 60, the plaintiffs contracted with the defendant for him to play a lead role in their film production. Before the film was completed the defendant breached the contract and pulled out of the film. In this case it was very difficult (impossible) to calculate damages on the expectation interest (the position the plaintiffs would have been in had the contract not been breached). To award damages on the expectation interest would have required the court to predict how much profit would have been made had the film been released. Instead, the court awarded damages on the reliance interest (the position they would have been in had they not entered into the contract). On this basis the plaintiffs were able to recover their wasted expenditure.

In **Anglia TV v Reed**, given the speculative nature of the damages, the only basis on which damages could be awarded was on the reliance interest. However, the claimant will generally have the choice of whether to pursue an action for damages on either the expectation or reliance interest. This may be desirable as one measure may be more generous in some cases than others. However, as in **Anglia TV v Reed**, if the damages are so speculative then the court will decide the issue and rule that damages can only be claimed on the reliance interest.

The restitutionary interest

14-024 The nature of an award of damages in contract law is to compensate the innocent party for their loss. However, there may be circumstances in which the courts are unable to award damages on either the expectation or reliance interests. For example, loss may be too speculative to award damages on the expectation interest, and the claimant may not have suffered any quantifiable loss that can be awarded on the reliance interest. In these cases the courts may award damages on the restitutionary interest.

The restitutionary interest can best be described as a last resort for the courts and the courts will only award damages on this basis if neither the expectation nor reliance interests can be protected. At this point it is important not to confuse an award of damages on the "restitutionary interest" with the quasi-contractual remedy of "restitution". The remedy of restitution will be considered in more detail in Ch.15. The award of damages on the "restitutionary interest" seeks to return to the claimant the value of any benefit that has been received by the other party as a result of an unjust enrichment.

DISTINGUISHING THE RESTITUTIONARY INTEREST FROM THE RELIANCE INTEREST

14-025 At first glance there may seem little to differentiate an award of damages on the restitutionary interest from an award on the reliance interest. The principles behind an award on the restitutionary interest are to force a defendant to give up (disgorge) the benefit he receives as a result of breaching the contract. An award on the reliance interest seeks to put the innocent party into the position he would have been in had the contract not been breached. To this extent both measures appear to be backward looking. However, the focus of these two measures is quite different. An award on the reliance interest is *claimant focused*; it seeks to put the *claimant* into his pre-contractual position. An award on the restitutionary interest is *defendant focused*; it seeks to prevent the defendant from benefiting from their wrongful act and the defendant will be held to account any the profit they have made as a result.

It is perhaps misleading to refer to an award of damages on the restitutionary basis as "compensation". In the majority of cases where this has been argued, the claimant has not suffered any quantifiable loss. Rather, the court will hold the wrongdoer to *account* for any profit they have made as a result of their breach. An action to hold the wrongdoer to account is perhaps the more accurate way to describe the operation of the restitutionary interest. However, over the years the courts have slowly moved towards accepting the principles of "restitutionary damages". As we will see, it is only very recently that restitutionary damages have found a place within modern contract law and their availability has been severely limited to very "exceptional cases".

THE RELUCTANCE OF THE COURTS TO AWARD DAMAGES ON THE RESTITUTIONARY INTEREST

Historically, the courts have been very reluctant to award damages based on the restitutionary interest. For the courts to consider making an award on this basis the expectation or reliance interest must have been inadequate. There are a number of reasons for this reluctance, but one of the primary objections to an award of damages on the restitutionary interest is that the role of damages in contract law is to compensate the claimant for their loss. Damages are not intended to punish the defendant for their breach of contract. If damages are inadequate on the expectation or reliance interests then the claimant may not have suffered any quantifiable loss. Therefore, if the courts were to award damages on the restitutionary interest this may have the effect of punishing the defendant for their breach rather than compensating the claimant for their loss. In this way an award of damages on the restitutionary interest would be contrary to one of the most fundamental principles of damages (**Tito v Waddell (No2)** [1977] Ch. 106). Despite these objections, an analysis of the case law reveals a tentative move towards the recognition of restitutionary damages.

14-026

SURREY CC V BREDERO HOMES LTD

As mentioned above, the courts are reluctant to recognise an award of damages founded on restitutionary principles. The general principle was that it was irrelevant whether the defendant profited from the breach when determining the amount of compensation that the claimant can recover. This principle is demonstrated in **Surrey CC and Mole DC v Bredero Homes Ltd** [1993] 1 W.L.R. 1361. In this case the claimant council sold a plot of land to the defendant property developers. The council granted planning permission for 72 homes to be built on the land. In breach of this covenant the defendants built 77 homes on the plot of land. The coun-

14-027

cil claimed damages for the amount that the defendants would have had to pay to vary the planning permission.

There were a number of fundamental problems with the council's claim. Most importantly, the council had not actually suffered any loss. Damages could not be awarded on the expectation interest as the council was already in the position it would have been in had the contract not been breached. This posed an interesting problem for the court. Damages would not provide an adequate remedy, but at the same time the defendants had profited from their deliberate breach of the covenant. The court rejected the council's claim and refused to award damages on the restitutionary basis. The court was obviously concerned by the fact that an award of damages in this form would not actually compensate the council for its loss (as no actual loss had been suffered). Rather, an award of restitutionary damages would have the effect of punishing the defendants for the breach, which is contrary to the fundamental principle of an award of damages in contract.

WROTHAM PARK ESTATE CO LTD V PARKSIDE HOMES LTD

14-028   While the decision in **Surrey CC v Bredero Homes Ltd** represents the restrictive approach to an award of restitutionary damages, the door has not been closed completely. In fact, the earlier decision of **Wrotham Park Estate Co Ltd v Parkside Homes Ltd** [1974] 1 W.L.R. 798 recognised that restitutionary damages may be awarded in some cases. In this case the defendant built a house in breach of a restrictive covenant. The claimants (the owners of the estate on which the house was built) sought an injunction against the defendant. The injunction was refused but the court awarded the claimants damages.

Again, the claimants had not suffered any quantifiable loss. The value of the neighbouring property had not been reduced by the breach nor had the claimants suffered any other financial loss. Despite this, the court awarded the claimants five per cent of the profit that the defendant made from building the house in breach of the covenant. The figure of five per cent represented the amount that might reasonably have been charged to waive the restrictive covenant.

The case of **Wrotham Park Estate** is important as it provides a clear application of restitutionary principles in making an award of damages. In other words, the profit made by the *defendant* was relevant in determining the amount of damages to be awarded to the *claimant*. The defendant was required to account for this profit to the claimant.

RECONCILING SURREY CC V BREDERO HOMES WITH WROTHAM PARK ESTATE LTD

14-029   The facts of **Surrey CC v Bredero** and **Wrotham Park Estate** sound quite similar, but the courts came to quite different conclusions as to the amount of compensation that could be awarded.

Further, the cases are very similar in that neither of the claimants had suffered any actual loss that could be compensated by a traditional award of damages. So, why could the claimant recover compensation for the deliberate breach of covenant in **Wrotham Park Estate** but not in **Bredero Homes**? The answer seems to rest in the availability of further equitable remedies.

Despite the decision in **Wrotham Park Estate**, the court was still reluctant to label the award as being one of "restitutionary damages". Rather, damages were awarded *in lieu of* equitable remedies. We will consider these equitable remedies further in Ch.15, but for the moment we will be concerned with the equitable remedy of an injunction. An injunction is an equitable remedy that operates so as to prevent an individual from acting in a particular way. The claimants in **Wrotham Park** applied for an injunction, although this was refused by the court. Under the Senior Courts Act 1981 s.50 the court can award damages in lieu of equitable remedies such as an injunction. However, in **Bredero** an injunction could not have been granted as there was no interest that needed protection. The defendant was not in a position to breach the agreement further so an injunction would not have been an appropriate remedy. Therefore, damages could not be awarded *in lieu of* an injunction.

Damages in lieu of equitable relief is certainly one way of explaining the differing outcomes between **Wrotham Park** and **Bredero**, but it also preserves the stance that "restitutionary damages" are merely a way of awarding compensation based on normal contractual principles.

AN ACCOUNT FOR PROFITS AND THE DECISION IN ATTORNEY GENERAL V BLAKE

The most recent authority to consider this issue is the House of Lords decision in **Attorney General v Blake** [2001] 1 A.C. 268. This case concerned the actions of a former British Secret Intelligence Service agent, George Blake, who defected to the Soviet Union. As part of his defection, Blake passed information to the Soviet Government. This was a breach of his contract of employment with the British Secret Intelligence Service but was also a breach of the Official Secrets Act 1911. Blake was charged with and convicted of treason and was sentenced to 42 years in prison. He escaped from prison and returned to Russia.

14-030

Some 20 years later Blake entered into a contract with a publisher to release his autobiography. The total contract price was £150,000. The contents of the autobiography also revealed information that breached the Official Secrets Act. The Attorney General brought an action to prevent the autobiography from being released. The House of Lords allowed the Attorney General to recover £90,000, which represented the amount that was still to be paid to Blake.

Again, the facts of **Blake** provide an example of when traditional contractual damages would not have been available. The publication of the book would not have caused any quantifiable loss to the State. Despite this, the House of Lords awarded the Attorney General compensation as a result of Blake's unjust enrichment and Blake was held to account for this profit. The

House of Lords based its decision on the fact that the publication of the autobiography was in breach of Blake's fiduciary duty to the State to observe the provisions of the Official Secrets Act. A fiduciary duty arises out of a relationship of trust and confidence, and even though his contract of employment had been terminated many years before the publication, Blake's fiduciary duty to the State continued to bind him. In fact, this duty would continue to bind him for life.

The decision in **Blake** is interesting for a number of reasons. The House of Lords approved the decision in **Wrotham Park Estate** and recognised that damages can be awarded on restitutionary principles when the claimant has suffered no actual loss that could be compensated by an award of damages on the expectation or reliance interests. In these cases, if the defendant has profited as a result of his deliberate breach of duty then the court can hold the defendant to account for that profit. However, at the same time, the House of Lords was also keen to stress that damages can only be awarded in this way in "exceptional circumstances". To this extent, there appear to be two key limitations on the ability of the courts to hold an individual to account for profits:

1. Damages must be inadequate on both the expectation and reliance interests.
2. The claimant must have a "legitimate interest" in preventing the defendant from profiting from the breach.

These limitations on an account for profit have, unsurprisingly, narrowed the availability of such an award. Since the decision in **Blake**, there have been a number of cases where the courts have had to grapple with this new interpretation of an account for profits in exceptional circumstances.

AN ACCOUNT FOR PROFITS POST-*BLAKE*

14-031   While in **Blake** the House of Lords recognised the possibility of compensating a claimant by holding the defendant to account for profits, the limitations on this award meant that it fell short of forming a wide-ranging general principle. Despite this, **Blake** has been followed by subsequent case law giving greater weight to a shift towards the recognition of "restitutionary damages". In **Esso Petroleum Co Ltd v Niad Ltd** [2001] All E.R. 324, Niad entered into a price agreement with Esso. Niad breached this agreement and sold petrol for more than the agreed price. The court held Niad to account for the profit he made in selling the petrol in breach of the price agreement.

The court applied the decision in **Blake** and decided, first, that damages would not be an adequate remedy in this situation. It was difficult to ascertain what loss the breach had caused to Esso as it was not possible to identify every sale that had been affected by the breach. Secondly, Esso had a "legitimate interest" in preventing the defendant from profiting from the breach. The whole purpose of the price agreement was to preserve Esso's strong position in the marketplace. A breach of this agreement undermined this interest and justified holding Niad to account for the profit made as a result of the breach.

In contrast, the court refused to hold the defendants to account in **Experience Hendrix LLC v PPX Enterprises Inc** [2003] EWCA Civ 323. In this case the defendants breached a licence agreement and released some unauthorised copies of Jimi Hendrix material. The claimants sought and were granted an injunction preventing the defendants from releasing material in the future, but they also sought damages for the breaches that occurred before the injunction was granted. Again, the claimants had suffered no actual loss following the breach of the licence agreement so any compensation would have to be awarded by holding the defendants to account for their profits. Even though damages would not have been appropriate on either the expectation or reliance interests, and even though the claimants had a legitimate interest in preventing the defendants from profiting from their breach, the court held that the facts were not "exceptional" so as to justify holding the defendants to account.

Although the court refused to hold the defendants to account the court did award the claimants damages on the same basis as in **Wrotham Park**. The claimants were awarded an amount that represented the amount that the defendants would have to pay in order for the claimants to waive the licence agreement. So, while this decision is consistent with **Wrotham Park**, it is inconsistent with the way in which the House of Lords calculated the amount of damages in **Blake**. As you will recall, the damages awarded in **Blake** represented the amount by which the defendant was to profit from the publication of the autobiography. In **Wrotham**, damages were awarded to represent the amount the defendant would reasonably have been expected to pay in order for the covenant to be varied.

The decision in the **Hendrix** case is unfortunate as it amplifies the uncertain aspect of the decision in Blake, that the facts must be "exceptional" (such as involving national security or breach of a fiduciary duty) before the court will hold an individual to account for profit. Further, it also illustrates the confusion that still exists as to how damages are calculated on restitutionary principles in contract law.

The ability to recover for non-pecuniary loss

14-032

We have seen that even where damages are quite speculative the courts are still able to award damages for this loss. A loss of opportunity provides a good example of this approach, as in **Chaplin v Hicks**. However, the courts have adopted a stricter approach to other types of loss and have demonstrated their reluctance to award damages for emotional distress caused by a breach of contract. Such loss is referred to as "non-pecuniary" because it is difficult to quantify as it will generally have no economic value. If a contract is of a commercial nature, then the courts are very reluctant indeed to award damages for any non-pecuniary loss that may have been suffered as a result of the breach.

DAMAGES FOR DISAPPOINTMENT/INJURED FEELINGS

14-033 As noted above, the courts have adopted a restrictive approach to the ability to recover non-pecuniary loss in commercial contracts. This approach is demonstrated in the case of **Bliss v South East Thames RHA** [1985] I.R.L.R. 308. In this case a surgeon claimed damages for emotional distress as a result of his wrongful dismissal at work. His employer requested that he take part in a psychiatric examination following an allegation at work. When the surgeon refused he was suspended from duty. The Court of Appeal held (reversing the decision at first instance) that it was not possible to recover damages for emotional distress for wrongful dismissal.

The approach in **Bliss** is to some extent inconsistent with the law of tort, which allows a claimant to recover for emotional distress following a breach of duty. This inconsistency was recognised by Lord Denning in **Jarvis v Swans Tours Ltd** [1973] Q.B. 233 and this decision marks the beginning of a more lenient approach to damages for emotional distress in contracts that are to provide for a pleasurable experience. In **Jarvis**, the claimant booked a holiday that promised to provide a "great time" and would include such events as a "house party" (and yodelling!). None of these events took place as described and the claimant sued for damages. The price of the holiday was £63, but the court awarded the claimant £125 to reflect his disappointment suffered when the contract did not provide what was promised.

This decision was affirmed in **Jackson v Horizon Holidays** [1975] 1 W.L.R. 1468. We have already discussed this case as an exception to the rule of privity of contract (see above at p.125). In this case a husband was able to claim damages for disappointment for the inadequate facilities provided on the family holiday on behalf of himself *and* his family. Again, this decision is based on the fact that the purpose of the contract was to provide for a pleasurable experience. When this was not provided the husband was able to claim for loss of his expectation under the contract. The purpose of the contract was to provide a pleasurable experience not simply for the husband but for the whole family, and damages were awarded to reflect this disappointment.

The decisions in **Jarvis** and **Jackson** are examples of where the courts awarded damages for disappointment, as the "primary purpose" of the contract was to provide for an enjoyable experience. However, the courts have also adopted a more lenient approach where an important (not primary) element of the contract was to guard against disappointment or injured feelings. The leading case on this issue is **Farley v Skinner (No.2)** [2002] 2 A.C. 732. Here, the claimant entered into a contract with a surveyor who was to conduct a number of inspections of a property that the claimant wished to purchase. The claimant specifically requested that the surveyor inspect for aircraft noise. The surveyor reported back to the claimant and made no mention of any aircraft noise. The claimant purchased the house only to find that property was in fact located on the flight path to Gatwick airport!

The House of Lords had to consider a claim for non-pecuniary loss, more specifically a claim for the distress caused by the aircraft noise. This was a claim purely for non-pecuniary loss as the value of the property had not been adversely affected by the aircraft noise so the claimant had not suffered any traditional quantifiable loss. The House of Lords awarded the claimant £10,000 for non-pecuniary loss. Again, decision is based on the need to protect the expectations of the parties under the contract. One of the important elements of the contract was for the surveyor to investigate whether the property was affected by aircraft noise. The surveyor failed to discover that the property was so affected and as a result the claimant was able to recover non-pecuniary loss for his distress.

The decision in **Farley v Skinner** is an important step in the ability of claimants to recover for non-pecuniary loss. Prior to this decision the court had recognised only two limited situations in which a claimant could recover for such loss when the "primary purpose" of the contract was to guard against such disappointment. In **Watts v Morrow** [1991] 1 W.L.R. 1421, the court identified these two situations as follows:

- Where the very object of the contract is to provide pleasure, relaxation, peace of mind or freedom from molestation; or
- Where physical inconvenience and discomfort was caused by the breach.

The loss suffered in **Farley** did not strictly fall within the first exception as the very object of the contract was not to guard against aircraft noise. However, the House of Lords in **Farley** gave a more flexible interpretation to this first exception and interpreted it as applying to contracts where an "important" object of the contract was to provide for pleasure, relaxation etc. In effect, the House of Lords widened the scope of damages for non-pecuniary loss and brought it closer to the approach adopted by the courts in **Jarvis v Swans** Tours and Jackson where the very purpose of the contract was to provide for a pleasurable experience.

Damages agreed between the parties: "Liquidated damages"

It is quite possible (and common) for the parties to agree between themselves the amount of damages that will be awarded in the event of breach. If the parties freely agree this amount then the principles of freedom of contract would support the approach of the courts in giving effect to this agreement. Damages that are agreed between the parties are referred to as "liquidated damages", as the amount of damages that will be awarded in the event of breach have been agreed up front and in advance between the parties.

14-034

It is common in commercial agreements for the contract to contain a liquidated damages clause. Being aware of potential liability before the contract is breached means that each party can make provision to meet such loss should it arise. Risk allocation devices such as insurance provisions can be put in place to protect the defaulting party in the event of breach. Also, liquidated damages clauses have the advantage of speeding up any disputes between the parties.

The court will not have to embark upon the task of determining remoteness of damage as this issue has already been agreed by the parties.

> ## Over to you. . .
>
> As we will see, the courts have developed principles so as to limit the validity of liquidated damages clauses. Can you think why such restrictions could be justified?

While liquidated damages clauses play an important role in commercial contracts they are, of course, also open to abuse. As with the use of exclusion clauses, a party in a weaker bargaining position may have little choice but to agree to the terms imposed by the party in a stronger bargaining position. In fact, liquidated damages clauses and exclusion clauses operate in a very similar way: they are both examples of where liability has been freely agreed between the parties. However, it is important to distinguish a liquidated damages clause from an exclusion clause. Essentially, a liquidated damages clause is recognition of liability and represents the intention of the parties as to the actual amount of damages that will be recoverable. This amount will be recoverable irrespective of the actual loss suffered. On the other hand an exclusion clause is a denial of liability and sets the maximum amount of liability that the defaulting party will incur (and will usually seek to exclude liability completely).

Given the potential abuse with liquidated damages clauses the courts have responded and placed limitations on the principles of freedom of contract. The courts draw a distinction between liquidated damages clauses (which are quite lawful) and penalty clauses (which are unlawful). Even if the parties freely agreed to a clause it will not be enforceable by the court if the court construes it is a penalty clause.

- A liquidated damage clause = lawful and the court will give effect to the intention of the parties.
- A penalty clause = unlawful and the court will not enforce the clause.

Distinguishing a liquidated damages clause from a penalty clause

14-035   The courts have developed a number of methods by which to distinguish a liquidated damages clause from a penalty clause. The basic approach is to compare the actual loss following the breach of contract against the amount claimed by way of liquidated damages. For example, in Cellulose Acetate Silk Co Ltd v Widnes Foundry (1925) Ltd [1933] A.C. 20, the claimant sought to recover his loss for the delay in the completion of a plant within the specified time. The contract provided that the plant should be completed within 18 weeks and the contract provided that £20 would be payable for every week of delay beyond those 18 weeks. The plant was completed 18 weeks late which would have given £600 in liquidated damages. The claimant's actual loss was £5,800. As the amount agreed (£600) was less than the actual loss suffered, the court held that the clause was a liquidated damages clause, despite the fact that it was labelled as a "penalty" in the contract.

There are a number of problems with the approach in **Cellulose Acetate**. First, the decision to construe the clause as a liquidated damages clause meant that the claimant could only recover the amount that was agreed (£600). The claimant could not choose to ignore the liquidated damages clause and recover his actual losses. In most cases this will not be objectionable; however in this case the amount agreed was so unrepresentative of the anticipated loss that it was more akin to a limitation clause than a liquidated damages clause. Secondly, this approach is inconsistent with the approach of the court in **Dunlop Pneumatic Tyre Co Ltd v New Garage and Motor Co Ltd** [1915] A.C. 79 which was subsequently approved in **Philips Hong Kong Ltd v Attorney General of Hong Kong** (1993) 61 B.L.R. 49. Following **Dunlop Pneumatic Tyre**, in order for a clause to be classed as a liquidated damages clause it must be a "genuine pre-estimate of loss". Again, as the amount agreed was substantially less than the actual loss it is difficult to see how this could be construed as a genuine pre-estimate of loss.

The guidelines in *Dunlop Pneumatic Tyre*

The difficult task for the court is to distinguish a liquidated damages clause from a penalty clause. To assist with this task the courts have developed a number of guidelines to use when drawing this distinction. The leading authority is **Dunlop Pneumatic Tyre Co Ltd v New Garage and Motor Co Ltd** [1915] A.C. 79, in which Lord Dunedin formulated the following guidelines:

14-036

> "1. Though the parties to a contract who use the words 'penalty' or 'liquidated damages' may prima facie be supposed to mean what they say, yet the expression used is not conclusive. The Court must find out whether the payment stipulated is in truth a penalty or liquidated damages[. . .].
> 2. The essence of a penalty is a payment of money stipulated as in terrorem of the offending party [to scare the other party]; the essence of liquidated damages is a genuine covenanted pre-estimate of damage[. . .].
> 3. The question whether a sum stipulated is penalty or liquidated damages is a question of construction to be decided upon the terms and inherent circumstances of each particular contract, judged of as at the time of the making of the contract, not as at the time of the breach[. . .].
> 4. To assist this task of construction various tests have been suggested, which if applicable to the case under consideration may prove helpful, or even conclusive. Such are:
>   (a) it will be held to be penalty if the sum stipulated for is extravagant and unconscionable in amount in comparison with the greatest loss that could

> conceivably be proved to have followed from the breach[. . .].
>
> (b) It will be held to be a penalty if the breach consists only in not paying a sum of money, and the sum stipulated is a sum greater than the sum which ought to have been paid[. . .].
>
> (c) There is a presumption (but no more) that it is penalty when 'a single lump sum is made payable by way of compensation, on the reccurrence of one or more or all of several events, some of which may occasion serious and others but trifling damage'[. . .].
>
> (d) It is no obstacle to the sum stipulated being a genuine pre-estimate of damage, that the consequences of the breach are such as to make precise pre-estimation almost an impossibility. On the contrary, that is just the situation when it is probable that pre-estimated damage was the true bargain between the parties[. . .]".

Distilling these principles, the key test in distinguishing a liquidated damages clause from a penalty clause will be to assess whether the amount agreed is a "genuine pre-estimate of loss". To decide whether the amount is a "genuine pre-estimate of loss" the court will compare the amount agreed against the maximum loss that could have been suffered as a result of the breach. If the amount agreed is *extravagant* in comparison to this maximum loss, then the clause will be a penalty clause and will be unenforceable.

Now, we can apply these principles to the facts of **Dunlop** itself. Here, the contract provided that the defendant would pay the claimant £5 for each tyre that was sold under the list price. This demonstrates the problems identified in Lord Dunedin's final guideline. It was difficult to pre-estimate the actual loss that would be suffered if this agreement were breached. For example, if a tyre were sold at £1 then this would have caused a loss of £4 to the claimants. If a tyre were sold at £4, then only £1 loss would have been suffered. Despite the problems in assessing the precise loss, the court held that the figure of £5 represented a genuine pre-estimate of loss and the clause was thus construed as a liquidated damages clause.

Contributory negligence

14-037   Contributory negligence is another method by which damages can be reduced. Essentially, in a claim of contributory negligence it is alleged that the claimant is also partially responsible for the loss suffered by failing to act with reasonable care. The position in the law of tort is quite settled and the court can reduce the amount of damages that the claimant is able to recover to reflect the claimant's fault that contributed to the loss suffered. However, the position in contract law is less certain. At first glance it would seem doubtful that the same tortious principles would apply to an award of damages in contract law. For example, we have assessed in detail the differences in how damages are awarded in contract and tort. Generally, damages will be awarded on different measures and different tests of remoteness will apply to an award of damages in contract and tort.

The starting point in analysing contributory negligence in contract law is to consider the provisions of the Law Reform (Contributory Negligence) Act 1945. Section 1(1) provides:

> "Where any person suffers damage as the result partly of his own fault and partly of the fault of another person or persons, a claim in respect of that damage shall not be defeated by reason of the fault of the person suffering the damage, but the damages recoverable in respect thereof shall be reduced to such extent as the court thinks just and equitable having regard to the claimant's share in the responsibility for the damage".

The key to assessing contributory negligence in contract law lies in interpreting the issue of "fault". In the law of tort a claimant will be at "fault" when they act negligently (failing to act with reasonable care and skill). However, in contract law "fault" can be based on strict liability. If an individual is "strictly liable" then there is no need to prove "fault" in order to pursue an action for damages. This fact was recognised in **Forsikringsaktieselskapet Vesta v Butcher** [1989] A.C. 852, in which Hobhouse J. held that where the only obligation is a strict contractual obligation then damages *cannot* be reduced as a result of contributory negligence. This was confirmed by the Court of Appeal in **Barclays Bank Plc v Fairclough Building Ltd** [1995] Q.B. 214.

The decision in **Vesta** highlights the fundamental difference between contractual and tortious liability. The law of contract recognises strict contractual liability and in doing so this distinguishes contractual liability from that in tort. As such, it would be unjust to apply tortious principles to a contractual claim when the two bases of liability are clearly different. However, if the claimant in a contractual claim has breached the contract by acting negligently (in breach of a duty of care) then the court can of course take this into account when awarding damages.

Particular problems arise, however, when the nature of the obligation is based partly on contractual and partly on tortious principles. For example, if there is no duty of care between the claimant and defendant, but the claimant nevertheless breaches the contract by acting negligently, then it is questionable whether damages could be reduced based on the contributory negligence of the claimant. There is no strong authority on this point and despite the recommendations of the Law Commission it is still uncertain whether contributory negligence would apply in such cases.

Mitigation of loss

14-038   Finally, a claimant must take reasonable steps to mitigate (reduce) their loss. It is not enough for the claimant to simply sit back and watch the loss get bigger and bigger following a breach of contract. The principle of mitigation requires the claimant to act reasonably to reduce the loss. For example, think back to the case of **Victoria Laundry v Newman**. You will recall that this case concerned the late delivery of a boiler which caused the claimant to suffer ordinary business loss and also to lose a lucrative dyeing contract with the Ministry of Defence. In this case, had the claimants been able to hire a replacement boiler in the meantime for a reasonable price but declined to do so, then the amount of damages might have been reduced to reflect their failure to mitigate their loss.

However, the claimant must act reasonably to mitigate his loss. If the claimant acts unreasonably then the court may reduce the amount of damages awarded to almost zero, as happened in **Brace v Calder** [1895] 2 Q.B. 253. In this case the defendants employed the claimant as a manager of their business. Owing to several acquisitions and restructuring of the business, the partnership that employed the defendant was dissolved. The dissolution of the partnership operated to dismiss the claimant from his position as manager. The claimant offered to re-employ the defendants but he refused and brought an action for wrongful dismissal. The court rejected this claim on the basis that the claimant had failed to mitigate his loss. It would have been reasonable for the claimant to have accepted the offer of continued employment. By refusing, the claimant had acted unreasonably and as a result was only able to recover nominal damages for the breach of contract.

Again, in **Payzu Ltd v Saunders** [1919] 2 K.B. 581, the refusal to accept an offer for payment in cash for the delivery of goods (instead of the monthly payment that had been agreed) was held to be unreasonable. In this time the goods had risen in price so the loss suffered would have been greatly reduced and thus the amount of damages awarded was reduced to reflect this unreasonable behaviour.

Summary

The measure of damages

1. Damages are the primary remedy for a breach of contract and seek to compensate the innocent party for their loss.

2. Contractual damages are usually awarded on the expectation interest and thus seek to put the claimant into the position they would have been in had the contract not been breached. Expectation damages are therefore described as being *forward looking*.

3. In some cases, particularly where expectation damages are too speculative, a claimant may be able to recover damages on the reliance interest. Reliance damages seek to put the claimant into the position they would have been in had they not entered into the contract. Reliance damages are therefore described as being *backward looking*.

4. Exceptionally, if damages would not be adequate on either the expectation or reliance interests, the court may apply restitutionary principles and hold the defendant to account for any profit they have made as a result of the breach. Such an award is sometimes referred to as restitutionary damages, as the effect is to compensate the claimant based on the defendant's gain.

Limitations on the award of damages

1. There are a number of factors that limit an award of damages in contract law. The most fundamental of these is the principle of remoteness of damage. Losses that are too remote from the breach will not be recoverable, even though they may have *in fact* been caused by the breach of contract.

2. There has been considerable debate as to the appropriate test of remoteness in contract law. The leading authority is **Hadley v Baxendale**, but this decision has been modified over the years into a single principle of remoteness (see **Victoria Laundry**). In order for loss to be recoverable it must have been in the *reasonable contemplation* of the parties at the time the contract was formed (**The Heron II**).

3. There was an attempt by Lord Denning in **Parsons v Uttley** to introduce the tortious test of reasonable forseeability when the claimant suffered physical harm, irrespective of whether the cause of action rested in contract or tort. This distinction was not accepted by the majority and it is clear that the stricter test of reasonable contemplation applies to contractual claims for damages.

4. The parties are free to agree the amount of damages before the breach occurs. These damages are referred to as liquidated damages. However, the courts distinguish a liquidated damages clause (which is lawful) from a penalty clause (which is unlawful). The key test is whether the amount agreed is a "genuine pre- estimate of loss" compared to the maximum loss that could have been suffered as a result of the breach.

5. Finally, a claimant's damages may also be reduced owing to contributory negligence or a failure to act reasonably in mitigating their loss.

Key Cases Grid

Case	Court	Key Issue
Hadley v Baxendale (1854)	Court of Exchequer	Establishes the test of remoteness of damage for breach of contract. In order for loss to be recoverable it must have been in the *reasonable contemplation* of both parties at the time the contract was formed.
Victoria Laundry (Windsor) Ltd v Newman Industries [1949]	Court of Appeal	Normal loss will be recoverable as a natural consequence of eh breach. Abnormal loss will be recoverable if it was within the reasonable contemplation of both parties when entering into the contract. The relevant knowledge of the parties will determine whether such loss was reasonably contemplated.
Parsons (Livestock) Ltd v Uttley Ingham & Co Ltd [1978]	Court of Appeal	The majority view was that only *type* of harm, not the extent of that harm, needs to be within the reasonable contemplation of the parties. Note the approach of Lord Denning M.R., who was of the view that the relevant test of remoteness should be determined by the type of harm suffered, drawing a distinction between physical and economic harm.
Dunlop Pneumatic Tyre Co Ltd v New Garage and Motor Co Ltd [1915]	House of Lords	In distinguishing between liquated damages and a penalty clause, the court should have regard to whether the amount agreed is a genuine pre-estimate of loss. The court will interpret the clause of a penalty if the sum stipulated is extravagant in comparison with the greatest loss that could conceivably be proved to have followed from the breach.

End of Chapter Question

Mary enters into a contract with Weather-King Ltd for the purchase of 1,000 umbrellas. The contract provides that the umbrellas are to be delivered by April 1, and that Weather-King Ltd is to pay Mary £5,000 for every week that the umbrellas are delivered late. Mary made clear to Weather-King Ltd that the umbrellas had to be delivered by April 1, in order for her to meet the high demand during April and also to meet a lucrative contract with an outdoor activity centre.

Due to a delay in Weather-King Ltd placing their order with the supplier, the umbrellas are delivered three weeks late. Had Mary been able to sell the umbrellas she would have expected to have made profits of £3,000 in relation to general sales and £7,000 from the contract with the activity centre.

Mary is now claiming £15,000 damages from Weather-King Ltd.

Advise Weather-King Ltd.

Points of Answer

♦ Damages agreed between the parties are referred to as "liquidated damages". Apply the principles from **Dunlop Pneumatic Tyre** to decide whether the amount agreed is a "genuine pre-estimate of loss", or whether it is extravagant so as to amount to a penalty.

♦ If the clause is construed as a penalty then consider the recovery of unliquidated damages.

♦ Apply the two branches of **Hadley v Baxendale** to the two losses suffered. Following the approach in **Victoria Laundry**, the loss flowing naturally from the breach will be recoverable, but would the loss of the contract with the activity centre have been in the reasonable contemplation of Weather-King Ltd?

Further Reading

Krishnaprasad, V. "From the mill shaft to the coal cruiser: contractual damages after the Achilleas." I.C.C.L.R. 2011, 22(7), 218-223

> This article provides an overview of the legal principles of remoteness of damage and considers the application of Hadley v Baxendale in light of the decision in Transfield Shipping Inc v Mercator Shipping Inc (The Achilleas).

Naravane, S. "The implications of Transfield for concurrent liability in tort and contract. J.B.L. 2012, 5, 404–419.

While this article is not confined to the strict boundaries of contract law, concurrent liability inevitably blurs the artificial distinctions between contract and. This article provides an analysis of the impact of the decision in Transfield Shipping Inc v Mercator Shipping Inc (The Achilleas) in such cases.

Stone, R. and Cunnington, R. *Text, Cases and Materials on Contract Law* (London: Routledge-Cavendish, 2014), Chapter 15.

Treitel, G. *The Law of Contract*, 13th edn (London Sweet & Maxwell, 2011), Chapter 20.

Other Remedies

15

CHAPTER OVERVIEW

In this chapter we:

- discuss the alternative remedies to damages at common law and equity

- consider the equitable remedies of specific performance and injunctions

- introduce the "quasi-contractual" principles of Restitution

Summary

Key Cases Grid

Further Reading

Introduction

15-001 The primary remedy for breach of contract is for the court to make an award of damages. The court will seek to put the innocent party into the position they would have been in had the contract not been breached, thereby protecting the innocent party's "expectation" interest. There are circumstances, however, when an award of damages will not be an adequate or appropriate remedy. The innocent party may seek alternative remedies from the court that have the effect of making the party in breach of contract perform his obligations under the contract, rather than the innocent party receiving compensation for the other party's failure to perform those obligations.

There are common law and equitable remedies that have the effect of forcing the party in breach of contract to perform obligations under the contract. The results can often be similar to an award of damages, but the principles on which these remedies are based are quite different from those that govern an award of damages. We will first consider the position at common law and then analyse the remaining equitable remedies.

Common law

Action for an agreed sum

15-002 As part of their contractual obligations, a party may be required to pay a sum of money should a specific event occur. The most obvious example is where a party must pay a sum of money when the other party performs their contractual obligations. This may arise in the context of a unilateral contract where the defendant has promised the claimant a reward should the claimant perform a certain act. If the claimant performs the required act and the defendant refuses to pay then the claimant may bring an action to recover the sum that was promised.

> **Over to you. . .**
>
> Can you think of why pursuing an action for an agreed sum may be more advantageous than claiming a traditional assessment of contractual damages?

There are several advantages in pursuing an action for an agreed sum instead of damages. As you will recall, there are a number of limitations on an award of damages. The most notable of these limitations is remoteness of damage. The claimant may recover less than his actual loss on the basis that this was not reasonably contemplated by the other party as resulting from the breach. However, in an action for an agreed sum, the claimant will be able to claim the full amount promised under the contract. In addition, the claimant may *also* be able to claim damages for any loss caused by the defendant's late payment.

An action for an agreed sum may have a very similar effect to an award of damages in terms of the amount of money that is ultimately awarded by the court. However, an action for an agreed sum is very different in principle to an award of damages. If the defendant agreed to pay a specific amount should an event occur then the innocent party will bring an action for an agreed sum to recover the money that is now due under the contract.

An award of damages seeks to compensate the innocent party for the defendant's breach. An action for an agreed sum allows an innocent party to recover an amount that was promised under the contract and which is now due to be paid.

Equitable remedies

. . . .

Specific performance

The effect of an award of an agreed sum at common law is to require the defendant to perform his obligations under the contract and pay the amount he promised to pay should a specific event occur. However, this is the only action at common law that will have the effect of compelling a defendant to perform his obligations under a contract. If a claimant wishes to compel the defendant to perform any obligations other than the payment of an agreed sum, then he will have to rely on the equitable remedy of specific performance.

15-003

Specific performance is an equitable remedy and as such is not available as of right (unlike an award of damages). The court will have a discretion to make an award of specific performance and there are a number of factors that the court will take into account when deciding whether to exercise this discretion.

The requirements for an award of specific performance are as follows.

1. Damages must not be an adequate remedy.
2. There must be mutuality.
3. Court supervision must not be required.
4. It must be equitable to grant the remedy of specific performance.
5. Specific performance will not be granted in contracts for personal services.
6. There must not be an undue delay in claiming specific performance.

DAMAGES MUST NOT BE AN ADEQUATE REMEDY

As noted above, an action for damages is the primary remedy for a breach of contract and the courts will only exercise their discretion to award specific performance if damages are an inadequate remedy. If damages would provide an adequate remedy at common law then the equitable remedy of specific performance will not be available.

15-004

The courts have adopted a rather strict approach to the availability of specific performance in relation to contracts for the sale of goods. The reason for this strict approach is that damages will generally be an adequate remedy to compensate the claimant for his loss of bargain. The relevant "market value" will determine the amount of damages that the purchaser can recover if a seller fails to deliver goods. The purchaser will be able to recover the difference between the market value of the goods and the price agreed in the contract. However, the courts are more willing to award specific performance for the non-delivery of goods that are unique or where there is no market value by which to assess the appropriate amount of damages.

Section 52 of the Sale of Goods Act 1979 expressly allows an award of specific performance in relation to ascertained (specific) goods, rather than general goods. However, there are situations in which the courts grant equitable relief in relation to unascertained (or general) goods. In **Sky Petroleum v VIP Petroleum** [1974] 1 W.L.R. 576, the defendants withdrew the plaintiffs' supply of oil during an oil crisis and the court granted an injunction to prevent the defendants from withholding the supply. In this case damages would not have been an adequate remedy for the plaintiffs. The plaintiffs could not purchase oil from another supplier because of the oil crisis, so the unstable market justified the award of an equitable remedy.

Further, there may be circumstances in which damages cannot be recovered owing to a rule of law. For example, a claimant cannot generally recover damages for loss suffered by a third party. In these cases the claimant has not actually suffered any loss (or such loss will only be nominal) so the amount of damages that are recoverable will be minimal at best. Would these cases justify an award of specific performance on the grounds that damages are not an adequate remedy?

In **Beswick v Beswick** [1968] A.C. 58, an uncle sold his business to his nephew with the agreement that the nephew would make payments to the uncle and his wife. When the uncle died the nephew refused to make the payments to the wife. The wife could not claim damages under the contract as she was a third party to the contract and the privity of contract rule prevented her from pursuing a claim. The House of Lords granted specific performance to compel the nephew to make the agreed payments. If the House of Lords had not granted specific performance there would have been no remedy for the wife at all, so specific performance was used by the House to avoid the inequitable operation of the privity of contract rule. Note that the decision in **Beswick** now needs to be assessed in the light of the Contracts (Rights of Third Parties) Act 1999.

Despite the equitable result in **Beswick**, this decision does create problems in how the courts assess whether damages are an adequate remedy. Take the example of where the market value of particular goods were to mean that only nominal damages could be recovered for breach of contract. The claimant will still be able to recover damages (there is no rule of law preventing a recovery of damages) but he may only recover nominal damages because of the prevailing market price. If specific performance was granted on the grounds that damages were an inadequate remedy, following **Beswick**, this would shift the emphasis away from whether damages would be an *adequate* remedy to whether damages would be a *favourable* remedy.

THERE MUST BE MUTUALITY

The court will only make an award of specific performance if the remedy is available to *both* parties. If for some reason one of the parties cannot claim specific performance then there is a lack of mutuality and the court will refuse to make an award of specific performance.

15-005

In **Price v Strange** [1978] Ch. 337, the defendant subleased property to the plaintiff. In return the plaintiff agreed to undertake internal and external repair work to the property. The plaintiff completed the internal repairs but was not able to complete the external repairs as the defendant had already carried out these repairs herself. The defendant sought to terminate the agreement and the plaintiff brought an action for specific performance. Initially, the claim of specific performance was rejected on the grounds that at the time of the contract, the plaintiff would not have been able to compel the defendant to carry out the repairs. The Court of Appeal reversed this decision and held that the appropriate time of assessment should be at trial. At the time of the trial the plaintiff would not be able to enforce the obligations under lease without the defendant also being able to require the plaintiff to complete the repair work. As both parties would be able to compel performance there was the necessary element of mutuality to grant specific performance.

COURT SUPERVISION MUST NOT BE REQUIRED

The court will be reluctant to grant specific performance if the award would require continuing supervision over a period of time to ensure that the parties are performing their obligations under the contract. In **Ryan v Mutual Tontine Westminster Chambers Association** [1893] 1 Ch. 116, the contract placed an obligation on a landlord to ensure that a porter was "constantly in attendance" at the property. Specific performance would not be granted in these situations as the court would have to constantly monitor the agreement to ensure that a porter was in attendance at the property.

15-006

Further, in **Cooperative Insurance Society Ltd v Argyll Stores (Holdings) Ltd** [1998] A.C. 1, a lease over retail premises required that the defendants were to keep the shop open for the usual hours of business. When the business started to make a loss the defendants took the decision to close the business. The plaintiffs brought an action for specific performance to compel the defendants to keep the business open. The House of Lords again refused to grant specific performance on the grounds that it would require constant supervision of the court to ensure that the obligations under the lease were being met.

The decision in **Argyll Stores** also revealed a further reluctance of the court to grant specific performance. Not only would continuing supervision be required, but the court may also have to make numerous awards of specific performance to ensure that the obligations under the lease were met. Each time the defendant failed to meet these obligations he could potentially face an action for contempt of court in failing to perform the acts demanded of him by the court. This was seen as most undesirable and also explains the reluctance of the courts to continuously monitor such contractual relationships.

IT MUST BE EQUITABLE TO GRANT THE REMEDY OF SPECIFIC PERFORMANCE

15-007   As specific performance is an equitable remedy, the court will not grant specific performance if it would be *inequitable* to do so. For example, if the award of specific performance was to result in unnecessary hardship for one party then to make such an award would be contrary to the equitable principles that govern specific performance.

In **Patel v Ali** [1984] Ch. 283, the vendors agreed to sell their house to the purchaser. A number of unfortunate events followed: the vendor's husband was made bankrupt and the vendor's leg was amputated after contracting bone cancer. The purchaser was then awarded specific performance to compel the sale of the house. On appeal the court refused to grant specific performance on the grounds of hardship. The vendor was disabled and relied on a close network of her friends to support her: she would suffer undue hardship if she were forced to move. The purchaser was therefore awarded damages in place of specific performance.

Further, the equitable maxim of "he who comes to equity must do so with clean hands" will prevent a party from receiving an equitable remedy if it would be unjust for that party to do so. The courts will not grant specific performance if the party claiming the award has acted inequitably. For example, taking advantage of a mistake when making an offer (**Webster v Cecil** (1861) 30 Beav. 62) or a mistake as to the value of property (**Walters v Morgan** (1861) 45 E.R. 1056) are both grounds for refusing a claim of specific performance on the basis that it would be inequitable to grant such relief.

SPECIFIC PERFORMANCE WILL NOT BE GRANTED IN CONTRACTS FOR PERSONAL SERVICES

15-008   The general rule of law is that the law cannot compel a party to work for an employer. As we have seen with the use of restraint of trade clauses, the law can prevent a person from working for another employer, but the law cannot force a party to meet their contractual obligations. This position is now also supported by the Trade Union and Labour Relations (Consolidation) Act 1992, which will prevent an award of specific performance in relation to a contract for personal services.

These statutory provisions are also based on the practicalities and realities of a contract of employment. If an employer has to resort to the courts to compel an employee to perform his contractual obligations then this is strong evidence that the relationship of trust and confidence between the parties has broken down.

THERE MUST NOT BE AN UNDUE DELAY IN CLAIMING SPECIFIC PERFORMANCE

Again, as specific performance is an equitable remedy, there must not be undue delay in seeking the remedy. You will recall that the equitable remedy of rescission can be lost following a lapse of time (see above at p.137). The same principles apply to an award of specific performance. The equitable principle that "delay defeats equity" will prevent a claim. It is difficult to reach a firm conclusion as to the length of delay required before the courts will refuse a claim of specific performance. The overriding principle is that the result must be just and equitable, so the courts have demonstrated a broad approach to undue delay.

15-009

. . . .

Injunctions

The remedy of specific performance has the effect of compelling a party to meet their contractual obligations. Closely related to this remedy is the use of injunctions. An injunction is an equitable remedy which can have one of two effects depending on the *type* of injunction.

15-010

1. A mandatory injunction: this has the effect of compelling the defendant to act in a particular way, usually to remedy the results of his breach of obligations.
2. A prohibitory injunction: this has the effect of preventing a party from acting in a particular way, usually to prevent the defendant from breaching (or continuing to breach) their contractual obligations.

MANDATORY INJUNCTIONS

If a defendant has breached their contractual or legal obligations then the court may grant a mandatory injunction to compel them to correct the wrong committed. Mandatory injunctions are quite rare as the consequences of granting them can be quite severe at times. For example, in **Wakeham v Wood** (1982) 43 P. & C.R. 40, the defendant built a house on land that was subject to a restrictive covenant. The restriction on building was in place to protect the view of the ocean from the plaintiff's property. The defendant's building blocked this view so the plaintiff sought an injunction. The court awarded a mandatory injunction that required the defendant to tear down the house that had been built in breach of the restrictive covenant. Damages would not have provided an adequate remedy to the plaintiff so in this situation the court was prepared to grant an injunction.

15-011

PROHIBITORY INJUNCTIONS

15-012 A prohibitory injunction will have the effect of compelling the defendant to meet his contractual obligations. This sounds quite similar to an award of specific performance which also has the effect of compelling an individual to act. However, a prohibitory injunction operates so as to hold a party to a negative obligation under a contract. As we will see, many of the cases involve contracts for personal services (for which specific performance cannot be granted) but a prohibitory injunction will have the effect of preventing a breach of a negative obligation not to work for anther employer, rather than compelling that party to work for a particular employer.

Bear in mind that:

1. specific performance enforces positive obligations;
2. a prohibitory injunction enforces negative obligations.

In **Warner Bros Pictures v Nelson** [1937] 1 K.B. 209, the Hollywood actress Bette Davis contracted to work exclusively for Warner Brothers. In breach of this agreement she agreed to appear in a production arranged by a third party. The court granted an injunction preventing her from working elsewhere for the duration of the agreement. The court was of the opinion that she could seek alternative employment apart from as an actor to make a living.

Similarly, in **Lumley v Wagner** (1852) 1 De G.M. & G. 604, the defendant agreed to sing exclusively in the plaintiff's theatre for three months. When the defendant was offered more money to appear in another production the plaintiff brought an action to prevent her from appearing in that production. The court granted an injunction that had the effect of preventing the defendant from working for anyone else during her three month agreement with the plaintiff.

Over to you. . .

Consider the approach of the courts in *Warner Bros Pictures v Nelson* and *Lumley v Wagner*. Do you agree with these decisions? Can you identify any criticisms as the granting of injunctions in these cases?

The decisions in **Warner Bros v Nelson** and **Lumley v Wagner** are certainly open to criticism. It is questionable whether the effect of the injunctions was to prevent the defendants from working for anyone else or whether the true effect was to *compel* them to work for the plaintiffs. There is a fine line indeed between "encouraging" and "compelling" performance. This nettle was finally grasped by the High Court in **Page One Records Ltd v Britton** [1968] 1 W.L.R. 157.

In this case the pop group, The Troggs, agreed with the plaintiff that he would be their manager for five years and that they would not employ any other manager during that time. The group breached the agreement when they employed another manager. Interestingly, the court refused to grant an injunction in this case. The reasoning was that to do so would effectively *compel* the manager to work exclusively for the group. This was particularly undesirable as the relationship of trust and confidence between the group and the manager had broken down. To grant an injunction would be to accept specific performance in relation to a contract for service by the backdoor.

Restitution

Finally, we turn to the remedy of restitution. We have left this remedy to last as it is often described as a quasi-contractual remedy. An award in restitution is not strictly based on contractual principles. In fact, there may not even be a contract on which the law of restitution can operate.

15-013

The primary aim of an award in restitution is to reverse an unjust enrichment. We have seen in the previous chapter that the courts will exceptionally compensate the claimant based on a defendant's unjust enrichment by holding the defendant to account for profit he has made as a result of the breach.

A total failure of consideration

Restitution provides a remedy for when there has been a total failure of consideration. So, if one party has provided something of value under the contract but has received nothing in return the court may use the principles of restitution to prevent a party from benefiting from the lack of consideration. We have already discussed this position in relation to frustration and the decision in **The Fibrosa** (see above at p.329). A restitutionary remedy will be available where money has been paid under a contract that is then frustrated but where one party has not received any of what was bargained for under the contract. In these cases restitution will operate so as to reverse the unjust enrichment of one of the parties.

15-014

Further, in **Rowland v Divall** [1923] 2 K.B. 500, the claimant was able to recover the money paid for a car which later was discovered to be stolen. Again, there had been a total failure of consideration as no title to the car could have passed to the claimant under s.12 of the Sale of Goods Act 1979 (as the car was stolen the seller did not have good title to pass to the claimant).

Quantum meruit claims

A claimant may be able to recover money on a quantum meruit basis (money paid for work done). For example, in **Planche v Colbourn** (1831) 8 Bing.14, the claimant was able to claim half the amount promised by his publisher for writing a book when the publisher took the decision to abandon the series in which his book was to appear. The claimant was awarded a reasonable amount to reflect the work that he had done in anticipation that the book would be published.

15-015

If work is carried out under a contract that is subsequently declared void, the claimant can also recover an amount to reflect the work undertaken on a quantum meruit basis. This is demonstrated in cases such as **Craven-Ellis v Canons Ltd** [1936] 2 K.B. 403, in which a company director was awarded an amount of money on a quantum meruit basis to reflect the work he had provided before some irregularities in his appointment were discovered and he was forced to step down as a director.

Summary

1. Damages are the primary remedy in contract law and are awarded at common law. However, in some situations damages may not provide an adequate remedy and the court will have a discretion to award equitable remedies.

2. The court can order specific performance which has the effect of requiring the defendant to meet their obligations under the contract. However, as specific performance is an equitable remedy it is not available as of right and is subject to the following limitations.

    (a) Damages must not be an adequate remedy.

    (b) There must be mutuality.

    (c) Court supervision must not be required.

    (d) It must be equitable to grant the remedy of specific performance.

    (e) Specific performance will not be granted in contracts for personal services.

    (f) There must not be an undue delay in claiming specific performance.

3. An injunction is another equitable remedy and can also have the effect of compelling or preventing the defendant from acting in a particular way. It is important to distinguish between the different types of injunction.

    (a) A mandatory injunction: this has the effect of compelling the defendant (usually to remedy the consequences of his actions).

    (b) A prohibitory injunction: this has the effect of preventing a party from acting in a particular way, usually to prevent the defendant from breaching their contractual obligations.

4. Beyond contractual and equitable principles, the law of restitution operates so as to reverse an unjust enrichment and will generally be available where there has been a total failure of consideration.

5. Finally, a claimant may recover compensation on a quantum meruit basis. Such an award can be made where the claimant has either paid money under a contract or provided services under a contract. The claimant will be able to recover a reasonable sum to reflect the efforts he has exhausted in performance of the contract which may fail to materialise.

Key Cases Grid

Case	Court	Key Issue
Beswick v Beswick [1968]	House of Lords	When considering their discretion to award the equitable remedy of specific performance, the court must assess whether damages are an adequate remedy. If the common law remedy of damages would provide an adequate remedy then an award of specific performance will not be made.
Patel v Ali [1984] Ch. 283	Chancery Division	The court will not grant specific performance if it would be *inequitable* to do so, such as if the award would result in unnecessary hardship.
Fibrosa Spolka Akcyjna v Fairbairn Lawson Combe Barbour Ltd (The Fibrosa) [1943]	House of Lords	Restitution provides a remedy for when there has been a total failure of consideration.

Further Reading

Stone, R. and Cunnington, R. *Text, Cases and Materials on Contract Law* (London: Routledge-Cavendish, 2014), Chapter 15.

Treitel, G *The Law of Contract*, 13th edn (London Sweet & .Maxwell, 2011), Chapter 21 (Specific Remedies) and Chapter 22 (Unjust Enrichment).

Index

This index has been prepared using Sweet and Maxwell's Legal Taxonomy. Main index entries conform to keywords provided by the Legal Taxonomy except where references to specific documents or non-standard terms (denoted by quotation marks) have been included. These keywords provide a means of identifying similar concepts in other Sweet & Maxwell publications and online services to which keywords from the Legal Taxonomy have been applied. Readers may find some minor differences between terms used in the text and those which appear in the index.

Suggestions to **taxonomy@sweetandmaxwell.co.uk**.

(All references are to paragraph number)

Acceptance
see also **Offers**
battle of the forms, 2–026
communication
email, 2–049
introduction, 2–027
modern methods, 2–040—2–049
postal rule, 2–028—2–039
counter-offers, 2–022
cross-offers, 2–024
effective time, 2–027
email, by
generally, 2–049
introduction, 2–040
fax, by, 2–040
ignorance of offer, in, 2–057
introduction, 2–021
modern methods of communication
email, 2–049
fault, 2–046
generally, 2–040
inside office hours, 2–047
introduction, 2–027
outside office hours, 2–048
rules, 2–041—2–044
time of formation of contract, 2–045
postal rule
absurd result, 2–035
checklist, 2–040
development, 2–029
displacement, 2–034—2–036
general rule for acceptance, 2–033
generally, 2–028
letter properly posted, 2–032
limitations, 2–031—2–036
offeror may explicitly displace, 2–034
prescribed method of acceptance, 2–036

rationale, 2–030
reasonable to use post to accept, 2–031
silence, and, 2–053
summary, 2–039
withdrawal of acceptance, and, 2–038
withdrawal of offer, and, 2–037
request for information, 2–023
silence
bilateral contracts, and, 2–051
exceptions to rule, 2–052—2–054
generally, 2–050
inertia selling, and, 2–052
postal rule, and, 2–053
unilateral contracts, and, 2–054—2–056
statement of minimum price, 2–025
summary, 2–060
unilateral contracts
'continuing act', 2–056
generally, 2–054
problems, 2–055
voice message, by, 2–040
Account of profits
generally, 14–030—14–031
Actual undue influence
generally, 10–013
Advertisements
auctions, of, 2–017
construed as offers, 2–013
introduction, 2–010
invitation to treat, and, 2–006
manufacturers, from, 2–012
'multi-acceptance' issue, 2–011
Affirmation
misrepresentation, 8–033
Agency
privity of contract, 5–005
Agreements
see also **Acceptance, Offers**

definition of contract, 1–003
enforceability, 1–005
self-regulatory nature, 1–010
formation, 1–004
Ambiguity
certainty, 3–005
Assignment
privity of contract, 5–006
Auctions
advertisement, 2–017
contract terms, 6–010
generally, 2–014
with reserve, 2–016
without reserve, 2–015
Automated machines
see **Vending machines**
Battle of the forms
see **Standard terms**
Bilateral contracts
generally, 1–012
Blue pencil test
illegal contracts, 11–026
Certainty
ambiguity, 3–005
incomplete agreements
generally, 3–006
reconciling case law, 3–007
sale of goods, 3–008
introduction, 3–001
meaningless phrases, 3–003
negative obligations, and, 3–004
overview, 3–014
resolution of ambiguity, 3–005
sale of goods, 3–008
vague terms of agreement, 3–002
Change of circumstances
misrepresentation, 8–011
Collateral contracts
generally, 6–010
Common law
exclusion clauses

generally, 7–004
incorporation, 7–005—7–014
introduction, 7–002
reasonableness, and, 7–041
satisfy relevant statutory
    provisions, 7–026—7–059
test of 'construction',
    7–015—7–025
privity of contract
    agency, 5–005
    assignment, 5–006
    introduction, 5–004
remedies
    action for an agreed sum, 15–002
    generally, 15–001
Common mistake
introduction, 9–004
quality, as to
    *Associated Japanese Bank v Credit
      du Nord*, 9–009
    generally, 9–008
    limited acceptance, 9–010
subject-matter of contract, as to
    destruction of subject-matter,
      9–006
    generally, 9–005—9–006
title, as to, 9–007
Competition law
illegal contracts, 11–006
Concurrent liability
generally, 1–008
Conditions
identification, 6–024
identification by parties, 6–026
identification by statute, 6–025
importance to contract, 6–027
introduction, 6–022
Consideration
see also **Promissory estoppel**
adequacy, 4–005
definition, 4–002
economic duress
    performance of duty owed to
      same promissory, 4–017
    promise to perform duty to third
      party, 4–023
economic value, 4–006
introduction, 4–001
moves from promisee, 4–007
part-payment of debt
    generally, 4–024
    Pinnel's case, 4–025—4–026
    problems, 4–028
    Williams v Roffey decision, 4–027
past consideration

exceptions, 4–011
generally, 4–009—4–010
Pao On v Lau Yiu Yong, 4–012
requested performance, 4–011
performance of duty owed to same
    promissory
    economic duress, and, 4–017
    exceeding existing duty, 4–016
    generally, 4–015
    Williams v Roffey principles,
      4–018—4–020
performance of duty owed to third
    parties, 4–021
performance of existing duties
    introduction, 4–013
    owed to same promissor,
      4–015—4–020
    owed to third parties, 4–021
    public duty, 4–014
performance of public duty, 4–014
'price of the promise', 4–003
promise to perform duty to third party
    economic duress, and, 4–023
    generally, 4–022
promissory estoppel, and, 4–031
rules
    adequacy, 4–005
    consideration moves from
      promisee, 4–007
    economic value, 4–006
    generally, 4–004
    sufficiency, 4–005
sufficiency
    generally, 4–008
    introduction, 4–005
    past consideration, 4–009—4–
      012
    performance of existing duties,
      4–013—4–021
    promise to perform duty to third
      party, 4–022—4–023
Construction of contracts
see **Interpretation**
Consumer contracts
unfair contract terms
    ambiguity of terms, 7–059
    application, 7–050
    appropriateness of price, 7–054
    automatically unfair terms, 7–053
    background, 7–048
    bar on exclusion or restriction of
      liability, 7–055
    'consumer', 7–051
    'consumer contracts', 7–050
    'consumer notices', 7–050

    contracts affected, 7–050
    definitions, 7–050—7–051
    different meanings, 7–059
    exclusion from assessment of
      fairness, 7–054
    exclusion of liability, 7–055
    fairness of terms and notices,
      7–052—7–054
    goods contracts, 7–056
    'grey list' of terms, 7–053
    installation of goods, 7–057
    introduction, 7–049
    negligence liability, 7–055
    notices affected, 7–050
    'person', 7–051
    restriction of liability, 7–055
    services contracts, 7–058
    subject matter of contract, 7–054
    terms with different meanings,
      7–059
    'trader', 7–051
Contra proferentem
generally, 7–016
liability irrespective of negligence,
    7–024
negligence, and, 7–017—7–021
only basis for liability is negligence,
    7–023
strict liability, and, 7–018
Contract terms
auctions, 6–010
collateral contracts, 6–010
conditions
    identification, 6–024
    identification by parties, 6–026
    identification by statute, 6–025
    importance to contract, 6–027
    introduction, 6–022
express terms, 6–011
implied terms
    'business efficacy', 6–014
    implied by court, 6–017—6–018
    implied by custom, 6–020
    implied by law, 6–016—6–019
    implied by statute, 6–019
    implied in fact, 6–013—6–015
    introduction, 6–012
    necessity, 6–014
    'officious bystander' test, 6–015
    reasonableness, 6–015
incorporation
    express, 6–012
    implied, 6–012—6–020
    generally, 6–011
innominate terms

advantages, 6–030
disadvantages, 6–031
example, 6–029
generally, 6–028
introduction, 6–001
parol evidence rule
  collateral contracts, 6–010
  generally, 6–005
representations, and
  breach of collateral contract,
    6–010
  generally, 6–002
  guiding factors, 6–003
  importance of statement, 6–007
  introduction, 6–002
  invite to verify statement, 6–009
  lapse of time, 6–008
  parol evidence rule, 6–005
  presumptions, 6–003
  reduction to writing, 6–004
  specialist skill or knowledge,
    6–006
summary, 6–031
types
  conditions, 6–022
  innominate terms, 6–028—6–031
  introduction, 6–021
  warranties, 6–023—6–027
warranties
  identification, 6–024
  identification by parties, 6–026
  identification by statute, 6–025
  importance to contract, 6–027
  introduction, 6–023

Contracts
see also **Collateral contracts**,
    Unilateral contracts
bilateral contracts, 1–012
classical theory
  generally, 1–011
  problems, 1–012
concurrent liability, 1–008
construction
  flexible approach, 11–024
  generally, 11–022
  literal approach, 11–023
contract law
  introduction, 1–001—1–002
  restitution, and, 1–009
  self-regulatory nature, 1–010
  sources, 1–006
  tort, and, 1–007
definition, 1–004
freedom of contract, 1–013
illegality

common law, at, 11–009—11–013
introduction, 11–001
performance, and,
    11–002—11–004
public policy, 11–010—11–013
restraint of trade, and,
    11–014—11–027
statute, under, 11–005—11–008
introduction, 1–001—1–002
legally binding agreement, 1–005
meaning, 1–003
objectivity, 1–004
restitution, and, 1–009
self-regulatory nature, 1–010
sources of law, 1–006
tort, and, 1–007
unilateral contracts, 1–012

**Contracts (Rights of Third Parties) Act
    1999**
see **Privity of contract**
defences, 5–011
exceptions, 5–012
generally, 5–008
rescission of contract, 5–010
term that purports to confer a
    benefit, 5–009
variation of contract, 5–010

Contributory negligence
generally, 14–037

Counter-offers
generally, 2–022
request for information, and, 2–023

Damages
account of profits, 14–030—14–031
'agreed' sums
  generally, 14–034
  guidelines in *Dunlop Pneumatic
    Tyre*, 14–036
  penalty clause distinguished,
    14–035
awards
  compensatory aim, 14–015
  expectation interest,
    14–016—14–019
  restitutionary interest,
    14–024—14–031
  speculative loss, 14–020—14–023
contributory negligence, 14–037
disappointment, 14–033
expectation interest
  cost of the cure, 14–018
  introduction, 14–016
  market price, 14–017
  *Ruxley Electronics & Construction
    Ltd v Forsyth*, 14–019

speculative loss, and,
    14–020—14–0
fraudulent misrepresentation, for,
    8–038
injured feelings, 14–033
introduction, 14–001
limitations, 14–002
liquidated damages
  generally, 14–034
  guidelines in *Dunlop Pneumatic
    Tyre*, 14–036
  penalty clauses, and, 14–035
loss of chance, 14–021
measure of damages, 14–038
misrepresentation
  fraudulent misrepresentation, for,
    8–038
  introduction, 8–037
  negligent misstatement, for,
    8–039
  s.2(1) Misrepresentation Act 1967,
    under, 8–040
  s.2(2) Misrepresentation Act 1967,
    under, 8–041
mitigation of loss, 14–038
negligent misstatement, for, 8–039
non-pecuniary loss
  disappointment, 14–033
  generally, 14–032
  injured feelings, 14–033
reliance interest
  distinction from restitutionary
    interest, 14–025
  generally, 14–022
  speculative damages, and,
    14–023
penalty clauses, 14–035
remoteness
  generally, 14–003
  Hadley v Baxendale test,
    14–004—14–007
  Heron II, The, 14–008
  justification for differing tests,
    14–009
  Parsons v Uttley, 14–010—14–013
  *Transfield Shipping Inc v Mercator
    Shipping Inc*, 14–014
restitutionary interest
  account of profits,
    14–030—14–031
  Attorney General v Blake,
    14–030
  distinction from reliance interest,
    14–025
  introduction, 14–024

reluctance of court to award
    damages, 14–026
  Surrey CC v Bredero Homes Ltd,
    14–027
  *Wrotham Park Estate Co Ltd
    v Parkside Homes Ltd*,
    14–028–14–029
speculative loss
  introduction, 14–020
  loss of opportunity, 14–021
  reliance interest, 14–022–14–023
summary, 14–038
Delay
  misrepresentation
    generally, 8–006
    rescission, 8–034
Discharge
  agreement, by
    bilateral discharge, 12–003
    generally, 12–002
    unilateral discharge, 12–004
  bilateral, 12–003
  breach, by
    anticipatory breach, 12–013
    generally, 12–012
  construction of contract, and
    introduction, 12–007
    partial performance, 12–009
    severable obligations, 12–008
    substantial performance, 12–010
  introduction, 12–001
  partial performance, 12–009
  performance, by
    exactitude, 12–006
    introduction, 12–005
    partial, 12–009
    precision, 12–006
    prevention, 12–011
    substantial, 12–010
  severable obligations, 12–008
  substantial performance, 12–010
  summary, 12–013
  unilateral, 12–004
Display of goods
  internet transactions, 2–020
  generally, 2–008
  shop window, in, 2–009
Duress
  see also **Undue influence**
  economic duress
    development, 10–006
    introduction, 10–005
    lawful act, and, 10–008
    realistic alternatives, 10–007
  introduction, 10–001

threats
  effect on claimant, 10–004
  generally, 10–002
  nature sufficient to amount to
    duress, 10–003
Economic duress
  see also **Undue influence**
  consideration
    performance of duty owed to
      same promissory, 4–017
    promise to perform duty to third
      party, 4–023
  development, 10–006
  introduction, 10–005
  lawful act, and, 10–008
  realistic alternatives, 10–007
Electronic mail
  acceptance
    email, 2–049
    fault, 2–046
    generally, 2–049
    inside office hours, 2–047
    introduction, 2–040
    outside office hours, 2–048
    rules, 2–041–2–044
    time of formation of contract,
      2–045
Equitable remedies
  generally, 15–001
  injunctions
    effects, 15–010
    mandatory, 15–011
    prohibitory, 15–012
  specific performance
    court supervision not required,
      15–006
    court's discretion, 15–003
    damages not an adequate
      remedy, 15–004
    delay in claim, 15–009
    grant, 15–007
    mutuality, 15–005
    personal services, 15–008
    requirements for award, 15–003
  summary, 15–015
Estoppel
  see also **Promissory estoppel**
  generally, 4–030
Exclusion clauses
  see also **Unfair contract terms**
  common law, at
    generally, 7–004
    incorporation, 7–005–7–014
    introduction, 7–002
    reasonableness, and, 7–041

satisfy relevant statutory
  provisions, 7–026–7–059
test of 'construction',
  7–015–7–025
construction
  contra proferentem,
    7–016–7–024
  fundamental breach, 7–025
  generally, 7–015
  introduction, 7–003
Consumer Rights Act 2014, under
  ambiguity of terms, 7–059
  application, 7–050
  appropriateness of price, 7–054
  automatically unfair terms, 7–053
  background, 7–048
  bar on exclusion or restriction of
    liability, 7–055
  'consumer', 7–051
  'consumer contracts', 7–050
  'consumer notices', 7–050
  contracts affected, 7–050
  definitions, 7–050–7–051
  different meanings, 7–059
  exclusion from assessment of
    fairness, 7–054
  exclusion of liability, 7–055
  fairness of terms and notices,
    7–052–7–054
  goods contracts, 7–056
  'grey list' of terms, 7–053
  installation of goods, 7–057
  introduction, 7–049
  negligence liability, 7–055
  notices affected, 7–050
  'person', 7–051
  restriction of liability, 7–055
  services contracts, 7–058
  subject matter of contract, 7–054
  terms with different meanings,
    7–059
  'trader', 7–051
contra proferentem
  generally, 7–016
  liability irrespective of negligence,
    7–024
  negligence, and, 7–017–7–021
  only basis for liability is
    negligence, 7–023
  strict liability, and, 7–018
freedom of contract, and, 7–001
fundamental breach, 7–005
incorporation
  generally, 7–005
  introduction, 7–004

notice, by, 7–007—7–011
previous dealings, via,
7–012—7–014
signature, by, 7–006
introduction, 7–001
liability irrespective of negligence,
7–024
negligence
approach of courts , 7–019
Canada Steamship, 7–024
contra proferentem rule, and,
7–017
express reference in clause,
7–020
introduction, 7–017
no express reference in clause,
7–021
strict liability, and, 7–018
UCTA 1977, and, 7–039—7–040
notice, by
contractual document, in, 7–011
generally, 7–007
reasonableness, 7–008
'red hand rule', 7–010
timing, 7–009
unusual clauses, 7–010
only basis for liability is negligence,
7–023
previous dealings, by
consistency, 7–014
generally, 7–012
sufficient notice of clause, 7–013
reasonableness
guidelines for application of test,
7–040
introduction, 7–038
limitation clauses, 7–039
'red hand rule', 7–010
signature, by, 7–006
statutory provisions
Consumer Rights Act 2014,
7–048—7–059
generally, 7–026
introduction, 7–002
Unfair Contract Terms Act 1977,
7–027—7–041
Unfair Terms in Consumer
Contracts Regulations 1999,
7–042—7–047
strict liability
generally, 7–018
UCTA 1977, and, 7–032
three–stage approach, 7–003
Unfair Contract Terms Act 1977,
under

background, 7–026
business liability, 7–029
'dealing as consumer', 7–029,
7–034
hire purchase, 7–033—7–036
'in the course of business', 7–036
introduction, 7–027
limitation clauses, 7–039
negligence liability,
7–030—7–031
overview, 7–028
reasonableness test,
7–038—7–040
sale of goods, 7–033—7–036
strict liability, 7–032
supply of goods, 7–037
types of liability, 7–028
Unfair Terms in Consumer Contracts
Regulations 1999, under
companies, and, 7–043
'consumer', 7–043
consumer contracts, 7–043
core terms, 7–047
enforcement, 7–046
generally, 7–026
'good faith' requirement, 7–045
introduction, 7–042
unfair terms, 7–044
use, 7–002
Exclusion of liability
see also **Exclusion clauses**
misrepresentation, 8–042
Exclusive service agreements
illegal contracts, 11–021
Express terms
generally, 6–011
False statements
see also **Misrepresentation**
change of circumstances, 8–011
fact, of
basic principle, 8–013
fact or opinion, 8–014
generally, 8–013
statements of future intention,
8–016
statements of law, 8–015
fact that induced the contract, of
generally, 8–017
representation material to
contract decision, 8–018
representation relied on, 8–019
generally, 8–008
half-truths, 8–010
silence, 8–009
utmost good faith, 8–012

Fax
acceptance, 2–040
Fraudulent misrepresentation
damages, for, 8–038
generally, 8–021
Misrepresentation Act 1967, under,
8–028
Freedom of contract
exclusion clauses, 7–001
generally, 1–013
Frustration
absolute obligations doctrine
generally, 13–003
limitations, 13–004
allocation of risk, 13–017
common law position
effect, 13–021
Fibrosa case, 13–022—13–023
generally, 13–020
total failure of consideration,
13–022
death, 13–013
delay, 13–018
destruction of subject matter, 13–008
development of doctrine
absolute obligations,
13–003—13–004
construction of obligations,
13–006
implied-term theory, 13–005
introduction, 13–002
effect
common law position,
13–020—13–023
generally, 13–019
statutory position,
13–024—13–032
Fibrosa case, 13–022—13–023
frustrating events
coronation cases, 13–010
destruction of subject matter,
13–008
illegality, 13–012
introduction, 13–007
non-availability of parties, 13–013
non-occurrence of event,
13–009—13–011
leases, and, 13–014
illegality, 13–012
illness, 13–013
implied-term theory, 13–005
introduction, 13–001
Law Reform (Frustrated Contracts)
Act 1943
application of s.1(3),

13–027—13–031
common law effect of frustration,
and, 13–032
generally, 13–024
operation of s.1(2), 13–025
part performance,
13–027—13–031
recovery of benefits conferred by
partial performance, 13–026
recovery where sum paid or
payable before frustrating
event, 13–025
leases, and, 13–014
limitations on doctrine
allocation of risk, 13–017
delay, 13–018
generally, 13–015
self-induced frustration, 13–016
meaning, 13–001
non-availability of parties, 13–013
non-occurrence of event
coronation cases, 13–010
Herne Bay Steam Boat Company,
13–010—13–011
introduction, 13–009
Krell v Henry, 13–010—13–011
part performance
Appleby v Myers, 13–031
award of 'just sum', 13–029
BP v Hunt (No 2), 13–030
calculation of 'valuable benefit',
13–028
generally, 13–027
introduction, 13–026
self-induced frustration, 13–016
summary, 13–032
total failure of consideration, 13–022

Fundamental breach
exclusion contracts, 7–025

Gambling contracts
illegal contracts, 11–007

Good faith
misrepresentation, 8–012

Husband and wife
see **Spouses**

Ignorance
offer and acceptance, 2–057

Illegal contracts
'blue pencil' test, 11–026
breach of statutory requirements,
11–008
common law, at
immorality, 11–010—11–013
introduction, 11–009
public policy, 11–010—11–013

competition law, 11–006
contract obligations unaffected,
11–004
contract rendered unenforceable,
11–003
exclusive service agreements, 11–021
frustration, and, 13–012
gambling contracts, 11–007
introduction, 11–001
jurisdiction of the court, and, 11–013
performance, and
contract obligations unaffected,
11–004
contract rendered unenforceable,
11–003
generally, 11–002
public policy
introduction, 11–010
jurisdiction of the court, 11–013
sanctity of marriage, 11–012
sexually immoral contracts, 11–011
restraint of trade, and
'blue pencil' test, 11–026
construction of contract,
11–022—11–024
duration of restriction, 11–020
exceptions to general rule, 11–016
exclusive service agreements,
11–021
extent of restriction, 11–020
flexible construction, 11–024
general rule, 11–015
guiding factors assessing
reasonableness, 11–020
introduction, 11–014
literal construction, 11–023
nature of interest protected,
11–020
reasonable as to protection of
parties, 11–018
reasonable as to public policy,
11–019
reasonableness, 11–017
severance, 11–025—11–027
sanctity of marriage, and, 11–012
severance
altering nature of contract,
11–027
'blue pencil' test, 11–026
generally, 11–025
sexually immoral contracts, 11–011
statute, under
breach of statutory requirements,
11–008
competition law, 11–006

introduction, 11–005
wagering contracts, 11–007
summary, 11–027
wagering contracts, 11–007

Illegality
see **Illegal contracts**

Implied terms
'business efficacy', 6–014
implied by court, 6–017—6–018
implied by custom, 6–020
implied by law, 6–016—6–019
implied by statute, 6–019
implied in fact, 6–013—6–015
introduction, 6–012
necessity, 6–014
'officious bystander' test, 6–015
reasonableness, 6–015

Impossibility
misrepresentation, 8–035

Incomplete agreements
generally, 3–006
reconciling case law, 3–007
sale of goods, 3–008

Incorporation
contract terms
express, 6–012
implied, 6–012—6–020
generally, 6–011
exclusion clauses
generally, 7–004
notice, by, 7–007—7–011
previous dealings, via,
7–012—7–014
signature, by, 7–006
exclusion clauses by notice
contractual document, in, 7–011
generally, 7–007
reasonableness, 7–008
'red hand rule', 7–010
timing, 7–009
unusual clauses, 7–010
exclusion clauses by previous
dealings
consistency, 7–014
generally, 7–012
sufficient notice of clause, 7–013
notice, by
contract terms, 6–011
exclusion clauses, 7–007—7–011
previous dealings, by
contract terms, 6–011
exclusion clauses, 7–012—7–014
signature, by
contract terms, 6–011
exclusion clauses, 7–006

Inertia selling
see **Unsolicited goods**
Injunctions
effects, 15–010
mandatory, 15–011
prohibitory, 15–012
Innocent misrepresentation
generally, 8–029
Innominate terms
see **Intermediate terms**
Intention
misrepresentation, 8–003
offers
assessment, 2–005
generally, 2–004
Intention to create legal relations
commercial agreements,
3–013
domestic agreements, 3–011
generally, 3–009
introduction, 3–001
overview, 3–014
presumptions, 3–010
social agreements, 3–012
Intermediate terms
advantages, 6–030
disadvantages, 6–031
example, 6–029
generally, 6–028
Internet
offers, 2–020
Interpretation
contra proferentem
generally, 7–016
liability irrespective of negligence,
7–024
negligence, and,
7–017—7–021
only basis for liability is
negligence, 7–023
strict liability, and, 7–018
fundamental breach, 7–025
generally, 7–015
Invitations to tender
offers, 2–018
Invitation to treat
see also **Offers**
generally, 2–006
Liquidated damages
generally, 14–034
guidelines in *Dunlop Pneumatic Tyre*,
14–036
penalty clauses, and, 14–035
Loss of chance
generally, 14–021

Mandatory injunctions
effect, 15–010
generally, 15–011
Marriage
illegal contracts, 11–012
Measure of damages
generally, 14–038
Misrepresentation
affirmation, 8–033
categories, 8–020—8–029
change of circumstances, 8–011
contracts of utmost good faith,
8–012
damages
fraudulent misrepresentation, for,
8–038
introduction, 8–037
negligent misstatement, for,
8–039
s.2(1) Misrepresentation Act 1967,
under, 8–040
s.2(2) Misrepresentation Act 1967,
under, 8–041
distinguishing term of contract from
representation
intention, 8–003
introduction, 8–002
lapse of time, 8–006
reduction of contract to writing,
8–004
specialist skill or knowledge,
8–005
exclusion of liability, 8–042
false statements
change of circumstances, 8–011
generally, 8–008
half-truths, 8–010
silence, 8–009
utmost good faith, 8–012
false statements of fact
basic principle, 8–013
fact or opinion, 8–014
generally, 8–013
statements of future intention,
8–016
statements of law, 8–015
false statements of fact that induced
the contract
generally, 8–017
representation material to
contract decision, 8–018
representation relied on, 8–019
fraudulent misrepresentation
damages, for, 8–038
generally, 8–021

Misrepresentation Act 1967,
under, 8–028
half-truths, 8–010
identification
false statements, 8–008—8–012
false statements of fact,
8–013—8–016
false statements of fact that
induced the contract,
8–017—8–
introduction, 8–007
impossibility, 8–035
innocent misrepresentation, 8–029
intention, 8–003
introduction, 8–001
lapse of time
generally, 8–006
rescission, 8–034
Misrepresentation Act 1967, under
claimants case, 8–025
damages under, 8–040—8–041
defence evidence, 8–006
'fiction of fraud', 8–027
generally, 8–024
scope, 8–028
negligent misrepresentation
common law, at, 8–023
damages, 8–039—8–041
generally, 8–022
Misrepresentation Act 1967,
under, 8–024—8–028
negligent misstatement
damages, 8–039
generally, 8–023
pre-contractual statements
intention, 8–003
introduction, 8–002
lapse of time, 8–006
reduction to writing, 8–004
specialist skill or knowledge,
8–005
reduction of contract to writing,
8–004
remedies
damages, 8–037—8–041
introduction, 8–030
rescission, 8–031—8–036
rescission
affirmation, 8–033
bars, 8–032—8–03
generally, 8–031
impossibility, 8–035
lapse of time, 8–034
third party rights, 8–036
silence, 8–009

specialist skill or knowledge, 8–005
statements of future intention, 8–016
statements of law, 8–015
structured approach, 8–043
summary, 8–043
third party rights, 8–036
types, 8–020—8–029
utmost good faith, 8–012
voidable contracts, 8–001
Mistake
agreement mistakes
generally, 9–011
mutual mistake, 9–012—9–013
unilateral mistake, 9–014—9–025
attributes, as to, 9–020
boundaries, 9–002
categories, 9–003
common mistake
introduction, 9–004
quality, as to, 9–008—9–010
subject-matter of contract, as to,
9–005—9–006
title, as to, 9–007
contracts *inter absentes*, 9–019
contracts *inter praesentes*, 9–021
cross-purposes
cause of mistake, 9–013
generally, 9–012
destruction of subject-matter, 9–006
documents signed by mistake, 9–031
existence of subject-matter of
contract, as to
destruction of subject-matter,
9–006
generally, 9–005
face-to-face contracts
generally, 9–021
rebutting presumption, 9–022
identity, as to
attributes, as to, 9–020
contracts *inter absentes*, 9–019
contracts *inter praesentes*, 9–021
effect on contract, 9–023
face-to-face contracts,
9–021—9–022
fundamental importance, 9–018
importance of contract being
declared void, 9–017
Ingram v Little, 9–024—9–025
introduction, 9–016
written contracts, 9–019
introduction, 9–001
mistaken identity
attributes, as to, 9–020
contracts *inter absentes*, 9–019

contracts *inter praesentes*, 9–021
effect on contract, 9–023
face-to-face contracts,
9–021—9–022
fundamental importance, 9–018
importance of contract being
declared void, 9–017
Ingram v Little, 9–024—9–025
introduction, 9–016
written contracts, 9–019
mutual mistake
cause, 9–013
generally, 9–012
non est factum, 9–031
quality, as to
*Associated Japanese Bank v Credit
du Nord*, 9–009
generally, 9–008
limited acceptance, 9–010
res extincta
destruction of subject-matter,
9–006
generally, 9–005
res sua, 9–007
Shogun Finance v Hudson
consequences of decision,
9–030
facts, 9–026
majority decision, 9–027—9–028
minority view, 9–029
subject-matter of contract, as to
destruction of subject-matter,
9–006
generally, 9–005
summary, 9–031
term of contract, as to, 9–015
types, 9–003
unilateral mistake
attributes, as to, 9–020
identity, as to, 9–016—9–024
introduction, 9–014
term of contract, as to, 9–015
vitiating factor, as, 9–001
void contracts
introduction, 9–001
mistaken identity, and, 9–017
voidable contracts
introduction, 9–001
mistaken identity, and, 9–017
written contracts, 9–019
Mistaken identity
attributes, as to, 9–020
contracts *inter absentes*, 9–019
contracts *inter praesentes*, 9–021
effect on contract, 9–023

face-to-face contracts,
9–021—9–022
fundamental importance, 9–018
importance of contract being
declared void, 9–017
Ingram v Little, 9–024—9–025
introduction, 9–016
written contracts, 9–019
Mitigation
generally, 14–038
Mutual mistake
see **Mutual misunderstanding**
Mutual misunderstanding
cause, 9–013
generally, 9–012
Negligence
exclusion clauses
approach of courts , 7–019
Canada Steamship, 7–024
contra proferentem rule, and,
7–017
express reference in clause,
7–020
introduction, 7–017
no express reference in clause,
7–021
strict liability, and, 7–018
UCTA 1977, and, 7–030—7–031
Negligent misrepresentation
common law, at, 8–023
damages, 8–039—8–041
generally, 8–022
Misrepresentation Act 1967, under,
8–024—8–028
Negligent misstatement
damages, 8–039
generally, 8–023
Non est factum
generally, 9–031
Non-pecuniary loss
disappointment, 14–033
generally, 14–032
injured feelings, 14–033
Notice
exclusion clauses
contractual document, in, 7–011
generally, 7–007
reasonableness, 7–008
'red hand rule', 7–010
timing, 7–009
unusual clauses, 7–010
undue influence, 10–025
Offers
see also **Acceptance**
advertisements

auctions, of, 2–017
construed as offers, 2–013
introduction, 2–010
manufacturers, from, 2–012
'multi-acceptance' issue, 2–011
auctions
advertisement, 2–017
generally, 2–014
with reserve, 2–016
without reserve, 2–015
automated machines, 2–019
counter-offers, 2–022
cross-offers, 2–024
display of goods
generally, 2–008
shop window, in, 2–009
identification , 2–002
ingredients of offer
contractual intent,
2–004—2–005
introduction, 2–003
intention
assessment, 2–005
generally, 2–004
internet transactions, 2–020
introduction, 2–001
invitation to treat, and, 2–006
machines, 2–019
'offeree', 2–001
'offeror', 2–001
presumptions
advertisements, 2–010—2–013
auctions, 2–014—2–017
automated machines, 2–019
display of goods, 2–008—2–009
generally, 2–007
internet transactions, 2–020
introduction, 2–006
tenders, 2–018
revocation
generally, 2–058
third party, by, 2–059
unilateral contracts, and, 2–060
shop window, in, 2–009
tenders, 2–018
Parol evidence
collateral contracts, 6–010
generally, 6–005
Part payments
generally, 4–024
Pinnel's case, 4–025—4–026
problems, 4–028
Williams v Roffey decision, 4–027
Part performance
Appleby v Myers, 13–031

award of 'just sum', 13–029
BP v Hunt (No 2), 13–030
calculation of 'valuable benefit',
13–028
generally, 13–027
introduction, 13–026
Parties
frustration
death or illness, 13–013
Past consideration
exceptions
generally, 4–011
requested performance exception,
4–011
generally, 4–009—4–010
Pao On v Lau Yiu Yong, 4–012
Penalty clauses
generally, 14–035
Performance
consideration
introduction, 4–013
owed to same promissor,
4–015—4–020
owed to third parties, 4–021
public duty, 4–014
duty owed to same promissory, of
economic duress, and, 4–017
exceeding existing duty, 4–016
generally, 4–015
Williams v Roffey principles,
4–018—4–020
duty owed to third parties, of, 4–021
illegal contracts
contract obligations unaffected,
11–004
contract rendered unenforceable,
11–003
generally, 11–002
public duty, of, 4–014
Postal rule
absurd result, 2–035
checklist, 2–040
development, 2–029
displacement, 2–034—2–036
general rule for acceptance, 2–033
generally, 2–028
letter properly posted, 2–032
limitations
absurd result, 2–035
general rule for acceptance,
2–033
introduction, 2–031
letter properly posted, 2–032
offeror may explicitly displace,
2–034

prescribed method of acceptance,
2–036
reasonable to use post to accept,
2–031
offeror may explicitly displace, 2–034
prescribed method of acceptance,
2–036
rationale, 2–030
reasonable to use post to accept,
2–031
silence, and, 2–053
summary, 2–039
withdrawal of acceptance, and,
2–038
withdrawal of offer, and, 2–037
Pre-contractual misrepresentation
intention, 8–003
introduction, 8–002
lapse of time, 8–006
reduction to writing, 8–004
specialist skill or knowledge, 8–005
Presumed undue influence
Class 2A relationships,
10–015—10–017
becoming finding, 10–021
generally, 10–014
introduction, 10–012
husband and wife, 10–017
'manifest disadvantage' requirement,
10–020
recognised relationships, 10–016
relationship giving rise to automatic
presumption, 10–015—10–017
relationship may give rise to
presumption, 10–018—10–020
*Royal Bank of Scotland v Etridge (No
2)*, 10–012
summary, 10–021
Privity of contract
agency, 5–005
assignment, 5–006
Beswick v Beswick, 5–002
common law, at
agency, 5–005
assignment, 5–006
introduction, 5–004
Contracts (Rights of Third Parties)
Act 1999
defences, 5–011
exceptions, 5–012
generally, 5–008
rescission of contract, 5–010
term that purports to confer a
benefit, 5–009
variation of contract, 5–010

effects, 5–001
exceptions
  common law, at, 5–004—5–006
  generally, 5–003
introduction, 5–001
justifications, 5–002
rescission of contract, 5–010
summary, 5–012
term that purports to confer a
    benefit, 5–009
third parties, and
  defences, 5–011
  exceptions, 5–012
  generally, 5–008
  rescission of contract, 5–010
  term that purports to confer a
    benefit, 5–009
  variation of contract, 5–010
  Tweddle v Atkinson, 5–002
variation of contract, 5–010
Prohibitory injunctions
effect, 15–010
generally, 15–012
Promissory estoppel
consideration, and, 4–031
detrimental reliance on promise,
  4–042
development, 4–032—4–037
existing legal relationship, 4–041
Foakes v Beer, 4–036
High Trees House , 4–032—4–035
Hughes v Metropolitan Railway Co,
  4–038
introduction, 4–029
Jordan v Money, 4–039
limitations
  detrimental reliance, 4–042
  equity of promise, 4–043
  existing legal relationship,
    4–041
  generally, 4–040
  suspension of rights, 4–045
  use, 4–044
meaning, 4–030
principle, 4–029
summary, 4–045
suspension of rights, 4–045
use as 'shield not sword', 4–044
Proprietary estoppel
generally, 4–030
Public policy
illegal contracts, and,
  introduction, 11–010
  jurisdiction of the court, 11–013
  restraint of trade, and, 11–019

sanctity of marriage, 11–012
sexually immoral contracts,
  11–011
Quality
mistake, and
  *Associated Japanese Bank v Credit
    du Nord*, 9–009
  generally, 9–008
  limited acceptance, 9–010
Quantum meruit
claims, 15–015
Reasonableness
Unfair Contract Terms Act 1977,
  under
  guidelines for application of test,
    7–040
  introduction, 7–038
  limitation clauses, 7–039
Remedies
misrepresentation
  damages, 8–037—8–041
  introduction, 8–030
  rescission, 8–031—8–036
Remoteness
damages
  generally, 14–003
  Hadley v Baxendale test,
    14–004—14–007
  Heron II, The, 14–008
  justification for differing tests,
    14–009
  Parsons v Uttley, 14–010—14–013
  *Transfield Shipping Inc v Mercator
    Shipping Inc*, 14–014
Representations
see **Statements**
Requests for information
counter-offers, and, 2–023
Rescission
affirmation, 8–033
bars, 8–032—8–03
generally, 8–031
impossibility, 8–035
lapse of time, 8–034
privity of contract, 5–010
third party rights, 8–036
Restitution
generally, 15–013
introduction, 1–009
summary, 15–015
total failure of consideration, 15–014
Restraint of trade
'blue pencil' test, 11–026
construction of contract
  flexible approach, 11–024

generally, 11–022
  literal approach, 11–023
duration of restriction, 11–020
exceptions to general rule, 11–016
exclusive service agreements, 11–021
extent of restriction, 11–020
flexible construction, 11–024
general rule, 11–015
guiding factors assessing
  reasonableness, 11–020
introduction, 11–014
literal construction, 11–023
nature of interest protected, 11–020
reasonable as to protection of parties,
  11–018
reasonable as to public policy,
  11–019
reasonableness, 11–017
severance
  altering nature of contract, 11–027
  'blue pencil' test, 11–026
  generally, 11–025
Revocation
offers, of
  generally, 2–058
  third party, by, 2–059
  unilateral contracts, and, 2–060
Severance
illegal contracts
  altering nature of contract, 11–027
  'blue pencil' test, 11–026
  generally, 11–025
Signatures
exclusion clauses, 7–006
Silence
acceptance
  bilateral contracts, and, 2–051
  exceptions to rule, 2–052—2–054
  generally, 2–050
  inertia selling, and, 2–052
  postal rule, and, 2–053
  unilateral contracts, and,
    2–054—2–056
misrepresentation, 8–009
Social and domestic agreements
intention to create legal relations
  domestic agreements, 3–011
  introduction, 3–010
  social agreements, 3–012
Sources of law
contracts, 1–006
Specific performance
court supervision not required,
  15–006
court's discretion, 15–003

Spouses
  damages not an adequate remedy,
    15–004
  delay in claim, 15–009
  grant, 15–007
  mutuality, 15–005
  personal services, 15–008
  requirements for award, 15–003
  summary, 15–015

Spouses
  undue influence
    generally, 10–024—10–025
    presumption of influence, 10–017

Standard terms
  acceptance, 2–026

Statements
  breach of collateral contract, 6–010
  generally, 6–002
  guiding factors, 6–003
  importance of statement, 6–007
  introduction, 6–002
  invite to verify statement, 6–009
  lapse of time, 6–008
  parol evidence rule, 6–005
  presumptions, 6–003
  reduction to writing, 6–004
  specialist skill or knowledge,
    6–006

Statements of law
  misrepresentation, 8–015

Strict liability
  exclusion clauses
    generally, 7–018
    UCTA 1977, and, 7–032

Sufficiency
  consideration
    generally, 4–008
    introduction, 4–005
    past consideration,
      4–009—4–012
    performance of existing duties,
      4–013—4–021
    promise to perform duty to third
      party, 4–022—4–023
  past consideration
    exceptions, 4–011
    generally, 4–009—4–010
    Pao On v Lau Yiu Yong, 4–012
    requested performance, 4–011
  performance of duty owed to same
    promissory
    economic duress, and, 4–017
    exceeding existing duty, 4–016
    generally, 4–015
    Williams v Roffey principles,
      4–018—4–020

performance of duty owed to third
  parties, 4–021
performance of existing duties
  introduction, 4–013
  owed to same promissor,
    4–015—4–020
  owed to third parties, 4–021
  public duty, 4–014
performance of public duty, 4–014
promise to perform duty to third
  party
  economic duress, and, 4–023
  generally, 4–022

Tenders
  offers, and, 2–018

Terms
  see **Contract terms**

Third parties
  privity of contract
    defences, 5–011
    exceptions, 5–012
    generally, 5–008
    rescission of contract, 5–010
    term that purports to confer a
      benefit, 5–009
    variation of contract, 5–010
  revocation of offers, 2–059
  undue influence
    bank put on inquiry,
      10–023—10–024
    notice and constructive notice,
      10–025
    presumption of influence, 10–017
    steps to take to avoid notice,
      10–025
    threats

Threats
  effect on claimant, 10–004
  generally, 10–002
  nature sufficient to amount to duress,
    10–003

Torts
  contract law, and, 1–007

Undue influence
  see also **Duress**
  actual undue influence, 10–013
  categories, 10–010
  concept, 10–011
  introduction, 10–009
  presumed undue influence
    Class 2A relationships,
      10–015—10–017
    becoming finding, 10–021
    generally, 10–014
    introduction, 10–012

husband and wife, 10–017
'manifest disadvantage'
  requirement, 10–020
recognised relationships, 10–016
relationship giving rise to
  automatic presumption,
  10–015—10–017
relationship may give rise to
  presumption, 10–018—10–020
summary, 10–021
*Royal Bank of Scotland v Etridge (No
  2)*, 10–012
spouses
  generally, 10–024—10–025
  presumption of influence, 10–017
summary, 10–025
third parties, and
  bank put on inquiry,
    10–023—10–024
  notice and constructive notice,
    10–025
  presumption of influence, 10–017
  steps to take to avoid notice,
    10–025
threats
  effect on claimant, 10–004
  generally, 10–002
  nature sufficient to amount to
    duress, 10–003

Unfair contract terms
  see also **Exclusion clauses**
  Consumer Rights Act 2014, under
    ambiguity of terms, 7–059
    application, 7–050
    appropriateness of price, 7–054
    automatically unfair terms, 7–053
    background, 7–048
    bar on exclusion or restriction of
      liability, 7–055
    'consumer', 7–051
    'consumer contracts', 7–050
    'consumer notices', 7–050
    contracts affected, 7–050
    definitions, 7–050—7–051
    different meanings, 7–059
    exclusion from assessment of
      fairness, 7–054
    exclusion of liability, 7–055
    fairness of terms and notices,
      7–052—7–054
    goods contracts, 7–056
    'grey list' of terms, 7–053
    installation of goods, 7–057
    introduction, 7–049
    negligence liability, 7–055

notices affected, 7–050
'person', 7–051
restriction of liability, 7–055
services contracts, 7–058
subject matter of contract, 7–054
terms with different meanings,
7–059
'trader', 7–051
generally, 7–026
introduction, 7–002
Unfair Contract Terms Act 1977,
under
background, 7–026
business liability, 7–029
'dealing as consumer', 7–029,
7–034
hire purchase, 7–033–7–036
'in the course of business',
7–036
introduction, 7–027
limitation clauses, 7–039
negligence liability,
7–030–7–031
overview, 7–028
reasonableness test,
7–038–7–040
sale of goods, 7–033–7–036
strict liability, 7–032
supply of goods, 7–037
types of liability, 7–028

Unfair Terms in Consumer Contracts
Regulations 1999, under
companies, and, 7–043
'consumer', 7–043
consumer contracts, 7–043
core terms, 7–047
enforcement, 7–046
generally, 7–026
'good faith' requirement,
7–045
introduction, 7–025
unfair terms, 7–044
Unilateral contracts
acceptance
'continuing act', 2–056
generally, 2–054
problems, 2–055
generally, 1–012
revocation of offers, 2–060
Unilateral mistake
attributes, as to, 9–020
identity, as to
attributes, as to, 9–020
contracts *inter absentes*, 9–019
contracts *inter praesentes*, 9–021
effect on contract, 9–023
face-to-face contracts,
9–021–9–022
fundamental importance,
9–018

importance of contract being
declared void, 9–017
Ingram v Little, 9–024–9–025
introduction, 9–016
written contracts, 9–019
introduction, 9–014
term of contract, as to, 9–015
Utmost good faith
misrepresentation, 8–012
Variation
privity of contract, 5–010
Vending machines
offers, 2–019
Void contracts
introduction, 9–001
mistaken identity, 9–017
quantum meruit claims, 15–015
Voidable contracts
introduction, 9–001
misrepresentation, 8–001
mistaken identity, and, 9–017
Wagering contracts
illegal contracts, 11–007
Warranties
identification
by parties, 6–026
by statute, 6–025
generally, 6–024
importance to contract, 6–027
introduction, 6–023